SPORTING STATS

GUIDE

RYDER CUP
1927-2002

ABSOLUTE
PUBLISHING LTD

SPORTING STATISTICS

GUIDE TO THE

RYDERCUP
1927-2002

First published in Great Britain in 2002 by Absolute Publishing Ltd.

© Absolute Publishing 2002

ABSOLUTE PUBLISHING LTD
197-199 CITY ROAD, LONDON, EC1V 1JN, UK

Printed and bound in Great Britain by Cox & Wyman, Reading, Berkshire

ISBN: 0 9542304 1 8

EDITOR ANDY SWALES
PUBLISHER PETER LEVINGER
SUB EDITORS ROB FURBER, GUY WOODWARD
SERIES EDITORS GLYN WILMSHURST, ANDY TONGUE
ART EDITOR JOHN PAUL YETTON
DESIGNER DAMON COGMAN
COVER PHOTOGRAPHY GETTY IMAGES

CONTENTS

FOREWORD BY
ANGUS LOUGHRAN

My first memories of the Ryder Cup are at Walton Heath back in 1981 when despite the decision taken two years earlier to allow Europeans to join the Great Britain and Northern Ireland side, the home side were once again soundly thrashed – not helped by the absence of European number one Seve Ballesteros because of a row over appearance money.

In fact the Ryder Cup had become a joke and tickets were given away like confetti in an attempt to drum up public interest. The contest was going nowhere fast.

But two years later, perhaps more by luck the luck than judgement came the turning point. Although there was limited television coverage of the 1983 contest, Tony Jacklins's side made it into a cracking match with a thrilling finish and were only edged out at the death when Tom Watson saw off future European skipper Bernard Gallacher.

1985 was a golden year for European golf with Sandy Lyle's Open Championship victory at Sandwich followed by the Ryder Cup triumph at the Belfry, which signalled the start of a roller-coaster Ryder Cup ride, propelling the match to the top of the sporting calender and not just the golfing one. Sam Torrance holed the winning putt but it was an all-round tremendous team performance from Jacklin's men.

Despite all the excitement and the hype of 1985, Europe were still 4-1 outsiders in 1987 when they arrived at the Jack Nicklaus designed Muirfield village in 1987. I made my first transatlantic trip there and found the place exhilarating from the moment I arrived until the day after I left.

The Americans were beaten by a European side that had an intense will to win for Jacklin. In particular, the Spanish pair Ballesteros and Jose-Marie Olazabal (who showed great maturity) were outstanding. Irishman Eamonn Darcy was a true hero in his final day singles match with Ben Crenshaw, who used a one-iron as a putter for the majority of the match, after braking his intended club in a fit of rage. Darcy was oblivious to all the shenanigans going on around him and held his nerve in a difficult situation to earn a vital point for the visitors.

But it was the middle day which stands out in my mind as Lyle and Bernhard Langer finished in the dusk to claim a vital fourballs win which gave Europe vital breathing space going into the final day.

The contest not only made golf a big name sport in Europe but profoundly changed the way the US public saw the contest. Previously their attitude had been "We're going to win – it's just a question of by how many." That victory increased awareness of the Ryder Cup among the US golfing fraternity, many of whom knew remarkably little about the contest and in the coming years would provide us with a biennial competition to evoke perhaps a little too much emotion and hostility.

Certainly it created a rivalry that had never before been witnessed in a golf team event.

FOREWORD

The 1989 match at the Belfry was a classic, with the tie backed at 20-1 before the tournament by some shrewd punters who had realised that if it finished all-square Europe would retain the trophy. The atmosphere was electric, with golf of an extremely high standard played. As the packed galleries left the Midlands that Sunday night there was only one question on everybody's minds "How do I get tickets for Kiawah Island in two years time?"

There was bad blood in the air throughout the run-up to what the local press tagged the 'War on the Shore' and as usual the Ryder Cup lived right up to its billing. Kiawah was a classic golf course and the Americans were desperate for victory.

In the end it all came down to Langer's six foot putt on the last green for another tie to enable Europe to again hold onto the trophy. His miss was greeted with ecstasy by the US side and the packed home galleries, and the Ryder Cup went back across the Atlantic.

Two years later I returned to the Belfry and another close match was not quite close enough for the home side as the US side ran out 15-13 victors, though the winners were given more than a scare.

Oak Hill in 1995 provided one of the great Ryder Cups and really caught the public imagination. There was real drama and quality golf on show as Europe sneaked home by a point to regain the cup and bring back memories of 1987.

Two years later, the commercially astute move was made to take the contest to Valderrama in Spain. Not even the horrendous conditions which provided anything but Spanish sun could dampen the enthusiasm and spirits of the golf fans.

The European win took football off the back pages of the British press and even made the front page of some of the tabloids which was previously unheard of for golf.

The events of Brookline in 1999 are well documented but I found them particularly strange as I had considered US skipper Crenshaw and Europe's Mark James to be good friends. And there is no more charming man in American golf than 'gentle Ben'.

Europe were quick out of the traps but on the final day the US completed the mother of all comebacks. Over the years the US have generally had the stronger side but lacked the passion and will to win of their European counterparts. But that US side deserved immense credit for their final day showing despite Tom Lehman leading the unacceptable scenes on the 17th green after the match-winning putt from Justin Leonard.

The tragedy of September 11th forced the postponement of the contest last year and all credit to the European Tour and the USPGA for making the decision to keep the same dates and move the Ryder Cup from its traditional odd years to even.

With some players on both sides clearly out of form the US are hot favourites at 1-2 with Europe a sporting bet at an attractive looking 15-8. The last 20 years suggest that it will be close and once again I expect that prediction to come true. So I'm going to plump for Europe to win 15-13, which is available at around 10-1.

Padraig Harrington looks good value at 6-1 with some firms to be top points scorer for Europe. For the Americans, I would take David Toms – 2001 USPGA Championship – who is always hard to beat. Tiger Woods is the obvious favourite to top the US scoring charts and should certainly not be opposed in the Sunday singles but anything is possible in the foursomes and fourballs and he has not sparkled in either of his two previous Ryder Cup appearances at Valderrama and Brookline.

RYDER CUP FORMAT

The Ryder Cup is split into three different types of match: foursomes (two man teams playing alternate shots), fourballs (two man teams taking the better player's score) and singles (18 holes of matchplay). The order of play during the first two days of competition (foursomes or fourballs) is determined through the mutual agreement of both team captains. There are a total of 28 matches over the three days.

All games are scored by matchplay, which is played by holes. A hole is won by the team which holes its ball in the fewer strokes. The score is kept by the number of holes up (won) and the number of holes to play. (e.g.: Europe two-up, with four to play.)

When a team is up (winning) by more holes than there are holes remaining, then the match is closed out and a point is awarded. One point is awarded for each match won. If the match is tied or 'halved' through 18 holes of play, each team receives half a point.

There are 28 points to play for so 14½ points is enough to win the Cup. In the event of a tie at 14-14 the side defending the Ryder Cup retains the trophy (in this case the US).

The current format has been in use since 1979 and the trend has been for Europe to build up a lead during the foursomes and fourballs over the first two days before the Americans strike back in the final day singles due to their greater strength in depth.

FOURSOMES

In foursomes, two golfers compete on a team against two other golfers and each side plays one ball. The golfers play alternate shots (player A hits tee shot, player B hits second shot, etc.) until the hole is played out. Team members alternate playing the tee shots, with one golfer hitting the tee shot on odd-numbered holes, and the other hitting

RULES & FORMAT

the tee shot from the even-numbered holes. The team with the better score wins the hole. Should the two teams tie for best score, the hole is halved.

FOURBALLS
In fourballs, each member of the two man team plays their own ball. Four balls are in play per hole with each of the four players recording a score on the hole. The team whose player posts the best score on that hole wins the hole. Should players from each team tie for the best score, the hole is halved.

SINGLES
In the final day singles players from the two sides go head to head. A player wins the match when he is up by more holes than there are holes remaining to play.

Each team captain submits the order of play for his team to the appointed tournament official. The lists from each captain are matched, resulting in the pairings. The particular players in pairings can be modified by the team captains at any time prior to the beginning of a match. Should a player injure himself over the first two days and not be able to take part in the final day singles then a nominated player drops out from the other side and that match is halved.

FRIDAY 27TH SEPTEMBER
MORNING **FOURSOMES**

FRIDAY 27TH SEPTEMBER
AFTERNOON **FOURBALLS**

SATURDAY 28TH SEPTEMBER
MORNING **FOURSOMES**

SATURDAY 28TH SEPTEMBER
AFTERNOON **FOURBALLS**

SUNDAY 29TH SEPTEMBER
SINGLES

PAST RESULTS

YEAR	VENUE
1999	THE COUNTRY CLUB, BROOKLINE, MASS
1997	VALDERRAMA GC, SOTOGRANDE, SPAIN
1995	OAK HILL CC, ROCHESTER, NY
1993	THE BELFRY, WEST MIDS, ENGLAND
1991	THE OCEAN COURSE, KIAWAH ISLAND, S CAROLIN.
1989	THE BELFRY, WEST MIDS, ENGLAND
1987	MUIRFIELD VILLAGE GC, COLUMBUS, OHIO
1985	THE BELFRY, WEST MIDS, ENGLAND
1983	PGA NATIONAL GC, PALM BEACH GDNS, FL
1981	WALTON HEATH GC, SURREY, ENGLAND
1979	THE GREENBRIER, WEST VIRGINIA
1977	ROYAL LYTHAM & ST. ANNES, LANCS, ENGLAND
1975	LAUREL VALLEY GC, LIGONIER, PA
1973	MUIRFIELD, GULLANE, SCOTLAND
1971	OLD WARSON CC, ST. LOUIS, MO
1969	ROYAL BIRKDALE GC, LANCS, ENGLAND
1967	CHAMPIONS GC, HOUSTON, TEXAS
1965	ROYAL BIRKDALE GC, LANCS, ENGLAND
1963	EAST LAKE CC, ATLANTA, GA
1961	ROYAL LYTHAM & ST. ANNES, LANCS, ENGLAND
1959	ELDORADO CC, PALM DESERT, CA
1957	LINDRICK GC, YORKSHIRE, ENGLAND
1955	THUNDERBIRD CC, PALM SPRINGS, CA
1953	WENTWORTH GC, SURREY, ENGLAND
1951	PINEHURST CC, NORTH CAROLINA
1949	GANTON GC, SCARBOROUGH, ENGLAND
1947	PORTLAND GC, PORTLAND, OREGON
1939-1945	NO MATCHES PLAYED DUE TO WORLD WAR II
1937	SOUTHPORT & AINSDALE GC, ENGLAND
1935	RIDGEWOOD CC, RIDGEWOOD, N.J.
1933	SOUTHPORT & AINSDALE GC, ENGLAND
1931	SCIOTO CC, COLUMBUS, OHIO
1929	MOORTOWN GC, LEEDS, ENGLAND
1927	WORCESTER CC, WORCESTER, MASS

1961 saw all matches reduced from 36 holes to 18, which has remained the position since. In 1963,

PAST RESULTS – AT A GLANCE

WINNER	
US 14½	EUROPE 13½
EUROPE 14½	US 13½
EUROPE 14½	US 13½
US 15	EUROPE 13
US 14½	EUROPE 13½
EUROPE 14	US 14
EUROPE 15	US 13
EUROPE 16½	US 11½
US 14½	EUROPE 13½
US 18½	EUROPE 9½
US 17	EUROPE 11
US 12½	GB & IRE 7½
US 21	GB & IRE 11
US 19	GB & IRE 13
US 18½	GB 13½
US 16	GB 16
US 23½	GB 8½
US 19½	GB 12½
US 23	GB 9
US 14½	GB 9½
US 8½	GB 3½
GB 7½	US 4½
US 8	GB 4
US 6½	GB 5½
US 9½	GB 2½
US 7	GB 5
US 11	GB 1
US 8	GB 4
US 9	GB 3
GB 6½	US 5½
US 9	GB 3
GB 7	US 5
US 9½	GB 2½

fourball matches were introduced and the overall match extended to three days from the previous two.

THE GREAT SURVIVOR

BY ANDY SWALES

The Ryder Cup celebrated its 75th birthday in June 2002. Yet, for much of its life, the competition has teetered on the edge of extinction. Even in its debut year of 1927, its founder Samuel Ryder had to stump up some of the cash to pay for the British and Irish team to travel across the Atlantic. The rest of the money was collected through public donations, a full list of which was printed in national newspapers at the time. When the event resumed after the Second World War, the British team needed more financial help to make the trip to Oregon. This time an American called Robert Hudson baled them out.

It was a similar story in 1965 when Royal Birkdale member Brian Park came to the rescue, using his own money to promote the contest and pay for a tented village.

Even in the late 1970s, when the scale of American domination was at its height, the match appeared to be beyond redemption. But thanks to the foresight of Jack Nicklaus, and others, the match was revamped. After 50 years of Great Britain and Ireland (until 1977), the team's boundaries were extended to incorporate the continent of Europe.

Since then, players such as Seve Ballesteros, Bernhard Langer, Jose-Maria Olazabal, Jesper Parnevik and Sergio Garcia have been allowed to grace the fairways of the Ryder Cup. And to bring the story up to date, the terrible events of September 11th last year meant that the match had to be postponed. But 12 months later, the 24 players who should have played at The Belfry last September will finally make that journey.

However, since the mid-1980s, the Ryder Cup has not merely survived, it has positively flourished, becoming one of the highlights of the sporting calendar – even if it is only for three days, every couple of years. Yet the build-up to this year's match has been strangely subdued. So far, there has been little of the hype normally associated as Ryder Cup week approaches. With the teams already selected, there has been none of the usual week-in, week-out, coverage of the qualifying process.

And, as the teams were picked last summer, it is interesting to look at the players who may have forced themselves into contention had qualifying been in existence this season. For the hosts, Justin Rose has made great strides in 2002 while Jose Maria Olazabal is the fifth highest European in the World Ranking (in early August).

Even at number 50 in the world, Nick Faldo may have been called-up for his 12th Ryder Cup cap. His experience would certainly have come in handy. Although far from his championship-winning form of the late-Eighties and early-Nineties, Faldo is enjoying his best season for a long time. Perhaps one of the two Danish Hansens would have also forced their way into the team.

One player who has travelled in the other direction is Lee Westwood. In early August 2001, he was 10th in the World Ranking but on August 1st, 2002, he is not in the top 100. For the Americans, players such as Bob Estes and Chris DiMarco – both inside the world's top 20 – and Jerry Kelly may have qualified on this year's form. Their fall guy is Hal Sutton who has slipped more than 80 places down the ranking in 12 months.

INTRODUCTION

As for the two captains, both will arrive at The Belfry with good and bad memories of the venue. European skipper Sam Torrance will always be remembered for holing a birdie putt, on the 18th green in 1985, that won back the Ryder Cup after a gap of 28 years. But in 1993, the Scot was injured and had to withdraw from his singles, as Europe were beaten 15-13 with the visitors making one of their customary final day recoveries.

Curtis Strange, his American counterpart, was part of the losing 1985 team, as well as the US side that failed to regain the trophy four years later when the match finished all square 14-14. But, on a positive note, Strange has won both his singles at the Midlands venue, including the last tie of the 1989 meeting when he beat Ian Woosnam to bring the scores level. The Americans had earlier trailed 14-10 and appeared to be heading for a third straight defeat until a late quartet of victories salvaged some lost pride.

In all, Torrance has played in eight Ryder Cup matches, three of which ended in joy, four in tears, with one stalemate. His most recent memory of the match was at Oak Hill where European happiness meant anguish for Strange who lost a key singles to Faldo. Strange, who was one-up on Faldo at the 17th tee, bogied each of the final two holes and was criticised by the media for losing America the Ryder Cup.

Even six months later he was still being heckled at tournaments and on one occasion Faldo, who happened to be one of Strange's playing partners, was forced to remonstrate with a vocal member of the public.

Strange has played in five Ryder Cup matches but only on his debut in 1983 has he tasted team glory. From a European perspective, let's hope that his wait for another triumph goes on a little longer.

THEN AND NOW.....

WORLD RANKING COMPARISON

EUROPE	at 1/9/01	at 1/8/02	UNITED STATES	at 1/9/01	at 1/8/02
Sergio Garcia	7	5	Tiger Woods	1	1
Padraig Harrington	15	8	Phil Mickelson	2	2
Darren Clarke	8	14	David Toms	10	6
Colin Montgomerie	11	15	Davis Love III	6	7
Bernhard Langer	25	30	David Duval	3	9
Niclas Fasth	47	32	Jim Furyk	9	12
Thomas Bjorn	14	36	Scott Verplank	27	20
Jesper Parnevik	21	44	Scott Hoch	19	25
Paul McGinley	45	57	Paul Azinger	23	41
Phillip Price	58	85	Mark Calcavecchia	20	43
Pierre Fulke	41	92	Stewart Cink	26	48
Lee Westwood	13	107	Hal Sutton	17	99
Average:	25.42	43.75	Average:	13.58	26.08

BETTING ANALYSIS

BY ANDY SWALES

For those wishing to place a bet on the final outcome of this year's Ryder Cup, it is worth remembering one key statistic. Not once in the last seven matches has the winning margin been greater than two points. So, if recent history is to repeat itself at The Belfry, there can only be five different options from which to choose: a European victory by one or two points, an American success by either one or two points, or a tie. Judging by the closeness of these results it is surprising that a draw has not occurred more often.

VICTORY MARGINS
(1987-1999)

	SCORE	MARGIN
1987	15-13	2
1989	14-14	0
1991	14.5-13.5	1
1993	15-13	2
1995	14.5-13.5	1
1997	14.5-13.5	1
1999	14.5-13.5	1

THE TIGER FACTOR

Another key area for gamblers to mull over is the likely performance of Tiger Woods, who has so far struggled in two Ryder Cup appearances. In 10 ties overall, Woods has a disappointing success rate of 35 per cent. Yet it is hard to imagine the world number one losing another three matches at The Belfry. In fact, 'the law of averages' – if it exists! – probably means he will be the major player in the Midlands and could well be the difference between the two sides.

When he made his Spanish debut five years ago, Woods was already a top player, having won one Major championship. By Massachusetts in September 1999, he'd won two Major titles. This time, he goes into the match with eight Major triumphs behind him and is a far more powerful player than he was at the time of his previous Ryder Cup starts.

Surely Tiger will register at least three and a half points out of five. Perhaps he may complete the match with a 4-1 record. If this is the case, would Europe be able to make-up this three-point deficit from the other 23 matches, bearing in mind that the widest winning margin in the last 15 years is only two points? If Europe are looking for a crumb of comfort in all of this then Tiger's record in the Presidents Cup may provide it. In two appearances (1998 & 2000), his record stands at 50 per cent (five wins and five losses).

BETTING ANALYSIS

In the 2000 match, played in Virginia in October, when Tiger was three-quarters of his way towards holding all four Major titles at the same time, his tally was a fairly moderate three wins, two losses. But for a player who proved his liking for matchplay golf when he won an unprecedented three successive US Amateur Championships, surely it is only a matter of time before he clicks into top gear at the Ryder Cup.

FOURSOMES & THE FIRST DAY

Since the Ryder Cup became competitive in 1983, the outcome of the foursomes has been too close to call. Over the last nine matches (72 foursomes in all), the sides are divided by just two points, with Europe holding sway 37-35 (table 1). This year's hosts have had the edge in the last four meetings but what is more interesting is the split between the teams over the two sessions of foursomes. While the Americans perform better in the first series – usually on the first morning – Europe undoubtedly save their best till the second round of games. In the second foursomes session Europe enjoy a 21-15 advantage having lost just one (1991) of nine since 1983 (table 2). Possibly the most important aspect of all this is not which team is better than the other at foursomes, but rather that the US come out of the blocks better than Europe.

Only once since 1983 have Europe won the first session, for which the States enjoy a cumulative five-point advantage (table 3). Europe's quick start in 1999 ended 26 years of first morning blues. By the end of the first day the table has usually turned, with Europe on top more times than not (table 4). Possibly the key foursomes partnership for Europe will be the Irish pairing of Padraig Harrington and Paul McGinley – providing the latter can find some reasonable form. The duo won three of their four games in April's Seve Trophy. For the Americans, Hal Sutton's foursomes record is hard to beat. In Ryder Cup and Presidents Cup combined, his cumulative tally is: Played 8, Won 6, Halved 1, Lost 1. Sutton also plays well on the first morning, having won all three of his games in the opening session of play. The only drawback regarding a punt on Hal is his current form.

FOURSOMES POINTS (table 1)

	EUR	USA
1983	4	4
1985	4	4
1987	4.5	3.5
1989	3	5
1991	2	6
1993	5	3
1995	5	3
1997	5	3
1999	4.5	3.5
Total	37	35

2nd FOURSOMES SESSION (table 2)

	EUR	USA
1983	2	2
1985	3	1
1987	2.5	1.5
1989	2	2
1991	1	3
1993	3	1
1995	3	1
1997	2.5	1.5
1999	2	2
Total	21	15

BETTING ANALYSIS

1st SESSION OF PLAY (table 3)

	EUR	USA
1983	2	2
1985	1	3
1987	2	2
1989	1	3
1991	1	3
1993	2	2
1995	2	2
1997	2	2
1999	2.5	1.5
Total	15.5	20.5

1st DAY POINTS (table 4)

	EUR	USA
1983	4.5	3.5
1985	3.5	4.5
1987	6	2
1989	5	3
1991	3.5	4.5
1993	4.5	3.5
1995	3	5
1997	4.5	3.5
1999	6	2
Total	40.5	31.5

FOURSOMES RECORDS

NAME	Pld	W	H	L
AZINGER PAUL	5	2	-	3
CALCAVECCHIA MARK	4	4	-	-
CLARKE DARREN	2	1	-	1
DUVAL DAVID	1	-	-	1
FURYK JIM	2	-	-	2
GARCIA SERGIO	2	2	-	-
HARRINGTON PADRAIG	2	-	1	1
HOCH SCOTT	2	2	-	-
LANGER BERNHARD	16	10	-	6
LOVE DAVIS	6	2	1	3
MICKELSON PHIL	2	-	1	1
MONTGOMERIE COLIN	9	6	-	3
PARNEVIK JESPER	4	2	2	-
SUTTON HAL	6	4	1	1
WESTWOOD LEE	4	2	-	2
WOODS TIGER	4	1	1	2

Thomas Bjorn has never played a Ryder Cup foursomes.

BETTING ANALYSIS

FOURBALLS

On paper, the Europeans usually come out on top in this category. Since 1983 Europe have enjoyed better fourball results in six out of nine matches, while suffering a deficit only twice.

On two occasions the Europeans even posted clean sweeps (4-0), with the Americans having to return to 1971 to locate the last time they won all four ties in a fourball session.

Historically, fourballs was always considered a format that favoured the Americans, but that doesn't appear to be the case any more (table 5).

FOURBALL POINTS (table 5)

	EUR	USA
1983	4	4
1985	5	3
1987	6	2
1989	6	2
1991	6	2
1993	3.5	4.5
1995	2	6
1997	5.5	2.5
1999	5.5	2.5
Total	43.5	28.5

FOURBALL RECORDS

NAME	Pld	W	H	L
AZINGER PAUL	6	1	1	4
BJORN THOMAS	1	1	-	-
CALCAVECCHIA MARK	4	-	-	4
CLARKE DARREN	3	2	-	1
DUVAL DAVID	2	-	1	1
FURYK JIM	2	-	-	2
GARCIA SERGIO	2	1	1	-
LANGER BERNHARD	13	5	2	6
LOVE DAVIS	7	1	2	4
MICKELSON PHIL	6	3	1	2
MONTGOMERIE COLIN	9	3	2	4
PARNEVIK JESPER	3	2	1	-
SUTTON HAL	5	1	2	2
WESTWOOD LEE	4	2	-	2
WOODS TIGER	4	1	-	3

Padraig Harrington and Scott Hoch have never played in a Ryder Cup fourball tie.

BETTING ANALYSIS

SINGLES

Little European glory to mention in this category. The last match proved to be Europe's worst singles performance since 1979 and even in the glory years of 1987 and 1997, Europe took a terrible hammering on singles day.

Since 1983, the United States have 'won' the singles seven times out of nine, collecting 60.5 points out of a total of 108 (table 6).

SINGLES POINTS (table 6)

	EUR	USA
1983	5.5	6.5
1985	7.5	4.5
1987	4.5	7.5
1989	5	7
1991	5.5	6.5
1993	4.5	7.5
1995	7.5	4.5
1997	4	8
1999	3.5	8.5
Total	47.5	60.5

SINGLES RECORDS

NAME	Pld	W	H	L
AZINGER PAUL	3	2	1	-
BJORN THOMAS	1	-	1	-
CALCAVECCHIA MARK	3	1	1	1
CLARKE DARREN	2	-	-	2
DUVAL DAVID	1	1	-	-
FURYK JIM	2	2	-	-
GARCIA SERGIO	1	-	-	1
HARRINGTON PADRAIG	1	1	-	-
HOCH SCOTT	1	-	1	-
LANGER BERNHARD	9	3	3	3
LOVE DAVIS	4	3	-	1
MICKELSON PHIL	3	3	-	-
MONTGOMERIE COLIN	5	3	2	-
PARNEVIK JESPER	2	-	-	2
SUTTON HAL	3	1	1	1
WESTWOOD LEE	2	-	-	2
WOODS TIGER	2	1	-	1

BETTING ANALYSIS

KEY SESSIONS

If anyone is looking to find a session of play that mirrors the entire match, then the third session is usually a vital one. Since 1983, the second morning's play has been foursomes on six occasions, and three times it has hosted the second round of fourballs. But only once (out of nine) has a team lost the third session and gone on to win the match (table 7).

For Europe, their form is at its height in sessions two and three, in which over the past 19 years they have enjoyed a success rate of 64 per cent. The Americans usually shine at both ends of the match (sessions 1 & 5). Europe's performance at Oak Hill – where they lost neither the opening foursomes nor the singles – is apparently no more than a collector's item (table 9).

SESSIONS 2 & 3 (table 8)

	EUR	USA
1983	4	4
1985	5	3
1987	6.5	1.5
1989	6	2
1991	3.5	4.5
1993	5.5	2.5
1995	4	4
1997	6	2
1999	5.5	2.5
Total	46	26

SESSIONS 1 & 5 (table 9)

	EUR	USA
1983	7.5	8.5
1985	8.5	7.5
1987	6.5	9.5
1989	6	10
1991	6.5	9.5
1993	6.5	9.5
1995	9.5	6.5
1997	6	10
1999	6	10
Total	63	81

THE VITAL THIRD SESSION (table 7)

	EUR	USA
1983	1.5	2.5
1985	2.5	1.5
1987	2.5	1.5
1989	2	2
1991	1	3
1993	3	1
1995	3	1
1997	3.5	0.5
1999	2	2
Total	21	15

BETTING ANALYSIS

EUROPE'S MOST PRODUCTIVE SESSION
Day One (afternoon)

	EUR	USA
1983	2.5	1.5
1985	2.5	1.5
1987	4	0
1989	4	0
1991	2.5	1.5
1993	2.5	1.5
1995	1	3
1997	2.5	1.5
1999	3.5	0.5
Total	25	11

OVERALL RECORDS

NAME	Pld	W	H	L
AZINGER PAUL	14	5	2	7
BJORN THOMAS	2	1	1	-
CALCAVECCHIA MARK	11	5	1	5
CLARKE DARREN	7	3	-	4
DUVAL DAVID	4	1	1	2
FURYK JIM	6	2	-	4
GARCIA SERGIO	5	3	1	1
HARRINGTON PADRAIG	3	1	1	1
HOCH SCOTT	3	2	1	-
LANGER BERNHARD	38	18	5	15
LOVE DAVIS	17	6	3	8
MICKELSON PHIL	11	6	2	3
MONTGOMERIE COLIN	23	12	4	7
PARNEVIK JESPER	9	4	3	2
SUTTON HAL	14	6	4	4
WESTWOOD LEE	10	4	-	6
WOODS TIGER	10	3	1	6

BETTING ANALYSIS

ROOKIES & WILDCARDS

Tony Jacklin's claim, that nothing beats experience when it comes to surviving the excruciating pressure of the Ryder Cup, certainly seems to be a case of wise words indeed. In his final three matches as European captain (1985-87-89), Jacklin was fortunate to have a total of only four rookies in his team. In none of those three matches were Europe beaten, though two of Jacko's wild card selections were indeed rookies. Young talent Jose Maria Olazabal was chosen in 1987, while another Spaniard, Jose Rivero, was picked in 1985 because he'd won a European Tour event at The Belfry some 14 months previously.

It may also be no coincidence that when Europe won at Oak Hill in 1995, there were only two debutants in the team.

Overall, American rookies do marginally better than their European counterparts, but since 1983 neither groups have won more than 50 per cent of their games.

Where Europe's rookies tend to fall down is in the singles. In 1997, when Europe were victorious, none of the five rookies won, with four not even getting as far as the 18th tee.

Two years later, five of the seven rookies were beaten, although in mitigation, three of them weren't even given the opportunity to acclimatise themselves competitively on days one and two.

Generally, the team with fewer rookies end up winning and at The Belfry, European debutants outnumber American ones by four to three.

Regarding wildcards, American captains tend to fair better than European ones. In the last 20 years, US wildcards have enjoyed a success rate of 56 per cent, compared to 45 per cent for Europe. This year, however, may be the exception with Sergio Garcia and Jesper Parnevik likely to perform better than either Scott Verplank or Paul Azinger.

EUROPEAN ROOKIES

	NO.	W-H-L
1983	4	4-2-7
1985	1	1-0-1
1987	2	4-1-4
1989	1	1-0-2
1991	5	6-2-6
1993	4	4-0-7
1995	2	2-0-3
1997	5	5-6-6
1999	7	8-5-8
Total	31	35-16-44

AMERICAN ROOKIES

	NO.	W-H-L
1983	5	9-2-7
1985	4	3-1-9
1987	5	6-2-7
1989	5	10-1-6
1991	3	1-0-5
1993	4	5-0-6
1995	5	11-0-6
1997	4	4-4-7
1999	1	1-1-2
Total	36	50-11-55

PLAYERS IN FOCUS
UNITED STATES

PAUL AZINGER Normally a slow starter in the Ryder Cup. None of his five wins have come in sessions one or two, while in five matches on day one, the Zinger has only been able to muster half-a-point in total.

MARK CALCAVECCHIA An enigma. With his strong attacking play, fourballs should be more his forte than foursomes. Yet the opposite is the case. Calcavecchia has won all four of his Ryder Cup foursomes, while losing in each of his quartet of fourballs. On his last outing in 1991, he lost the final four holes of his singles to halve with Colin Montgomerie.

STEWART CINK Yet to play in the Ryder Cup, but on his Presidents Cup debut in 2000, won all four of his matches.

DAVID DUVAL Under performed in 1999 when his only victory came on singles day. However, he normally churns out more than his fair share of birdies which makes him a fourball star waiting to happen.

JIM FURYK Making his third straight Ryder Cup appearance. Is yet to win at either foursomes or fourballs but is 100 per cent in singles. Is a similar story in the Presidents Cup in which he has won both his singles but remains only 50 per cent overall.

SCOTT HOCH In three Presidents Cup appearances his record stands at seven wins, one half, four losses (62.5 per cent). And in his only Ryder Cup match he remained unbeaten in three games – although was fortunate to get away with a half against Colin Montgomerie at Valderrama. Is another accurate performer off the tee which would make him a good foursomes player. Hoch turns 47 in November, but that shouldn't be a hindrance as he seems to get better with age. Back in 1993, Ray Floyd won three of his four games at the age of 51.

DAVIS LOVE Has a strange Ryder Cup record. Lost all four of his games at Valderrama, while remaining unbeaten at Brookline. Yet, for a player of his ability, should have a better success rate than 44 per cent. But he makes up for this at the Presidents Cup in which he has lost just five of 19 games. His strength appears to be singles where in both Ryder and Presidents matches he has won three of his four ties.

PHIL MICKELSON Protects a 100 per cent singles record. This birdie machine is considered by his various captains as a better prospect at fourballs than in foursomes. Hasn't missed a fourball session to date, but has played in only two of six foursomes. In the Presidents Cup has only lost one of seven fourballs, while suffering defeat in four of seven foursome matches.

HAL SUTTON After tasting defeat in his two previous Ryder Cup matches (1985 and 1987), was finally a winner two years ago when he was arguably the best player in either team. Ended the match with the best win/loss ratio of holes played of all 24 golfers. His tally reads: 20 wins, 12 losses in 85 holes. Has a good foursomes record of four wins from six matches in Ryder Cup play, while winning both his foursomes in the Presidents Cup.

DAVID TOMS Has never played in either the Ryder Cup or Presidents Cup. However, his accurate tee-to-green play should make him a great foursomes partner. Could well be one of the unsung heroes of the American team.

TIGER WOODS Has a remarkably bad fourball record. In the Ryder Cup has lost three out of four, while in the Presidents version has been defeated in four out of four.

SCOTT VERPLANK A former US Amateur champion who tasted international team glory in 1985 when he played in the Walker Cup. Colin Montgomerie was a member of the losing Great Britain and Ireland team that year.

PLAYERS IN FOCUS
EUROPE

THOMAS BJORN Not intimidated by big name Americans, although it is always difficult to gauge his mood and form. Played well in this year's Open Championship where he remained in contention until the final few holes. Finished in a tie for eighth, two shots out of a play-off. At the 2001 Dubai Classic, partnered Tiger Woods for all 72 holes to win the title by two strokes from the world number one. However, in 10 Seve Trophy games has a success rate of less than 50 per cent. Yet, on his week, is one of the best players in the world.

DARREN CLARKE Yet to win a Ryder Cup singles but did beat Tiger Woods in the final of the Andersen Consulting Matchplay Championship at La Costa, California, two years ago. But remains an enigma in every sense. Likely to partner Lee Westwood at The Belfry. In four foursomes and fourball matches at Brookline in 1999, the pair had a 50 per cent record.

NICLAS FASTH Making his Ryder Cup debut. Reached the last 16 of the Accenture Matchplay Championship in California earlier this year, losing to Paul Azinger at the second extra hole. Suffered three defeats in four Seve Trophy matches this season when his meagre tally for a week's work came to half-a-point. But he is one of only three members of the European team whose world ranking has improved in the last 12 months.

PIERRE FULKE Finalist in last year's Accenture Matchplay Championship down under since when his form has been inconsistent.

SERGIO GARCIA Currently heads the 'Total Driving' category on the US Tour. This combines driving accuracy with length, which should be a vital asset in the Ryder Cup, particularly in the unusual format of foursomes where consistency is they key. The only doubt is his form with the putter, which cost him dearly in The Open Championship at Muirfield. At the 1999 Ryder Cup, enjoyed the best win/loss ratio for holes played by a European — winning 21 and losing 14 of the 84 hoes he contested.

PADRAIG HARRINGTON Likely to be one of the stars of this year's Ryder Cup. Despite one or two wobbles in strokeplay events, is now Europe's second highest player in the world ranking — inside the top 10. Has a great matchplay pedigree having played in three Walker Cup matches (1991-93-95). In the 1995 match at Royal Porthcawl he won three of his four matches, including a foursomes victory over 19-year-old Tiger Woods. In the 2002 Seve Trophy beat matchplay specialist Jose Maria Olazabal in the singles (3&2) while ending the week with four wins out of five.

BERNHARD LANGER Although the German has won more matches than he has lost during his Ryder Cup career, with an overall success rate of 54 per cent, his record at The Belfry is below par with only five points from 12 games (42 per cent). Has won 10 of 16 foursomes overall, with three from five victories at The Belfry. However, after four fourball matches in the Midlands, is still looking for his first win. His Belfry fourball record reads two halves and two defeats. Goes into the match as easily the most experienced Ryder Cupper on either side.

PAUL MCGINLEY After finishing a career best eighth in last year's European Order of Merit, his form has been on the slide in 2002. At the start of August was outside the top 50 in the Tour money list, and is on course to suffer his lowest finish since his rookie year of 1992. On the plus side, however, was his excellent performance in this year's Seve Trophy when he posted four wins and one defeat in five games.

COLIN MONTGOMERIE Unbeaten at singles, Monty also has a good foursomes record with six wins in nine matches. He lost his first foursomes back in 1991, since when his only two defeats have been by the smallest margin possible (one hole). His solid tee-to-green play is certainly the key to his form in the alternate shot format.

JESPER PARNEVIK Another European who is suffering his worst spell of form for many a year. Despite losing both his Ryder Cup singles, remains unbeaten in both foursomes and fourballs, in which his cumulative tally reads: four wins and three halves from seven games.

PHILLIP PRICE At the beginning of August was a moderate 40th in the European Order of Merit. In the 2000 Seve Trophy he collected two and a half points out of four.

LEE WESTWOOD Experiencing his worst form since turning professional in 1993. At the start of August was not even in the top 80 of the European Order of Merit. The one glimmer of hope is that earlier this season he did win three of his four games in the Seve Trophy. Maybe friend and likely Ryder Cup partner Darren Clarke can coax some decent performances out of him.

SAMUEL RYDER

Samuel Ryder, the man whose name adorns the biennial contest between Europe and the US, was a successful businessman who made his fortune selling packets of seeds through the post – a pre-war mail order pioneer.

Born in 1858 in Manchester, England, he worked for the family firm – corn merchants – before moving south to seek his fortune.

He formed his seed company along with his younger brother James and became a respected and valued member of the local community, fulfilling the posts of Town Mayor, Justice of the Peace and church deacon among other roles.

Ryder did not take up golf until the age of 50, when he was forced to give up his favourite pastime of cricket through ill-health.

He elected to join his local golf club, Verulam in St Albans, in preference to bowls and undertook lessons six days a week from club pro Abe Mitchell, whom he paid a generous £1,000 a year. The only stipulation was that Ryder, a deeply religious man, would not play on Sundays.

In 1923 his company sponsored a tournament for the first time, at Verulam. Ryder caused astonishment in some quarters by paying all competitors the princely sum of £5. This enabled him to attract the top players in the country including Harry Vardon, James Braid and George Duncan.

With this clutch of top British players challenging their US counterparts, talk in the clubhouses up and the down the country often turned to which nation was the stronger and some kind of contest became inevitable.

Ryder was not the first man to come up with the idea of the top professionals from the US and Great Britain challenging each other but he was the first one with the drive and determination to see it through to fruition.

Officially, the first competition took place in 1927 in Worcester, Massachusetts, but a match of some sorts took place a year earlier at Wentworth in Surrey – and naturally Ryder was involved.

A group of top American players were in the area, pre-qualifying for that year's Open Championship at nearby Sunningdale, and they were invited to form a side to take on the top British players.

In the event the visitors were crushed 13½-1½ in a very informal atmosphere. Some reports claim that the Ryder Cup was presented to the winners but the US PGA refused to officially recognise a heavy defeat for their men under such informal conditions. Consequently, an official contract was drawn up to oversee the running of the competition, which began the following year across the Atlantic.

Samuel Ryder died in January 1936, aged 77, with his competition well established. Yet even he could not have imagined just how big the contest would become over the next 66 years.

RYDER CUP
OUTRIGHT BETTING

PRICES CORRECT
AS OF 13/08/02

	Europe	USA	Tie
LADBROKES	7/4	1/2	10-1
WILLIAM HILL	13/8	4/7	9-1
BLUE SQUARE	7/4	4/7	10-1
SPORTINGODDS.COM	7/4	4/7	10-1
EUROBET	13/8	8/13	8-1
TOTALBET	7/4	4/7	8-1
UKBETTING	7/4	4/7	9-1
BET 365	13/8	8/13	10-1
BETINTERNET	15/8	1/2	10-1
VICTOR CHANDLER	7/4	4/7	9-1

VICTOR CHANDLER SPECIALS –
Europe to lead after 1st day: 6/5   Europe to lead after 2nd day: Evens   Europe to win final day singles: 9/4

26

CANTOR SPORT BETTING SPREADS

• 25POINTS WIN • 10 POINTS TIE

USA 15-16.5
EUROPE 7-8.5
TIE 6-9

WHO WILL SCORE THE MOST POINTS?
• WIN=50 • 2ND=30 • 3RD=20 • 4TH=10

USA

WOODS 26-29
MICKELSON 14-17
LOVE 10-13
DUVAL 8-11
TOMS 8-11
FURYK 7-9
VERPLANK 6-8
HOCH 7-9
CALCAVECCHIA 4-6
CINK 4-6
AZINGER 2-4
SUTTON 1-3

EUROPE

GARCIA 20-23
MONTY 12-15
CLARKE 11-14
HARRINGTON 11-14
PARNEVIK 11-14
BJORN 7-9
LANGER 7-9
FASTH 6-8
WESTWOOD 5-7
MCGINLEY 2-4
FULKE 1-3
PRICE 2-4

TOP EUROPEAN
POINTS SCORER

Dead heat rules apply.
Each-way 1/4 the
odds a place 1-2-3.

	Eurobet	Totalbet	UKbetting	Betinternet	Victor Chandler
GARCIA	3/1	3/1	10/3	3/1	10/3
MONTGOMERIE	5/1	11/2	5/1	5/1	6/1
CLARKE	5/1	11/2	11/2	6/1	6/1
HARRINGTON	6/1	11/2	11/2	11/2	4/1
PARNEVIK	8/1	8/1	8/1	8/1	6/1
BJORN	8/1	9/1	10/1	9/1	9/1
WESTWOOD	14/1	14/1	14/1	14/1	9/1
LANGER	14/1	12/1	12/1	14/1	14/1
FASTH	16/1	14/1	14/1	14/1	14/1
MCGINLEY	22/1	22/1	20/1	22/1	12/1
PRICE	25/1	33/1	33/1	28/1	16/1
FULKE	28/1	28/1	25/1	28/1	25/1

PRICES CORRECT AS OF 13/08/02

TOP US POINTS SCORER

Dead heat rules apply.
Each-way 1/4 the odds a place 1-2-3.

	Eurobet	Totalbet	UKbetting	Betinternet	Victor Chandler
WOODS	2/1	2/1	2/1	2/1	5/2
MICKELSON	4/1	9/2	4/1	4/1	4/1
DUVAL	7/1	13/2	7/1	7/1	13/2
LOVE	8/1	15/2	8/1	8/1	13/2
TOMS	10/1	9/1	10/1	8/1	8/1
FURYK	10/1	11/1	12/1	11/1	14/1
HOCH	14/1	18/1	16/1	14/1	20/1
CINK	16/1	16/1	20/1	16/1	20/1
VERPLANK	16/1	20/1	14/1	20/1	12/1
CALCAVECCHIA	20/1	18/1	20/1	20/1	20/1
AZINGER	25/1	25/1	25/1	25/1	28/1
SUTTON	33/1	33/1	33/1	33/1	40/1

PRICES CORRECT AS OF 13/08/02

US QUALIFYING TABLE

(Top Ten qualify automatically plus two captain's wild-card picks)

1	**TIGER WOODS**	2,447.5
2	**PHIL MICKELSON**	1,710.63
3	**DAVID DUVAL**	1,016.67
4	**MARK CALCAVECCHIA**	765.38
5	**DAVID TOMS**	755.00
6	**DAVIS LOVE III**	749.50
7	**SCOTT HOCH**	657.00
8	**JIM FURYK**	647.88
9	**HAL SUTTON**	613.00
10	**STEWART CINK**	586.63
11	**TOM LEHMAN**	543.75
12	**STEVE LOWERY**	542.00
13	**CHRIS DIMARCO**	534.00
14	**SCOTT VERPLANK**	508.50
15	**JOE DURANT**	505.00
16	**BRAD FAXON**	496.50
17	**FRANK LICKLITER II**	452.41
18	**ROCOO MEDIATE**	450.00
19	**BILLY ANDRADE**	426.25
20	**JEFF SLUMAN**	394.50

Wild-cards: **Scott Verplank and Paul Azinger**

EUROPE QUALIFYING TABLE

1	**DARREN CLARKE** (N.IRE)	2,281,476.75
2	**PADRAIG HARRINGTON** (IRE)	1,846,760.62
3	**THOMAS BJORN** (DEN)	1,684,002.63
4	**COLIN MONTGOMERIE** (SCOT)	1,488,625.42
5	**PIERRE FULKE** (SWE)	1,287,876.99
6	**LEE WESTWOOD** (ENG)	1,255,619.96
7	**PAUL MCGINLEY** (IRE)	1,087,584.01
8	**NICLAS FASTH** (SWE)	1,076,272.04
9	**BERNHARD LANGER** (GER)	1,072,119.74
10	**PHILLIP PRICE** (WAL)	858,944.71
11	**IAN POULTER** (ENG)	830,018.67
12	**MIGUEL ANGEL JIMENEZ** (SP)	770,071.69
13	**ANDREW OLDCORN** (SCOT)	737,106.98
14	**ANDREW COLTART** (SCOT)	732,210.42
15	**THOMAS LEVET** (FR)	730,846.18
16	**IAN WOOSNAM** (WAL)	702,890.96
17	**MATHIAS GRONBERG** (SWE)	701,193.84
18	**SERGIO GARCIA** (SP)	665,367.58
19	**JOSÉ MARIA OLAZABAL** (SP)	663,038.97
20	**ROBERT KARLSSON** (SWE)	662,148.70

Wild-cards: **Jesper Parnevik and Sergio Garcia**

PLAYER PROFILES

BY ANDY TONGUE

EUROPE | U.S.

EUROPE	U.S.
THOMAS BJORN	PAUL AZINGER
DARREN CLARKE	MARK CALCAVECCHIA
NICLAS FASTH	STEWART CINK
PIERRE FULKE	DAVID LOVE III
SERGIO GARCIA	DAVID DUVAL
PADRAIG HARRINGTON	JIM FURYK
BERNHARD LANGER	SCOTT HOCH
PAUL MCGINLAY	PHIL MICKELSON
COLIN MONTGOMERIE	HAL SUTTON
JESPER PARNEVIK	DAVID TOMS
PHILLIP PRICE	SCOTT VERPLANK
LEE WESTWOOD	TIGER WOODS

Thomas Bjorn

CAREER WINS

2001	DUBAI DESERT CLASSIC
2000	BMW INTERNATIONAL OPEN
1999	THE SARAZEN WORLD OPEN
1998	PEUGEOT OPEN DE ESPANA
	HEINEKEN CLASSIC
1996	LOCH LOMOND WORLD INVITATIONAL

Thomas Bjorn became the first Dane to represent Europe in the Ryder Cup at Valderrama in 1997 and, although he missed out on a place in the side two years later, will be regarded as one of the senior players on Sam Torrance's side at The Belfry. Bjorn played in just two matches under Seve Ballesteros but was arguably underutilised and will surely play a much more prominent part in 2002.

He teamed up with Ian Woosnam on the Saturday morning for a 2&1 foursomes victory over Justin Leonard and Brad Faxon, then earned a half against Leonard on the final day as Europe sealed a one point victory.

The Dane used the Challenge Tour as his platform to launch a successful career on the European Tour, winning four titles on his way to winning the Challenge Tour in 1995 with what was then a record total of 65,059 Euros (£46,471). Blessed with a solid, powerful game, he emerged as a genuine top class player by capturing the Loch Lomond World Invitational in 1996 over one of the most demanding courses on the European Tour. He became a major force in 2000, finishing tied second behind Tiger Woods in the Open Championship at St Andrews, and outright third behind the same player in the USPGA Championship at Valhalla. Bjorn started playing at age six because his parents played the game and his brother Síren is also a talented golfer. Thomas rubber-stamped his potential with two wins in 1998 but he struggled with a neck injury in the first half of 1999, which meant he missed out on the Ryder Cup that year. He returned to form with a victory in the Sarazen World Open at PGA Golf de Catalunya in October 1999, and then captured the Dunlop Phoenix tournament in Miyazaki, Japan, with a fourth extra-hole birdie to beat Sergio Garcia in a play-off. Began working with highly respected coach, Pete Cowen, midway through 2000 season and was rewarded with a victory in the BMW International Open. He produced arguably the best performance of his career in the 2001 Dubai Desert Classic, playing all four rounds in the company of Tiger Woods and emerging on top by two shots. He qualified automatically for his second Ryder Cup appearance, finishing third in the rankings behind Darren Clarke and Padraig Harrington.

A first round 68 at Muirfield meant B jorn was in with a real shout at this year's Open Championship but he was unable to make a real impression on the leaderboard with second and third round scores of 70 and 73, though he came back strongly in the final round with a 69, to eventually finish just two strokes behind the leaders in joint eighth place for an £81,000 paycheck.

Bjorn is bullish about Europe's chances in the Ryder Cup despite the Americans being favourites: "I think we look very strong. We knew last time that we were – we had to build a team for the future, and that was the thinking behind the team last time," he says.

"They came very close. There weren't many people that thought the team that went to America were going to go close, but they came very close and that shows their strength – how strong the Europeans were in strength and depth on our Tour – and we have come two years since then and we are even stronger now.

"So, I think we've got one of the best chances ever going into the Ryder Cup, and the Ryder Cup always shows different. Even though we are underdogs by ten points sometimes, we go into this Ryder Cup stronger than we ever have."

Unlike some Europeans, Bjorn understands why the US players tend to stick to their side of the Atlantic.

"If I was American and I could play 15 tournaments in America for three times the prize money we do in Europe, I wouldn't get my passport out. I would just stay there. There is no reason for them to come over here," he says.

"And you've got to understand why they stay at home. I feel it's a shame when some of them start saying poor things about The Open and other tournaments that are some of the best tournaments around. The Open is probably the best tournament in the world.

"But I can understand why they like to be in America and play in America. But the Open, taken aside, we don't really have the tournaments that compete with their biggest tournaments. In general, they are playing for a lot more money over there, and I tell you what, when you play over there and you finish 12th in a normal tournament, tied with seven others and you go home with $70,000, you feel quite happy."

Darren Clarke

CAREER WINS

2002	COMPASS GROUP ENGLISH OPEN
2001	DIMENSION DATA PRO-AM
	CHUNICHI CROWNS
	SMURFIT EUROPEAN OPEN
2000	WGC-ANDERSEN CONSULTING MATCH PLAY CHAMPIONSHIP
	COMPASS GROUP ENGLISH OPEN
1999	COMPASS GROUP ENGLISH OPEN
1998	BENSON & HEDGES INTERNATIONAL OPEN
	VOLVO MASTERS
1996	LINDE GERMAN MASTERS
1993	ALFRED DUNHILL BELGIAN OPEN

PLAYER PROFILES – EUROPE

The talented but tempremental Ulsterman Darren Clarke, rated one of the best matchplay golfers in the world, is now a senior member of the European team and will be making his third Ryder Cup appearance.

He made his bow in the competition at Valderrama in 1997 and teamed up with Colin Montgomerie in the fourballs on the second morning to defeat Fred Couples and Davis Love III.

But in his singles match on the final day he was edged out 2&1 by Phil Mickelson.

Two years later, he played the maximum possible five clashes. He partnered Lee Westwood in all four foursomes and fourballs matches and the pair won twice and lost twice. In the afternoon fourballs on the opening day they saw off the crack American pair Tiger Woods and David Duval – ranked number one and two in the world – by one hole in one of the most riveting clashes of the whole week.

But Clarke was exhausted by the final day, like Westwood, and he tamely surrendered 4 & 2 to Hal Sutton in the singles.

His finest moment came in the WGC-Accenture Match Play two years ago. In the knock-out format he disposed of a mighty impressive list of players: Paul Azinger, Mark O'Meara, Thomas Bjorn, Hal Sutton and David Duval, before beating Tiger Woods in the 36-hole final to claim the title.

"He did to Tiger what Tiger has been doing to everyone else," said swing coach Butch Harmon, who works with Clarke and Woods.

The fact that the final was played over 36 holes made Woods hot favourite. The American press believed that Darren's chubbiness would tell against the supremely fit Woods. The morning round between Clarke and Woods was nip-and-tuck. Woods led briefly with a birdie at No. 3. Clarke holed a 15-foot chip shot out of deep grass, with a bad lie, for birdie at No. 6 and a short- lived lead. They were even after 18 holes.

Clarke said he didn't want to walk down the hill to the practice range during the brief break between rounds. He was sighted taking a call on his cell phone and eating a banana. Early in the afternoon session Clarke took control as Woods fought his swing much of the time.

"I just couldn't quite hit the shots I wanted," Woods said. "I just wasn't able to put a lot of pressure on him." The deficit was just too big to overcome, even for Woods, who routinely pulls miracles out of his bag. It was the worst individual match-play loss as a pro for Woods since Italy's Costantino Rocca beat him four holes up with two to play at the 1997 Ryder Cup in Spain.

He had a fine 1999, winning The Compass Group English Open, then in the Smurfit European Open he became the first player on The European Tour to shoot 60 for a second time. He equalled three records – most birdies (12), consecutive birdies (eight), and the lowest round on The European Tour (it was the ninth time 60 had been achieved).

A year before he had won the Benson and Hedges International Open to set up a bold attack on the Volvo Order of Merit title. He almost succeeded in knocking Colin Montgomerie off his perch but in the end had to settle for second place.

Clarke showed his social concience by helping to organise a special pro-am at

Portmarnock in September 1998 in aid of the victims of the Omagh bombing tragedy.

Clarke is often described as 'fun-loving' and likes to play hard off the course as well as on it. He has always been keen on fast cars and is a familiar sight in his gleaming Ferrari with the registration DC 60 – a reference to those low rounds.

He retained The Compass Group English Open in 2000, coming from six shots behind on the last day to beat Michael Campbell and Mark James. After another consistent season he led the Volvo Order of Merit race going into the final week at Valderrama but his position of tied 17th in the WGC-American Express Championship was not sufficient to prevent his good friend Westwood from claiming the title of Europe's Number One.

Clarke won in South Africa for the first time at the start of 2001, capturing the Dimension Data Pro-Am and also triumphed at the Chunichi Crowns tournament in Japan before winning his first European Tour title of the year on home soil in the Smurfit European Open at The K Club in July – becoming the first Irishman to win in Ireland since John O'Leary 19 years earlier.

His form in 2002 has been solid, if not spectacular, with a third victory in his favourite tournament, The Compass Group English Open, but apart from that only a top ten finish in the Dubai Desert Classic. He came tied for 24th in the US Open with a respectable four days work but a third-round 77 in the rain and gales wrecked his Open challenge at Muirfield – like that of Tiger Woods. Even after a final round 69 he was disappointed.

"Birdie chances went begging at 9, 10, 13, 14, everywhere. I played easily well enough to shoot 65 and I walked off with a 69. It is disappointing," he said.

He had a great chance of Open glory a year earlier at Royal Lytham & St Annes when he was eventual winner David Duval's closest challenger in the final round until a double bogey six on the 17th hole. Clarke had to settle for joint third place, four shots behind Duval and one behind 2002 Ryder Cup team-mate Niclas Fasth of Sweden.

Having learnt his golf on the links courses of Northern Ireland he is tipped to win the Open one day. Clarke makes reference to his fiery nature when he says: "I'm like someone who built a fire but forgot to put a chimney in. I need a way to let the smoke out or I get very frustrated."

Like Westwood and Montgomerie he has the game to win a Major but was riled when former Ryder Cup skipper Tony Jacklin suggested the trio lacked the desire.

"I can assure you it's 15 or 20 out of ten. I do want to win a Major," he says. "I'm not out here to win tournaments and have a nice time. I want to win Majors. That is what I want to do and the Open is the one I'd want most."

RYDER CUP FACTS

In 1999 Andrew Coltart was the only player on either team not to win a single hole during the three days of competition. In his only match he was beaten by Tiger Woods 3&2, losing three and halving 13 of the 16 holes played

Niclas Fasth

CAREER WINS
2000   MADEIRA ISLAND OPEN

One of four European players set to make their debut in the 2002 Ryder Cup, Fasth is the latest in the line of Swedes, who have fought their way into the European side. He follows in the footsteps of Per-Ulrik Johansson, Joachim Haeggman, Jarno Sandelin and team-mates Jesper Parnevik and fellow debutant Pierre Fulke – this year being the first time that Sweden has supplied three members in the same European team.

He earnt his spot in Sam Torrance's side on the back of a solid 2000 and a stunning performance at the 2001 Open at Royal Lytham & St Annes, where he finished an impressive second behind David Duval. Fasth shot 69-69-72 in the first three rounds, then four birdies on the front nine in the final round put him top of the leaderboard.

Fasth, unaware of what had happened to Ian Woosnam, who was deducted two shots for carrying too many clubs in his bag, went to the turn in 31 and then birdied the long 11th as well to lead.

He was bunkered off the tee at the 14th and that brought Duval and Billy Mayfair into the joint lead on seven under, a position Duval changed with two putts, birdieing both the sixth and seventh.

Fasth knew, though, that he was at the crucial holes, the finishing stretch, and his four pars for a 67 were good, but might have been even better in the event as a 60-footer on the 17th and 40-footer on the last both grazed the edge of the cup. He was in at 4.15pm and there was over two hours for him to wait to discover his fate – Open title or near-miss. He thought it would be the latter and he was proved right.

Afterwards he said: "I had a great time out there today. I played very well and gave it all I had. I did not get too nervous. A couple of times I was affected, but nothing bad. I kept it under control. I really do like these situations, I guess that helps you a lot. I have been playing well for a long time. I have been up there most weeks, had good tournaments."

Amazingly, it was the first time Fasth had played in a Major after five failed attempts to qualify for the Open Championship, his four days work reaping him a cool £360,000.

His Open performance came in the middle of a spell of hot form on the European Tour which saw him tied for second in the Murphy's Irish Open and tied for 14th in the Scottish Open at Loch Lomond in the run-up to the big one. He also recorded top ten finishes in the Madeira Island Open, Algarve Portuguese Open and the Victor Chandler British Masters at Woburn.

And he continued to show good form in the aftermath of Lytham. His first tournament after his Open Championship heroics was the Volvo Scandinavian Masters where he finished a highly creditable 14th in front of an expectant home crowd.

His next outing took him to the USPGA Championship where, competing in his first Major Championship in America, he led the European charge over the first two days before eventually finishing joint 29th. Only Paul McGinley and Parnevik from the European contingent finished higher.

Unlike some of the rookie players whose form has tailed off alarmingly this season, Fasth has again shown he is made of the kind of stern stuff that will be needed at The Belfry. He came second in the Dubai Desert Classic behind Ernie Els and made a real impression on the South African.

Fasth wiped out Els' three-shot advantage after three rounds within seven holes, with an eagle on the third and birdie on the seventh, but then dropped four behind after running up a triple-bogey seven on the eighth that all high-handicap amateurs could identify with.

He refused to buckle, however, and reduced his deficit by half, only to drop another shot on the 16th as Els made the birdie that sealed victory.

"I've heard some comments that people have made about him and he's got to go out there and show them, and he's doing that at the moment," said Els.

"He's an excellent player, an excellent ball striker, a great putter. He really played well, kept on being aggressive and he wasn't scared. I guess he's going to be a great asset for the European team."

Fasth finished an extremely respectable ninth (tied) in the WGC-Accenture World Matchplay a week earlier. He has also shown encouraging form in the past couple of months with a tied second place in the Murphy's Irish Open, where he had finished second a year earlier, followed by another top ten spot in the Smurfit European Open, before a decent enough tie for 28th place in the Open at Muirfield.

The Monaco-based player came close to becoming the first player to win the European Tour Qualifying School twice. In 1996, he lost his card by one place and a small matter of 1,120 Euros (£800), but reclaimed his card by taking first place at San Roque.

Three years on, he was back on the Costa del Sol with a one shot lead going into the last day, but finished second to Alastair Forsyth. A three-time winner on the Challenge Tour in 1993, he finished 17th to gain his card in US PGA Tour School in 1997. He tried to follow Parnevik's lead and play in both America and Europe in 1998 and admitted it was a mistake,

"I spent all my time on a plane," he recalls. The decision to re-focus totally on Europe paid off with victory in the Madeira Island Open in 2000.

Fasth took up the game of golf at the tender age of ten, and was a product of the Swedish national team system. Fasth worked his way up to the Tour by spending a few years on the Asian Tours.

Pierre Fulke

CAREER WINS

2000	SCOTTISH PGA CHAMPIONSHIP
	VOLVO MASTERS
1999	TROPHÉE LANCÔME

This debutant Swede is one of the unknowns in the European side, and worryingly for Sam Torrance he has struggled with his form in 2002. Indeed he looked out of touch for much of 2001 having secured his place on the back of a good year two seasons ago, and a second place in the WGC-Accenture Matchplay Championship in January 2001. He is still without a win since the Volvo Masters in November 2000.

He hinted at a return to form in the 2001 Open at Royal Lytham & St Annes but that exploded in his face in the final round. He had hardly done a thing in the previous six months and spoke of personal problems.

But he says: "I think my game will hold up. I know I can beat these guys out there. It's been a pretty bad five months. It's down to a lot of things. I said don't worry about the Ryder Cup. I will be ready for September."

Fulke began the final day just one shot off the lead on five under par, easily his best performance since finishing runner-up in the World Matchplay in Melbourne in January 2001, a result which guaranteed his place in the Ryder Cup team and seemed to be close to his best after rounds of 69, 67 and 72.

But playing alongside fellow Swede and Ryder Cup team-mate Jesper Parnevik, he collapsed to a closing 83, 12 over par, that left him in a tie for 62nd place.

Bogeys at the first four holes set the tone for a bad day that got worse with an awful eight on the par three 12th, the same hole where Tiger Woods took a triple bogey six, and which all added up to 39 shots for the front nine and an inward half of 44.

A year prior to his appearance in the Matchplay Championship in Melbourne the Swede was at a low ebb, his career threatened by a back problem.

But all that changed during the first week of January. Although he eventually lost to American Steve Stricker in the final, his performance throughout the week saw him draw admiring glances from many quarters.

Fulke's performance also saw him gather an abundance of Official World Golf Ranking Points too, raising the former European Challenge Tour player to 32nd on the list at the time – a far cry from the 203rd place he occupied just one week prior to the 1999 Ryder Cup at The Country Club, Brookline.

The 30 year old's Antipodean exploits continued a glorious five-month spell following his victories in 2000 at the Scottish PGA Championship at Gleneagles and the Volvo Masters at Montecastillo.

Before that, his first European Tour title had come in France in September 1999 when he captured the Trophée Lancôme but, in between times, he had the real worry of a potentially serious injury with which to contend.

"The problem was that the vertebrae in my neck and back were in the wrong place and therefore were sending out the wrong signals to the rest of my body," says Fulke. "I went to see a chiropractor in Stockholm called Michael Jansch – he just put them back in place and everything was fine."

The Swede admitted that during his darkest hours, it had occurred to him that he might never play golf at the highest level again. "It came into my mind, very briefly, in Dubai at the beginning of the 2000 season," he says. "I had only hit about 300 balls in six days and the problem recurred. You do think about things like that, but thankfully everything is fine now."

At The Belfry, the Swede will follow in the footsteps of his fellow Ryder Cup countrymen Joakim Haeggman, Jesper Parnevik, Per-Ulrik Johansson and Jarmo Sandelin, something he admitted he is more than looking forward to.

"Before Metropolitan there was no pressure on me to make the team, at least not from myself, so doing what I did was a bonus. To be honest I didn't actually realise it until some press guys told me after the tournament that I was probably in the Ryder Cup team now.

"It was a great feeling though, knowing that you are in the team at such an early stage, because you can prepare properly for it. And I did things. I wanted to go over to America a little bit and try that out.

"I played four tournaments over there, so my schedule turned out completely different to what it would have been had I not got in the Ryder Cup team that early. But I would definitely say that you can really prepare for the Ryder Cup in a much easier way when you qualify that early, for sure."

Fulke is the son of a Swedish national swimming champion and golf was not his preferred sport as a youngster. Handball was a bigger lure until he caught the golf bug and won junior and senior amateur honours. He changed coach in 1997 to Swedish Federation's Steffan Johansson and became more positive.

Success came in the Trophée Lancôme with a last hole 25 foot putt at Saint Nom la Bretèche – after his mother, Christina, had a premonition that he would triumph.

He went on to consolidate that victory by taking the Scottish PGA Championship at Gleneagles in 2000, soon after his competitive return following a seven-month absence with what he believed to be an injury to his left wrist a week after winning the Trophée Lancôme.

The problem was later diagnosed as an injury to the neck and back vertebrae being out of alignment. Once cured, he won at Gleneagles, then added the Volvo Masters title, producing the Canon Shot of the Year – a 215-yard five wood at the 70th hole at Montecastillo – to edge out Darren Clarke.

His only top ten finish this year was a tied second place in the Johnnie Walker Classic and he will be hoping to rediscover his touch in the run-up to the clash at The Belfry.

Sergio Garcia

CAREER WINS

2002	MERCEDES CHAMPIONSHIPS
2001	MASTERCARD COLONIAL
	BUICK CLASSIC
	TROPHEE LANCOME
	NEDBANK GOLF CHALLENGE
1999	MURPHY'S IRISH OPEN
	LINDE GERMAN MASTERS

Nicknamed 'El Nino' Sergio Garcia is the latest in the recent long line of great Spanish players to grace the Ryder Cup. Although only 22, and still yet to win a Major, he has already proved a worthy successor to Ballesteros, Olazabal et al.

On his Ryder Cup debut at Brookline in 1999 as the youngest ever participant, the then 19-year-old teamed up with Sweden's Jesper Parnevik and the pair produced a stunning three and a half points from a possible four over the first two days.

On the opening morning they scored a confidence-inducing 2&1 fourballs win over Tom Lehman and Tiger Woods before edging Jim Furyk and Phil Mickelson by a single hole in a tense foursomes clash after lunch.

It was a case of more of the same on the Saturday as they saw off Justin Leonard and Payne Stewart 3&2 in the morning's fourballs before they were held to a tie by David Duval and Davis Love III, presumably as a bit of fatigue set in. Unfortunately, by the final day's singles, both were tired and Garcia went down 4&3 to Furyk, while Parnevik also lost.

European captain Sam Torrance will have to avoid falling into a similar trap when he decides upon his combinations for the pairs on the first two days.

Garcia got 2002 off to the perfect start when he won the Mercedes Championships in Hawaii, the curtain-raising tournament on the US Tour.

He sank a ten-foot birdie putt on the first extra hole of a play-off to defeat reigning US PGA Champion David Toms and give himself his third victory in eight months in America.

He had started the day four shots off the pace but moved to the top of the leaderboard with an excellent final round 64 for an 18-under-par total of 274 which put him alongside the American who had closed with a 66.

It meant the pair had to return to the 663-yard 18th and Garcia wasted little time in banking the $720,000 first prize, chipping his third shot ten feet past the hole and rolling in the winning birdie putt after Toms had two-putted for par.

He had also finished 2001 on a high, winning his fourth event of the year at the Lancome Trophy, coming out on top of a thrilling head-to-head battle with US Open champion Retief Goosen.

Garcia was four shots behind with four holes to play but finished in a flurry with birdies on 15, 16 and 17, while Goosen stumbled with bogeys on the final two holes to hand Garcia a one shot victory. Those four victories – two in the United States, one in Europe and one in South Africa – elevated him from 16th to sixth in the World Ranking, earning him $5.5 million worldwide in the process.

There isn't a player on the planet, Tiger Woods included, who drives the ball as effectively as Garcia, who averages almost 290 yards off the tee and hits three out of four fairways. In the PGA Tour driving statistic that combines distance and accuracy, Garcia finished third in 2000 and first in 2001. After finishing 176th in greens in regulation two years ago, he improved to 54th last year.

Garcia announced his arrival as a serious player back in 1999 in an extraordinary four-week period. First he suffered the humiliation of an 89 in the first round of the 1999 Open Championship at Carnoustie after which he sobbed on the shoulder of his mother in front of the world's media.

But a month later he was trading blows with Woods down the final stretch at the US PGA Championship, a tournament forever highlighted by Garcia's miraculous six-iron from behind a tree, right of Medinah's 16th fairway. He jackknifed his ball 185 yards off the base of the trunk and onto the green then dashed up the fairway to witness the shot, leaping in the air to determine its exact whereabouts, which turned golf's rising star into an instant action hero with the American golf public.

Earlier in 1999, competing at Augusta as the reigning British Amateur champion, he was the only non-professional to make the US Masters cut (in joint 38th place) and one month later he made his professional debut in the Spanish Open. A relatively inauspicious share of 25th place gave little indication of the furore to follow, and the extraordinary fulfilment of his four objectives in 1999: secure US and European Tour cards for 2000; win a European Tour event; and make the Ryder Cup team. He thus became the youngest player to tee up in a Ryder Cup and acquitted himself brilliantly before moving on to Scotland to captain Spain to its first victory in the Dunhill Cup – teaming up with Miguel Angel Jimenez and José María Olazabal. By the end of the year he was third in the European Tour rankings, ahead of illustrious players who had competed in twice as many tournaments throughout the season.

The results were less spectacular in 2000, as he combined his time between the European and US Tours, but the highlight of his season came in the "Battle of Bighorn" in August, when he beat Tiger Woods by one hole in a made-for-TV match in California and collected a cheque for $1.1 million.

The driving force behind Garcia has always been his father Victor, a former caddie at Club de Campo in Madrid, who worked his way up to a head professional. No successful player in the game's history has leaned so heavily on his dad as a coach. Victor, 51, is one of the rare fathers you'll see on the PGA Tour practice range.

He is the reason Sergio sharpened his English as a youngster by memorizing Ballesteros' victory speech from the 1988 British Open, and why Sergio began playing an international schedule at age 13. Victor's playing career stalled on the backstreets of Europe in the mid-1970s. Shy and unsophisticated, armed with little confidence and only a few crumbs of continental experience, he decided to teach his boy everything he could not have known himself.

Padraig Harrington

CAREER WINS

2001	VOLVO MASTERS
2000	BBVA OPEN TURESPANA MASTERS COMUNIDAD DE MADRID
	BRAZIL SAO PAULO 500 YEARS OPEN
1996	PEUGEOT SPANISH OPEN

Ireland's Padraig Harrington is rated one of the most promising players on the European Tour and he acquitted himself admirably on his Ryder Cup debut at Brookline two years ago.

On the opening morning, playing with Miguel-Angel Jimenez, he halved a foursomes clash with David Love III and Payne Stewart.

Although the pair lost narrowly to Steve Pate and Tiger Woods in the corresponding foursomes on the second morning, he bounced back superbly amidst the carnage all around him during the singles to beat Mark O'Meara by a hole. The first six Europeans out had crashed to defeat as the US mounted an incredible comeback but Harrington's heroics at least gave Mark James' men some hope, though it was extinguished by Justin Leonard later in the afternoon.

With a bit of luck and the benefit of hindsight Harrington could be going to The Belfry as Open Champion after coming agonisingly close at Muirfield in July.

Going into the final few holes he was hot on the heels of leader Ernie Els as the big South African uncharacteristically wobbled.

Harrington halved his lead with birdies at the 15th and 17th, but Els responded with a nine-foot putt at the 12th to go eight under. Harrington then elected to hit driver down the 449-yard 18th, but as soon as it left the clubface he knew it was heading for one of the bunkers down the left.

Unbeknown to him, Els found a pot bunker on the short 13th – the same trap he had failed to get out of on the Friday. The force was with Els, however. He splashed out brilliantly to within a foot of the hole to save his par and stay two in front.

Harrington's mistake was fatal. He had to go out sidewards and settle for a bogey, which meant he finished one shot off the lead and so missed out on a play-off with Els, Frenchman Thomas Levet, Stuart Appleby of Australia, and his compatriot Steve Elkington.

Afterwards the Irishman said it was only his performance on the greens which let him down in his bid to land that first Major.

"It is a full package you need to win a Major, I just didn't have the putting this week but I felt very comfortable out there and I don't think I need anything else."

In the week prior to the Open he finished tied for second in the Murphy's Irish Open, and also finished tied for third place in the Benson & Hedges International Open earlier in the season.

His only disappointment was the Volvo PGA Championship where he missed the cut back in May. Together with top ten finishes in the US Masters and the US Open, those performances have propelled him to fifth place in the Volvo Order of Merit, with Colin Montgomerie the only European player ahead of him.

Born in Dublin and part of a big family with four brothers, Harrington took up golf at age four at Stackstown Golf club in Dublin, but mixed it with other sports until aged 15 when he played in his first amateur tournament 'the Connaught Boys Championship', where he was beaten in the final on the 22nd hole.

He then made steady progress under the Golfing Union of Ireland training scheme to achieve a scratch handicap at age 15 and representative honours for Ireland.

His amateur victories included the West of Ireland Championship, Irish Close Championship & Irish Stroke Play Championship. He showed early signs of matchplay pedigree with three Walker Cup appearances: 1991 at Portmarnock, 1993 at Interlacken, and 1995 at Royal Porthcawl, where Europe were the surprise winners. He also studied and passed his exams to be an accountant during this period. He then went to the European Tour School in 1995 and finished 14th. His first full year on tour was in 1996 and he won the Spanish Open. He has followed that up with another three individual victories: 2000 Sao Paulo Open, 2000 Turespana Masters, and the 2001 Volvo Masters.

He has also played Dunhill Cup and World Cup for Ireland on six occasions and won the World Cup for Ireland in 1997 with 2002 Ryder Cup team-mate Paul McGinley.

Harrington was sensationally disqualified in the 2001 Benson & Hedges International for failing to sign his first round card. At the time he held a five stroke lead going into the final round.

It will never happen again: "Now, every time I sign my scorecard twice. Once at the top over my name and once at the bottom. Then I know I can't go wrong. I sign it as soon as I go in to record and then I check it again next to my name, because the only thing that can go wrong is if I've signed the wrong card."

His best finish in a Major prior to Muirfield was also fifth place – in the 1997 Open Championship. He has also tied for fifth place in the 2000 US Open Championship and 2002 US Masters, proving that he can mix it with the best of the Americans. Last season he finished second seven times and seemed destined to be whatever the male equivalent of a bridesmaid is – an usher, perhaps? – without ever becoming the groom.

He did not break this bogy until he won the season-ending Volvo Masters Andalucia at the beginning of November. It was no more than natural justice at work when he prevailed finally to nail down second place in the Order of Merit. He was also defeated in the final of the Cisco World Match Play Championship by Ian Woosnam.

Harrington has undergone some swing adjustments which he believes have added yards to his game and now undertakes a strict fitness regime and insists that he is "fitter than ever".

He is regarded as one of the slowest players in Europe. He insists he is not guilty of not being ready to play or practicing his technique too long, though he admits he is sometimes indecisive: "because I'm trying so hard."

Bernhard Langer

CAREER WINS

2001	THE TNT OPEN	1989	PEUGEOT SPANISH OPEN
	LINDE GERMAN MASTERS		GERMAN MASTERS
2000	LINDE GERMAN MASTERS	1988	EPSON GRAND PRIX OF EUROPE
1997	CONTE OF FLORENCE	1987	WHYTE & MACKAY PGA
	ITALIAN OPEN		CHAMPIONSHIP
	BENSON & HEDGES		CARROLL'S IRISH OPEN
	INTERNATIONAL OPEN	1986	GERMAN OPEN
	CHEMAPOL TROPHY CZECH OPEN		LANCOME TROPHY
	LINDE GERMAN MASTERS	1985	US MASTERS
	ARGENTINIAN MASTERS		SEA PINES HERITAGE
1995	VOLVO PGA CHAMPIONSHIP		LUFTHANSA GERMAN OPEN
	DEUTSCHE BANK OPEN TPC		PANASONIC EUROPEAN OPEN
	OF EUROPE		AUSTRALIAN MASTERS
	SMURFIT EUROPEAN OPEN	1984	PEUGEOT OPEN DE FRANCE
1994	MURPHY'S IRISH OPEN		KLM DUTCH OPEN
	VOLVO MASTERS		CARROLL'S IRISH OPEN
1993	VOLVO PGA CHAMPIONSHIP		BENSON & HEDGES
	VOLVO GERMAN OPEN		SPANISH OPEN
	US MASTERS	1983	ITALIAN OPEN
1992	HEINEKEN DUTCH OPEN		GLASGOW GOLF CLASSIC
	HONDA OPEN		ST. MELLION TIMESHARE TPC
1991	BENSON & HEDGES		CASIO WORLD OPEN [JAPAN]
	INTERNATIONAL OPEN	1982	LUFTHANSA GERMAN OPEN
	MERCEDES GERMAN MASTERS	1981	GERMAN OPEN
1990	CEPSA MADRID OPEN		BOB HOPE BRITISH CLASSIC
	AUSTRIAN OPEN	1980	DUNLOP MASTERS

Bernhard Langer returns to the European team to make his tenth Ryder Cup appearance after being controversially left out in 1999 – the first time since 1979 that he had not been involved – when Mark James' side threw away a commanding lead on the final day. Many observers thought that the experience and quality of the German was sorely missed.

Langer has criticised the European selection which has often meant taking on the might of the US without some of the continent's best players.

"The system is old and overdue. We have so many players playing on the American system and it only counts European [Tour] prize money, Majors and World Golf Championships. We need to change the system so that it allows the best 12 players to make the team and not the players who play week after week on the European [Tour].

I personally think we should change to a system that takes the top 12 players from the world rankings."

Langer describes, in his own words, how he came to start playing golf: "I grew up in a very small town on a very small golf course, a nine-hole golf course. I started caddying at 8 1/2 years old because my older brother caddied. I enjoyed earning money and I also enjoyed the game of golf. It was a challenge. The first time I caddied, I was caddying for the club champion and he took a liking to me, and I to him. Every time he showed up, he asked for my name. So I just really learned by watching him play."

In 1985 Langer won the first of his two Majors, both US Masters victories, by shooting a three-under-par 33 on the back nine on the final day while closest rival Curtis Strange was stumbling to a 39. The 27-year-old native of Augsburg fired his second consecutive four-under-par 68 to finish four rounds with a six-under-par 282 total.

Langer has conquered putting 'yips' to reach the top, and has hovered in the upper echelons of the game for over 20 years.

Stories about Langer almost always focus on his putting, which has been so erratic for a world class player. By his count, he has gone through four drastic styles in a never-ending battle with the yips.

"Many years ago, Sam Torrance told me I should go to the long putter. I said, no way. It feels like a snake in my hands," recalls Langer.

"It wasn't that I didn't like the look or I cared about tradition, I just couldn't get a feel for it. So, I went to cross-handed. That worked for a while, then I started using the split cross-handed grip. People thought I was crazy, that I looked like I came from Mars.

"But I won the Masters in 1993 with it, which has the toughest greens in the world. You don't get style points for looking pretty. After a while, that stopped working and I finally tried the long putter. It felt good in short range, and that's what counts."

Since 1980, he has only been outside the top 30 in the Volvo Order of Merit on one occasion in 1996. His Czech-born father settled in Bavaria after jumping a Russian prisoner-of-war train bound for Siberia. Langer has won 41 times in Europe, the last six with a broom handle putter which he adopted towards the end of 1996. A devout Christian, he helps organise the regular meetings of the Tour Bible Class. Won his 40th European Tour title, his first in four years, when he took The TNT Open at Noordwijkse in July, beating Warren Bennett in a play-off, and won a second title of the year when he won the Linde German Masters, the tournament he co-promotes with this brother Erwin, for a fourth time. It was his 11th victory on home soil.

In 1996, the only time he has been outside the top 30 in the Volvo Order of Merit since 1980, he finished 39th. Three years earlier he won his second Masters, by four strokes over Chip Beck. His Ryder Cup record stretches back to 1981 but he will unfortunately be best remembered for the missed six-foot putt on the final green against Hale Irwin at Kiawah Island during the 1991 'War on the Shore', which cost Europe a tie and handed the trophy to the US.

Afterwards Seve Ballesteros said: "Nobody could have holed that putt. Not Nicklaus in his prime. Not me. The pressure was just unbelievable."

He has played on four winning teams – in 1985, 87, 95 and 97 – and contributed an individual record of 18 wins, 15 loses and five halved matches.

His most impressive contest was in 1983 at Palm Beach, Florida when he won four out of five points – three in partnership with Nick Faldo and a singles victory on the final day as Europe just slipped to defeat by one point in the closest match for two decades.

He was in equally fine form at The Belfry two years later in Europe's famous win, with a crucial final day singles win over Hal Sutton and only one loss in his four pairs games. On the Saturday afternoon, in partnership with Ken Brown, he saw off the vastly experienced US pair Raymond Floyd and Lanny Wadkins 3&2.

Twelve years later at Valderrama and Langer was able to exorcise the ghost of Kiawah Island with a vitally important win in the singles over Brad Faxon as Europe's overnight lead began to evaporate and Ballesteros' team held on for victory by the most slender of margins.

He also played his part to the full at the Oak Hill Country Club, New York two years earlier with wins in the foursomes with Per-Ulrik Johansson and David Gilford respectively.

This season the consistent German has not been at his best but has put in respectable performances in two of the big pressure tournaments – the US Open and the Open – and will be sure to put in another Ryder Cup performance befitting his status as Europe's senior player.

Paul McGinley

CAREER WINS

2001	WALES OPEN WINNER	
1997	OKI PRO-AM	
1996	HOKE BRUKE AUSTRIAN OPEN WINNER	

Paul McGinley suffered more than most because of the postponement of the Ryder Cup last year. At that time he was in hot form and was sure to play an important role in the European side. 12 months on he is hopelessly out of form and like fellow out-of-form rookie Phillip Price, the likelihood is that McGinlay will play no part at The Belfry until the singles on the final day. McGinley rededicated himself to golf at age 19, after a broken kneecap forced him to give up his first love, Gaelic football.

Six years later, he helped Liam White beat Phil Mickelson and Bob May in the 1991 Walker Cup, and shortly thereafter earned his Tour card. Steady progress led to World Cup and Dunhill Cup berths representing Ireland in 1994, followed by his first European Tour victory at the 1996 Hoke Bruke Open.

Seeking greater consistency and improvement, he built an extensive home gym and hired a personal conditioning coach in 1999.

McGinlay went on to post his best season yet in 2000, with eight top-tens, finishing 18th on the Volvo Order of Merit. And he bettered this in 2001, with ten top-ten finishes, along with his European Tour win at the 2001 Wales Open – the victory that elevated him to his first Ryder Cup selection.

The relief was palpable as the 34-year-old absorbed the knowledge that he was about to take part in the greatest team event in golf. Victory came following two previous play-off defeats and the significance of his win was not lost on him.

He says: "That was the first play-off I'd won so obviously I was thrilled. It was a huge difference between first place and second in terms of Ryder Cup points and that was really a lot of pressure and that's what drove me on.

"Oh yes, it was on my mind. I would be lying if I said it wasn't. Since the Ryder Cup points list started I felt I could make the team. Obviously I've been under the microscope and everybody was looking to see how I was doing and there's been a lot of pressure on myself."

McGinley had previously won two European Tour titles, but his most cherished moment came in the 1997 World Cup of Golf when he and Padraig Harrington triumphed amid the sand dunes of Kiawah Island. He and Harrington were feted wherever they went in Ireland, but McGinley is under no illusion that the Ryder Cup is a different proposition to that tournament.

"It was a totally different kind of pressure to winning the World Cup because then we were in a no-lose situation" he recalls. "Three of the four Major winners of 1997 were in the field. It was a particularly strong field and we went out and didn't play with a whole lot of pressure because we weren't expected to win.

"Now I've done the opposite in terms of the Ryder Cup. I've been playing with a lot of pressure. Everybody knows how much I want to play in the Ryder Cup. Everybody knows the position I've been in. Everybody knows what I had to do."

McGinley admits that his decision to take up a golf scholarship in San Diego assisted his move into the professional game. He reveals: "It was the make or break for me. I had been working for a year before that having graduated from a college in Dublin with a diploma in marketing and I had to give up football because of my injury and I had played golf during that year I was working.

"And I was starting to get pretty good at it, so I had come to a crossroads: was I going to play golf and or was I going to go into business? And at the time there was a 20 per cent chance I'd go into golf. So, that's why America was perfect for me. I was able to kill two birds with one stone.

"I got my degree over there and I also played more or less full-time golf for two years competitively, and at the end of those years I was at the crossroads. I made the decision to turn pro and I've been here ever since."

McGinley believes he wasn't good enough to make previous teams, but has improved to the point where he can compete. He adds: "I'm very comfortable in a team position. My record as a team player has been very strong. I think a lot of that emanates from my years as a footballer, and hurling. I played at a very high level.

"So, I've always enjoyed team sports. I've always enjoyed being part of a package, if you know what I mean. Obviously, I won the World Cup with Padraig at Kiawah and we've always performed well in the Dunhill Cup. Team sports is something I certainly enjoy and I'm looking forward to being part of another team in the Ryder Cup."

His consistency in 2001 was something to be admired. He finished tied for ninth at the Dubai Desert Classic, then eighth at the Moroccan Open, before a joint second place at the B&H International Open. That was followed by a tenth place in the TPC of Europe and the same placing at the Compass Group English Open, before he secured third spot in the Scottish Open at Loch Lomond. He then finished tenth at the BMW International Open before further top spots in the Dunhill Links Championship and the Volvo Masters Andalucia.

Unfortunately he has been unable to repeat that form in 2002. He has managed just one top ten finish – back in the Dunhill Championship – and has missed an alarming five cuts. Hardly the kind of form to have the Americans quaking in their boots. European captain Sam Torrance will be hoping that McGinley can scramble together his game in time for the Ryder Cup.

Colin Montgomerie

CAREER WINS

2001	VOLVO SCANDINAVIAN MASTERS	1997	ANDERSEN CONSULTING WORLD CHAMPIONSHIP OF GOLF
	MURPHY'S IRISH OPEN		MURPHY'S IRISH OPEN
	ERICSSON MASTERS		COMPAQ EUROPEAN GRAND PRIX
2000	VOLVO PGA CHAMPIONSHIP	1997	NEDBANK MILLION DOLLAR CHALLENGE (SUN CITY)
	NOVOTEL PERRIER OPEN DE FRANCE		CANON EUROPEAN MASTERS
1999	CISCO WORLD MATCH PLAY CHAMPIONSHIP		MURPHY'S IRISH OPEN
			DUBAI DESERT CLASSIC
	BMW INTERNATIONAL OPEN	1995	TROPHÉE LANCÔME
	VOLVO SCANDINAVIAN MASTERS		VOLVO GERMAN OPEN
	STANDARD LIFE LOCH LOMOND	1994	VOLVO GERMAN OPEN
	VOLVO PGA CHAMPIONSHIP		MURPHY'S ENGLISH OPEN
	BENSON AND HEDGES INTERNATIONAL OPEN		PEUGEOT OPEN DE ESPANA
		1993	VOLVO MASTERS
1998	LINDE GERMAN MASTERS		HEINEKEN DUTCH OPEN
	ONE 2 ONE BRITISH MASTERS	1991	SCANDINAVIAN MASTERS
	VOLVO PGA CHAMPIONSHIP	1989	PORTUGUESE OPEN TPC

Regarded, along with US opponent Phil Mickelson, as the best current player in the world not to have won a Major, that tag has weighed heavily on his shoulders in the past few years but there are signs recently that he has come to terms with it despite blowing a great position after two rounds in last year's Open at Royal Lytham & St Annes.

Born in Glasgow, Montgomerie, whose father was secretary at Royal Troon, was introduced to golf from an early age. Even though he attended a public school throughout his formative years, he still found time to compete as an amateur. He had a successful amateur career, winning national championships and serving on two Walker Cup squads. He attended Houston Baptist University, Texas under a golf scholarship where he studied business management and law. He turned professional in 1987 and gained his first victory in the 1989 Portuguese Open. By 1991, he topped the European Order of Merit and did so again in 1994. He has also been awarded the Vardon trophy on three occasions. However, he has never won a Major. His best attempts were second and third in the US Open, in 1994 and 1997 respectively, and second in the US PGA in 1995, when he lost out in a play-off to Steve Pate.

In spite of that, he is a valuable member of the Ryder Cup squad and has represented Europe three times already. He does not practise as much as some other players because Montgomerie is a natural golfer rather than a technician.

He eventually surrendered his Volvo Order of Merit crown in 2000 to Lee Westwood after an unprecedented seven successive titles – a record which may never be surpassed. He received unstinting praise for his leadership qualities on and off the golf course at the 1999 Ryder Cup, in which he accrued three and a half points and beat the late Payne Stewart on the last green to maintain his unbeaten record in five Ryder Cup singles despite receiving horrendous abuse from drunken American fans throughout the round.

Attended investiture ceremony at Buckingham Palace in November 1998 to receive MBE from Her Majesty The Queen. Won six times in 1999 and twice in 2000, making a superb defence of his Cisco World Match Play title before being edged out by Westwood at the 38th hole of the final. Won the Ericsson Masters at the start of 2001 to capture his first title Down Under. Returned to winning ways in emphatic style when he claimed his 25th European Tour title in the Murphy's Iris and has now amassed over £9 million in prize money making him the leading money winner on the European Tour ever.

On his Ryder Cup debut at Kiawah Island in 1991 he was four down to Mark Calcavecchia with four to play in the singles but fought back, including a pitch-in from a bunker at the 16th, to win all four of the closing holes to grab a memorable half. He also teamed up with Bernhard Langer on the Saturday afternoon to earn a vital fourballs win over the volatile Corey Pavin and Pate. In 1993 he played in all five matches possible and repaid the faith shown in him by skipper Bernard Gallacher with three and half points from his partnership with Nick Faldo, and a singles win over Lee Janzen.

Two years later he bounced back from three defeats out of four in the first two days to overcome Ben Crenshaw 3&1 on the final day as Europe recorded only their second victory on US soil. Then at Valderrama in 1997 he enjoyed his finest Ryder Cup hour. On the final hole of his singles clash with Scott Hoch, scores level and needing a half to ensure Europe retained the trophy, the Scot hit a perfect drive and approach to 20 feet, while Hoch was unable to make the green in two and pitched to 15 feet. Montgomerie putted to within inches of the hole and then sportingly walked across to Hoch to concede the half. It was a fitting gesture to end a memorable contest, one which also saw the Scot finish the contest as top points scorer of the 24 players on show.

From rookie in 1991, Montgomerie graduated to senior figure at Brookline, assuming the mantle of the oldest player in the team, taking debutant Paul Lawrie under his wing and striking up a highly effective partnership which yielded two and a half points out of four, in addition to his brave, but ultimately futile, singles win over Stewart in the most trying of conditions.

Montgomerie is a big fan of the Ryder Cup and thinks the format should not be tampered with. He also believes that the events of September 11th 2001 have put the match into context and that should prevent a repitition of what he had to endure at Brookline.

"I think the event would have been softened by what happened at Brookline, but the events of 11 September will have softened it further. By all means, have a rivalry. But not a hatred. What we saw at Brookline was something very different from a sporting rivalry. The sooner we get away from that the better, and maybe taking a year out will be a blessing in disguise."

But he says the decision to postpone the contest for 12 months was the right one. "It was just too soon to have an American team competing against their allied continent," he says. "Rather than being opponents, the United States against Europe, there would have been a different atmosphere. You cannot have the Ryder Cup without competitiveness and fire. But when we do meet, we will be wearing our Ryder Cup 2001 shirts. It will just be 2002, that's all."

Jesper Parnevik

CAREER WINS

2001	HONDA CLASSIC
2000	BOB HOPE CHRYSLER CLASSIC
	GTE BYRON NELSON CLASSIC
1999	GREATER GREENSBORO CHRYSLER CLASSIC
1998	PHOENIX OPEN
1997	JOHNNIE WALKER SUPER TOUR
1996	TROPHEE LANCOME
1995	SCANDINAVIAN MASTERS
1993	SCOTTISH OPEN

The instantly recognisable Swede, with his signature, extravagantly-peaked baseball cap and drainpipe chequered trousers, has become one of Europe's leading players over the past decade. He won 14 times of which six came on the US Tour, which he joined in 1993 and is arguably considerably tougher than its European counterpart.

He has been picked for the third successive Ryder Cup as a 'wild card', and could prove to be Sam Torrance's ace in the pack at The De Vere Belfry with his experience and knowledge of Europe's opponents.

Parnevik's father, Bo, is Sweden's most famous comedian. He learned the game by hitting floating golf balls into lake behind the family home and has a son named

Phoenix, where Jesper first won on the US Tour in 1998.

His first European Tour win came at the Bell's Scottish Open in 1993 a year after he joined the Tour. A year later he should have won the British Open at Turnberry 1994. He held a two-stroke lead at the final hole but made a bogey to finish on 269, 11-under-par. Nick Price went eagle-birdie-par on the final three holes to capture a one-stroke victory. After further wins in 1995 and 1996 it was the following year (1997) that he moved up among the game's elite.

He finished in the top-25 in 11 of 19 events that he entered. He came runner-up five times and third once. In the Open he fired a third-round 66 to open a two-stroke lead over Darren Clarke and a five-stroke margin over Justin Leonard heading into the final round. His final round 73 was not good enough to hold off Leonard, so he had to settle for second place for the second time in his career. Later that summer he made his Ryder Cup debut at Valderrama when he was picked as one of Seve Ballesteros's 'wild cards' and joined compatriot Per-Ulrik Johansson in the team.

Parnevik's first match in the Ryder Cup arena was a titanic battle as he and Johansson took on the formidable partnership of Tom Lehman and Jim Furyk in the longest match in Ryder Cup history – five hours and 43 minutes – but the end was worth waiting for from a European standpoint as Parnevik holed from 20 feet on the 17th and even more bravely from ten feet on the last to edge the American pair by just one hole.

In the foursomes, Parnevik joined forces with Ignacio Garrido, whose father Antonio had played in the first Europe v USA match in 1979. The following morning, the first time a United States team failed to win a match all day, they secured a tough half with left hander Phil Mickelson and Lehman.

In the second set of foursomes matches Parnevik and Garrido were again paired together and again they held on for a half, this time with the reigning Masters and Open champions, Tiger Woods and Justin Leonard. Parnevik, as he had done on the first day, holed a crucial putt late in the match, this time from eight feet for an improbable birdie at the 17th after a wicked drive.

A tired Parnevik was defeated in his singles match by Mark O'Meara but by then Europe were on the way to victory.

In 1998 that first US Tour title came at the Phoenix Open, a three-stroke victory over Tommy Armour III, Steve Pate, Brent Geiberger and Tom Watson. He became only the second Swede to win in America following Gabriel Hjertstedt at the 1997 B.C. Open.

The following year he earned his second US title by two strokes over Jim Furyk at the Greater Greensboro Chrysler Classic, winning in wire-to-wire fashion, becoming the first player since Ernie Els at the 1997 Buick Classic to accomplish the feat. His final-round 70 earned him the victory and tournament record and he lit a victory cigar on the 18th green before holing his final putt.

He was an obvious choice as a wild card selection for Europe's Ryder Cup defence at Brookline and again contributed fully to the agonisingly close contest. He secured three and a half points from a possible four with the young Spaniard Sergio Garcia in the most effective pairing of the match.

Second out on the opening day, they could hardly have faced tougher opposition but the European pair fought back from two down to win on the 17th against Woods and Lehman.

In the afternoon they defeated Mickelson and Furyk on the final hole and their partnership continued to flourish on the second day as they first defeated the late Payne Stewart and Leonard and then, in an enthralling match against Davis Love III and David Duval, Garcia won the final hole to secure a half point.

Unfortunately he was extremely fatigued by the final day singles, as in Spain two years earlier, but this time it proved more expensive for Europe as he crashed 5&4 to David Duval at the heart of the US comeback.

In 2000 he won twice despite dealing with increasing hip pain that eventually required corrective surgery, and his eighth-place finish on the money list was his first year among the top ten.

He won his first tournament of the year at the Bob Hope Chrysler Classic by one-stroke from Rocco, then a second win came at the GTE Byron Nelson Classic in nail-biting fashion. He outlasted Davis Love III and Phil Mickelson with a par on the third play-off hole to win the largest winning purse of his career ($720,000).

The fine form continued in 2001 as he won a tour event for the fourth consecutive season, leading the Honda Classic for all the final three rounds. He was one off the lead after 54 holes in the Open at Royal Lytham & St Annes, but fired a final-round 71 to finish tied for ninth. This season his best performance has been a second-place finish at the BellSouth Classic, four strokes behind Retief Goosen.

Phillip Price

CAREER WINS

2001	PORTUGUESE OPEN
1994	PORTUGUESE OPEN

Debutant Phillip Price is another European player who has shown a worrying lack of form in 2002 and his participation at The Belfry may be limited to a singles match on the final day.

Apart from an impressive third place at the Victor Chandler British Masters at Woburn, he has not finished in the top ten of any event this year and he has missed four cuts including the Open Championship at Muirfield.

The Welshman had established a reputation on the European Tour as something of a journeymen, finishing comfortably within the top 115 places which would ensure he had a workplace for the following season but never seriously troubling the big names in the game.

However, Price made a conscious decision in 1998 to shed that slightly unflattering label. He embraced the work ethic and enjoyed a quick pay off by finishing 15th on the

Volvo Order of Merit that season, helped by a couple of runner-up finishes.

Suddenly, the journeyman was no more. Price gained respect wherever he played and although 1999 saw a slight dip in his fortunes, when he came 36th on the Volvo Order of Merit, four second place finishes in 2000 elevated him to eighth position and a place in all four Major championships in 2001.

The second European Tour title, which eluded him in 2000 after Gary Orr eagled the final hole in the Algarve Portuguese Open, finally arrived in that same event earlier this year when he closed in style with a 64 to capture the crown.

If ever Price needed a stage to showcase his abilities, it came in last year's World Golf Championships-NEC Invitational at Firestone Country Club in Akron. Although Tiger Woods retained the title with a barely credible 21-under-par total of 259, Price was the man who chased him home.

As darkness descended, causing Price to drop two shots in the last four holes, the Welshman kept his composure and tied Justin Leonard for second, securing him the biggest pay cheque of his career, 482,466 Euros (£293,722).

That outstanding finish provided the boost to Price's confidence and self-belief that he needed. There were few more consistent performers during the Ryder Cup qualifying campaign, where Price hovered around the tenth place mark for much of the closing months of the campaign.

In the end, it all came down to the BMW International Open in Munich. Although Price missed the cut, so did Ian Poulter and Miguel Angel Jiménez, who occupied 11th and 12th places going into the last counting tournament.

Thomas Levet of France and Scotland's Dean Robertson both made strong challenges to win the event which would have secured them tenth and last place, but they came up just short behind John Daly and Padraig Harrington.

As realisation dawned that he had achieved his life's ambition, Price said: "I feel a bit subdued at the moment. I don't really know how to feel. It's been such a long couple of months. We've got the champagne open, though, and we're going to party tonight. I have loads of friends and family coming round.

"I hope that by tomorrow I will have settled down and can enjoy the experience of being in the team. I wouldn't say that I felt the pressure so much in Munich as felt tired from the efforts of the last few months. Obviously I have felt it at certain times over the last few weeks and I think I tried too hard and that didn't help the cause.

"I figured anything I did this week would help but I felt it would come down to what others did rather than anything I did. I wanted to show up and give it my best shot. I am so tired. I am taking the week off, going to St Louis, then taking another week off so that I am fit and fresh and ready to play for my life at The Belfry."

A former short hitter Price hits much longer after he started using two-piece golf balls. He switched balls in 1999 and now hits his drives ten yards further: "It has transformed my game really," says Price, who does not speak Welsh.

He also works with sports psychologist Alan Fine. "We play a game and it's called 'act as if'. The idea is that you always act confidently even if you don't feel that way inside. Sometimes it helps if I think of certain players. For example, when I'm chipping I sometimes think I'm Seve Ballesteros."

Lee Westwood

CAREER WINS

2000	DEUTSCHE BANK-SAP OPEN		DEUTSCHE BANK-SAP OPEN
	CISCO WORLD MATCHPLAY		ENGLISH OPEN
	EUROPEAN GRAND PRIX		JAPAN TAIHEIYOU MASTERS
	EUROPEAN OPEN		USA FREEPORT-MCDERMOTT
	SCANDINAVIAN OPEN		CLASSIC
	BELGACOM OPEN	**1997**	MALAYSIAN OPEN
1999	DUTCH OPEN		JAPAN TAIHEIYO MASTERS
	EUROPEAN OPEN		AUSTRALIAN OPEN
	EUROPEAN MASTERS	**1996**	SCANDINAVIAN MASTERS
1998	BELGIAN OPEN		VOLVO MASTERS
	LOCH LOMOND INVITATIONAL		JAPAN VISA TAIHEIYO MASTERS

Westwood has suffered something of an alarming slump in form this season after being one of the hottest players in the world over the previous few years, having plunged out of the top 100 from the heady heights of being world No 4 just 14 months ago. In part this can be attributed to the lengthy break he took from the game at the start of 2001 following the birth of his first son Samuel Bevan. European supporters will be hoping he can rediscover his top form in time for The Belfry come September as he is one of the few players around the world who has proved he can go head-to-head with the likes of Tiger Woods and come out on top.

1996 was the highlight of Westwood's career when he holed a huge putt from just off the green to win the Scandinavian Masters at the second extra hole in a three-man play-off, his first PGA European Tour victory.

Westwood is a former British Youths' Champion, who has ten GCE O-levels. Aged 16, he was offered but turned down, a scholarship at Augusta. He married Andrew Coltart's sister Laurae on 9th January 1999, at St Anne's Church in Worksop. A keen snooker player, his first car was a Ford Fiesta but he now owns a number of cars ranging from BMWs and Mercedes to Ferraris.

He rounded off 2000 by securing his first Volvo Order of Merit crown, so ending Colin Montgomerie's seven-year tenure at the top. Won seven times in total, and equalled the European Tour record of six victories in a year, with a new record of 3,125,147 Euros (£1,858,602) to his name. In the process he edged his close friend and stable-mate, Darren Clarke, into second place after a dramatic race which went down to the wire.

During 2000 Westwood won the Dimension Data Pro-Am tournament in South Africa before going on to emulate the feats of Seve Ballesteros, Nick Faldo and Montgomerie by winning six times in Europe. He had also broken through in America in 1998 by taking the Freeport McDermott Classic. However, 2001 proved to be less profitable, as he was unable to record a win during the season in which he parted company with long time coach, Pete Cowen, and linked up with Bob Torrance. Westwood took up the game aged 13 with a half set bought by his grandparents, and he has now won on every continent. He returned to South Africa in December 2000 and was pipped by Ernie Els in a play-off for the $2 million prize in the Nedbank Golf Challenge. Westwood's strengths are his long straight driving, accurate iron play and superb putting. Indeed his overall game is now first class after improvements in a couple of weak areas.

He finished second at the season-ending American Express Championship to overtake Darren Clarke for the 2000 European Order of Merit. His victory ended Colin Montgomerie's seven-year reign atop the list as he won both the European Grand Prix and the European Masters, giving him consecutive victories heading into the 2000 British Open. He then shot a final-round 64 to pass Woods and win the 2000 Deutsche Bank-SAP Open for the second time in three years. In the process, he became only the second player to win when Woods took a lead into final round of an event.

Won the 1999 European Masters, aided by a final round eagle at the 15th. This win was his third straight, matching the consecutive wins mark set by Faldo seven years earlier.

He is now one of the senior figures in Sam Torrance's European team. He made his debut four years ago at Valderrama and was placed under the wing of the most experienced Ryder Cup player of all time, six time Major championship winner Faldo.

The English pair formed a solid partnership, losing their opening fourball match but fighting back in a rain-affected afternoon foursomes against Tiger Woods and Mark O'Meara, which Westwood sealed the following morning by holing a ten foot birdie putt that he had all night to ponder. He subsequently went on to play in all four remaining matches, securing two valuable points.

Two years on there was no Faldo but Westwood could easily stand on his own two feet among the world's best. Captain Mark James partnered him with his close friend Clarke and the pair formed the bedrock of the European team over the first two days, playing all four series of matches together and securing two points out of a possible four, including a famous victory over Tiger Woods and David Duval on the opening day fourballs.

On the final day Westwood went out first but the exhaustion from the first two days took its toll and he lost to an in-form Tom Lehman as the American team began the greatest comeback in the history of the Ryder Cup.

When questioned about his loss of form Westwood insists that the good times are just round the corner again. "No, it doesn't prey on the mind. Why should it?" he says. "You just go out there and work on the things that have stood you in good stead in the past. You know you must have a certain ability to have won those tournaments in the past, so you just have to rely on that." He claims that the efforts of the past five or six years have simply caught up with him but he will bounce back.

"I was peaking for three years," he says. "I won seven tournaments, then five, then seven again. That's a lot of high performing. Then last year there was none. Did I pay mentally for those three years? Well, you wonder. I almost switched off. The body tells you you can't keep it going at that level of intensity. You know, the pressures don't change when you're not winning. You still have the press to do, you still have to look after your sponsors. And people expect you to go out there and shoot 66 as well."

Paul Azinger

CAREER WINS

2000	SONY OPEN IN HAWAII	1989	CANON GREATER HARTFORD OPEN
1993	MEMORIAL TOURNAMENT	1988	HERTZ BAY HILL CLASSIC
	NEW ENGLAND CLASSIC	1987	PHOENIX OPEN
	PGA CHAMPIONSHIP		PANASONIC LAS VEGAS
1992	THE TOUR CHAMPIONSHIP		INVITATIONAL
	BMW INTERNATIONAL		CANON SAMMY DAVIS JR.
1991	AT&T PEBBLE BEACH		GREATER HARTFORD OPEN
	NATIONAL PRO-AM		
1990	MONY TOURNAMENT		
	OF CHAMPIONS		
	BMW INTERNATIONAL		

The story of Paul Azinger is one to admire regardless of what he achieves on the golf course during the remainder of his career. Diagnosed in 1993 with cancer in the right shoulder he fought to overcome the disease and returned full time to the US Tour, re-establishing himself as one of the leading players on the circuit.

This will be his fourth Ryder Cup appearance but his first since the 1993 contest – coincidentially the last time the match was hosted by The Belfry.

In 1994 and 1995, he served as host for the Zinger Stinger Pro-Am, which raised money for lymphoma research and was the recipient of the GWAA Ben Hogan Award in 1995, given to the individual who has continued to be active in golf despite physical handicap or serious illness. His book, 'Zinger,' is about his fight against cancer.

Azinger started playing golf at aged five, but he couldn't break 40 until he was a high school senior. He gave the eulogy at long-time friend Payne Stewart's Memorial Service in 1999.

He announced his arrival in golf's big-time in 1987 with three wins, when he finished second on the money list behind Curtis Strange. He also finished runner-up at the British Open, narrowly missing out behind then world number one Nick Faldo.

In 1989 he made his Ryder Cup debut and captured a magnificent singles victory over Seve Ballesteros, though it was ultimately futile as Europe tied the match 14-14 to retain the trophy. In addition, he also formed an impressive partnership with Chip Beck on the Saturday to defeat Gordon Brand Jnr and Sam Torrance in the foursomes before lunch, and Ian Woosnam and Faldo in the fourballs afterwards.

Two years later he again earnt his place in the US team, despite missing nine tournaments during the middle of the season after having surgery on his right shoulder. He played in the maximum possible five matches and won a crucial singles match against Jose Maria Olazabal at Kiawah Island during the 'War on the Shore', though his partnership with Beck did not work so well this time round as they lost both a foursomes and fourballs clash on the opening day.

Azinger was also at the centre of controversy during a bad-tempered foursomes clash with Beck against Olazabal and Seve Ballesteros. The Americans played the wrong ball, which they considered gamesmanship but Ballesteros was convinced was cheating. Afterwards the equally volatile Spaniard said: "The American team has 11 nice guys and Paul Azinger."

Then, in 1993, a bitter-sweet year saw him enjoy the finest season of his career before suddenly being diagnosed with lymphoma in his right shoulder blade in December of that year.

He captured his first Major by defeating Greg Norman on the second hole of a sudden-death play-off at the PGA Championship at Inverness after earlier winning the Memorial Tournament in dramatic fashion, holing out from a greenside bunker on the 72nd hole to defeat Corey Pavin by one stroke and Payne Stewart by two.

His ten top-three finishes in 1993 were the most since Tom Watson in 1980 and he finished second on the money list to Nick Price, and then halved a dramatic final day singles clash with Faldo at The Belfry as the US held onto the Ryder Cup. That was a relief for Azinger, who had lost three out of the four matches he played in on the Friday and the Saturday and only managed to halve the other so he definitely owed his team-mates something.

The following year he played in only four events because of chemotherapy and radiation treatments but he bravely fought off the disease showing the same will and determination that he displayed on the golf course and he bounced back in 1995. In his first event of the season, he tied for fourth at the United Airlines Hawaiian Open.

After a quiet spell as he re-adjusted to life on the tour he returned to top form in 1998, finishing a best-ever fifth place in the US Masters and recording places in the top fifteen in both the US Open and the PGA Championship.

"In 1995, 1997, and 1999, in respect to the Ryder Cup teams, I asked the captains not to consider me because I was not playing well," he says.

"The Ryder Cup was a non-event as far as the public was concerned, until the late 80s. It has come a long way in a short time."

In 2000, he captured his 12th career victory at the Sony Open in Hawaii, which was his first victory since the 1993 PGA Championship. He qualified for the Tour Championship for the first time since 1993 and his 27th-place finish on the Official Money List was also a best since finishing second in 1993.

So far this year his best finish has been fourth in the WGC-Accenture Match Play Championship. Azinger has also proved he can perform in Europe by twice winning on the continent – the 1990 and 1992 BMW International.

Azinger is 16th on the PGA Tour career money list with nearly $10 million of prize money, having won 12 events and two international titles. He is considered one of the game's finest short-game players and his mere presence in the US side will remind the players that it is only a game and should help prevent a repetition of the ugly scenes that were witnessed in 1991 and 1999.

Mark Calcavecchia

CAREER WINS

2001	PHOENIX OPEN		1989	THE OPEN
1998	HONDA CLASSIC			PHOENIX OPEN
1997	GREATER VANCOUVER OPEN			NISSAN LOS ANGLES OPEN
	SUBARU SARAZEN WORLD OPEN		1988	BANK OF BOSTON CLASSIC
1995	BELLSOUTH CLASSIC			AUSTRALIAN OPEN
	ARGENTINE OPEN		1987	HONDA CLASSIC
1993	ARGENTINE OPEN		1986	SOUTHWEST GOLF CLASSIC
1992	PHOENIX OPEN			

The vastly experienced Mark Calcavecchia returns to the US side to make his first Ryder Cup appearance since the infamous 'War on the Shore' at Kiawah Island over a decade ago. He is likely to be a reliable performer but Europe will remember that his last Ryder Cup act was to allow Colin Montgomerie to recover from five down with five to play to snatch an unlikely half, and give Bernhard Langer the chance to tie the contest on the final day. Calcavecchia was in tears as the German lined up that famous six foot putt, convinced he had cost his country the trophy, but they turned to tears of joy as Langer's putt just stayed out.

He deserved to be on the winning side though having won two out of the three pairs matches he played in on the opening two days. Combining with Payne Stewart he defeated Nick Faldo and Ian Woosnam in the opening foursomes, before he and Corey Pavin crashed 5&4 to Mark James and Steven Richardson in the afternoon fourballs, but he was reunited with Stewart to gain revenge on the English pairing in the Saturday foursomes.

On his Ryder Cup debut in 1987 he beat Faldo in the singles on the final day but was earlier beaten in a foursomes with Andy Bean by Sandy Lyle and Bernhard Langer.

Two years later, when reigning Open champion, he played in all five matches, winning two and losing three. An opening victory with Ken Green over Langer and Ronan Rafferty was cancelled out by defeat against Faldo and Woosnam with Mark McCumber in the afternoon fourballs. The next day he and Green were again victorious, this time over Rafferty and Christy O'Connor Jnr but that afternoon the pair slipped to defeat against the Spanish combination Seve Ballesteros and Jose Marie Olazabal. And on the final day Rafferty had his revenge with a one hole victory in the singles.

He started playing when he was six years old. Calcavecchia grew up in a small town in Nebraska and it had a nine-hole course he played on regularly.

In 1986 his first tour victory came at the Southwest Golf Classic, by three strokes over Tom Byrum. Calcavecchia has a reputation as a big tournament player and in 1988 he was runner-up to Sandy Lyle in the US Masters before earning his third career victory in the Bank Of Boston Classic.

His most successful season came some 13 years ago when he won his only Major –

the Open Championship at Royal Troon. He defeated Wayne Grady and Greg Norman in a play-off, sealing victory with a five-iron shot to seven feet on the fourth and final play-off hole.

He had won twice in the US earlier that year. He finished with 65-64 to win the Phoenix Open by seven strokes over Chip Beck and then, after trailing Lyle by two strokes after the third round of the Nissan Los Angeles Open, a final-round 68 was good enough for a one-stroke victory.

Three years later he won the Phoenix Open again following a final-round 63 and he set a course record for the Augusta National back-nine at the US Masters with 29, a record since equalled by 2002 Ryder Cup team-mate David Toms.

The mid-to-late nineties were something of a barren spell as he failed to make the Ryder Cup teams, although he did taste victory several times.

In December 1993 a skiing accident hampered him for much of the following year, but he came back to finish tied for ninth at the Buick Invitational of California after cartilage damage and a torn achilles were surgically repaired.

Then, in 1995, after trailing Jim Gallagher Jr. and Stephen Keppler by two shots entering the final day, he fired a 66 for a two-stroke victory at the BellSouth Classic and teamed up with Australia's Steve Elkington to win the Franklin Templeton Shootout. Three years later he earned his ninth tour title at the Honda Classic, winning by three strokes. He also shot a final-round 66 to finish second by one stroke at the Las Vegas Invitational.

But it was the turn of the millennium that marked a turning point in Calcavecchia's fortunes. He earned $1,597,317 to finish 23rd on the official money list and qualify for his 11th Tour Championship as well as getting back in Ryder Cup contention. He finished second at the Canon Greater Hartford Open and tied for second at the SEI Pennsylvania Classic, marking his sixth career season with multiple runner-up finishes. Altogether there were nine top-ten finishes, which was his most since nine in 1990.

He finished tied for ninth at the World Golf Championships-Accenture Match Play Championship after posting victories in matches over Nick Price and Olazabal before eventually losing to Paul Lawrie. He became the tenth player in tour history to top the $10 million mark in career earnings after winning $84,390 for a tied seventh finish at the Honda Classic.

Calcavecchia has been in reasonable form so far this season. Rounds of 72-66-71-69 resulted in a tie for fifth in the Mercedes Championships and he was inducted into the Phoenix Open Hall of Fame, which he has won twice, becoming only the 15th person and sixth golfer put into the Hall which was established in 1985. The others are Arnold Palmer, Gene Littler, Byron Nelson, Ben Hogan and Ken Venturi. He finished ninth in the WGC-Accenture Match Play Championship after losing to Olazabal (2up) in the third round, having defeated Chris DiMarco and Jerry Kelly in the first two rounds.

A third top-ten finish of the season came at the Worldcom Classic-The Heritage of Golf, where a final-round 65 placed him in a tie for tenth and he followed that up with a runner-up finish at the Greater Greensboro Chrysler Classic, having held the first-round lead after an opening 65. He tied the tour record for the fewest putts in a 72-hole event (Kenny Knox, 1989 MCI Heritage Classic) with just 93 over the four rounds.

Stewart Cink

CAREER WINS
2000   MCI CLASSIC
1997   CANON GREATER HARTFORD OPEN

US rookie Stewart Cink is best known for an 18-inch miss that cost him a spot in the 2001 US Open play-off. After running his par attempt 18 inches past the hole, Cink marked his ball and went through his routine, looking to clear the stage for Retief Goosen, who had a 12-footer for birdie but could two-putt and win by a stroke.

The 18-inch miss became the most important meaningless putt in US Open history, the miss nobody remembers, the miss Stewart Cink isn't allowed to forget. He tapped in for double bogey, then saw Goosen roll his birdie try two and a half feet past the hole. When Goosen fanned the return putt, missing it badly to the right, a relatively uneventful Major championship had disintegrated into an ugly game of hot potato within two minutes.

"When Retief knocked it past, I told my caddie (Frank Williams): 'That's a play-off.' Then he missed and it took me a second to realise I could have been in the play-off, too." Cink recalls.

The 18-hole Monday play-off pitted Goosen against Mark Brooks with the South African winning.

A father at the age of 20, a PGA Tour Rookie of the Year at 24, Cink seemed to realise that there's much more to life than an 18-inch putt. Even one that costs you a shot at the national championship.

He has won just twice in his five and a half years on tour, which suggests he is an underachiever given that he is blessed with a smooth swing and that even temperament. But Cink has never finished lower than 32nd on the money list, making him an inconspicuous model of consistency. The high point of his career might be the 2000 Presidents Cup, when he went 4-0-0 in his first international team competition, which suggests he is more than comfortable in high-pressure matchplay competitions.

Perhaps we will learn more this September at The Belfry, when the pressure of a Ryder Cup will test Cink's mental toughness.

"I think he has an unbelievable attitude," says Ryder Cup team-mate Paul Azinger. "It is to be admired. The thing at the US Open was just a blunder. What's he supposed to do, tell the press everything he is feeling? You can't do that. There's only a couple of Phil Mickelsons and John Dalys running around, telling you every single thing they're thinking."

Adds US captain Curtis Strange, no stranger to intensity: "Would Stewart go out and wrestle a tree? No, but he's got plenty of fire in his belly."

The conflict draws its roots from Cink's potential to be a star and his commitment to become one. At Georgia Tech, he beat Tiger Woods and swept the college player-of-the-year awards in 1995.

In 1995 he tied for 18th place in his first professional start at the Canon Greater Hartford Open.

He won the same honour on the junior US Tour – the Nike Tour – in 1996 and tied for 16th place at the US Open to earn an invitation to the 1997 US Masters, then was named the top first-year player on the big tour in 1997. At the Canon Greater Hartford Open that year, he rallied from four strokes down on the Sunday, shot a 66 and beat Brandel Chamblee by a shot. He was the only rookie to qualify for the Tour Championship and finished the season ranked 29th in the official earnings.

The following year he recorded six top-ten finishes and almost became the first player to successfully defend the Canon GHO title as a final-round 67 moved him into a play-off with Olin Browne and Larry Mize, but Browne won with a chip-in birdie.

In 1999 he finished 32nd on the final money list and missed earning a place in the Tour Championship by one spot. He defeated Payne Stewart and Craig Parry before losing to Tiger Woods in the third round of the World Golf Championships-Accenture Match Play Championship and earned a share of the lead after three rounds at the BellSouth Classic, but a closing 70 left him one stroke behind the winner David Duval. At the PGA Championship, he shot 69-70-68-73, and finished tied for third place.

His second tour win came at the 2000 MCI Heritage Classic, as much a product of Ernie Els' closing 74 as anything Cink did.

He followed with second spot at the MasterCard Colonial, where he held a three-stroke lead through 54 holes but a final round 71 left him two strokes behind Phil Mickelson.

His eighth top-ten place was seventh spot at the WGC-NEC Invitational, where he closed with a 63, the second-lowest round of the event.

Cink sees himself as a player with the temperament and patience to win a Major and the US Open in particular. Before Southern Hills, he had been in contention three times: in 1997 (tied for 13th), 1998 (tied for tenth) and 2000 (tied for eighth).

Aside from his US Open disappointment, 2001 was a great year for Cink as he made 22 of 29 cuts on his way to $1,743,028 in earnings and 26th spot on the tour money list. The highlight of the season came when he posted three top-fives in June. He started the month with fourth place at the Memorial Tournament. Two weeks later he finished third at the US Open, then the next week an opening-round 65 at the Buick Classic gave him a one-stroke lead over Scott Hoch and Vijay Singh. He finished tied for third spot.

He started this season poorly and he was without a top-ten finish through the first 13 events before back-to-back top tens at the Memorial Tournament (T9) and the Buick Classic (T5).

"I tend to play my best when the situation is well defined," he says. "You have to have that combination of the attitude and the patience as well as the ability to buckle down and focus."

That attitude is sure to bode well for Cink and will be appreciated by his captain at The Belfry, Curtis Strange .

Davis Love III

CAREER WINS

2001	AT&T PEBBLE BEACH NATIONAL PRO-AM	1992	THE PLAYERS CHAMPIONSHIP MCI HERITAGE GOLF CLASSIC KMART GREATER GREENSBORO OPEN
1998	MCI CLASSIC		
1997	USPGA CHAMPIONSHIP BUICK CHALLENGE	1991	MCI HERITAGE GOLF CLASSIC
1996	BUICK INVITATIONAL	1990	THE INTERNATIONAL
1995	FREEPORT-MCMORAN CLASSIC	1987	MCI HERITAGE GOLF CLASSIC
1993	INFINITI TOURNAMENT OF CHAMPIONS LAS VEGAS INVITATIONAL		

The extravagantly-named David Love III was beginning to earn himself a reputation alongside Phil Mickelson and Colin Montgomerie as the best player not to have won a Major until he won the USPGA Championship in August 1997 by five strokes from Justin Leonard. To shoot 66 three times at Winged Foot – one of the hardest courses in America before the rough is grown high enough to swallow a small dog – ranks among the best performances of the last 20 years. After a decade of futility, after the valiant run at the 1995 Masters and the three-foot miss on the 72nd hole that cost him the 1996 US Open, Love finally had his Major.

That win helped Davis Love to shed the unfortunate tag of 'choker' but the player himself admits he has squandered countless chances to win tournaments.

"Just think if I'd won half my play-offs," he says. "Just think if I'd won half the times I had the lead going into Sunday, if I'd made a couple more putts along the way. How many more tournaments could I have won? I could be sitting here saying: 'Yeah, this Tiger Woods is a pretty good player, but I'm the No. 1 player in the world.' I've let a lot of opportunities get away. I've accomplished a lot of the things I wanted to accomplish, but I haven't come close to what I could have done."

He started playing golf as soon as he could walk, under the tutelage of his father Davis Love Jr., who was regarded as one of the premier teachers in the game, and who played in many USPGA Tour events in the 60s.

Davis III was born the day after his father finished tied for 31st in the 1964 US Masters.

By the time he was ten, there was no doubt in Love's mind that he would follow in his father's footsteps and become a professional golfer.

He did not have much success in junior golf, but things changed when he went to play college golf at North Carolina and he became a three-time All-American and played on the 1985 Walker Cup team, turning pro after that and finishing tied for seventh in the qualifying school. In his rookie season, Love earned $113,245 (ranked

77th) and led the tour in driving distance.

He won for the first time at the 1987 MCI Heritage Classic, and won $297,378 for the year (ranked 33rd). 1988 was an annus horribilis year for David Love both professionally, as he earned $156,068 on tour ranking him 75th, and personally, when his father and only teacher was killed in a plane crash. Shortly afterwards he wrote the book, 'Every Shot I Take,' to honour his dad's lessons and teachings on golf and life. It was named recipient of USGA's 1997 USGA International Book Award.

The following year he finished 44th on the money list with $278,760 despite missing six weeks with a broken bone in his left wrist which occurred that summer during the British Open.

Though he went without a victory for the first time in four years, the 1999 season was still a success. He finished third on the money list earning a career-high $2,475,328, and he had 13 top-ten finishes including four runner-up placings.

He has won consistently on the PGA Tour, highlighted by his first Major win at the PGA Championship at Winged Foot in 1997. He surpassed the million dollar mark in earnings for the fifth year in a row and sixth time in his career.

He is now one of the most established members of the US Ryder Cup side having played in the last four clashes (1993, 1995, 1997 and 1999) of which he was twice on the winning side and twice a loser.

In his first ever Ryder Cup match he was thrown in at the deep end alongside Tom Kite against the legendary Spanish pairing of Seve Ballesteros and Jose Marie Olazabal in a foursomes but the Americans triumphed 2&1. He's uniformly polite in victory or defeat.

During that contest Peter Baker's daughter fell violently ill and was taken to the hospital. Love wrote a note to the family expressing his family's support.

At Oak Hill two years later he played in all five matches, winning three and losing two as the US were surprisingly beaten on home soil by a point, but he had a far less happy time in Valderrama two years later. He arrived having just landed his first Major but crashed to four defeats out of four and was one of the players singled out for criticism by the US media. Teaming up with Phil Mickelson and Fred Couples he could make no impression on the Europeans in the pairs matches and he blew his chance to redeem himself on the final day, going down 3&2 to Per-Ulrik Johansson.

However, Davis Love made amends at Brookline last time out, halving both his pairs matches on the opening day and then, after resting on the Saturday, crushing the hapless Frenchman Jean Van de Velde 5&4 in the singles as part of the great US comeback.

This season he was the first-round leader at the US Masters after carding a bogey-free five-under-par 67. He eventually finished tied for 14th place, and then earned his first top-ten spot of the season with fifth place at the WC Classic-The Heritage of Golf. He posted runner-up finishes in back-to-back starts for the third time in his career with his tied second place at the Canon Greater Hartford Open and second at the Advil Western Open a week later, during which he shot seven of eight rounds in the 60s.

When relaxing off the golf course he owns and raises horses, with a seven-stall barn at home. His daughter Lexie is a nationally-ranked competitive rider in the adult division on Paso Fino horses.

David Duval

CAREER WINS

2001	OPEN CHAMPIONSHIP	1998	TUCSON CHRYSLER CLASSIC
2000	BUICK CHALLENGE		SHELL HOUSTON OPEN
1999	MERCEDES CHAMPIONSHIP		NEC WORLD SERIES OF GOLF
	BOB HOPE CHRYSLER CLASSIC		MICHELOB CHAMPIONSHIP
	THE PLAYERS CHAMPIONSHIP	1997	MICHELOB CHAMPIONSHIP
	BELLSOUTH CLASSIC		WALT DISNEY
			WORLD/OLDSMOBILE CLASSIC
			THE TOUR CHAMPIONSHIP

Like many others before him David Duval lost form the year after winning the Open Championship. The world No. 2 finally landed his first Major at Royal Lytham & St Annes last year but has subsequently struggled to rediscover that magic touch. Quiet and unassuming – one of the game's nice guys – his admirers would say. Somewhat dull and almost entirely lacking in charisma, those less endeared to the American might claim.

Duval made his decisive move in the third round, recording a best-of-the-day 65 to come from seven shots off the pace to joint leader, and then carded a final round 67 to finish on ten under par for a three-stroke victory over Niclas Fasth, which earnt the Swede a spot on the European side.

The win was extra sweet for Duval because the previous year (2000) at St Andrews he had mounted the biggest challenge to runaway winner Tiger Woods on the final day, but finished only 11th after running up an eight at the 71st hole – the famous Road Hole.

He was aided by a slice of luck in the final round at the 14th after one of his balls avoided landing in the rough when it bounced off a spectator's leg. Duval gave the spectator a personalised golf ball bearing the initials DD as a memento.

Duval's father, Bob, is a senior PGA tour player. David caddied for his dad at 1996 Transamerica, Bob's first tour event. He wears sunglasses on the golf course due to eye stigma which causes sensitivity to light.

As an amateur in 1992 he was Collegiate Player of the Year and winner of the prestigious Dave Williams Award. He held a two-stroke lead through 54 holes at the 1992 BellSouth Classic before closing with 79 and finishing tied for 13th place. While at Georgia Tech, he joined three others including Ryder Cup team-mate Phil Mickelson as the only four-time Division One first-team All-Americans.

In his debut season on the US Tour in 1995 he finished second three times, at the AT&T Pebble Beach National Pro-Am, the Bob Hope Chrysler Classic and the Memorial Tournament, and finished the season with eight top-tens and what was at that time record earnings for a player in his debut season.

PLAYER PROFILES – U.S.

Two years later he won the last three events to finish second in the official earnings list. He won the Michelob Championship at Kingsmill for his first tour title, followed that with victory at the Walt Disney World/Oldsmobile Classic, and then won the Tour Championship.

He became the first player since Nick Price in 1993 to win three consecutive starts and was the first player in PGA Tour history to win play-offs in consecutive weeks. He also became the first player since Billy Andrade in 1991 to win his first two titles back-to-back.

1999 was the year he joined the world's elite as he became the first player since Johnny Miller in 1974 to win four times before the US Masters and the first player since Nick Price (1993-94) to earn at least four victories in consecutive years. He eagled the last hole to win the Bob Hope Chrysler Classic and shoot 59, which matched Al Geiberger (1977) and Chip Beck (1991). His Players Championship victory came the same day that his father won the Emerald Coast Classic seniors event. The $900,000 paycheque made Duval the quickest to win $2 million in a season. He moved to No. 1 in the world rankings, ending Woods' run of 41 consecutive weeks at the top. He became the first to surpass $3 million in a season and then made his Ryder Cup debut at Brookline as part of the famous US comeback team.

He missed part of the 2000 season with back problems but bounced back to win the Buick Challenge, though the continuing pain caused him to withdraw from the PGA Championship. It was the first Major he had missed since his debut year of 1995, when he was not eligible for the Masters. Then last season he overcame an early season wrist injury to land the first Major of his career, finishing eighth in the earnings list, his sixth consecutive year in the top ten.

He also finished runner-up in the US Masters. He trailed by three strokes after 36 and 54 holes and eventually finished two behind Tiger Woods after a closing 67, where he was tied for the lead on the back nine until a bogey at the sixteenth.

He could only manage tied for 16th in the US Open, which prevented him from a top ten spot in all four Majors.

Duval is one of the new breed of American players who do not find the magic of the Ryder Cup in the way that many of his European opponents do. He has been at the forefront of the US members, suggesting that they ought to be paid for playing in the contest, and he has been quoted as saying he feels people get over-excited about it.

"I don't spend a lot of time thinking about it, because I haven't figured out why we make such a big deal about it. There's way too much emphasis on it, no question about that," he says.

"The Ryder Cup is an exhibition. The whole thing has become a little overcooked, but it's probably going to stay that way until players choose not to play."

And he hints darkly at potential boycotts by the American squad.

"Without the players, they're not going to have a Ryder Cup. Mark O'Meara got blasted for bringing up the compensation issue during the last Ryder Cup, and he was absolutely right.

"Meanwhile, the people criticizing him were being paid that week. They aren't donating their services to the cause. Why don't they work for free, too? Better yet, let's take some of that big Ryder Cup pot and cut it up and give it away to charity."

Jim Furyk

CAREER WINS

2002 MEMORIAL TOURNAMENT	1998 LAS VEGAS INVITATIONAL
2001 MERCEDES CHAMPIONSHIP	1997 ARGENTINE OPEN
2000 DORAL-RYDER OPEN	1996 UNITED AIRLINES HAWAIIAN OPEN
1999 LAS VEGAS INVITATIONAL	1995 LAS VEGAS INVITATIONAL

Jim Furyk has been a consistent performer on the US Tour for the past six or seven seasons, playing in the last two Ryder Cups. He made his debut in Valderrama in 1997 but began inauspiciously losing both a foursomes game in tandem with Tom Lehman against the Swedes Jesper Parnevik and Per Ulrik Johnasson, and a foursomes match alongside Lee Janzen against Colin Montgomerie and Bernhard Langer the next day. But he went some way towards making amends in the singles with a fine 3&2 victory over Nick Faldo.

Two years later Furyk again struggled in the pairs. He went down with Phil Mickelson to Parnevik again and Sergio Garcia in the fourballs on the first afternoon, then lost to Darren Clarke and Lee Westwood with Mark O'Meara in the foursomes the next morning. However, he again bounced back in the final day singles – this time to crush Garcia 4&3 as the US came back to win.

So his pairs record stands played four, lost four but he has won both singles matches he has played.

Furyk made his Open debut at Royal Lytham & St Annes in 1996 and finished a respectable tied 44th. But at Troon 12 months later he finished fourth and then at Birkdale in 1999 he was fourth again, hinting that his first Major title could come this side of the Atlantic. A tenth place at Carnoustie in 2000 highlighted his love for this tournament with his weird swing seeming to hold up well in windy conditions.

In 1994 he recorded three top-tens as a rookie, including a tied for seventh at the Northern Telecom Open, his first start of the year. His first tour win came the next year at the Las Vegas Invitational with a one-stroke victory over Billy Mayfair.

During a very successful 1997 he set a then-tour record for the most money earned without a victory with $1,619,480, fourth on money list. His 13 top-ten finishes matched Davis Love III for the most on the tour and included eight in a row. He had an impressive run in the Majors that year: tied fifth at the US Open, fourth at the Open Champiosnhip, and tied sixth at the PGA Championship.

In 1999 he won a third Las Vegas Invitational title, becoming the first player to successfully defend the title and the following year he missed only one cut all season, at the SEI Pennsylvania Classic and earned his fifth tour victory at the Doral-Ryder Open.

Last year he captured a sixth tour title at the Mercedes Championship, marking his fourth consecutive season with a victory. He was four strokes down at the start of the final round but holed a ten-foot birdie putt on the 72nd hole in Kapalua that put him in the lead as Rory Sabatini missed a three-foot birdie that would have forced a play-off.

The victory came after a slight cartilage tear in the right wrist forced him to withdraw from the 2000 Tour Championship, the 2001 WGC-American Express Championship, and the Accenture Match Play Championship.

He suffered the injury the previous autumn while trying to intercept a pass in the parking lot of a Baltimore Ravens NFL game. At the US Masters, rounds of 69-71-70-69 produced sixth spot and another top-ten position came at the PGA Championship with a tie for seventh.

After opening with scorss of 70-71 at the Tour Championship, he posted a third-round nine-under-par 62 and was only three strokes behind after three rounds but a closing 69 left him tied for seventh. The 62 set a Champions 18-hole course record and a Tour Championship record.

Completely out of character, he missed four cuts in six starts across March, April and May at the start of this season, although an ear infection which caused dizzy spells was partly to blame.

But anyone writing him off was put in their place when he produced a final round charge to capture the Memorial back in May thanks to a final-round 65 that included a chip-in for birdie on the par-three 12th hole and an eagle from the front bunker on the par-five 15th hole. He won by two strokes over John Cook and David Peoples. Furyk recorded a third-round hole-in-one with a five-iron from 192 yards on the fourth hole. He followed that up with a top ten finish in the Buick Classic.

Anyone looking at Furyk's unconventional swing would be amazed to learn that his father is one of the leading golf coaches in the US.

"He is my swing coach but also throughout my game. I've learned some short game and putting on my own," says Furyk.

"But he has seen me play so much and he can notice the little differences and help me out. As far as a family member, it can be easy and difficult at times. It is sometimes easier with an outsider because you listen more.

"When you listen to a parent you can be a child and think you know it all and don't listen as well. It has brought us closer now but when I was younger we had many arguments. But because of those arguments we are closer and get along better on the golf course. It is not that we didn't get along then, but we had some rocky times."

He also uses an unconventional cross-grip when putting.

"I started that as a child. That is how I began and that is how my father taught me to grip the putter. During a pro-am my father talked to both Arnold Palmer and Jack Nicklaus and they both said if they could have started over they would have tried the cross-over. Being a golf pro that is how my father taught me. Now a conventional grip is uncomfortable for me."

And he is relishing the contest at The Belfry in September: "Playing in Europe after what is supposed to have happened in Boston, it will be fierce competition and a tough crowd. That is an area I would like to test myself in."

Scott Hoch

CAREER WINS

2001	GREATER GREENSBORO CHRYSLER CLASSIC ADVIL WESTERN OPEN	1990	KOREAN OPEN
1997	GREATER MILWAUKEE OPEN	1989	LAS VEGAS INVITATIONAL
1996	MICHELOB CHAMPIONSHIP	1986	JAPAN CASIO WORLD OPEN
1995	GREATER MILWAUKEE OPEN	1984	MILLER HIGH LIFE QCO
	HEINEKEN DUTCH OPEN	1982	USF&G CLASSIC
1994	BOB HOPE CHRYSLER CLASSIC		JAPAN PACIFIC MASTERS
1991	KOREAN OPEN		JAPAN CASIO WORLD OPEN
		1980	QUAD CITIES OPEN

Another experienced US campaigner, Scott Hoch is best remembered by European fans for missing a short putt in a US Masters play-off which handed Nick Faldo the Green Jacket in 1989.

"If I had made that putt in 1989 to win the play-off, it would have changed a lot," he recalls.

"I think about what might have been. Everybody says 18 inches or two feet, but it was more like 30 inches. I knew the Masters was mine if I made it, and I missed it. I could probably make 90 to 95 out of 100 of those, but not that one on No. 10. I lined it up to the left, I think."

But it would be a mistake to think that Hoch is a big match choker. In his only previous Ryder Cup contest, at Valderrama in 1997, he won two-and-a-half points out of a possible three as the better known stars such as Tiger Woods, Justin Leonard and Davis Love III struggled.

On the first afternoon he teamed up with Lee Janzen to defeat Jose Marie Olazabal and Costantino Rocca in the foursomes, then the next day he repeated the dose with Jeff Maggert against Nick Faldo and Lee Westwood, with a 2&1 victory. In the singles he was left with the task of beating Colin Montgomerie to keep the US's hopes of winning alive. Hoch was two holes up early in the match but the Scot had fought back to level by the 14th. Hoch then bogeyed the 16th but a birdie at the par-five 17th squared things up again and he knew he had to win the last hole. Montgomerie found the green in regulation – Hoch didn't – and as the Scot two-putted for the half-point to give Europe victory he conceded a generous putt to allow Hoch a halved match.

At the relatively advanced golf age of 46, he's punctuating his remarkably consistent career with an exclamation point.

Last year he won twice in the same year – the Greater Greensboro Classic and the Western Open – for the first time since he turned pro in 1979. He was the first 45-year-old to accomplish that feat since Hale Irwin in 1990. If not for nagging wrist and ankle injuries, he might have won enough to be challenging Tiger Woods for the

2001 money title.

Since 1982, Hoch has finished among the top 40 on the money list every year except 1992, when he had shoulder surgery. His career resume features ten tour wins and 149 top-tens, including ten this year. He won the Quad City Classic in his debut season on the Tour in 1980 and also won events in 1982 and 1984. Then a quiet period followed until 1989 when, in addition to his US Masters runners-up spot, he won the Las Vegas Invitational in a play-off over Robert Wrenn and had a first money list top-ten finish. Then in 1994, after four years without a victory, he captured the Bob Hope Chrysler Classic. Later that year, he was runner-up to Jose Maria Olazabal at the NEC World Series of Golf.

His best year yet on the Tour was in 1997 when he won a second Greater Milwaukee Open and had a career-best 11 top-ten finishes, including second at the Players Championship and third at the Nissan Open.

Last year was his best ever in money earned with $2,875,319 (seventh on money list). He held a third-round lead at the Greensboro Chrysler Classic, finishing with a 69 that made him the oldest tour winner since Tom Watson won the 1998 MasterCard Colonial aged 48. He also supplanted defending champion Hal Sutton (41) as the oldest Greater Greensboro Chrysler Classic winner since 52-year-old Sam Snead. A final-round 64 at the Advil Western Open produced his tenth tour title and second of the season as he edged DavisLove III by one stroke. His 267 total broke the tournament record set by Sam Snead in 1949 and the $648,000 payday was the largest of his career.

So far in 2002 he has continued to show some good form. His first top-ten finish came at the Bay Hill Invitational, seven strokes behind champion Tiger Woods, then he tied for fourth at the Players Championship – a fifth top-ten there in the last six years.

He did not defend his title at the Greater Greensboro Chrysler Classic due to trouble with his right eye from LASIK surgery and had two operations to fix an astigmatism.

He returned to action in the Buick Classic and a week later, tied for a career best with a fifth place finish at the US Open, closing with a one-under-par 69. He also tied for fifth at the 1993 US Open at Baltusrol GC, won by Lee Janzen. On the Sunday, sporting a stars and stripes golf shirt dedicated to New York City, he recorded an ace with a three-iron on the 207-yard 17th hole, one of three holes-in-one during the week.

"My strength has been longevity and the calibre of play I've maintained through the years," says Hoch, who turns 46 on November 24. "I don't consider myself an elite player. You have to win a Major to be great. I haven't done that. I've been a good, consistent player."

Hoch has gone on-record criticising the way standards in the Ryder Cup have degenerated over the past decade, culminating in the disgraceful scenes at Brookline in 1999. "The Ryder Cup has become something it wasn't intended to be. The media and fans have taken respect and sportsmanship out of it. That's why I prefer playing the Presidents Cup, which is just about golf," he says.

And the abrasive American has no qualms about upsetting British golf fans. He once said of the hallowed Old Course at St. Andrews, Scotland: "I think they had some sheep and goats there that died, and they just covered them over. It's the biggest piece of mess I've ever seen."

Phil Mickelson

CAREER WINS

2000	MASTERCARD COLONIAL	1995	NORTHERN TELECOM
	BELLSOUTH CLASSIC	1994	MERCEDES CHAMPIONSHIP
	BUICK INVITATIONAL	1993	SPRINT INTERNATIONAL
1998	AT&T PEBBLE BEACH		BUICK INVITATIONAL
	MERCEDES CHAMPIONSHIP	1991	NORTHERN TELECOM OPEN
1997	SPRINT INTERNATIONAL		
	BAY HILL INVITATIONAL		
1996	NEC WORLD SERIES		
	GTE BYRON NELSON		
	PHOENIX OPEN		
	NORTEL OPEN		

Regarded as the greatest player to have never won a Major – Europe's Colin Montgomerie is usually reckoned to be the second best never to have triumphed – Mickelson would surely have picked up several titles already were it not for a certain Tiger Woods. Mickelson is also unique in that he is the only top golfer in the world who plays left-handed.

Born to be a golfer is how his friends describe Mickelson, who aged one-and-a-half was already swinging a homemade cut-down club, mirroring his father in their San Diego backyard. At age three, he tried to run away from home because his parents didn't think he was old enough to join his father for a weekend golf game at the local public course.

That same spirit of not wanting the game to end led him to a phenomenal junior career that saw Mickelson capture 34 San Diego County titles, followed by an amateur career highlighted by three NCAA Championships, a US Amateur title and a win on the PGA Tour's Northern Telecom Open as a collegian.

Other than 1999, the year his daughter was born, Mickelson has captured at least one victory on the US Tour in every full season as a professional.

Winning continues to be the priority on the course and a hunger still remains for making his imprint on golf history, but being a winner off the course is just as important for Mickelson, who is renowned as someone who spends more time signing autographs than anyone else on the US Tour.

Mickelson is one of only three golfers to win the NCAA Championship and US Amateur Championships in the same year: the other two are Jack Nicklaus and Tiger Woods.

In 1990, he became the only left-handed player to win the US Amateur Championships and was also the first amateur since Scott Verplank in 1985 to win a tour event when he triumphed at the 1991 Northern Telecom Open, by one stroke over

Tom Purtzer. Then, in 1993, he won his first two titles as a professional, the Buick Invitational in his hometown of San Diego, and the International.

Two years later he won the Northern Telecom Open for the second time, following his 1991 victory as an amateur, and then made his first appearance as a member of the Ryder Cup team, which was surprisingly beaten at Oak Hill. But the leftie could not be faulted, his record over the contest was a stunning won 3 halved 0 lost 0 – the best of any player on either side.

After teaming up with Corey Pavin to destroy Bernhard Langer and Per-Ulrik Johansson 6&4 in the opening fourballs, he repeated the trick with Jay Haas to see off Seve Ballesteros and David Gilford the following afternoon.

Then, in the singles, he beat Johansson but his efforts were in vain as his team-mates could not match his feats. In 1996 he won four times, including two of his first three starts, successfully defending the Nortel Open title and defeating Justin Leonard in a play-off to win the Phoenix Open.

In 1997 he won twice, at the Bay Hill Invitational and Sprint International, and finished in the top 25 in 15 of the 21 tournaments he entered. He was a mainstay of the US team, which went down in Valderrama, finishing with a creditable 1-2-1 record from his four matches and again, triumphing in the singles on the last day.

The following year he was able to hold off the charging pair of Mark O'Meara and Tiger Woods on Sunday with a final-round 68 to win the Mercedes Championships. He also won the weather-postponed AT&T Pebble Beach National Pro-Am.

Despite failing to win a tour competition in 1999 he had another impressive year and had memorable performance in the US Open at Pinehurst. With wife Amy's delivery of their first child imminent, he lost by one stroke to Payne Stewart.

He then produced another exceptional Ryder Cup performance as the US came back from the dead to regain the trophy at Brookline. Mickelson had a 2-2-0 record in his third appearance, including a 4&3 defeat of Jarmo Sandelin in Sunday's singles to give him the impressive record of having won all three of his Ryder Cup singles contests.

In 2000 he ended Woods' consecutive victory string at six with a four-stroke win at the Buick Invitational, and captured the Tour Championship at Atlanta's East Lake Golf Club with a final-round 66.

He captured the Bob Hope Chrysler Classic in his first appearance of the 2002 season, overcoming a four-shot deficit with a 64 on the final day to finish tied with David Berganio Jr. He defeated Berganio with a birdie on the first play-off hole with another birdie, bringing his play-off record on the tour to 5-1. Victory, worth $720,000, was the 20th of his career.

Then he shot a final-round 64 at the Canon Greater Hartford Open, including a birdie on the final hole, to beat Davis Love III and Jonathan Kaye by one stroke, becoming the first player ever to win the Hartford in consecutive years.

His third-place finish at the US Masters was his sixth top-ten finish at the Augusta National and fourth consecutive top ten. After entering the final round four strokes behind Woods and Retief Goosen, he birdied the first two holes to close within two strokes of Woods but finished with a one-under-par 71, four behind Woods.

Hal Sutton

CAREER WINS

2001	HOUSTON OPEN	1986	PHOENIX OPEN
2000	PLAYERS CHAMPIONSHIP		MEMORIAL TOURNAMENT
2000	GT GREENSBORO CLASSIC	1985	ST. JUDE
1999	CANADIAN OPEN		SOUTHWEST CLASSIC
1998	TEXAS OPEN	1983	PLAYERS CHAMPIONSHIP
	TOUR CHAMPIONSHIP		PGA CHAMPIONSHIP
1995	B.C. OPEN	1982	WALT DISNEY CLASSIC

Hal Sutton burst onto the golfing scene in the mid-eighties winning a Major and making two successive Ryder Cup appearances before fading into obscurity in the late eighties and early nineties. But he fought back to return to the US team in 1999 and is set to make his fourth appearance in the 2002 contest.

Born and raised in Shreveport, Lakota, to a well-to-do oil family, his prodigious talent did little to liberate Sutton, the 1980 US Amateur champion, from the shadow of his father, Howard. Hal won the PGA Championship, the Players Championship and the PGA Tour money title at the age of 25 in 1983.

He made his Ryder Cup debut at The Belfry and played four matches, losing a vital singles clash with Bernhard Langer on the final day.

Two years later Sutton was the only single player in the US team at Muirfield Village and he stayed with Jack Nicklaus and his wife, Barbara, for the weekend.

"It was a unique opportunity for me, because I was staying with my idol. Every morning, Barbara would cook breakfast and Jack and I would talk about everything under the sun. It was a great week for me and I'll never forget it, but I was also very disappointed we didn't win. The golf course was set up perfectly for us."

Sutton again performed solidly, halving his singles clash with Gordon Brand Jnr and earning two points from a possible four overall but, as in 1985, he could not stop the US slipping to defeat.

When he returned to the US side 12 years later at Brookline as one of the senior 'enforcers' Sutton says he thought (European captain) Mark James made a tactical error, putting the three guys who hadn't played (Jarmo Sandelin, Andrew Coltart and Jean Van de Velde), near the front of the line-up on the final day's singles.

"That placed a tremendous burden on those three. He had to know we were going to be pretty top-heavy – we were trying to win every match we could right off the bat. If Tom (Lehman) and I won the first two matches, we were going to have a lot of momentum," he says.

Sutton showed his ability to play under the most intense pressure by comfortably defeating Darren Clarke 4&2 in the singles having played in all four matches on the first two days – a remarkable feat of stamina for a 41-year-old. Playing with Jeff Maggert he won two and lost one match before teaming up with Justin Leonard to halve against the Spanish pair Miguel Angel Jimenez & Jose Maria Olazabal.

Sutton believes that 1999 captain Ben Crenshaw succeeded in creating a team unity that was lacking in his two previous appearances.

"The first two teams didn't come together like a family the way this last one did. Before, you showed up and you played. Ben and Julie did a great job of bringing us together, making motivational tapes, getting Governor [George W.] Bush to talk to us," he says.

In his debut season on the tour Sutton claimed three second places, a third and, in the final event of his season at the Walt Disney World Golf Classic, his first victory.

Then, the following year, in just his second on the circuit, he finished top of the money list with $426,668 on the strength of victories in the Players Championship and the PGA Championship, where he led from start to finish, defeating Jack Nicklaus by one stroke. He trailed John Cook by four strokes entering the final round of the Players Championship before a closing 69 gave him a one-stroke victory.

In 1985 and 1986 he won two tournaments each before a dramatic loss of form seemed to signal the end of his career as a top player.

He was winless for the next eight years after 1986, with the low point coming, when his earnings for the year fell to a paltry $39,324 in 1992.

His comeback began two years later when he made $540,162 over the season and twice finished second. Then, in 1995, he returned to the winner's circle at the B.C. Open. His closing ten-under-par 61 was the best final round by a winner since Johnny Miller at the 1975 Dean Martin Tucson Open.

Three years later in 1998 he had his best money-list finish since 1983, when he was first, earning a ninth tour victory with a one-stroke win over Justin Leonard and Jay Haas at the Westin Texas Open. Victory boosted him from 31st to 15th place on the money list. Then he defeated Vijay Singh in a play-off with a birdie on the first extra hole to capture the Tour Championship at East Lake GC.

In 1999 he had another fine year with a career-best 13 top-tens, including a three-stroke victory over Dennis Paulson in the Bell Canadian Open.

His form then got even better the following year with another two wins, one after going head-to-head with Tiger Woods at the Players Championship, where he came away with a one-stroke win. Sutton and Woods played in the last group on the Sunday and Sutton held a three-stroke lead on the 12th hole when lightning suspended play for the day.

On the Monday morning, Woods fell four back but pulled to within one with an eagle on the par-five 16th hole before both players parred the closing two holes. That victory came 17 years after his first Players win in 1983.

His second victory of the season came at the Greater Greensboro Chrysler Classic with a three-stroke win over Andrew Magee. Additionally his tenth place in the US Masters was the first time he had made the cut at Augusta since 1985.

David Toms

CAREER WINS

2001	COMPAQ CLASSIC OF NEW ORLEANS
	USPGA CHAMPIONSHIP
	MICHELOB CHAMPIONSHIP
2000	MICHELOB CHAMPIONSHIP
1999	SPRINT INTERNATIONAL
	BUICK CHALLENGE
1997	QUAD CITY CLASSIC

David Toms gatecrashed the Ryder Cup party by winning the 2001 USPGA Championship, which lifted him from 14th to fourth on the qualification list and pushed out Tom Lehman in the process.

The PGA Championship was the sixth victory of Toms' career and the second of the season for the softly-spoken man from Shreveport.

Toms shot 66-65-65 to hold the lead after three rounds, which included a hole-in-one on the par-three 15th in Saturday's third round. He went head-to-head with playing partner Phil Mickelson in the final round and holding a one-stroke lead over Mickelson on the par-four 18th hole, he chose to lay up short of a water hazard in front of the green after studying a poor lie from 213 yards away. He wedged to 12 feet and sank the par putt for the win after Mickelson's long birdie putt rolled just short.

Earlier that year, he became the first Louisiana native to win the Compaq Classic of New Orleans. The win also meant he had won six times in the previous five years – a feat only David Duval, Tiger Woods, Phil Mickelson and Hal Sutton matched or bettered during that stretch.

Toms has been a professional since 1989 but spent the first few years on the US Tour flitting between the main tour and the second-string Nike Tour. It was only in 1997 that he made his breakthrough by winning the Quad Cities Classic. He birdied the last two holes at Castle Pines GC to defeat David Duval by three points.

He attributes much of his recent success to the lessons learnt on the junior tours.

"I think you have to go back to college golf. I cannot tell you how important that was. Getting in the travelling, playing more tournaments. That helped get me prepared. Then playing the Hogan Tour and playing in Asia and appreciating what I had here in the States. It made me hungry to play and willing to work hard at it to achieve success. It also taught me about the travelling and being away from home as well as everything else."

Toms was playing regularly by the age of 11. By 17, he had racked up junior championships at a Tiger Woods-like pace. In fact, his name joins Woods' on the list of winners of the Junior World Championship in San Diego. Toms also joined future PGA Tour players Bob Estes, Brian Watts, Billy Mayfair and Bob May on the American Junior

Golf Association's 1984 All-American team.

As good as Toms has become, he's still undersized in a sport where 300-yard drives are increasingly common. He gets all the yardage he can out of his 172 pounds, but in the last three years he has failed to crack the top 60 on tour in driving distance. During that span, however, he has ranked in the top 15 in greens in regulation and birdies per round, pushing his worldwide ranking to eighth -- above players like Colin Montgomerie, Jim Furyk and Jesper Parnevik.

When Woods won the 2000 British Open, he was paired with Toms during Saturday's third round. Despite facing the game's No. 1 player, a worldwide television audience and in his first Open Championship, Toms shot a one-under-par 71 at St. Andrews that day, and ultimately finished tied for fourth.

It left a lasting impression on the other guy in the pairing that day.

"I'm surprised he hasn't won more out here," Woods said at the time. "He's got talent, but more importantly, he doesn't back down."

And he doesn't like to give up. Toms, playing in the US Masters for the first time in 1998, had no chance of winning that tournament and even told his wife Sonya that it was okay for her to fly home before his final round was complete. As soon as she left, he made six straight birdies starting at the 12th hole for a 29, a final-round 64 and a tie for sixth with Jack Nicklaus. His round was one off the Augusta National course record and one shy of the record for any Major championship, while the back-nine 29 tied the tournament record, as did his six consecutive birdies on holes 12 through to 17.

In the PGA Tour stop in New Orleans in May 2001, Toms again showed his mettle as he overcame a six-shot deficit to overtake Mickelson and win by two strokes.

Talking about the Ryder Cup clash Toms says: "I am very excited. I am looking forward to playing for the US and with my fellow tour players. It will be good to play for my country and talk strategy with Curtis Strange and the others. It is a wonderful opportunity, and I look forward to it."

As for having to wait an extra 12 months to make his debut in the contest he is philosophical about the situation.

"I want to have my game in good shape to go over there and perform well because I am really looking forward to it.," he says.

"I hope all 12 guys are the top 12 guys on the money list so you don't have to answer any questions about whether or not you are fielding the best team. I hope that's the way it works out."

His form has been extremely impressive in 2002. In the Mercedes Championship he lost to Ryder Cup opponent Sergio Garcia on the first play-off hole. That runner-up finish earned him a cool $432,000. He then added a second top-ten in as many weeks, with a tied fourth place at the Sony Open in Hawaii. He finished in joint fifth in the WGC-Accenture Match Play Championship after losing to Kevin Sutherland (3&2) in the quarter-finals, having defeated Steve Flesch, Rocco Mediate and Rory Sabbatini in the first three rounds before closing with a 66 for tied fourth at the Verizon Byron Nelson Classic, his fourth top-five finish of the season. Aided by weekend rounds of 64-66, he earned a sixth top ten in 14 events with a runners-up finish at the MasterCard Colonial, moving into third place on the 2002 Tour Money List.

Scott Verplank

CAREER WINS

2001	BELL CANADIAN OPEN
2000	RENO-TAHOE OPEN
1988	BUICK OPEN
1985	WESTERN OPEN

Scott Verplank was a surprise choice of US skipper Curtis Strange as the second of his two captain's picks – the first time a debutant has been a captain's pick. It was thought to be a choice between the hero of 1999 Justin Leonard and the veteran Tom Lehman.

"I knew he (Strange) was interested for the couple of weeks before the team was announced. He called and said he wanted me on the team, but I needed to show him something the last couple times I was playing," says Verplank.

In those two events, the Buick Open and the PGA Championship, Verplank finished 14th and seventh, respectively.

"I know you've got to drive the ball pretty straight. I talked to Curtis a little bit about that. I know The Belfry is a little bit more of an American-style golf course for over there."

But he doesn't expect the British and European fans to reciprocate the poor behaviour of the American public in 1999.

"If they're heckling, they're heckling. But I think the fans over there are a little different than ours. I'm sure there will be some guys that maybe have a pint or two too many," he says.

"Our fans, particularly now in golf, are a lot more mainstream sports fans. It's continually getting louder and more abrasive."

Verplank is a diabetic, who has a pump attached to his back belt to regulate his insulin intake, while on the course. He became the first amateur to win an event on the US Tour when he triumphed in the 1985 Western Open, beating Jim Thorpe in a play-off.

But the Texan's early days on the PGA Tour were positively Springsteenesque: one step up and two steps back. Showing the grit of someone who has had to deal with diabetes since the age of nine, plus overcome three career-threatening elbow surgeries, Verplank, since 1998, has clawed back into the upper echelon of the PGA Tour. He's remarkably consistent and possesses a short game to be admired, envied, or both.

Three year later in 1992 he earned his second tour title at the Buick Open, where a final-round 66 produced a two-stroke victory over Doug Tewell.

However, the next few years were plagued by injuries and a somewhat barren time for Verplank.

He missed most of the 1992 season and the prior year due to first elbow surgery and after several further poor years lost his place on the tour in 1996. In 1997 he finished as a medalist at the 1997 Tour Qualifying Tournament to regain his card.

But 1998 was the turning point for Verplank. He managed ten top-ten finishes, including two runner-ups and one third spot. He lost a play-off to Trevor Dodds at the Greater Greensboro Chrysler Classic on the first extra hole, then finished fifth at the Tour Championship.

Earnings of $1,223,436 placed him 18th on the money list, the highest finish by a qualifying school graduate since John Daly was 17th in 1991.

Along with Daly, he represented the United States in the World Cup of Golf and won the individual title with a nine-under-par 279, one stroke better than Nick Faldo and Costantino Rocca. To cap it all off he was chosen by his peers as the Tour Comeback Player of the Year.

In 2000 he returned to the winner's circle for the first time since 1988 with victory at the Reno-Tahoe Open. His time between victories (12 years, 27 days) is the fourth longest in the history of the tour. He trailed the third-round leader Jean Van de Velde by five strokes after 54 holes but a final-round 67 earned a tie with Van de Velde and Verplank won the play-off with an eight-foot birdie putt on the fourth extra hole.

After missing the cut at the PGA Championship, he won the next week at Reno and started a stretch in which he finished in the top-ten in four of his final eight appearances. He was ranked third in Driving Accuracy (78.8 per cent).

Last season he finished in the top ten on the money list and earned over $2 million for the first time in his career, completing the season with a victory at the Bell Canadian Open. A second-round 63, after an opening 70, lifted him into contention before a third-round 66 put him one stroke ahead of Paul Gow and Dicky Pride. A final round 67 produced a three-stroke victory over Bob Estes and Joey Sindelar. His 63 broke the Royal Montreal course record (64) set earlier in the day by Pride. He also narrowly missed out on winning the Verizon Byron Nelson Classic, losing a play-off to Robert Damron.

This year he shared the third-round lead at the Mercedes Championship. but a final-round 73 dropped him into eighth place. He was named the winner of the 2002 Ben Hogan Award, given by the Golf Writers Association of America to an individual who has continued to be active in golf despite a physical handicap or serious illness.

He fired a hole-in-one at the par-three fifth hole at Tamarisk CC during the third round of the Bob Hope Chrysler Classic, while opening and closing rounds of 67 helped him to joint fifth place at the Worldcom Classic-The Heritage of Golf.

Verplank attributes his fine form over the past couple of years to improved health.

"The main factor is that my health has been consistently better. I'm in better shape physically than I've been in the past, and most important, this insulin pump I've been wearing [since the fall of 1999] has made me feel a lot better and has made my health a lot more stable. I really haven't played that much different this year than I did last year."

He says his strength recently has been his consistency.

"Last year, I really drove the ball beautiful, really nice and straight. This year, I'm not driving the ball quite as straight. But I have no glaring weaknesses at the moment. I hit a good amount of fairways, hit a good amount of greens. I'm good at chipping and putting."

Tiger Woods

CAREER WINS

2002 BUICK OPEN	**1999** BUICK INVITATIONAL
BAY HILL INVITATIONAL	MEMORIAL TOURNAMENT
PRESENTED BY COOPER TIRES	MOTOROLA WESTERN OPEN
US MASTERS TOURNAMENT	USPGA CHAMPIONSHIP
US OPEN	WGC NEC INVITATIONAL
BUICK OPEN	NATIONAL CAR RENTAL
2001 BAY HILL INVITATIONAL	GOLF CLASSIC/DISNEY
THE PLAYERS CHAMPIONSHIP	THE TOUR CHAMPIONSHIP
US MASTERS	WGC AMERICAN EXPRESS
MEMORIAL TOURNAMENT	CHAMPIONSHIP
WGC-NEC INVITATIONAL	DEUTSCHE BANK OPEN
DEUTSCHE BANK - SAP OPEN	WORLD CUP OF GOLF
2000 MERCEDES CHAMPIONSHIPS	**1998** BELLSOUTH CLASSIC
AT&T PEBBLE BEACH	JOHNNIE WALKER CLASSIC
NATIONAL PRO-AM	**1997** MERCEDES CHAMPIONSHIPS
BAY HILL INVITATIONAL	US MASTERS
MEMORIAL TOURNAMENT	GTE BYRON NELSON GOLF CLASSIC
US OPEN	MOTOROLA WESTERN OPEN
OPEN CHAMPIONSHIP	ASIAN HONDA CLASSIC
USPGA CHAMPIONSHIP	**1996** LAS VEGAS INVITATIONAL
WGC-NEC INVITATIONAL	WALT DISNEY
BELL CANADIAN OPEN	WORLD/OLDSMOBILE CLASSIC
JOHNNIE WALKER CLASSIC	

Regarded as the greatest player of all-time despite being just 26-years-old, Woods has now won eight Majors (3 US Masters, 2 US Opens, 2 US PGAs, and 1 Open), though he still has some way to go to beat Jack Nicklaus' total of 19. He was tipped to complete the Grand Slam of all four Majors this year and but for being caught in a Scottish gale during the third round of the Open, would surely have added that to the US Masters and US Open that he had already captured.

Strangely though, Woods' record in his two Ryder Cup contests is unimpressive. He made his debut at Valderrama in 1997 and was one of the players who stuggled to read the greens and was criticised by the US press for not having played the course enough.

Playing three times with long-time friend Mark O'Meara on the opening two days they only won one match, losing the other two, and then combined with Justin Leonard for a half against Jesper Parnevik and Ignacio Garrido in the Saturday afternoon foursomes. On the last day he crashed to a comprehensive 4&2 loss against the Italian Costantino Rocca.

Two years later he played in all four pairs but lost three and only managed a solitary win with Steve Pate against Colin Montgomerie and Paul Lawrie on the Saturday afternoon. But it was a crucial point as it at least kept the US side in touch and he easily defeated Andrew Coltart 3&2 in the singles as the US came back to win dramatically.

His overall Ryder Cup record is played ten, won three, halved one, lost six and he will be keen to improve on that at The Belfry.

In 2000, he matched the record of Ben Hogan in 1953 in winning three professional Major championships in the same year. Having won the PGA Championship in 1999, this gave him the unofficial Grand Slam.

In winning the British Open, Woods became the youngest to complete the career Grand Slam of professional Major championships and only the fifth ever to do so, following Hogan, Gene Sarazen, Gary Player and Jack Nicklaus. He was the youngest Masters champion ever, at the age of 21 years, three months and 14 days, and was the first Major championship winner of African or Asian heritage.

Woods holds or shares the record for the lowest score in relation to par in each of the four Major championships. His records are 270 (18 under par) in the Masters, 272 (12 under par) in the US Open, 269 (19 under par) in the British Open, and he shares the record of 270 (18 under par) with Bob May in the 2000 PGA Championship, which Tiger won by one stroke in a three-hole play-off.

The US Open and Masters victories came by record margins, 15 strokes and 12 strokes respectively, and the US Open triumph swept aside the 13-stroke Major championship standard which had stood for 138 years, established by Old Tom Morris in the 1862 British Open. The record margin for the US Open had been 11 strokes by Willie Smith in 1899. In the Masters, Woods broke the record margin of nine strokes set by Jack Nicklaus in 1965. Tiger won the British Open by eight strokes, the largest margin since J.H. Taylor in 1913.

Woods' five professional Major championships and three US Amateur titles bring his total to eight Major championships at the age of 24, three more than Nicklaus at that age. Nicklaus had three professional Major victories and two US Amateur titles.

He compiled one of the most impressive amateur records in golf history, winning six USPGA national championships.

He is the son of Earl Woods, a retired lieutenant colonel in the US Army, and his wife, Kultida, a native of Thailand. He was nicknamed Tiger after a Vietnamese soldier and friend of his father, Vuong Dang Phong, to whom his father had also given that nickname.

Born on December 30, 1975, Woods grew up in Cypress, California, 35 miles south-east of Los Angeles. He was not out of the crib before he took an interest in golf, at the age of 6 months, watching as his father hit golf balls into a net and imitating his swing. He appeared on the Mike Douglas Show at the age of two, putting with Bob Hope.

Tiger played in his first professional tournament in 1992, at the age of 16, the Nissan Los Angeles Open, and in three more PGA Tour events in 1993. He made the 36-hole cut and tied for 34th place in the 1994 Johnnie Walker Asian Classic in Thailand, and had three additional PGA Tour appearances. He entered Stanford University in 1994 and in two years he won ten collegiate events, concluding with the NCAA title. His other amateur victories included the 1994 Western Amateur. He represented the United States in the 1994 World Amateur Team Championships in

France and the 1995 Walker Cup Match in Wales.

He played his first Major championships in 1995, making the cuts in the Masters and the British Open, but had to withdraw from the US Open because of an injured wrist. He played in three more Major championships in 1996, making the cuts in two. After missing the cut in the Masters, he led the US Open after 13 holes of the first round before finishing tied for 82nd place.

The week after winning his third US Amateur title, Woods played his first tournament as a professional in the Greater Milwaukee Open. In the remaining six tournaments that year he won twice, becoming the first rookie since 1990 to win twice, and the first player since 1982 to have five consecutive top-five finishes.

Starting 1997 in spectacular fashion, he won the season-opening Mercedes Championships with a birdie in a play-off over Tom Lehman with a six-iron shot that drew perfectly to the flag, landing two feet right of the hole and spinning back to within inches. Including the Masters, Woods won four tour events in 1997, plus one overseas, and was the leading money winner with a then-record $2,066,833. He won $2,440,831 worldwide in 25 events.

On June 15, 1997, in his 42nd week as a professional, Woods became the youngest-ever World No. 1 golfer aged 21 years, 24 weeks. The previous youngest was Bernhard Langer, age 29 years, 31 weeks in 1986.

In 1998 Woods won one event on the PGA Tour and three times overall. He was fourth on the money list with $1,841,117 and earned $2,927,006 worldwide in 26 events. His most dramatic triumph was over Ernie Els in the Johnnie Walker Classic in Thailand. He rallied with 65 in the final round after starting tied for 18th place, eight strokes behind Els, whom he beat with a birdie on the second play-off hole. He had been 11 strokes behind Els after two rounds.

In his third full season as a professional, in 1999, Woods won eight times on the PGA Tour, including the PGA Championship, and earned $6,616,585. He had a margin of $2,974,679 over runner-up David Duval, a figure greater than the previous single-year PGA Tour record. His dominance was such that Woods won an astounding 52 per cent of all the prize money he could have won. He won 81.7 per cent more than the runner-up, the highest margin since Byron Nelson in 1945 (87.2 per cent) and Ben Hogan in 1946 (85 per cent). He was the first to have as many as eight PGA Tour victories in one year since Johnny Miller won eight in 1974. His total has been exceeded only five times.

He won four consecutive PGA Tour events to end 1999, and started 2000 with two more victories for a total of six in succession. He had to come from behind for the fifth and sixth victories. He played the last three holes in four under par at the Mercedes Championships, then defeated Els in a play-off with a 40-foot birdie putt. He trailed Matt Gogel by seven strokes with seven holes left in the AT&T Pebble Beach National Pro-Am, then played the last four holes in four under par to win by two strokes. There has been only one longer winning streak, Nelson's 11 consecutive wins in 1945.

Woods' 11 worldwide victories in 1999 represented a total not achieved since the primes of Nelson, Hogan and Sam Snead in the 1945-50 period. He earned $7,681,625 worldwide in 25 events. The founding members of the World Sports Academy, in voting for the Laureus Sports Awards, selected Tiger as the 1999 World Sportsman of the Year.

SAM TORRANCE

Sam Torrance is a man who knows the importance of the Ryder Cup. "It was a fabulous honour to be named captain," he says. "When it happened it was an indescribable feeling. It's tremendous for myself, my family, my parents and for Scotland. It's the pinnacle of my career, without a doubt.

"Of course, I was one of Mark James' assistants in the 1999 Ryder Cup and I learned a great deal from that experience. It taught me about the job I would be doing, the whole atmosphere – everything really.

"Hopefully I can take a little of what I've learned from all the Cup captains. You can't define any one thing because they were all so different – John Jacobs, Bernard Gallacher and Tony Jacklin – but they all had great points. Hopefully some of it has sunk in with me."

Torrance was destined to become a golfer. His father, Bob, was a pro and he's been Sam's one and only coach. Torrance junior started under his father's guidance at Rossendale in Lancashire when he was seven. At the age of 10 the family moved back to Largs in Ayrshire.

One of Torrance's recollections as a 10-year-old was scaling up a lamppost at St Andrews when Tony Lema won the 1964 Open Championship. By then golf was already up in lights for him.

He remembers the unorthodox first tip given to him by his father.

"He told me to take the biggest shoulder turn I could, and to hit the ball as hard as I could," recalls Torrance.

After leaving school, the young Scot got a job at Sunningdale for a year before going on the Tour. Although he turned professional at 16, which was a young age, it wasn't so unusual in those days. He missed the first nine cuts on Tour before the big breakthrough came at the John Player Trophy, where he was leading with nine holes to play, before finishing ninth.

Torrance was European Tour Rookie of the Year in 1972 and won his first tournament, the Zambian Open, in 1975. He won 21 events on the European Tour but says the victories that really stand out are the Irish Opens in 1981 and 1995. In 1981 the event was held at Port Marnock and drew enormous crowds, giving it the feel of a Major. He won by five shots.

Probably the best win in his career though, was at the Australian PGA Championship in 1980 when he beat Seve Ballesteros into second and had

Greg Norman back in third.

The last time Torrance won on the Tour was the 1998 French Open. He became the first golfer to notch up 600 European Tour tournaments when he played at the Lancombe Trophy in the same year, but he has also played over 300 outside Europe, making a total nearer 1,000. A pioneer of the broom handle putter, Torrance was awarded the MBE in 1996.

This year's European captain made his Ryder Cup debut in 1981, when he was thrown in at the deep end against the so-called American dream team, which boasted an incredible 36 Majors between them and included Jack Nicklaus, Ray Floyd, Lee Trevino and Tom Watson. Torrance played Jerry Pate – who was in awesome form at the time – and Trevino, who he recalls never let him hit a shot without first offering his advice.

Overall, Torrance played in eight Ryder Cups and was part of the European team that won the event in 1985, 1987 and 1995. Unsurprisingly, he says that the 1985 contest was the highlight of his playing career.

"I holed the winning putt at The Belfry in 1985. It was a 15-footer against Andy North on the 18th and everyone thinks that was a great putt. But the hardest putt I've ever had in my life was on the 17th green – a six-footer.

"I was one down and that was to win the hole. I knew we needed one more point and if I didn't hole it I could only get half a point. I holed it and that was important in winning the Cup. To end Europe's 28-year drought in the tournament was great because it helped revive the worldwide interest in the event."

Two years later he was part of the side that went over and beat America's finest in their own backyard. "Their captain was Jack Nicklaus, who was my hero, and we hammered them. We started strongly and kept going. It was the finest European performance in any Ryder Cup. 1995 came close, but 1987 was so very special," he says.

"I remember the Opening Ceremony that year in Ohio. There was a huge band which came up the 18th – it was magnificent. Each player walked around the car park in front of the crowd, and it was amazing. The atmosphere and the applause were incredible. My wife and I, who got engaged on the flight over, actually walked round again because it was so good."

Torrance says he will be careful not to let any of the players who do not feature on the first two days feel left out of such an atmosphere. "One of the worst things I've ever experienced was playing in the Ryder Cup, but being dropped and having to go out and watch. I was full of negative thoughts," he says.

"I've appointed Ian Woosnam as one of my vice-captains and he's just fantastic. I feel confident with the people I've got around me. Woosie's been a dear friend for 30 years, he's a tremendous character and I want him with me," Torrance says.

"There's nobody with more fire than him. He'll talk to the youngsters, he'll talk to the older players, he'll be anywhere I want him to be. I think he'll be a great asset. I've never made a secret of how much I enjoy being part of the Ryder Cup. I enjoy the adrenaline and the fire that goes with it – there's no event like it and I love it."

CURTIS STRANGE

The idea of Curtis Strange being appointed US Ryder Cup captain would have seemed a fanciful notion at times during this fiery player's career. But he has mellowed with age and is now seen as the ideal choice as the US look to play hard but fair and avoid any repeat of the scenes of Brookline three years ago.

Strange has not always endeared himself to fans this side of the Atlantic with his somewhat forthright views on golf in the British Isles.

"Why should I take two weeks out of my life to play in bad weather on some terrible course like Turnberry?" he asked once.

"The British Open only counts if you win. Second place is as much use as a pat on the back. To be honest, I don't want to play in the British Open because every time I turn around some smart son of a bitch is telling me that I have to."

But three-time Ryder Cupper Tom Lehman is just one of those who thinks the US's new skipper will do just fine at The Belfry come September. "Curtis and the job are a perfect fit," says the 1996 British Open champion.

Then there are the adjectives used to describe the man himself. 'Remorseless' is one. 'Difficult' is another. But the one that comes up time after time is 'intense'.

Strange has always been a driven individual, especially during the decade or so when he was one of the best golfers on the planet. That accolade came in handy when he beat Nick Faldo in a play-off to win his first US Open in 1988.

Perhaps his finest moment, however, came at the 1989 Ryder Cup. Knowing he had to win his final day singles against Woosnam to tie the overall match, Strange birdied each of the last four holes to hold off the Welshman on the final green. It was an impressive display of gutsy golf under the severest pressure. And all without the look of stern intensity on his face altering one iota.

But that same passion could also lead to trouble. For Strange, the line between fervour and temper tantrum was always a fine one. "Curtis is the only player I've known who plays better when he's mad," says his college coach at Wake Forest, Jesse Haddock. There were, however, moments when Strange was unable to maintain control and do the right thing. In 1982, Arnold Palmer was provoked into writing a letter of protest to PGA Tour commissioner Deane Beman after Strange verbally and profanely abused a woman scorer and a photographer during Palmer's Bay Hill tournament. Strange, though, won't be altering his outlook.

"There is nothing wrong with being fiery," he says. "To be a leader you need a bit of that to inspire your players. I don't want to take any of the fight out of the players, but there must be civility on both sides." Strange refers, of course, to events at Brookline two years ago. The American side drew waves of criticism for their headlong rush across the 17th green at The Country Club in the wake of Justin Leonard's infamous putt against Jose Maria Olazabal. As captain, Strange knows he has a wider responsibility to the peerless etiquette of the game, as well as to his players and country.

"There is no doubt that we crossed the line at Brookline," he concedes. "And that must never happen again. But at the same time, that is why the Ryder Cup is so great. There is so much emotion there and that gets inside the players. That's why the world likes to watch it.

"I'm not saying what happened was right. We made a mistake. But spontaneous emotion is a wonderful thing. It happened and we apologised for it. That's all we can do.

"The atmosphere will be tough [this year] because they root for their own team. I've played twice at The Belfry, and any time you have people not so much rooting against you, but rooting hard for the other team, you take it personally. You can't help it. But you have to prepare yourself. They are not rooting so much against me; they are rooting for their team very hard. So when they cheer on a 4-foot missed putt, they are just cheering for their own team. That's the attitude I took.

"Sam and I are very sincere about what we are trying to do. I think the whole personality of the Ryder Cup matches starts with the two captains and filters to the players. And then we need the help of the press and the media; we really do, to get out our message to the people, to get our message to the American public. To start with, this isn't going to be a grudge match. There's different characters in this Ryder Cup than there were before."

His style of captaincy won't be as 'hands-on' as, say, Seve Ballesteros in 1997, but Strange will bring his own thoughts to what is a unique role in professional golf.

"I'll be there to motivate the players," he states. "To say the right thing at the right time and stay positive. To be upbeat, to have fun."

Strange was the winner of 17 PGA Tour events, including consecutive US Open titles. A year after he defeated Faldo in that play-off he became the first player to successfully defend the title since Ben Hogan (1950-51), with a one-stroke victory over Chip Beck, Mark McCumber and Ian Woosnam at Oak Hill in 1989.

When asked what it takes to win the US Open twice, Strange replied: "Guts and pars." He came close to a third US Open in 1994, but fell one stroke short of the Ernie Els/Loren Roberts/Colin Montgomerie play-off.

In 1988, he became the first player to surpass $1 million prize money in a season when he captured his third of three money titles. He won at least one tournament each year for seven years (1983-89). He also finished tied for second at the 1989 PGA Championship, one behind Payne Stewart. Strange was a five-time Ryder Cup team member with a 6-2-12 career record. He was voted 1985, 1987 and 1988 Golf Writers Association Player of the Year.

RECORDS

A COMPLETE LIST OF EACH 2002 COMPETITOR'S RYDER CUP PLAYING RECORD

PAUL AZINGER (USA)

YEAR	FORMAT	PARTNER	F	A	OPPONENTS		WON	SCORE
1989	Fourballs	C Strange	0	1	S Torrance	G Brand jnr	Eur	1 hole
1989	Foursomes	C Beck	1	0	S Torrance	G Brand jnr	USA	4&3
1989	Fourballs	C Beck	1	0	N Faldo	I Woosnam	USA	2&1
1989	Singles		1	0	S Ballesteros		USA	1 hole
1991	Foursomes	C Beck	0	1	S Ballesteros	JM Olazabal	Eur	2&1
1991	Fourballs	C Beck	0	1	S Ballesteros	JM Olazabal	Eur	2&1
1991	Foursomes	M O'Meara	1	0	N Faldo	D Gilford	USA	7&6
1991	Fourballs	H Irwin	0	1	I Woosnam	P Broadhurst	Eur	2&1
1991	Singles		1	0	JM Olazabal		USA	2 holes
1993	Foursomes	P Stewart	0	1	I Woosnam	B Langer	Eur	7&5
1993	Fourballs	F Couples	.5	.5	N Faldo	C Montgomerie	Hvd	
1993	Foursomes	F Couples	0	1	I Woosnam	B Langer	Eur	2&1
1993	Fourballs	F Couples	0	1	I Woosnam	P Baker	Eur	6&5
1993	Singles		.5	.5	N Faldo		Hvd	

THOMAS BJORN (EUR)

YEAR	FORMAT	PARTNER	F	A	OPPONENTS		WON	SCORE
1997	Fourballs	I Woosnam	1	0	J Leonard	B Faxon	Eur	2&1
1997	Singles		.5	.5	J Leonard		Hvd	

MARK CALCAVECCHIA (USA)

YEAR	FORMAT	PARTNER	F	A	OPPONENTS		WON	SCORE
1987	Fourballs	A Bean	0	1	S Lyle	B Langer	Eur	1 hole
1987	Singles		1	0	N Faldo		USA	1 hole

1989	Foursomes	K Green	1	0	B Langer	R Rafferty	USA	2&1
1989	Fourballs	M McCumber	0	1	N Faldo	I Woosnam	Eur	2 holes
1989	Foursomes	K Green	1	0	R Rafferty	C O'Connor jr	USA	3&2
1989	Fourballs	K Green	0	1	S Ballesteros	JM Olazabal	Eur	4&2
1989	Singles		0	1	R Rafferty		Eur	1 hole
1991	Foursomes	P Stewart	1	0	N Faldo	I Woosnam	USA	1 hole
1991	Fourballs	C Pavin	0	1	S Richardson	M James	Eur	5&4
1991	Foursomes	P Stewart	1	0	S Richardson	M James	USA	1 hole
1991	Singles		.5	.5	C Montgomerie		Hvd	

DARREN CLARKE (EUR)

YEAR	FORMAT	PARTNER	F	A	OPPONENTS		WON	SCORE
1997	Fourballs	C Montgomerie	1	0	F Couples	D Love	Eur	1 hole
1997	Singles		0	1	P Mickelson		USA	2&1
1999	Foursomes	L Westwood	0	1	J Maggert	H Sutton	USA	3&2
1999	Fourballs	L Westwood	1	0	D Duval	T Woods	Eur	1 hole
1999	Foursomes	L Westwood	1	0	J Furyk	M O'Meara	Eur	3&2
1999	Fourballs	L Westwood	0	1	T Lehman	P Mickelson	USA	2&1
1999	Singles		0	1	H Sutton		USA	4&2

DAVID DUVAL (USA)

YEAR	FORMAT	PARTNER	F	A	OPPONENTS		WON	SCORE
1999	Foursomes	P Mickelson	0	1	P Lawrie	C Montgomerie	Eur	3&2
1999	Fourballs	T Woods	0	1	D Clarke	L Westwood	Eur	1 hole
1999	Fourballs	D Love	.5	.5	S Garcia	J Parnevik	Hvd	
1999	Singles		1	0	J Parnevik	USA		5&4

JIM FURYK (USA)

YEAR	FORMAT	PARTNER	F	A	OPPONENTS		WON	SCORE
1997	Fourballs	T Lehman	0	1	J Parnevik	PU Johansson	Eur	1 hole
1997	Foursomes	L Janzen	0	1	C Montgomerie	B Langer	Eur	1 hole
1997	Singles		1	0	N Faldo		USA	3&2
1999	Fourballs	P Mickelson	0	1	S Garcia	J Parnevik	Eur	1 hole
1999	Foursomes	M O'Meara	0	1	D Clarke	L Westwood	Eur	3&2
1999	Singles		1	0	S Garcia		USA	4&3

PLAYER RECORDS

SERGIO GARCIA (EUR)

YEAR	FORMAT	PARTNER	F	A	OPPONENTS		WON	SCORE
1999	Foursomes	J Parnevik	1	0	T Lehman	T Woods	Eur	2&1
1999	Fourballs	J Parnevik	1	0	J Furyk	P Mickelson	Eur	1 hole
1999	Foursomes	J Parnevik	1	0	J Leonard	P Stewart	Eur	3&2
1999	Fourballs	J Parnevik	.5	.5	D Duval	D Love	Hvd	
1999	Singles		0	1	J Furyk		USA	4&3

PADRAIG HARRINGTON (EUR)

YEAR	FORMAT	PARTNER	F	A	OPPONENTS		WON	SCORE
1999	Foursomes	M Jimenez A	.5	.5	D Love	P Stewart	Hvd	
1999	Foursomes	M Jimenez A	0	1	S Pate	T Woods	USA	1 hole
1999	Singles		1	0	M O'Meara		Eur	1 hole

SCOTT HOCH (USA)

YEAR	FORMAT	PARTNER	F	A	OPPONENTS		WON	SCORE
1997	Foursomes	L Janzen	1	0	JM Olazabal	C Rocca	USA	1 hole
1997	Foursomes	J Maggert	1	0	N Faldo	L Westwood	USA	1 hole
1997	Singles		.5	.5	C Montgomerie		Hvd	

BERNHARD LANGER (EUR)

YEAR	FORMAT	PARTNER	F	A	OPPONENTS		WON	SCORE
1981	Foursomes	M Pinero	0	1	L Trevino	L Nelson	USA	1 hole
1981	Fourballs	M Pinero	1	0	H Irwin	R Floyd	Eur	2&1
1981	Foursomes	M Pinero	0	1	T Watson	J Nicklaus	USA	3&2
1981	Singles		.5	.5	B Lietzke		Hvd	
1983	Foursomes	N Faldo	1	0	L Wadkins	C Stadler	Eur	4&2
1983	Fourballs	N Faldo	0	1	T Watson	J Haas	USA	2&1
1983	Fourballs	N Faldo	1	0	B Crenshaw	C Peete	Eur	4&2
1983	Foursomes	N Faldo	1	0	T Kite	R Floyd	Eur	3&2
1983	Singles		1	0	G Morgan		Eur	2 holes
1985	Foursomes	N Faldo	0	1	C Peete	T Kite	USA	3&2
1985	Fourballs	JM Canizares	.5	.5	C Stadler	H Sutton	Hvd	
1985	Fourballs	S Lyle	.5	.5	C Stadler	C Strange	Hvd	
1985	Foursomes	K Brown	1	0	L Wadkins	R Floyd	Eur	3&2
1985	Singles		1	0	H Sutton		Eur	5&4
1987	Foursomes	K Brown	0	1	H Sutton	D Pohl	USA	2&1

PLAYER RECORDS

YEAR	FORMAT	PARTNER	F	A	OPPONENTS			WON	SCORE
1987	Fourballs	S Lyle	1	0	A Bean	M Calcavecchia		Eur	1 hole
1987	Foursomes	S Lyle	1	0	L Wadkins	L Nelson		Eur	2&1
1987	Foursomes	S Lyle	1	0	L Wadkins	L Nelson		Eur	1 hole
1987	Singles		.5	.5	L Nelson			Hvd	
1989	Foursomes	R Rafferty	0	1	M Calcavecchia	K Green		USA	2&1
1989	Fourballs	JM Canizares	0	1	T Kite	M McCumber		USA	2&1
1989	Singles		0	1	C Beck			USA	3&1
1991	Foursomes	M James	0	1	F Couples	R Floyd		USA	2&1
1991	Fourballs	C Montgomerie	1	0	C Pavin	S Pate		Eur	2&1
1991	Singles		.5	.5	H Irwin			Hvd	
1993	Foursomes	I Woosnam	1	0	P Stewart	P Azinger		Eur	7&5
1993	Fourballs	B Lane	0	1	L Wadkins	C Pavin		USA	4&2
1993	Foursomes	I Woosnam	1	0	P Azinger	F Couples		Eur	2&1
1993	Singles		0	1	T Kite			USA	5&3
1995	Foursomes	PU Johansson	1	0	B Crenshaw	C Strange		Eur	1 hole
1995	Fourballs	PU Johansson	0	1	P Mickelson	C Pavin		USA	6&4
1995	Foursomes	D Gilford	1	0	C Pavin	T Lehman		Eur	4&3
1995	Fourballs	N Faldo	0	1	C Pavin	L Roberts		USA	1 hole
1995	Singles		0	1	C Pavin			USA	3&2
1997	Fourballs	C Montgomerie	0	1	T Woods	M O'Meara		USA	3&2
1997	Foursomes	C Montgomerie	0	1	T Woods	M O'Meara		USA	5&3
1997	Foursomes	C Montgomerie	1	0	L Janzen	J Furyk		Eur	1 hole
1997	Singles		1	0	B Faxon			Eur	2&1

DAVIS LOVE (USA)

YEAR	FORMAT	PARTNER	F	A	OPPONENTS			WON	SCORE
1993	Foursomes	T Kite	1	0	S Ballesteros	JM Olazabal		USA	2&1
1993	Fourballs	T Kite	0	1	S Ballesteros	JM Olazabal		Eur	4&3
1993	Foursomes	T Kite	0	1	S Ballesteros	JM Olazabal		Eur	2&1
1993	Singles		1	0	C Rocca			USA	1 hole
1995	Foursomes	J Maggert	1	0	H Clark	M James		USA	4&3
1995	Fourballs	F Couples	1	0	N Faldo	C Montgomerie		USA	3&2
1995	Foursomes	J Maggert	0	1	C Rocca	S Torrance		Eur	6&5
1995	Fourballs	B Crenshaw	0	1	C Rocca	I Woosnam		Eur	3&2
1995	Singles		1	0	C Rocca			USA	3&2
1997	Fourballs	P Mickelson	0	1	JM Olazabal	C Rocca		Eur	1 hole
1997	Fourballs	F Couples	0	1	C Montgomerie	D Clarke		Eur	1 hole
1997	Foursomes	F Couples	0	1	JM Olazabal	C Rocca		Eur	5&4
1997	Singles		0	1	PU Johansson			Eur	3&2
1999	Foursomes	P Stewart	.5	.5	P Harrington	MA Jimenez		Hvd	
1999	Fourballs	J Leonard	.5	.5	P Lawrie	C Montgomerie		Hvd	
1999	Fourballs	D Duval	.5	.5	S Garcia	J Parnevik		Hvd	
1999	Singles		1	0	J Van De Velde			USA	6&5

PLAYER RECORDS

PHIL MICKELSON (USA)

YEAR	FORMAT	PARTNER	F	A	OPPONENTS		WON	SCORE
1995	Fourballs	C Pavin	1	0	PU Johansson	B Langer	USA	6&4
1995	Fourballs	J Haas	1	0	S Ballesteros	D Gilford	USA	3&2
1995	Singles		1	0	PU Johansson		USA	2&1
1997	Fourballs	D Love	0	1	JM Olazabal	C Rocca	Eur	1 hole
1997	Foursomes	T Lehman	.5	.5	J Parnevik	I Garrido	Hvd	
1997	Fourballs	T Lehman	.5	.5	JM Olazabal	I Garrido	Hvd	
1997	Singles		1	0	D Clarke		USA	2&1
1999	Foursomes	D Duval	0	1	P Lawrie	C Montgomerie	Eur	3&2
1999	Fourballs	J Furyk	0	1	S Garcia	J Parnevik	Eur	1 hole
1999	Fourballs	T Lehman	1	0	D Clarke	L Westwood	USA	2&1
1999	Singles		1	0	J Sandelin		USA	4&3

COLIN MONTGOMERIE (EUR)

YEAR	FORMAT	PARTNER	F	A	OPPONENTS		WON	SCORE
1991	Foursomes	D Gilford	0	1	L Wadkins	H Irwin	USA	4&2
1991	Fourballs	B Langer	1	0	C Pavin	S Pate	Eur	2&1
1991	Singles		.5	.5	M Calcavecchia		Hvd	
1993	Foursomes	N Faldo	1	0	R Floyd	F Couples	Eur	4&3
1993	Fourballs	N Faldo	.5	.5	P Azinger	F Couples	Hvd	
1993	Fourballs	N Faldo	1	0	L Wadkins	C Pavin	Eur	3&2
1993	Fourballs	N Faldo	0	1	J Cook	C Beck	USA	2 holes
1993	Singles		1	0	L Janzen		Eur	1 hole
1995	Foursomes	N Faldo	0	1	C Pavin	T Lehman	USA	1 hole
1995	Fourballs	N Faldo	0	1	F Couples	D Love	USA	3&2
1995	Foursomes	N Faldo	1	0	J Haas	C Strange	Eur	4&2
1995	Fourballs	S Torrance	0	1	F Couples	B Faxon	USA	4&2
1995	Singles		1	0	B Crenshaw		Eur	3&1
1997	Fourballs	B Langer	0	1	T Woods	M O'Meara	USA	3&2
1997	Foursomes	B Langer	1	0	T Woods	M O'Meara	Eur	5&3
1997	Fourballs	D Clarke	1	0	F Couples	D Love	Eur	1 hole
1997	Foursomes	B Langer	1	0	L Janzen	J Furyk	Eur	1 hole
1997	Singles		.5	.5	S Hoch		Hvd	
1999	Foursomes	P Lawrie	1	0	D Duval	P Mickelson	Eur	3&2
1999	Fourballs	P Lawrie	.5	.5	D Love	J Leonard	Hvd	
1999	Fourballs	P Lawrie	0	1	J Maggert	H Sutton	USA	1 hole
1999	Fourballs	P Lawrie	1	0	S Pate	T Woods	Eur	2&1
1999	Singles		1	0	P Stewart		Eur	1 hole

JESPER PARNEVIK (EUR)

YEAR	FORMAT	PARTNER	F	A	OPPONENTS		WON	SCORE
1997	Fourballs	PU Johansson	1	0	T Lehman	J Furyk	Eur	1 hole
1997	Foursomes	I Garrido	.5	.5	T Lehman	P Mickelson	Hvd	
1997	Foursomes	I Garrido	.5	.5	J Leonard	T Woods	Hvd	
1997	Singles		0	1	M O'Meara		USA	5&4
1999	Foursomes	S Garcia	1	0	T Lehman	T Woods	Eur	2&1
1999	Fourballs	S Garcia	1	0	J Furyk	P Mickelson	Eur	1 hole
1999	Foursomes	S Garcia	1	0	J Leonard	P Stewart	Eur	3&2
1999	Fourballs	S Garcia	.5	.5	D Duval	D Love	Hvd	
1999	Singles		0	1	D Duval		USA	5&4

CURTIS STRANGE (USA) (CAPTAIN)

YEAR	FORMAT	PARTNER	F	A	OPPONENTS		WON	SCORE
1983	Fourballs	R Floyd	0	1	S Ballesteros	P Way	Eur	1 hole
1983	Foursomes	J Haas	1	0	K Brown	B Waites	USA	3&2
1983	Singles		0	1	P Way		Eur	2&1
1985	Foursomes	M O'Meara	0	1	S Ballesteros	M Pinero	Eur	2&1
1985	Fourballs	C Stadler	.5	.5	B Langer	S Lyle	Hvd	
1985	Foursomes	P Jacobsen	1	0	I Woosnam	P Way	USA	4&2
1985	Singles		1	0	K Brown		USA	4&2
1987	Foursomes	T Kite	1	0	S Torrance	H Clark	USA	4&2
1987	Fourballs	T Kite	0	1	S Ballesteros	JM Olazabal	Eur	2&1
1987	Foursomes	T Kite	1	0	G Brand Jnr	J Rivero	USA	3&1
1987	Fourballs	T Kite	0	1	N Faldo	I Woosnam	Eur	5&4
1987	Singles		0	1	S Ballesteros		Eur	2&1
1989	Foursomes	T Kite	.5	.5	N Faldo	I Woosnam	Hvd	
1989	Fourballs	P Azinger	0	1	S Torrance	G Brand Jnr	Eur	1 hole
1989	Foursomes	T Kite	0	1	S Ballesteros	JM Olazabal	Eur	1 hole
1989	Fourballs	P Stewart	0	1	H Clark	M James	Eur	1 hole
1989	Singles		1	0	I Woosnam		USA	2 holes
1995	Foursomes	B Crenshaw	0	1	PU Johansson	B Langer	Eur	1 hole
1995	Foursomes	J Haas	0	1	N Faldo	C Montgomerie	Eur	4&2
1995	Singles		0	1	N Faldo		Eur	1 hole

91

HAL SUTTON (USA)

YEAR	FORMAT	PARTNER	F	A	OPPONENTS		WON	SCORE
1985	Foursomes	C Stadler	1	0	H Clark	S Torrance	USA	3&2
1985	Fourballs	C Stadler	.5	.5	B Langer	JM Canizares	Hvd	
1985	Foursomes	C Stadler	0	1	S Ballesteros	M Pinero	Eur	5&4
1985	Singles		0	1	B Langer		Eur	5&4
1987	Foursomes	D Pohl	1	0	K Brown	B Langer	USA	2&1
1987	Fourballs	D Pohl	0	1	N Faldo	I Woosnam	Eur	2&1
1987	Foursomes	L Mize	.5	.5	N Faldo	I Woosnam	Hvd	
1987	Fourballs	L Mize	1	0	S Ballesteros	JM Olazabal	USA	2&1
1987	Singles		.5	.5	G Brand Jnr		Hvd	
1999	Foursomes	J Maggert	1	0	D Clarke	L Westwood	USA	3&2
1999	Fourballs	J Maggert	0	1	MA Jimenez	JM Olazabal	Eur	2&1
1999	Foursomes	J Maggert	1	0	P Lawrie	C Montgomerie	USA	1 hole
1999	Fourballs	J Leonard	.5	.5	MA Jimenez	JM Olazabal	Hvd	
1999	Singles		1	0	D Clarke		USA	4&2

SAM TORRANCE (EUR) (CAPTAIN)

YEAR	FORMAT	PARTNER	F	A	OPPONENTS		WON	SCORE
1981	Fourballs	H Clark	.5	.5	T Kite	J Miller	Hvd	
1981	Fourballs	N Faldo	0	1	L Trevino	J Pate	USA	7&5
1981	Foursomes	P Oosterhuis	0	1	L Trevino	J Pate	USA	2&1
1981	Singles		0	1	L Trevino		USA	5&3
1983	Foursomes	JM Canizares	1	0	R Floyd	B Gilder	Eur	4&3
1983	Fourballs	I Woosnam	.5	.5	B Crenshaw	C Peete	Hvd	
1983	Fourballs	I Woosnam	0	1	T Watson	B Gilder	USA	5&4
1983	Foursomes	JM Canizares	0	1	G Morgan	L Wadkins	USA	7&5
1983	Singles		.5	.5	T Kite		Hvd	
1985	Foursomes	H Clark	0	1	C Stadler	Sutton Hal	USA	3&2
1985	Fourballs	H Clark	0	1	L Wadkins	R Floyd	USA	1 hole
1985	Fourballs	H Clark	1	0	T Kite	A North	Eur	2&1
1985	Singles		1	0	A North		Eur	1 hole
1987	Foursomes	H Clark	0	1	C Strange	T Kite	USA	4&2
1987	Singles		.5	.5	L Mize		Hvd	
1989	Fourballs	G Brand Jnr	1	0	C Strange	P Azinger	Eur	1 hole
1989	Foursomes	G Brand Jnr	0	1	C Beck	P Azinger	USA	4&3
1989	Singles		0	1	T Watson		USA	3&1
1991	Fourballs	D Feherty	.5	.5	L Wadkins	M O'Meara	Hvd	
1991	Foursomes	D Feherty	0	1	L Wadkins	H Irwin	USA	4&2

YEAR FORMAT	PARTNER	F	A	OPPONENTS		WON	SCORE
1991 Singles		0	1	F Couples		USA	3&2
1993 Foursomes	M James	0	1	L Wadkins	C Pavin	USA	4&3
1993 Singles		.5	.5	L Wadkins		Hvd	Eur Inj
1995 Foursomes	C Rocca	1	0	F Couples	J Haas	Eur	3&2
1995 Fourballs	C Rocca	0	1	J Maggert	L Roberts	USA	6&5
1995 Foursomes	C Rocca	1	0	D Love	J Maggert	Eur	6&5
1995 Fourballs	C Montgomerie	0	1	F Couples	B Faxon	USA	4&2
1995 Singles		1	0	L Roberts		Eur	2&1

LEE WESTWOOD (EUR)

YEAR FORMAT	PARTNER	F	A	OPPONENTS		WON	SCORE
1997 Fourballs	N Faldo	0	1	F Couples	B Faxon	USA	1 hole
1997 Foursomes	N Faldo	1	0	J Leonard	J Maggert	Eur	3&2
1997 Fourballs	N Faldo	1	0	T Woods	M O'Meara	Eur	2&1
1997 Foursomes	N Faldo	0	1	S Hoch	J Maggert	USA	1 hole
1997 Singles		0	1	J Maggert		USA	3&2
1999 Foursomes	D Clarke	0	1	J Maggert	H Sutton	USA	3&2
1999 Fourballs	D Clarke	1	0	D Duval	T Woods	Eur	1 hole
1999 Foursomes	D Clarke	1	0	J Furyk	M O'Meara	Eur	3&2
1999 Fourballs	D Clarke	0	1	T Lehman	P Mickelson	USA	2&1
1999 Singles		0	1	T Lehman		USA	3&2

TIGER WOODS (USA)

YEAR FORMAT	PARTNER	F	A	OPPONENTS		WON	SCORE
1997 Fourballs	M O'Meara	1	0	C Montgomerie	B Langer	USA	3&2
1997 Foursomes	M O'Meara	0	1	C Montgomerie	B Langer	Eur	5&3
1997 Fourballs	M O'Meara	0	1	N Faldo	L Westwood	Eur	2&1
1997 Foursomes	J Leonard	.5	.5	J Parnevik	I Garrido	Hvd	
1997 Singles		0	1	C Rocca		Eur	4&2
1999 Foursomes	T Lehman	0	1	S Garcia	J Parnevik	Eur	2&1
1999 Fourballs	D Duval	0	1	D Clarke	L Westwood	Eur	1 hole
1999 Foursomes	S Pate	1	0	P Harrington	MA Jimenez	USA	1 hole
1999 Fourballs	S Pate	0	1	P Lawrie	C Montgomerie	Eur	2&1
1999 Singles		1	0	A Coltart		USA	3&2

PLAYER FORM

EACH COMPETITOR'S TOUR FORM
SINCE JANUARY 2001

THOMAS BJORN

EUROPEAN TOUR RECORD
(Jan 1st, 2001 to Aug 1st, 2002)

Date	Event	Pos	1	2	3	4	Total
28-Jan-01	South African Open	3	72	67	71	72	282
04-Feb-01	Heineken Classic	8	67	71	73	69	280
04-Mar-01	Dubai Classic	1	64	66	67	69	266
11-Mar-01	Qatar Masters	23	69	71	70	75	285
08-Apr-01	US Masters	MC	70	76	0	0	146
13-May-01	Benson & Hedges International	7	69	68	75	72	284
20-May-01	Deutsche Bank (TPC of Europe)	73	67	75	71	76	289
28-May-01	PGA Championship	39	68	69	72	77	286
03-Jun-01	British Masters	27	69	75	69	72	285
17-Jun-01	US Open	22	72	69	73	72	286
01-Jul-01	Irish Open	5	66	69	72	66	273
08-Jul-01	European Open	2	73	71	65	67	276
15-Jul-01	Scottish Open	2	68	67	69	67	271
22-Jul-01	The Open Championship	MC	76	75	0	0	151
05-Aug-01	Scandinavian Masters	9	68	72	67	70	277
19-Aug-01	USPGA	63	67	71	73	73	284
26-Aug-01	NEC Invitational	31	66	79	73	71	289
02-Sep-01	BMW International	16	65	67	65	76	273
09-Sep-01	European Masters (Swiss Open)	Wd	66	71	0	0	137

PLAYER FORM SINCE JANUARY 2001

21-Oct-01	Dunhill Links Championship	13	70	67	71	69	277
28-Oct-01	Madrid Open	10	68	71	66	64	269
11-Nov-01	Volvo Masters	44	73	69	0	77	219
10-Mar-02	Dubai Classic	20	67	73	71	73	284
14-Apr-02	US Masters	18	74	67	70	77	288
05-May-02	French Open	55	70	71	75	74	290
12-May-02	Benson & Hedges International	51	71	70	80	70	291
20-May-02	Deutsche Bank (TPC of Europe)	6	73	65	71	66	275
26-May-02	PGA Championship	19	71	69	73	69	282
02-Jun-02	British Masters	Ret	70	0	0	0	70
16-Jun-02	US Open	37	71	79	73	71	294
30-Jun-02	Irish Open	5	71	68	63	70	272
07-Jul-02	European Open	MC	74	76	0	0	150
14-Jul-02	Scottish Open	MC	75	72	0	0	147
21-Jul-02	The Open Championship	8	68	70	73	69	280

BJORN IN THE STATES

26-Mar-01	Players Championship	MC	76	79	0	0	155
16-Apr-01	Worldcom Classic	12	69	70	71	67	277
24-Mar-02	Players Championship	22	74	72	75	68	289
31-Mar-02	Houston Open	MC	77	73	0	0	150
07-Apr-02	BellSouth Classic	12	66	70	69	77	282

DARREN CLARKE

EUROPEAN TOUR RECORD
(Jan 1st, 2001 to Aug 1st, 2002)

		Pos	1	2	3	4	Total
28-Jan-01	South African Open	MC	77	78	0	0	155
04-Mar-01	Dubai Classic	58	71	69	70	73	283
08-Apr-01	US Masters	24	72	67	72	73	284
22-Apr-01	Spanish Open	32	67	68	72	79	286
13-May-01	Benson & Hedges International	27	69	76	68	74	287
20-May-01	Deutsche Bank (TPC of Europe)	24	76	67	69	67	279
28-May-01	PGA Championship	8	72	69	68	70	279
03-Jun-01	British Masters	42	70	72	71	74	287
10-Jun-01	English Open	5	74	72	67	68	281
17-Jun-01	US Open	30	74	71	71	72	288
01-Jul-01	Irish Open	2	70	72	65	64	271
08-Jul-01	European Open	1	68	68	71	66	273
15-Jul-01	Scottish Open	7	69	67	68	69	273
22-Jul-01	The Open Championship	3	70	69	69	70	278
29-Jul-01	Dutch Open	56	68	70	73	74	285
05-Aug-01	Scandinavian Masters	16	66	70	70	73	279

19-Aug-01	USPGA	MC	73	69	0	0	142
26-Aug-01	NEC Invitational	3	66	68	68	69	271
07-Oct-01	German Masters	32	68	67	71	71	277
21-Oct-01	Dunhill Links Championship	24	72	67	70	70	279
28-Oct-01	Madrid Open	6	67	69	65	67	268
11-Nov-01	Volvo Masters	4	70	68	0	69	207
24-Feb-02	Accenture Matchplay Championship	33	0	0	0	0	0
10-Mar-02	Dubai Classic	7	72	73	68	69	282
17-Mar-02	Qatar Masters	24	70	70	70	71	281
14-Apr-02	US Masters	20	70	74	73	72	289
12-May-02	Benson & Hedges International	MC	74	73	0	0	147
20-May-02	Deutsche Bank (TPC of Europe)	16	67	68	73	70	278
26-May-02	PGA Championship	7	70	71	69	67	277
02-Jun-02	British Masters	76	73	70	70	75	288
09-Jun-02	English Open	1	65	70	68	68	271
16-Jun-02	US Open	24	74	74	72	71	291
30-Jun-02	Irish Open	27	71	70	65	73	279
07-Jul-02	European Open	20	74	70	76	67	287
14-Jul-02	Scottish Open	25	70	73	66	71	280
21-Jul-02	The Open Championship	37	72	67	77	69	285

CLARKE IN THE STATES

18-Mar-01	Bay Hill Invitational	MC	80	78	0	0	158
26-Mar-01	Players Championship	26	75	70	72	71	288
17-Feb-02	Los Angeles Open (Nissan)	MC	74	71	0	0	145
24-Mar-02	Players Championship	MC	76	73	0	0	149
31-Mar-02	Houston Open	2	69	65	67	71	272

NICLAS FASTH

EUROPEAN TOUR RECORD

(Jan 1st, 2001 - Aug 1st, 2002)		Pos	1	2	3	4	Total
04-Feb-01	Heineken Classic	64	73	72	79	72	296
11-Feb-01	Greg Norman Holden International	31	70	70	70	73	283
04-Mar-01	Dubai Classic	MC	74	68	0	0	142
11-Mar-01	Qatar Masters	MC	73	72	0	0	145
18-Mar-01	Madeira Island Open	3	69	63	72	70	274
22-Apr-01	Spanish Open	MC	78	73	0	0	151
29-Apr-01	Portuguese Open	9	66	72	68	73	279
13-May-01	Benson & Hedges International	MC	72	75	0	0	147
20-May-01	Deutsche Bank (TPC of Europe)	43	74	69	71	68	282
28-May-01	PGA Championship	14	69	68	69	75	281
03-Jun-01	British Masters	6	74	69	66	70	279

Date	Tournament	Pos	1	2	3	4	Total
01-Jul-01	Irish Open	2	68	71	69	63	271
08-Jul-01	European Open	45	69	75	68	74	286
15-Jul-01	Scottish Open	14	67	71	66	74	278
22-Jul-01	The Open Championship	2	69	69	72	67	277
05-Aug-01	Scandinavian Masters	13	67	69	72	70	278
19-Aug-01	USPGA	29	66	69	72	72	279
26-Aug-01	NEC Invitational	21	74	67	68	72	281
02-Sep-01	BMW International	60	67	71	71	72	281
23-Sep-01	Trophee Lancome	5	69	66	66	71	272
07-Oct-01	German Masters	25	72	69	68	67	276
11-Nov-01	Volvo Masters	21	72	67	0	74	213
27-Jan-02	Johnnie Walker Classic	27	72	72	78	72	294
03-Feb-02	Heineken Classic	31	73	68	69	75	285
10-Feb-02	ANZ Championship	11	0	0	0	0	0
24-Feb-02	Accenture Matchplay Championship	9	0	0	0	0	0
10-Mar-02	Dubai Classic	2	68	69	69	70	276
14-Apr-02	US Masters	MC	76	75	0	0	151
12-May-02	Benson & Hedges International	MC	70	80	0	0	150
20-May-02	Deutsche Bank (TPC of Europe)	29	71	72	72	66	281
26-May-02	PGA Championship	11	71	71	71	67	280
09-Jun-02	English Open	21	70	72	68	72	282
16-Jun-02	US Open	37	72	72	74	76	294
30-Jun-02	Irish Open	2	72	67	63	68	270
07-Jul-02	European Open	6	69	77	68	70	284
14-Jul-02	Scottish Open	41	70	68	79	65	282
21-Jul-02	The Open Championship	28	70	73	71	70	284

FASTH IN THE STATES

Date	Tournament	Pos	1	2	3	4	Total
17-Mar-02	Bay Hill Invitational	56	72	70	76	74	292
24-Mar-02	The Players Championship	MC	76	76	0	0	152

PIERRE FULKE

EUROPEAN TOUR RECORD

(Jan 1st, 2001 to Aug 1st, 2002)	Pos	1	2	3	4	Total
07-Jan-01 Accenture Matchplay Championship	2	0	0	0	0	0
04-Feb-01 Heineken Classic	23	67	76	69	73	285
11-Feb-01 Greg Norman Holden International	13	65	71	73	70	279
04-Mar-01 Dubai Classic	MC	73	69	0	0	142
08-Apr-01 US Masters	MC	73	79	0	0	152
13-May-01 Benson & Hedges International	64	75	68	77	72	292
20-May-01 Deutsche Bank (TPC of Europe)	MC	72	77	0	0	149
28-May-01 PGA Championship	67	71	70	79	71	291

Date	Event	Pos	1	2	3	4	Total
17-Jun-01	US Open	Ret	76	0	0	0	76
15-Jul-01	Scottish Open	MC	77	72	0	0	149
22-Jul-01	The Open Championship	62	69	67	72	83	291
05-Aug-01	Scandinavian Masters	25	68	71	71	71	281
19-Aug-01	USPGA	MC	71	78	0	0	149
26-Aug-01	NEC Invitational	17	73	71	65	70	279
02-Sep-01	BMW International	67	69	71	72	70	282
07-Oct-01	German Masters	32	67	70	69	71	277
21-Oct-01	Dunhill Links Championship	MC	71	66	79	0	216
11-Nov-01	Volvo Masters	44	73	72	0	74	219
27-Jan-02	Johnnie Walker Classic	2	72	70	74	66	282
03-Feb-02	Heineken Classic	MC	74	75	0	0	149
10-Feb-02	ANZ Championship	68	0	0	0	0	0
24-Feb-02	Accenture Matchplay Championship	33	0	0	0	0	0
10-Mar-02	Dubai Classic	20	69	73	74	68	284
05-May-02	French Open	MC	76	72	0	0	148
12-May-02	Benson & Hedges International	MC	77	70	0	0	147
20-May-02	Deutsche Bank (TPC of Europe)	12	69	70	66	72	277
26-May-02	PGA Championship	MC	71	76	0	0	147
09-Jun-02	English Open	39	74	68	70	73	285
07-Jul-02	European Open	Ret	82	0	0	0	82
14-Jul-02	Scottish Open	MC	74	71	0	0	145
21-Jul-02	The Open Championship	28	72	69	78	65	284
28-Jul-02	TNT Open	6	68	65	65	70	268

FULKE IN THE STATES

Date	Event	Pos	1	2	3	4	Total
01-Apr-01	BellSouth Classic	46	72	70	78	77	297
25-Jun-01	Buick Classic	MC	77	72	0	0	149

SERGIO GARCIA

US TOUR RECORD
(Jan 1st, 2001 to Aug 1st, 2002)

Date	Event	Pos	1	2	3	4	Total
28-Jan-01	Phoenix Open	13	67	71	70	66	274
04-Feb-01	ATT Pebble Beach Pro Am	59	68	70	75	76	289
25-Feb-01	Los Angeles Open (Nissan)	25	66	72	71	72	281
18-Mar-01	Bay Hill Invitational	4	71	66	68	74	279
26-Mar-01	Players Championship	50	73	74	74	72	293
08-Apr-01	US Masters	MC	70	76	0	0	146
16-Apr-01	Worldcom Classic	MC	72	71	0	0	143
13-May-01	Byron Nelson Classic	8	71	68	64	65	268
20-May-01	MasterCard Colonial	1	69	69	66	63	267
03-Jun-01	Memorial Tournament	2	68	69	70	71	278

17-Jun-01	US Open	12	70	68	68	77	283
24-Jun-01	Buick Classic	1	68	67	66	67	268
22-Jul-01	British Open	9	70	72	67	70	279
05-Aug-01	The International	11	0	0	0	0	0
19-Aug-01	PGA Championship	MC	68	75	0	0	143
09-Sep-01	Canadian Open	5	69	68	65	69	271
28-Oct-01	Buick Challenge	MC	70	74	0	0	144
04-Nov-01	Tour Championship	2	69	67	66	68	270
06-Jan-02	Mercedes Championship	1	73	69	68	64	274
13-Jan-02	Hawaiian Open (Sony)	40	71	66	69	71	277
17-Feb-02	Los Angeles Open (Nissan)	13	73	67	67	68	275
24-Feb-02	Accenture Matchplay Championship	9	0	0	0	0	0
03-Mar-02	Genuity Championship	33	73	70	71	72	286
17-Mar-02	Bay Hill Invitational	9	68	71	70	73	282
24-Mar-02	Players Championship	4	70	72	71	71	284
14-Apr-02	US Masters	8	68	71	70	75	284
21-Apr-02	Worldcom Classic	19	70	72	66	70	278
12-May-02	Byron Nelson Classic	MC	69	74	0	0	143
19-May-02	MasterCard Colonial	MC	76	74	0	0	150
26-May-02	Memorial Tournament	73	75	70	77	75	297
09-Jun-02	Buick Classic	12	68	70	70	71	279
16-Jun-02	US Open	4	68	74	67	74	283
23-Jun-02	Greater Hartford Open	20	69	67	69	70	275
21-Jul-02	British Open	8	71	69	71	69	280

GARCIA IN EUROPE

11-Feb-01	Greg Norman Holden International	2	64	69	70	68	271
22-Apr-01	Spanish Open	16	69	73	71	71	284
15-Jul-01	Scottish Open	14	69	69	69	71	278
02-Sep-01	BMW International	7	67	67	69	67	270
23-Sep-01	Trophee Lancome	1	68	65	68	65	266
27-Jan-02	Johnnie Walker Classic	3	69	73	72	69	283
28-Apr-02	Spanish Open	1	67	68	67	73	275

PADRAIG HARRINGTON

EUROPEAN TOUR RECORD

(Jan 1st, 2001 to Aug 1st, 2002)		Pos	1	2	3	4	Total
07-Jan-01	Accenture Matchplay Championship	33	0	0	0	0	0
18-Feb-01	Malaysian Open	2	70	66	68	70	274
25-Feb-01	Singapore Masters	5	63	67	71	66	267
04-Mar-01	Dubai Classic	2	66	69	64	69	268
08-Apr-01	US Masters	27	75	69	72	71	287

29-Apr-01	Portuguese Open	2	64	70	71	70	275
13-May-01	Benson & Hedges International	19	68	72	76	70	286
20-May-01	Deutsche Bank (TPC of Europe)	5	70	69	64	70	273
28-May-01	PGA Championship	45	67	75	69	76	287
17-Jun-01	US Open	30	73	70	71	74	288
01-Jul-01	Irish Open	2	67	72	68	64	271
08-Jul-01	European Open	2	70	67	69	70	276
22-Jul-01	The Open Championship	37	75	66	74	71	286
29-Jul-01	Dutch Open	9	67	67	71	71	276
19-Aug-01	USPGA	MC	75	74	0	0	149
26-Aug-01	NEC Invitational	17	68	66	73	72	279
02-Sep-01	BMW International	2	69	63	62	68	262
07-Oct-01	German Masters	19	70	67	67	71	275
21-Oct-01	Dunhill Links Championship	5	67	67	72	69	275
28-Oct-01	Madrid Open	25	63	72	69	69	273
11-Nov-01	Volvo Masters	1	67	71	0	66	204
24-Feb-02	Accenture Matchplay Championship	33	0	0	0	0	0
03-Mar-02	Malaysian Open	11	70	67	66	69	272
10-Mar-02	Dubai Classic	20	70	75	68	71	284
14-Apr-02	US Masters	5	69	70	72	71	282
12-May-02	Benson & Hedges International	3	71	70	70	69	280
20-May-02	Deutsche Bank (TPC of Europe)	12	71	70	66	70	277
26-May-02	PGA Championship	MC	76	72	0	0	148
02-Jun-02	British Masters	11	73	70	65	70	278
16-Jun-02	US Open	8	70	68	73	75	286
30-Jun-02	Irish Open	6	71	68	69	66	274
07-Jul-02	European Open	2	72	69	69	73	283
21-Jul-02	The Open Championship	5	69	67	76	67	279
28-Jul-02	TBT Open	3	66	67	64	68	265

HARRINGTON IN THE STATES

26-Mar-01	Players Championship	33	70	75	73	72	290
16-Apr-01	Worldcom Classic	59	70	71	72	72	285
12-Aug-01	Buick Open	6	67	67	65	69	268
24-Mar-02	Players Championship	22	70	72	77	70	289
07-Apr-02	BellSouth Classic	8	69	65	73	74	281

BERNHARD LANGER

EUROPEAN TOUR RECORD

(Jan 1st, 2001 to Aug 1st, 2002)	Pos	1	2	3	4	Total
07-Jan-01 Accenture Matchplay Championship	33	0	0	0	0	0
08-Apr-01 US Masters	6	73	69	68	69	279

PLAYER FORM SINCE JANUARY 2001

13-May-01	Benson & Hedges International	57	72	69	73	77	291
20-May-01	Deutsche Bank (TPC of Europe)	47	72	71	70	70	283
28-May-01	PGA Championship	MC	76	72	0	0	148
17-Jun-01	US Open	40	71	73	71	74	289
08-Jul-01	European Open	8	71	70	69	69	279
15-Jul-01	Scottish Open	Wd	70	69	0	0	139
22-Jul-01	The Open Championship	3	71	69	67	71	278
29-Jul-01	Dutch Open	1	69	67	67	66	269
19-Aug-01	USPGA	MC	69	73	0	0	142
26-Aug-01	NEC Invitational	11	69	67	68	73	277
02-Sep-01	BMW International	16	67	69	69	68	273
07-Oct-01	German Masters	1	67	64	68	67	266
11-Nov-01	Volvo Masters	7	69	70	0	69	208
24-Feb-02	Accenture Matchplay Championship	33	0	0	0	0	0
14-Apr-02	US Masters	32	73	72	73	74	292
12-May-02	Benson & Hedges International	24	72	70	73	72	287
20-May-02	Deutsche Bank (TPC of Europe)	60	73	71	71	73	288
16-Jun-02	US Open	35	72	76	70	75	293
07-Jul-02	European Open	MC	73	75	0	0	148
14-Jul-02	Scottish Open	MC	77	74	0	0	151
21-Jul-02	The Open Championship	28	72	72	71	69	284
28-Jul-02	TNT Open	53	71	69	69	69	278

LANGER IN THE STATES

14-Jan-01	Tucson Open	9	68	69	70	70	277
04-Feb-01	ATT Pebble Beach Pro Am	MC	74	77	72	0	223
11-Feb-01	Buick Invitational	25	71	69	67	70	277
04-Mar-01	Genuity Championship	40	68	70	73	73	284
11-Mar-01	Honda Classic	27	66	73	68	70	277
18-Mar-01	Bay Hill Invitational	34	72	70	70	74	286
26-Mar-01	Players Championship	3	73	68	68	67	276
16-Apr-01	Worldcom Classic	3	69	69	67	69	274
10-Jun-01	St Jude Classic	2	69	65	68	66	268
21-Oct-01	NCR Walt Disney Classic	36	67	72	67	70	276
04-Nov-01	Tour Championship	10	65	68	69	73	275
10-Feb-02	Buick Invitational	39	72	68	70	76	286
17-Feb-02	Los Angeles Open (Nissan)	MC	78	72	0	0	150
03-Mar-02	Genuity Championship	MC	75	71	0	0	146
10-Mar-02	Honda Classic	40	68	71	70	69	278
17-Mar-02	Bay Hill Invitational	31	72	71	76	69	288
24-Mar-02	Players Championship	22	75	71	72	71	289
21-Apr-02	Worldcom Classic	4	71	65	68	69	273
09-Jun-02	Buick Classic	MC	70	74	0	0	144

PAUL McGINLEY

EUROPEAN TOUR RECORD (Jan 1st, 2001 to Aug 1st, 2002)		Pos	1	2	3	4	Total
07-Jan-01	Accenture Matchplay Championship	33	0	0	0	0	0
21-Jan-01	Alfred Dunhill Championship	16	67	71	68	70	276
28-Jan-01	South African Open	21	71	72	70	74	287
04-Mar-01	Dubai Classic	9	70	64	67	72	273
11-Mar-01	Qatar Masters	13	71	67	71	74	283
15-Apr-01	Moroccan Open	8	67	75	70	72	284
29-Apr-01	Portuguese Open	37	71	69	70	73	283
06-May-01	French Open	7	72	67	69	65	273
13-May-01	Benson & Hedges International	2	66	72	70	70	278
20-May-01	Deutsche Bank (TPC of Europe)	10	69	65	72	69	275
28-May-01	PGA Championship	26	66	74	73	71	284
10-Jun-01	English Open	10	73	69	70	71	283
01-Jul-01	Irish Open	48	69	73	66	74	282
08-Jul-01	European Open	MC	72	74	0	0	146
15-Jul-01	Scottish Open	3	68	67	67	70	272
22-Jul-01	The Open Championship	54	69	72	72	76	289
29-Jul-01	Dutch Open	40	71	70	67	75	283
12-Aug-01	Wales Open	1	67	71	0	0	138
19-Aug-01	USPGA	22	68	72	71	67	278
26-Aug-01	NEC Invitational	26	68	73	71	72	284
02-Sep-01	BMW International	10	70	66	68	67	271
07-Oct-01	German Masters	8	70	67	68	66	271
21-Oct-01	Dunhill Links Championship	9	67	64	71	74	276
11-Nov-01	Volvo Masters	2	66	69	0	70	205
02-Dec-01	Hong Kong Open	26	65	66	74	68	273
20-Jan-02	Dunhill Championship	5	66	71	66	68	271
24-Feb-02	Accenture Matchplay Championship	17	0	0	0	0	0
14-Apr-02	US Masters	18	72	74	71	71	288
12-May-02	Benson & Hedges International	MC	74	81	0	0	155
26-May-02	PGA Championship	MC	71	74	0	0	145
02-Jun-02	British Masters	22	72	72	65	71	280
09-Jun-02	English Open	66	72	71	72	74	289
16-Jun-02	US Open	MC	75	79	0	0	154
07-Jul-02	European Open	MC	77	73	0	0	150
14-Jul-02	Scottish Open	14	69	73	68	68	278
21-Jul-02	The Open Championship	MC	72	74	0	0	146
28-Jul-02	TNT Open	MC	71	71	0	0	142
McGINLEY IN THE STATES							
17-Feb-02	Nissan Open		74	71	70	76	71	288

10-Mar-02 Honda Classic	MC	73	70	0	0	143
17-Mar-02 Bay Hill Invitational	25	74	68	68	76	286
24-Mar-02 The Players Championship	MC	75	72	0	0	147

COLIN MONTGOMERIE

EUROPEAN TOUR RECORD
(Jan 1st, 2001 to Aug 1st, 2002)

	Pos	1	2	3	4	Total
25-Feb-01 Singapore Masters	3	66	67	65	68	266
04-Mar-01 Dubai Classic	21	69	70	65	72	276
08-Apr-01 US Masters	MC	73	76	0	0	149
29-Apr-01 Portuguese Open	MC	73	72	0	0	145
13-May-01 Benson Hedges International	12	73	69	71	72	285
20-May-01 Deutsche Bank (TPC of Europe)	10	70	66	69	70	275
28-May-01 PGA Championship	17	73	69	69	71	282
03-Jun-01 British Masters	27	68	71	74	72	285
10-Jun-01 English Open	Ret	76	0	0	0	76
17-Jun-01 US Open	52	71	70	77	74	292
01-Jul-01 Irish Open	1	63	69	68	66	266
08-Jul-01 European Open	20	68	72	69	72	281
15-Jul-01 Scottish Open	28	70	67	69	74	280
22-Jul-01 The Open Championship	13	65	70	73	72	280
05-Aug-01 Scandinavian Masters	1	66	69	69	70	274
19-Aug-01 USPGA	Dq	71	69	74	0	214
26-Aug-01 NEC Invitational	4	66	71	66	70	273
02-Sep-01 BMW International	13	69	69	68	66	272
23-Sep-01 Trophee Lancome	MC	75	68	0	0	143
07-Oct-01 German Masters	15	70	70	68	66	274
21-Oct-01 Dunhill Links Championship	5	71	68	69	67	275
11-Nov-01 Volvo Masters	7	71	69	0	68	208
27-Jan-02 Johnnie Walker Classic	Ret	76	0	0	0	76
24-Feb-02 Accenture Matchplay Championship	33	0	0	0	0	0
10-Mar-02 Dubai Classic	MC	71	79	0	0	150
17-Mar-02 Qatar Masters	18	68	69	69	74	280
14-Apr-02 US Masters	14	75	71	70	71	287
05-May-02 French Open	23	67	72	71	74	284
12-May-02 Benson & Hedges International	3	71	67	73	69	280
20-May-02 Deutsche Bank (TPC of Europe)	2	66	68	65	69	268
26-May-02 PGA Championship	2	64	71	72	67	274
02-Jun-02 British Masters	4	70	69	68	67	274
16-Jun-02 US Open	MC	75	76	0	0	151
30-Jun-02 Irish Open	23	67	67	74	70	278
07-Jul-02 European Open	6	69	75	68	72	284

| 14-Jul-02 | Scottish Open | 14 | 72 | 71 | 69 | 66 | 278 |
| 21-Jul-02 | The Open Championship | 82 | 74 | 64 | 84 | 75 | 297 |

MONTGOMERIE IN THE STATES

18-Mar-01	Bay Hill Invitational	51	75	69	75	71	290
26-Mar-01	Players Championship	40	71	71	75	74	291
24-Mar-02	Players Championship	63	70	76	72	78	296
31-Mar-02	Houston Open	56	72	71	74	71	288
07-Apr-02	BellSouth Classic	17	69	70	70	74	283

JESPER PARNEVIK

US TOUR RECORD
(Jan 1st, 2001 to Aug 1st, 2002)

		Pos	1	2	3	4	Total
14-Jan-01	Mercedes Championship	23	76	66	72	71	285
21-Jan-01	Hawaiian Open (Sony)	MC	69	74	0	0	143
28-Jan-01	Phoenix Open	MC	67	74	0	0	141
04-Feb-01	ATT Pebble Beach Pro Am	72	72	70	71	80	293
25-Feb-01	Los Angeles Open (Nissan)	13	70	68	71	70	279
04-Mar-01	Genuity Championship	17	68	70	71	71	280
11-Mar-01	Honda Classic	1	65	67	66	72	270
26-Mar-01	Players Championship	MC	70	79	0	0	149
01-Apr-01	BellSouth Classic	21	72	71	75	71	289
08-Apr-01	US Masters	20	71	71	72	69	283
16-Apr-01	Worldcom Classic	28	68	69	72	70	279
13-May-01	Byron Nelson Classic	62	70	64	68	74	276
20-May-01	MasterCard Colonial	11	70	69	67	68	274
03-Jun-01	Memorial Tournament	30	68	75	73	71	287
10-Jun-01	St Jude Classic	8	67	64	71	69	271
17-Jun-01	US Open	30	73	73	74	68	288
22-Jul-01	British Open	9	69	68	71	71	279
19-Aug-01	PGA Championship	13	70	68	70	68	276
02-Sep-01	Air Canada Championship	19	67	71	72	67	277
09-Sep-01	Canadian Open	43	71	67	74	67	279
30-Sep-01	Texas Open	11	67	66	71	70	274
14-Oct-01	Invensys Classic (Las Vegas) (five rounds)	58	69	69 70	71	71	350
21-Oct-01	NCR Walt Disney Classic	6	71	65	67	67	270
28-Oct-01	Buick Challenge	31	73	69	67	71	280
06-Jan-02	Mercedes Championship	26	74	75	72	71	292
13-Jan-02	Hawaiian Open (Sony)	54	66	71	72	71	280
20-Jan-02	Bob Hope Classic	MC	68	70	68	71	277
27-Jan-02	Phoenix Open	MC	75	68	0	0	143
03-Feb-02	ATT Pebble Beach Pro Am	15	67	72	70	74	283

PLAYER FORM SINCE JANUARY 2001

Date	Event	Pos	1	2	3	4	Total
10-Feb-02	Buick Invitational	70	73	70	73	75	291
17-Feb-02	Los Angeles Open (Nissan)	29	65	69	73	72	279
24-Feb-02	Accenture Matchplay Championship	33	0	0	0	0	0
03-Mar-02	Genuity Championship	10	71	67	72	71	281
10-Mar-02	Honda Classic	MC	70	72	0	0	142
24-Mar-02	Players Championship	MC	74	74	0	0	148
07-Apr-02	BellSouth Classic	2	66	69	76	65	276
14-Apr-02	US Masters	29	70	72	77	72	291
05-May-02	Compaq Classic of New Orleans	62	71	70	72	74	287
12-May-02	Byron Nelson Classic	17	71	68	70	67	276
19-May-02	MasterCard Colonial	28	69	72	70	69	280
26-May-02	Memorial Tournament	Wd	77	0	0	0	77
09-Jun-02	Buick Classic	MC	72	76	0	0	148
16-Jun-02	US Open	54	72	76	69	80	297
21-Jul-02	British Open	28	72	72	70	70	284

PARNEVIK IN EUROPE

Date	Event	Pos	1	2	3	4	Total
15-Jul-01	Scottish Open	8	71	69	65	70	275
05-Aug-01	Scandinavian Masters	36	71	72	69	71	283

PHILLIP PRICE

EUROPEAN TOUR RECORD

(Jan 1st, 2001 to Aug 1st, 2002)		Pos	1	2	3	4	Total
07-Jan-01	Accenture Matchplay Championship	33	0	0	0	0	0
21-Jan-01	Alfred Dunhill Championship	MC	71	71	0	0	142
04-Feb-01	Heineken Classic	19	75	70	69	70	284
11-Feb-01	Greg Norman Holden International	8	66	69	74	69	278
04-Mar-01	Dubai Classic	21	66	72	69	69	276
11-Mar-01	Qatar Masters	Wd	78	0	0	0	78
22-Apr-01	Spanish Open	49	70	74	71	73	288
29-Apr-01	Portuguese Open	1	72	67	70	64	273
13-May-01	Benson & Hedges International	12	70	74	67	74	285
20-May-01	Deutsche Bank (TPC of Europe)	14	71	70	66	69	276
28-May-01	PGA Championship	4	65	69	72	71	277
10-Jun-01	English Open	35	74	75	70	71	290
17-Jun-01	US Open	Ret	0	0	0	0	0
01-Jul-01	Irish Open	30	75	65	73	66	279
08-Jul-01	European Open	8	70	72	70	67	279
15-Jul-01	Scottish Open	MC	73	71	0	0	144
22-Jul-01	The Open Championship	30	74	69	71	71	285
05-Aug-01	Scandinavian Masters	MC	75	70	0	0	145
12-Aug-01	Wales Open	14	70	72	0	0	142

PLAYER FORM SINCE JANUARY 2001

Date	Event	Pos	1	2	3	4	Total
19-Aug-01	USPGA	59	68	69	76	70	283
26-Aug-01	NEC Invitational	28	70	71	74	71	286
02-Sep-01	BMW International	MC	71	70	0	0	141
23-Sep-01	Trophee Lancome	11	70	67	66	72	275
21-Oct-01	Dunhill Links Championship	MC	71	69	76	0	216
28-Oct-01	Madrid Open	16	66	69	67	69	271
11-Nov-01	Volvo Masters	16	70	73	0	68	211
24-Feb-02	Accenture Matchplay Championship	33	0	0	0	0	0
10-Mar-02	Dubai Classic	46	73	71	72	72	288
17-Mar-02	Qatar Masters	34	72	69	69	73	283
07-Apr-02	Portuguese Open	60	74	78	0	0	152
12-May-02	Benson & Hedges International	11	71	70	70	73	284
20-May-02	Deutsche Bank (TPC of Europe)	MC	72	74	0	0	146
26-May-02	PGA Championship	19	72	72	68	70	282
02-Jun-02	British Masters	3	68	65	68	72	273
09-Jun-02	English Open	3	68	68	70	70	276
30-Jun-02	Irish Open	16	71	70	66	69	276
07-Jul-02	European Open	Ret	75	0	0	0	75
14-Jul-02	Scottish Open	41	73	69	69	71	282
21-Jul-02	The Open Championship	MC	75	74	0	0	149

PRICE IN THE STATES

Date	Event	Pos	1	2	3	4	Total
18-Mar-01	Bay Hill Invitational	MC	76	71	0	0	147
03-Feb-02	AT&T Pebble Beach Pro Am	24	70	70	73	72	285
20-Feb-02	Bob Hope Classic (five rounds)	31	65	69	68	66	71	339
28-Apr-02	Greater Greensboro Classic	MC	73	73	0	0	146

LEE WESTWOOD

EUROPEAN TOUR RECORD

(Jan 1st, 2001 to Aug 1st, 2002)	Pos	1	2	3	4	Total
04-Mar-01 Dubai Classic	17	66	70	69	70	275
13-May-01 Benson & Hedges International	57	73	68	76	74	291
20-May-01 Deutsche Bank (TPC of Europe)	52	66	71	70	77	284
28-May-01 PGA Championship	MC	73	73	0	0	146
03-Jun-01 British Masters	8	69	70	67	74	280
10-Jun-01 English Open	5	77	67	68	69	281
17-Jun-01 US Open	MC	75	76	0	0	151
24-Jun-01 The Great North Open	MC	81	74	0	0	155
08-Jul-01 European Open	62	71	74	73	71	289
15-Jul-01 Scottish Open	MC	72	72	0	0	144
22-Jul-01 The Open Championship	47	73	70	71	74	288
29-Jul-01 Dutch Open	MC	74	76	0	0	150

Date	Tournament	Pos	1	2	3	4	Total
05-Aug-01	Scandinavian Masters	2	67	67	69	72	275
19-Aug-01	USPGA	44	71	68	68	74	281
26-Aug-01	NEC Invitational	Wd	70	78	0	0	148
09-Sep-01	European Masters (Swiss Open)	16	70	69	69	72	280
07-Oct-01	German Masters	75	72	70	69	73	284
21-Oct-01	Dunhill Links Championship	MC	73	76	72	0	221
11-Nov-01	Volvo Masters	52	69	76	0	77	222
27-Jan-02	Johnnie Walker Classic	58	72	74	76	76	298
24-Feb-02	Accenture Matchplay Championship	17	0	0	0	0	0
14-Apr-02	US Masters	44	75	72	74	76	297
12-May-02	Benson & Hedges International	MC	79	71	0	0	150
20-May-02	Deutsche Bank (TPC of Europe)	MC	74	71	0	0	145
26-May-02	PGA Championship	MC	70	75	0	0	145
02-Jun-02	British Masters	45	71	70	71	71	283
09-Jun-02	English Open	Ret	0	0	0	0	0
30-Jun-02	Irish Open	19	67	68	72	70	277
07-Jul-02	European Open	16	72	71	72	71	286
14-Jul-02	Scottish Open	MC	76	74	0	0	150
21-Jul-02	The Open Championship	MC	72	73	0	0	145
28-Jul-02	TNT Open	71	70	66	72	75	283

WESTWOOD IN THE STATES

Date	Tournament	Pos	1	2	3	4	Total
18-Mar-01	Bay Hill Invitational	17	71	72	68	72	283
26-Mar-01	Players Championship	MC	73	75	0	0	148
17-Feb-02	Los Angeles Open (Nissan)	15	69	68	70	69	276
17-Mar-02	Bay Hill Invitational	MC	74	77	0	0	151
24-Mar-02	Players Championship	MC	75	75	0	0	150
07-Apr-02	BellSouth Classic	39	72	70	71	76	289

PAUL AZINGER

US TOUR RECORD

(Jan 1st, 2001 to Aug 1st, 2002)		Pos	1	2	3	4	Total
14-Jan-01	Mercedes Championship	17	70	70	68	75	283
21-Jan-01	Hawaiian Open (Sony)	MC	72	70	0	0	142
28-Jan-01	Phoenix Open	55	72	68	70	73	283
04-Feb-01	ATT Pebble Beach Pro Am	47	72	70	71	73	286
18-Feb-01	Bob Hope Classic (five rounds)	62	72	70	67	67	71	347
18-Mar-01	Bay Hill Invitational	15	71	70	71	70	282
26-Mar-01	Players Championship	7	66	70	74	72	282
08-Apr-01	US Masters	15	70	71	71	69	281
16-Apr-01	Worldcom Classic	12	69	71	68	69	277
03-Jun-01	Memorial Tournament	2	68	67	69	74	278

Date	Event	Pos	R1	R2	R3	R4	Total
17-Jun-01	US Open	5	74	67	69	71	281
24-Jun-01	Buick Classic	16	71	70	68	71	280
01-Jul-01	Greater Hartford Open	14	70	64	69	67	270
12-Aug-01	Buick Open	49	70	70	70	68	278
19-Aug-01	PGA Championship	22	68	67	69	74	278
26-Aug-01	NEC Invitational	5	67	70	65	72	274
23-Sep-01	Pennsylvania Classic	58	70	74	72	74	290
07-Oct-01	Michelob Championship	47	69	69	75	72	285
21-Oct-01	NCR Walt Disney Classic	16	70	69	67	66	272
28-Oct-01	Buick Challenge	17	68	72	70	68	278
27-Jan-02	Phoenix Open	28	70	67	67	73	277
03-Feb-02	ATT Pebble Beach Pro Am	52	74	72	70	73	289
17-Feb-02	Los Angeles Open (Nissan)	50	69	69	70	74	282
24-Feb-02	Accenture Matchplay Championship	4	0	0	0	0	0
03-Mar-02	Genuity Championship	11	69	72	71	70	282
17-Mar-02	Bay Hill Invitational	25	69	72	73	72	286
24-Mar-02	Players Championship	MC	72	78	0	0	150
14-Apr-02	US Masters	MC	75	73	0	0	148
28-Apr-02	Greater Greensboro Classic	67	71	73	76	74	294
26-May-02	Memorial Tournament	32	73	68	69	74	284
09-Jun-02	Buick Classic	64	69	74	73	72	288
16-Jun-02	US Open	MC	75	82	0	0	157
23-Jun-02	Greater Hartford Open	MC	68	74	0	0	142
30-Jun-02	St Jude Classic	54	73	66	68	72	279

MARK CALCAVECCHIA

US TOUR RECORD
(Jan 1st, 2001 to Aug 1st, 2002)

Date	Event	Pos	1	2	3	4	Total
14-Jan-01	Tucson Open	15	71	71	67	69	278
28-Jan-01	Phoenix Open	1	65	60	64	67	256
04-Feb-01	ATT Pebble Beach Pro Am	MC	76	73	68	0	217
18-Feb-01	Bob Hope Classic (five rounds)	3	64	66	69	65 66	330
11-Mar-01	Honda Classic	2	67	68	66	70	271
18-Mar-01	Bay Hill Invitational	31	66	72	75	72	285
26-Mar-01	Players Championship	MC	74	77	0	0	151
08-Apr-01	US Masters	4	72	66	68	72	278
16-Apr-01	Worldcom Classic	38	66	71	71	72	280
29-Apr-01	Greater Greensboro Classic	36	73	69	69	71	282
06-May-01	Compaq Classic of New Orleans	MC	71	72	0	0	143
20-May-01	MasterCard Colonial	MC	81	72	0	0	153
03-Jun-01	Memorial Tournament	40	69	73	74	73	289
17-Jun-01	US Open	24	70	74	73	70	287

01-Jul-01	Greater Hartford Open	29	68	68	71	66	273
22-Jul-01	British Open	54	72	70	72	75	289
05-Aug-01	The International	MC	0	0	0	0	0
12-Aug-01	Buick Open	MC	70	71	0	0	141
19-Aug-01	PGA Championship	4	71	68	66	65	270
26-Aug-01	NEC Invitational	36	72	69	72	79	292
23-Sep-01	Pennsylvania Classic	65	69	73	78	72	292
14-Oct-01	Invensys Classic (Las Vegas)	MC	71	71	72	0	214
04-Nov-01	Tour Championship	19	71	64	69	76	280
06-Jan-02	Mercedes Championship	5	72	66	71	69	278
20-Jan-02	Bob Hope Classic	MC	76	73	68	68	285
27-Jan-02	Phoenix Open	MC	68	74	0	0	142
17-Feb-02	Los Angeles Open (Nissan)	23	70	70	70	68	278
24-Feb-02	Accenture Matchplay Championship	9	0	0	0	0	0
03-Mar-02	Genuity Championship	MC	71	78	0	0	149
10-Mar-02	Honda Classic	21	72	67	70	67	276
17-Mar-02	Bay Hill Invitational	69	72	72	76	76	296
24-Mar-02	Players Championship	69	69	70	73	86	298
14-Apr-02	US Masters	MC	79	70	0	0	149
21-Apr-02	Worldcom Classic	10	68	70	73	65	276
28-Apr-02	Greater Greensboro Classic	2	65	69	69	72	275
12-May-02	Byron Nelson Classic	MC	73	71	0	0	144
26-May-02	Memorial Tournament	MC	75	76	0	0	151
02-Jun-02	Kemper Open	56	71	67	72	76	286
16-Jun-02	US Open	MC	74	77	0	0	151
23-Jun-02	Greater Hartford Open	20	68	70	68	69	275
14-Jul-02	Greater Milwaukee Open	27	70	67	68	68	273
21-Jul-02	British Open	80	74	66	81	74	295

STEWART CINK

US TOUR RECORD

(Jan 1st, 2001 to Aug 1st, 2002)	Pos	1	2	3	4	Total
07-Jan-01	Accenture Matchplay Championship	33	0	0	0	0	0
14-Jan-01	Mercedes Championship	12	69	71	69	72	281
21-Jan-01	Hawaiian Open (Sony)	MC	70	70	0	0	140
28-Jan-01	Phoenix Open	9	65	66	71	71	273
18-Feb-01	Bob Hope Classic	MC	71	67	72	68	278
25-Feb-01	Los Angeles Open (Nissan)	20	69	69	70	72	280
04-Mar-01	Genuity Championship	12	64	66	75	74	279
26-Mar-01	Players Championship	MC	78	79	0	0	157
01-Apr-01	BellSouth Classic	6	70	71	71	73	285
08-Apr-01	US Masters	MC	75	74	0	0	149

PLAYER FORM SINCE JANUARY 2001

Date	Tournament						
16-Apr-01	Worldcom Classic	10	69	71	70	66	276
22-Apr-01	Houston Open	13	73	70	71	71	285
29-Apr-01	Greater Greensboro Classic	MC	71	74	0	0	145
20-May-01	MasterCard Colonial	26	71	70	67	70	278
03-Jun-01	Memorial Tournament	4	72	69	67	71	279
10-Jun-01	St Jude Classic	37	70	69	71	68	278
17-Jun-01	US Open	3	69	69	67	72	277
24-Jun-01	Buick Classic	3	65	72	69	67	273
01-Jul-01	Greater Hartford Open	MC	68	76	0	0	144
22-Jul-01	British Open	30	71	72	72	70	285
05-Aug-01	The International	26	0	0	0	0	0
12-Aug-01	Buick Open	29	73	67	67	68	275
19-Aug-01	PGA Championship	59	68	72	71	72	283
26-Aug-01	NEC Invitational	13	69	67	70	72	278
23-Sep-01	Pennsylvania Classic	MC	74	74	0	0	148
14-Oct-01	Invensys Classic (Las Vegas) (five rounds)	20	71	71	67	66	67	342
21-Oct-01	NCR Walt Disney Classic	21	65	70	71	67	273
28-Oct-01	Buick Challenge	50	69	70	74	70	283
04-Nov-01	Tour Championship	13	70	70	67	69	276
20-Jan-02	Bob Hope Classic	MC	67	68	73	70	278
27-Jan-02	Phoenix Open	28	71	69	70	67	277
10-Feb-02	Buick Invitational	MC	74	75	0	0	149
17-Feb-02	Los Angeles Open (Nissan)	37	70	71	69	71	281
24-Feb-02	Accenture Matchplay Championship	33	0	0	0	0	0
03-Mar-02	Genuity Championship	24	67	74	74	70	285
17-Mar-02	Bay Hill Invitational	15	68	71	71	74	284
24-Mar-02	Players Championship	MC	73	74	0	0	147
07-Apr-02	BellSouth Classic	MC	71	75	0	0	146
14-Apr-02	US Masters	24	74	70	72	74	290
21-Apr-02	Worldcom Classic	MC	71	72	0	0	143
05-May-02	Compaq Classic of New Orleans	31	68	72	72	70	282
19-May-02	MasterCard Colonial	33	72	69	69	71	281
26-May-02	Memorial Tournament	9	66	70	69	73	278
09-Jun-02	Buick Classic	5	67	69	71	68	275
16-Jun-02	US Open	MC	70	82	0	0	152
23-Jun-02	Greater Hartford Open	33	69	72	67	69	277
21-Jul-02	British Open	59	71	69	80	69	289

CINK IN EUROPE

14-Jul-02	Scottish Open	MC	74	73	0	0	147

DAVID DUVAL

US TOUR RECORD

(Jan 1st, 2001 to Aug 1st, 2002)		Pos	1	2	3	4	Total
14-Jan-01	Mercedes Championship	7	73	71	65	70	279
28-Jan-01	Phoenix Open	MC	70	73	0	0	143
04-Feb-01	ATT Pebble Beach Pro Am	MC	75	70	71	0	216
18-Feb-01	Bob Hope Classic (five rounds)	51	65	68	70	68	74	345
04-Mar-01	Genuity Championship	63	69	69	77	72	287
08-Apr-01	US Masters	2	71	66	70	67	274
22-Apr-01	Houston Open	26	72	70	72	74	288
06-May-01	Compaq Classic of New Orleans	18	69	68	69	69	275
13-May-01	Byron Nelson Classic	3	64	65	70	67	266
20-May-01	MasterCard Colonial	46	69	68	73	71	281
17-Jun-01	US Open	16	70	69	71	74	284
24-Jun-01	Buick Classic	26	71	73	68	70	282
01-Jul-01	Greater Hartford Open	22	67	66	70	69	272
22-Jul-01	British Open	1	69	73	65	67	274
05-Aug-01	The International	24	0	0	0	0	0
19-Aug-01	PGA Championship	10	66	68	67	74	275
26-Aug-01	NEC Invitational	27	69	69	72	75	285
07-Oct-01	Michelob Championship	41	73	68	72	71	284
28-Oct-01	Buick Challenge	2	67	69	68	63	267
04-Nov-01	Tour Championship	7	69	69	63	71	272
06-Jan-02	Mercedes Championship	12	67	71	72	72	282
20-Jan-02	Bob Hope Classic (five rounds)	48	69	68	68	67	67	342
17-Feb-02	Los Angeles Open (Nissan)	Wd	67	69	70	0	206
24-Feb-02	Accenture Matchplay Championship	33	0	0	0	0	0
03-Mar-02	Genuity Championship	MC	72	73	0	0	145
17-Mar-02	Bay Hill Invitational	22	71	70	72	72	285
24-Mar-02	Players Championship	28	68	75	72	75	290
31-Mar-02	Houston Open	34	75	67	68	75	285
14-Apr-02	US Masters	MC	74	74	0	0	148
12-May-02	Byron Nelson Classic	15	66	70	72	67	275
19-May-02	MasterCard Colonial	MC	67	78	0	0	145
26-May-02	Memorial Tournament	4	75	69	67	66	277
09-Jun-02	Buick Classic	MC	72	73	0	0	145
16-Jun-02	US Open	MC	78	73	0	0	151
23-Jun-02	Greater Hartford Open	MC	73	71	0	0	144
21-Jul-02	British Open	22	72	71	70	70	283

JIM FURYK

US TOUR RECORD

(Jan 1st, 2001 to Aug 1st, 2002)		Pos	1	2	3	4	Total
14-Jan-01	Mercedes Championship	1	69	69	69	67	274
21-Jan-01	Hawaiian Open (Sony)	14	66	67	69	71	273
11-Feb-01	Buick Invitational	MC	73	73	0	0	146
18-Feb-01	Bob Hope Classic (five rounds)	22	68	68	67	67	69	339
04-Mar-01	Genuity Championship	17	69	72	66	73	280
11-Mar-01	Honda Classic	7	70	72	67	65	274
26-Mar-01	Players Championship	21	72	75	72	68	287
08-Apr-01	US Masters	6	69	71	70	69	279
29-Apr-01	Greater Greensboro Classic	9	69	72	66	69	276
13-May-01	Byron Nelson Classic	37	72	66	66	69	273
20-May-01	MasterCard Colonial	22	65	71	69	72	277
03-Jun-01	Memorial Tournament	24	69	69	74	74	286
17-Jun-01	US Open	62	70	70	71	82	293
24-Jun-01	Buick Classic	19	71	72	67	71	281
01-Jul-01	Greater Hartford Open	61	72	67	71	69	279
22-Jul-01	British Open	MC	77	75	0	0	152
12-Aug-01	Buick Open	2	64	69	66	66	265
19-Aug-01	PGA Championship	7	70	64	71	69	274
26-Aug-01	NEC Invitational	2	65	66	66	71	268
23-Sep-01	Pennsylvania Classic	11	72	72	68	68	280
07-Oct-01	Michelob Championship	MC	69	73	0	0	142
14-Oct-01	Invensys Classic (Las Vegas)	MC	76	70	70	0	216
28-Oct-01	Buick Challenge	MC	70	73	0	0	143
04-Nov-01	Tour Championship	7	70	71	62	69	272
06-Jan-02	Mercedes Championship	4	67	72	73	65	277
13-Jan-02	Hawaiian Open (Sony)	7	69	66	64	72	271
27-Jan-02	Phoenix Open	37	69	68	71	70	278
03-Feb-02	ATT Pebble Beach Pro Am	30	71	71	73	71	286
17-Feb-02	Los Angeles Open (Nissan)	37	70	71	71	69	281
24-Feb-02	Accenture Matchplay Championship	9	0	0	0	0	0
24-Mar-02	Players Championship	14	71	72	71	73	287
31-Mar-02	Houston Open	MC	76	72	0	0	148
14-Apr-02	US Masters	MC	73	77	0	0	150
21-Apr-02	Worldcom Classic	15	70	65	73	69	277
28-Apr-02	Greater Greensboro Classic	23	69	72	71	72	284
12-May-02	Byron Nelson Classic	MC	71	73	0	0	144
19-May-02	MasterCard Colonial	MC	73	71	0	0	144
26-May-02	Memorial Tournament	1	71	70	68	65	274
09-Jun-02	Buick Classic	9	68	69	74	67	278
16-Jun-02	US Open	MC	73	80	0	0	153
21-Jul-02	British Open	MC	71	76	0	0	147

SCOTT HOCH

US TOUR RECORD
(Jan 1st, 2001 to Aug 1st, 2002)

		Pos	1	2	3	4	Total
18-Feb-01	Bob Hope Classic (five rounds)	MC	69	70	72 0	69	280
25-Feb-01	Los Angeles Open (Nissan)	MC	70	74	0	0	144
04-Mar-01	Genuity Championship	MC	70	73	0	0	143
18-Mar-01	Bay Hill Invitational	8	68	72	69	71	280
26-Mar-01	Players Championship	7	67	70	71	74	282
08-Apr-01	US Masters	37	74	70	72	74	290
16-Apr-01	Worldcom Classic	28	67	69	71	72	279
22-Apr-01	Houston Open	16	72	72	67	75	286
29-Apr-01	Greater Greensboro Classic	1	68	68	67	69	272
06-May-01	Compaq Classic of New Orleans	11	69	72	63	70	274
28-May-01	Kemper Open	6	68	70	66	70	274
03-Jun-01	Memorial Tournament	10	70	69	69	74	282
10-Jun-01	St Jude Classic	10	68	68	67	69	272
17-Jun-01	US Open	16	73	73	69	69	284
24-Jun-01	Buick Classic	2	67	68	68	68	271
08-Jul-01	Western Open	1	69	68	66	64	267
15-Jul-01	Greater Milwaukee Open	10	67	68	68	68	271
22-Jul-01	British Open	MC	75	72	0	0	147
19-Aug-01	PGA Championship	7	68	70	69	67	274
26-Aug-01	NEC Invitational	21	71	70	69	71	281
23-Sep-01	Pennsylvania Classic	MC	73	73	0	0	146
07-Oct-01	Michelob Championship	MC	71	72	0	0	143
21-Oct-01	NCR Walt Disney Classic	MC	72	68	0	0	140
04-Nov-01	Tour Championship	29	74	71	70	72	287
06-Jan-02	Mercedes Championship	22	72	75	73	70	290
13-Jan-02	Hawaiian Open (Sony)	17	68	66	69	70	273
17-Feb-02	Los Angeles Open (Nissan)	50	68	72	70	72	282
24-Feb-02	Accenture Matchplay Championship	33	0	0	0	0	0
17-Mar-02	Bay Hill Invitational	9	71	68	70	73	282
24-Mar-02	Players Championship	4	67	77	68	72	284
31-Mar-02	Houston Open	MC	71	76	0	0	147
14-Apr-02	US Masters	MC	76	75	0	0	151
21-Apr-02	Worldcom Classic	58	72	69	73	70	284
09-Jun-02	Buick Classic	60	70	69	74	74	287
16-Jun-02	US Open	5	71	75	70	69	285
23-Jun-02	Greater Hartford Open	7	67	66	66	72	271
07-Jul-02	Western Open	MC	72	72	0	0	144
14-Jul-02	Greater Milwaukee Open	17	69	64	70	68	271
21-Jul-02	British Open	8	74	69	71	66	280

DAVIS LOVE

US TOUR RECORD

(Jan 1st, 2001 to Aug 1st, 2002)	Pos	1	2	3	4	Total
21-Jan-01 Hawaiian Open (Sony)	10	70	68	65	69	272
28-Jan-01 Phoenix Open	33	68	66	77	68	279
04-Feb-01 ATT Pebble Beach Pro Am	1	71	69	69	63	272
11-Feb-01 Buick Invitational	2	65	67	70	67	269
25-Feb-01 Los Angeles Open (Nissan)	8	68	67	68	75	278
04-Mar-01 Genuity Championship	6	65	70	69	71	275
26-Mar-01 Players Championship	MC	72	76	0	0	148
01-Apr-01 BellSouth Classic	11	70	71	71	74	286
08-Apr-01 US Masters	MC	71	75	0	0	146
16-Apr-01 Worldcom Classic	7	68	67	71	69	275
17-Jun-01 US Open	7	72	69	71	70	282
01-Jul-01 Greater Hartford Open	MC	77	70	0	0	147
08-Jul-01 Western Open	2	66	67	69	66	268
22-Jul-01 British Open	21	73	67	74	67	281
19-Aug-01 PGA Championship	37	71	67	65	77	280
26-Aug-01 NEC Invitational	5	68	68	70	68	274
14-Oct-01 Invensys Classic (Las Vegas) (five rounds)	4	69	65	68	69	61	332
21-Oct-01 NCR Walt Disney Classic	2	67	66	67	66	266
28-Oct-01 Buick Challenge	5	68	62	69	71	270
04-Nov-01 Tour Championship	15	70	72	66	69	277
06-Jan-02 Mercedes Championship	16	69	72	78	68	287
13-Jan-02 Hawaiian Open (Sony)	MC	75	67	0	0	142
27-Jan-02 Phoenix Open	28	72	69	68	68	277
03-Feb-02 ATT Pebble Beach Pro Am	MC	76	73	72	0	221
24-Feb-02 Accenture Matchplay Championship	17	0	0	0	0	0
03-Mar-02 Genuity Championship	MC	70	77	0	0	147
10-Mar-02 Honda Classic	30	69	71	69	68	277
17-Mar-02 Bay Hill Invitational	31	72	72	75	69	288
24-Mar-02 Players Championship	MC	73	74	0	0	147
07-Apr-02 BellSouth Classic	MC	72	75	0	0	147
14-Apr-02 US Masters	14	67	75	74	71	287
21-Apr-02 Worldcom Classic	5	62	69	72	71	274
12-May-02 Byron Nelson Classic	50	71	68	73	70	282
19-May-02 MasterCard Colonial	5	70	70	67	67	274
09-Jun-02 Buick Classic	55	71	69	72	74	286
16-Jun-02 US Open	24	71	71	72	77	291
23-Jun-02 Greater Hartford Open	2	68	64	68	67	267
07-Jul-02 Western Open	2	67	70	68	66	271
21-Jul-02 British Open	14	71	72	71	67	281

PHIL MICKELSON

US TOUR RECORD
(Jan 1st, 2001 to Aug 1st, 2002)

Date	Event	Pos	1	2	3	4	Total
14-Jan-01	Mercedes Championship	28	72	73	72	73	290
28-Jan-01	Phoenix Open	MC	71	72	0	0	143
04-Feb-01	ATT Pebble Beach Pro Am	3	70	66	66	73	275
11-Feb-01	Buick Invitational	1	68	64	71	66	269
25-Feb-01	Los Angeles Open (Nissan)	MC	73	74	0	0	147
11-Mar-01	Honda Classic	27	69	70	67	71	277
18-Mar-01	Bay Hill Invitational	2	66	72	70	66	274
26-Mar-01	Players Championship	33	73	68	72	77	290
01-Apr-01	BellSouth Classic	3	70	66	73	75	284
08-Apr-01	US Masters	3	67	69	69	70	275
06-May-01	Compaq Classic of New Orleans	2	66	66	64	72	268
13-May-01	Byron Nelson Classic	28	72	66	68	66	272
20-May-01	MasterCard Colonial	2	65	68	66	70	269
28-May-01	Kemper Open	3	68	67	72	65	272
10-Jun-01	St Jude Classic	MC	70	71	0	0	141
17-Jun-01	US Open	7	70	69	68	75	282
01-Jul-01	Greater Hartford Open	1	67	68	61	68	264
08-Jul-01	Western Open	42	66	74	67	76	283
22-Jul-01	British Open	30	70	72	72	71	285
05-Aug-01	The International	71	0	0	0	0	0
12-Aug-01	Buick Open	10	65	70	71	64	270
19-Aug-01	PGA Championship	2	66	66	66	68	266
26-Aug-01	NEC Invitational	8	67	66	70	72	275
20-Jan-02	Bob Hope Classic (five rounds)	1	64	67	70	65	64	330
27-Jan-02	Phoenix Open	23	72	66	70	68	276
03-Feb-02	ATT Pebble Beach Pro Am	MC	74	76	79	0	229
10-Feb-02	Buick Invitational	MC	73	75	0	0	148
24-Feb-02	Accenture Matchplay Championship	33	0	0	0	0	0
10-Mar-02	Honda Classic	11	70	66	68	71	275
17-Mar-02	Bay Hill Invitational	3	69	71	69	71	280
24-Mar-02	Players Championship	28	64	75	75	76	290
07-Apr-02	BellSouth Classic	3	65	68	71	73	277
14-Apr-02	US Masters	3	69	72	68	71	280
21-Apr-02	Worldcom Classic	3	65	64	72	71	272
05-May-02	Compaq Classic of New Orleans	9	73	66	71	68	278
12-May-02	Byron Nelson Classic	17	69	64	71	72	276
19-May-02	MasterCard Colonial	23	73	70	69	67	279
26-May-02	Memorial Tournament	9	73	66	70	69	278
09-Jun-02	Buick Classic	25	69	70	71	71	281

16-Jun-02	US Open	2	70	73	67	70	280
23-Jun-02	Greater Hartford Open	1	69	67	66	64	266
21-Jul-02	British Open	66	68	76	76	70	290

HAL SUTTON

US TOUR RECORD
(Jan 1st, 2001 to Aug 1st, 2002)

		Pos	1	2	3	4	Total
07-Jan-01	Accenture Matchplay Championship	33	0	0	0	0	0
14-Jan-01	Mercedes Championship	25	70	74	73	69	286
28-Jan-01	Phoenix Open	36	72	66	75	67	280
04-Feb-01	ATT Pebble Beach Pro Am	36	70	71	73	70	284
11-Feb-01	Buick Invitational	41	72	67	72	69	280
18-Feb-01	Bob Hope Classic (five rounds)	40	70	74	66	65	68	343
04-Mar-01	Genuity Championship	3	66	66	70	72	274
11-Mar-01	Honda Classic	18	69	68	67	72	276
26-Mar-01	Players Championship	5	72	71	68	70	281
08-Apr-01	US Masters	36	74	69	71	75	289
22-Apr-01	Houston Open	1	70	68	71	69	278
29-Apr-01	Greater Greensboro Classic	24	70	71	68	71	280
06-May-01	Compaq Classic of New Orleans	43	67	73	68	72	280
13-May-01	Byron Nelson Classic	28	68	70	66	68	272
20-May-01	MasterCard Colonial	40	73	69	66	72	280
03-Jun-01	Memorial Tournament	53	71	71	75	76	293
17-Jun-01	US Open	24	70	75	71	71	287
01-Jul-01	Greater Hartford Open	14	67	67	69	67	270
08-Jul-01	Western Open	31	70	71	70	70	281
12-Aug-01	Buick Open	MC	72	70	0	0	142
19-Aug-01	PGA Championship	44	67	71	73	70	281
26-Aug-01	NEC Invitational	11	69	71	67	70	277
09-Sep-01	Canadian Open	MC	74	73	0	0	147
30-Sep-01	Texas Open	30	69	69	69	70	277
28-Oct-01	Buick Challenge	MC	71	72	0	0	143
04-Nov-01	Tour Championship	26	70	73	70	73	286
06-Jan-02	Mercedes Championship	26	75	73	76	68	292
20-Jan-02	Bob Hope Classic	MC	73	69	71	68	281
27-Jan-02	Phoenix Open	MC	74	68	0	0	142
03-Feb-02	ATT Pebble Beach Pro Am	MC	74	75	71	0	220
17-Feb-02	Los Angeles Open (Nissan)	MC	72	73	0	0	145
24-Feb-02	Accenture Matchplay Championship	33	0	0	0	0	0
03-Mar-02	Genuity Championship	73	69	74	76	74	293
10-Mar-02	Honda Classic	MC	74	72	0	0	146
24-Mar-02	Players Championship	MC	73	74	0	0	147

31-Mar-02	Houston Open	23	72	67	74	69	282
07-Apr-02	BellSouth Classic	56	72	71	72	78	293
05-May-02	Compaq Classic of New Orleans	MC	77	73	0	0	150
12-May-02	Byron Nelson Classic	MC	73	72	0	0	145
19-May-02	MasterCard Colonial	12	69	68	71	69	277
02-Jun-02	Kemper Open	MC	72	75	0	0	147
09-Jun-02	Buick Classic	18	71	68	67	74	280
16-Jun-02	US Open	MC	77	77	0	0	154
30-Jun-02	St Jude Classic	MC	70	71	0	0	141
07-Jul-02	Western Open	MC	76	69	0	0	145
21-Jul-02	British Open	MC	74	75	0	0	149

DAVID TOMS

US TOUR RECORD

(Jan 1st, 2001 to Aug 1st, 2002)		Pos	1	2	3	4	Total
07-Jan-01	Accenture Matchplay Championship	17	0	0	0	0	0
14-Jan-01	Mercedes Championship	8	70	71	67	72	280
28-Jan-01	Phoenix Open	9	69	69	68	67	273
04-Feb-01	ATT Pebble Beach Pro Am	27	70	69	70	74	283
11-Feb-01	Buick Invitational	MC	72	71	0	0	143
18-Feb-01	Bob Hope Classic (five rounds)	18	67	68	66	69 68	338
04-Mar-01	Genuity Championship	21	73	68	71	69	281
18-Mar-01	Bay Hill Invitational	56	71	74	73	73	291
26-Mar-01	Players Championship	12	70	77	66	71	284
01-Apr-01	BellSouth Classic	17	69	69	74	75	287
08-Apr-01	US Masters	31	72	72	71	73	288
22-Apr-01	Houston Open	9	73	68	73	70	284
06-May-01	Compaq Classic of New Orleans	1	66	73	63	64	266
13-May-01	Byron Nelson Classic	11	68	71	62	68	269
20-May-01	MasterCard Colonial	8	67	70	66	70	273
10-Jun-01	St Jude Classic	53	70	68	73	70	281
17-Jun-01	US Open	66	71	71	77	75	294
08-Jul-01	Western Open	42	67	73	73	70	283
22-Jul-01	British Open	MC	74	73	0	0	147
05-Aug-01	The International	MC	0	0	0	0	0
12-Aug-01	Buick Open	35	68	69	70	69	276
19-Aug-01	PGA Championship	1	66	65	65	69	265
26-Aug-01	NEC Invitational	13	68	70	70	70	278
30-Sep-01	Texas Open	MC	74	73	0	0	147
07-Oct-01	Michelob Championship	1	64	70	67	68	269
21-Oct-01	NCR Walt Disney Classic	6	66	68	69	67	270
28-Oct-01	Buick Challenge	Wd	72	0	0	0	72

04-Nov-01	Tour Championship	2	73	66	64	67	270
06-Jan-02	Mercedes Championship	2	69	66	72	67	274
13-Jan-02	Hawaiian Open (Sony)	4	68	67	63	72	270
20-Jan-02	Bob Hope Classic (five rounds)	31	72	68	66	67	66	339
03-Feb-02	ATT Pebble Beach Pro Am	MC	73	75	70	0	218
24-Feb-02	Accenture Matchplay Championship	5	0	0	0	0	0
03-Mar-02	Genuity Championship	16	67	74	75	68	284
10-Mar-02	Honda Classic	30	72	68	70	67	277
24-Mar-02	Players Championship	19	69	72	70	77	288
31-Mar-02	Houston Open	17	69	72	67	73	281
07-Apr-02	BellSouth Classic	12	68	68	74	72	282
14-Apr-02	US Masters	36	73	74	76	71	294
05-May-02	Compaq Classic of New Orleans	9	69	69	71	69	278
12-May-02	Byron Nelson Classic	4	68	68	70	66	272
19-May-02	MasterCard Colonial	2	71	71	64	66	272
09-Jun-02	Buick Classic	12	70	68	68	73	279
16-Jun-02	US Open	45	74	74	70	77	295
30-Jun-02	St Jude Classic	4	68	68	65	68	269
07-Jul-02	Western Open	15	68	73	70	67	278
21-Jul-02	British Open	83	67	75	81	75	298

SCOTT VERPLANK

US TOUR RECORD

(Jan 1st, 2001 to Aug 1st, 2002)	Pos	1	2	3	4	Total
07-Jan-01	Accenture Matchplay Championship	17	0	0	0	0	0
14-Jan-01	Mercedes Championship	30	74	73	71	73	291
28-Jan-01	Phoenix Open	4	64	66	70	70	270
18-Feb-01	Bob Hope Classic (five rounds)	4	66	68	70	62	67	333
25-Feb-01	Los Angeles Open (Nissan)	33	72	70	71	69	282
04-Mar-01	Genuity Championship	12	67	71	69	72	279
26-Mar-01	Players Championship	44	69	75	72	76	292
08-Apr-01	US Masters	MC	69	78	0	0	147
16-Apr-01	Worldcom Classic	3	68	67	69	70	274
29-Apr-01	Greater Greensboro Classic	36	73	67	71	71	282
06-May-01	Compaq Classic of New Orleans	43	67	73	69	71	280
13-May-01	Byron Nelson Classic	2	62	67	68	66	263
20-May-01	MasterCard Colonial	Wd	74	0	0	0	74
03-Jun-01	Memorial Tournament	24	66	72	72	76	286
17-Jun-01	US Open	22	71	71	73	71	286
01-Jul-01	Greater Hartford Open	17	72	67	71	61	271
08-Jul-01	Western Open	15	69	69	70	71	279
22-Jul-01	British Open	30	71	72	70	72	285

PLAYER FORM SINCE JANUARY 2001

Date	Tournament	Pos	1	2	3	4	5	Total
12-Aug-01	Buick Open	14	68	67	68	68		271
19-Aug-01	PGA Championship	7	69	68	70	67		274
26-Aug-01	NEC Invitational	17	69	71	70	69		279
09-Sep-01	Canadian Open	1	70	63	66	67		266
23-Sep-01	Pennsylvania Classic	61	74	70	72	75		291
14-Oct-01	Invensys Classic (Las Vegas) (five rounds)	7	67	67	71	65	67	337
21-Oct-01	NCR Walt Disney Classic	46	68	70	70	69		277
04-Nov-01	Tour Championship	5	67	65	68	71		271
06-Jan-02	Mercedes Championship	8	67	69	70	73		279
20-Jan-02	Bob Hope Classic (five rounds)	42	69	69	67	65	71	341
27-Jan-02	Phoenix Open	22	69	65	67	74		275
17-Feb-02	Los Angeles Open (Nissan)	19	69	68	67	73		277
24-Feb-02	Accenture Matchplay Championship	17	0	0	0	0		0
03-Mar-02	Genuity Championship	MC	71	74	0	0		145
24-Mar-02	Players Championship	28	71	75	73	71		290
31-Mar-02	Houston Open	14	67	70	72	71		280
14-Apr-02	US Masters	43	70	75	76	75		296
21-Apr-02	Worldcom Classic	5	67	68	72	67		274
05-May-02	Compaq Classic of New Orleans	9	69	69	73	67		278
12-May-02	Byron Nelson Classic	50	68	71	72	71		282
19-May-02	MasterCard Colonial	19	67	70	72	69		278
26-May-02	Memorial Tournament	49	72	68	74	73		287
16-Jun-02	US Open	MC	75	78	0	0		153
23-Jun-02	Greater Hartford Open	4	65	70	63	71		269
07-Jul-02	Western Open	13	67	69	70	71		277
21-Jul-02	British Open	37	72	68	74	71		285

TIGER WOODS

US TOUR RECORD

(Jan 1st, 2001 to Aug 1st, 2002)		Pos	1	2	3	4	Total
14-Jan-01	Mercedes Championship	8	70	73	68	69	280
28-Jan-01	Phoenix Open	5	65	73	68	65	271
04-Feb-01	ATT Pebble Beach Pro Am	13	66	73	69	72	280
11-Feb-01	Buick Invitational	4	70	67	67	67	271
25-Feb-01	Los Angeles Open (Nissan)	13	71	68	69	71	279
18-Mar-01	Bay Hill Invitational	1	71	67	66	69	273
26-Mar-01	Players Championship	1	72	69	66	67	274
08-Apr-01	US Masters	1	70	66	68	68	272
13-May-01	Byron Nelson Classic	3	66	68	69	63	266
03-Jun-01	Memorial Tournament	1	68	69	68	66	271
17-Jun-01	US Open	12	74	71	69	69	283
24-Jun-01	Buick Classic	16	75	66	68	71	280

PLAYER FORM SINCE JANUARY 2001

Date	Tournament						
08-Jul-01	Western Open	20	73	68	68	71	280
22-Jul-01	British Open	25	71	68	73	71	283
19-Aug-01	PGA Championship	29	73	67	69	70	279
26-Aug-01	NEC Invitational	1	66	67	66	69	268
09-Sep-01	Canadian Open	23	65	73	69	69	276
21-Oct-01	NCR Walt Disney Classic	16	69	67	67	69	272
04-Nov-01	Tour Championship	13	70	67	69	70	276
06-Jan-02	Mercedes Championship	10	68	74	74	65	281
03-Feb-02	ATT Pebble Beach Pro Am	12	70	73	71	68	282
10-Feb-02	Buick Invitational	5	66	77	69	66	278
24-Feb-02	Accenture Matchplay Championship	33	0	0	0	0	0
03-Mar-02	Genuity Championship	2	67	70	70	66	273
17-Mar-02	Bay Hill Invitational	1	67	65	74	69	275
24-Mar-02	Players Championship	14	71	72	70	74	287
14-Apr-02	US Masters	1	70	69	66	71	276
12-May-02	Byron Nelson Classic	3	71	65	69	65	270
26-May-02	Memorial Tournament	22	74	70	72	66	282
16-Jun-02	US Open	1	67	68	70	72	277
21-Jul-02	British Open	28	70	68	81	65	284

WOODS IN EUROPE

04-Mar-01	Dubai Classic	2	64	64	68	72	268
20-May-01	Deutsche Bank (TPC of Europe)	1	69	68	63	66	266
20-May-02	Deutsche Bank (TPC of Europe)	1	69	67	64	68	268

RYDER CUP FACTS

Only two pairings can boast a 100 per cent record in multiple foursomes and fourballs over the years, and, strangely for formats in which the Europeans are considered to have the edge, both of them are American. Arnold Palmer and Gardner Dickinson won all five of their contests in 1967 and 1971, while the formidable partnership of Jack Nicklaus and Tom Watson emerged victorious from all four of their matches in 1977 and 1981. The most impressive record of all, though, belongs to the legendary Spanish pairing of Seve Ballesteros and Jose Maria Olazabal. The duo teamed up 15 times in their Ryder Cup career, and only lost twice, notching up 11 victories

Lanny Wadkins and Larry Nelson won all four of their matches when teaming up in 1979. Alas they couldn't repeat the feat when paired in 1987, losing both ties. Sergio Garcia and Jesper Parnevik came close to emulating the achievement in 1999, winning their first three matches before being held to a half by Davis Love and David Duval in the final fourballs

The biggest winning margin in singles play over 18 holes is 8&7, recorded by Fred Couples (over Ian Woosnam in 1997) and Tom Kite (from Howard Clark in 1989)

SKY'S THE LIMIT

This year's coverage of the Ryder Cup promises to be bigger and better than ever. The Ryder Cup is regarded by Sky as one of the jewels in the crown of its sports portfolio and no expense will be spared as the satellite channel covers every shot from the three-day clash at the Belfry.

The Outside Broadcast team will begin setting up at The Belfry a week before the contest starts.

Around 200 production staff from Sky will be on the ground. This is double the number for any other domestic golf competition, due to the size of the event and also because extra production staff are needed for interactive coverage.

Discussions on how the event would be covered first began two years ago. The first tour of the site took place in January 2001 when the Sky production crew responsible for the main broadcast studio visited the course. The main production crew first visited the site in May 2001.

The statistics involved make impressive reading. The production staff will use up to 20 vehicles consisting of:

2 x Sky Sports Production trucks - one for the world feed and one for the domestic feed
1 x graphics truck
1 x VT truck
1 x truck designated for Interactivity
1 x BT Uplink truck
1 x BT Satellite truck
Up to 12 support vehicles for catering, dining, cables, radio & cameras

The outside broadcast will use approximately 45 miles of cable and approximately 42 cameras.

In addition to Sky's coverage the BBC will broadcast comprehensive highlights each night.

BELFRY
COURSE GUIDE

Over the past 15 years The De Vere Belfry, Sutton Coldfield, Birmingham has become synonymous with the Ryder Cup. It first hosted the event in 1985 when Europe won the title for the first time since 1957, and magic moments such as Christy O'Connor's second to the 18th in his singles match against Fred Couples that year are now entwined in golfing folklore. But with increased competition from other courses, keen to muscle in and grab their piece of the increasingly lucrative Ryder Cup pie, officials at the West Midlands course are not sitting on their laurels, and the Brabazon Course is remarkably different now from when it last hosted the pan-Atlantic clash in 1993. The layout was designed by Peter Alliss and Dave Thomas and is situated on 15 former potato patches. Hardly the same illustrious history as St Andrews.

The Belfry is actually a hotel which was opened in 1959, becoming a favourite centre for wedding receptions and a place where, in the 1960s, such groups as Led Zeppelin, the Moody Blues, Slade and Status Quo performed live. In 1970 Thomas and Alliss were asked to design a Championship Course and a support course that could allow guests at the 59-room hotel to enjoy a round or two not far from their lodgings.

In 1975 the British PGA moved their headquarters from Kensington Oval to The Belfry, making it one of the most important golfing spots in the United Kingdom. The first official tournament to be held on the Brabazon course was the Hennessy Cup, a match between Great Britain and the Continent of Europe, played in September, 1978. In 1981 the course required the kiss of life, starting with the soil of the fairways being broken so that loose stones, which were causing so many complaints from players, could be removed. In 1989 the Europeans beat the Americans again at The Belfry, but lost out to the visitors from across the Atlantic in 1993, the last time the event was held on this famous course.

Now, following another eight years of continued refurbishment and, in particular, the remodelling of The Brabazon course, The De Vere Belfry is ready to host the Ryder Cup for a fourth time. There have been many changes since 1993 with an overall investment in excess of £48 million on the complex including 120 significant changes and £40 million spent on alterations and improvements to The Brabazon course. The outward nine holes were always regarded as far less interesting to players and spectators alike and serious modifications have been carried out, while on the spectacular back nine, with world-famous holes like 10 and 18, only a touch of tinkering has taken place.

BELFRY COURSE GUIDE

The opening tee is situated in front of the ivy-covered clubhouse and some imaginative design has lowered the tees by several metres to create an amphitheatre from which over 1,000 spectators can watch the players begin their rounds. Set 40 yards back from the normal tee, the 9th grandstand backs on to it. The drive is straight and fairly open. There are bunkers on the right and trees right and left but the rough is not too deep. Hit it right for the best approach. The fairway bottle necks into the green, which slopes from right to left. Enlarged and reshaped bunkers guard it on the left but it is a nice wide target. Regarded as a gentle opener, expect plenty of birdies as players on both sides look to grab the early initiative. In the Ryder Cup the visitors traditionally have the honour on the opening hole.

The 2nd is a par four, which dog-legs left and has been lengthened to increase its difficulty with the tee 22 yards further back than it was during the last Ryder Cup at the Belfry. There are trees on the right and also on the left meaning that this a narrow drive, probably with an iron. There are bunkers at driveable distance on the left and mounds on the right. The players will aim up the right to get the best view of the pin. The main feature of the hole is a small burn that guards the front of the green and will catch anything short (or huge drives). A cluster of bunkers – some enlarged – behind the burn make this a tough second shot to a small target but for most competitors it will be no more than a nine-iron or even a wedge for the likes of Woods, Davis Love III and Garcia.

Back in 1993 this was a long par four but the hole has since been redesigned as part of the changes to jazz up the outward nine, and it is now an exciting dog-leg par five, eminently reachable in two shots but with a large lake guarding the green which will surely trap some players as they go for the pin. This is particularly likely during the fourballs on the first two days. If they want to try to get on in two, they will have to carry at least 130 yards of water on to the green, probably from a long way back on the fairway. A big bank behind the green makes hitting long the sensible shot, though there are also bunkers either side of the green. The tee has been raised to give a view of the fairway bunkers in an attempt to intimidate the players, while there is a big chestnut tree on the right hand side that must also be avoided. The organisers hope this remodelled hole will become a favourite with competitors and fans alike, giving it similar status to the 10th and 18th.

BELFRY COURSE GUIDE

HOLE 4

To accommodate the previous hole being lengthened from a par four to par five the 4th, formerly an innocuous par five, has been redesigned as a tricky par four with conspicuous use of both water and sand. Only the 18th is longer of the par fours on the course with the Ryder Cup tee 35 yards back from the normal tee and cut into the lake leaving a drive over water.

The fairway slopes from right to left and there is more water down the right and rough and bunkers on the left with trees also cutting in on the left – all creating a very daunting drive. The new look, two-tier, sloping green is narrow and protected by a stream that has been widened. When it was a par five players could lay up short of the green. They do not have that option now and must go for the pin.

HOLE 5

This par four will be identified as definite birdie potential by the cream of Europe's and the US's golfers. Although not a short par four by any stretch of the imagination, the stream has been removed leaving a straight-forward drive with only the lake on the left-side to avoid, but that rarely comes into play. The tee is set back behind a lake forcing a short carry over water, but the real threat is water on the left of the fairway at 200 yards. Trees and bunkers on the right at 290 yards make the fairway very narrow.

The green is thin and wide with large bunkers guarding the front but overall the approach is not overly tough, being fairly open. The drive favours players who draw the ball and should leave a short iron to the small green, which is protected by three enlarged bunkers.

HOLE 6

Rated as one of the hardest holes on the Brabazon course, the 6th is very attractive with a very tight drive onto a camel's hump fairway avoiding the lake, which has been extended into the old fairway to tempt players to take an iron rather than a driver.

The water starts on the left of the hole at 180 yards, right on the line of the tee to green. The fairway then angles off to the right, and dog-legs back to the left before the green. Trees all down the right make the fairway very narrow, and there's a lake in there too, but a hook is the real shot to avoid. The reward for an accurate drive is that it leaves just an eight or nine iron into the green, in front of which water cuts in from the left and a big bunker protects the right. On the Sunday the pin will be tucked away behind this bunker.

BELFRY COURSE GUIDE

Depending on the wind, the players will take anything from a four to a seven iron approaching the tough looking target with its extravagant huge bunker snaking down the middle of the fairway and then ringing the front of the elevated, island-like green. The water down the right does not really come into play and is for aesthetic purposes rather than anything else. The green slopes down towards the back and any shots that are misjudged and hit too hard can roll down into the bunker at the rear. The 'railway sleepers' that used to guard the green in place of the monster bunker have long been discarded for health and safety reasons.

At first glance, it's difficult to see why this innocuous looking par four is rated the hardest on the course on the stroke index but its subtle nuances have been designed to negate the length off the tee that the top players hit these days. The hole is straight, and you drive down a fairly generous fairway, with rather forgiving rough, though the fairway bunkers on the right have been moved closer to the green narrowing the landing area and making a fade the ideal stroke. But once you get to the approach shot – a long one over water – you realise the quality of this hole. The green is protected by a wide, fast running stream and a large oak tree on the right which obstructs shots from that side. Playing safe with an iron off the tee leaves a tough, long second shot into the long and narrow green, which is guarded by deep bunkers on both sides, and is particularly difficult to play if the pin is near the back.

Another hole which has been tinkered with and another where water plays a major part. It's one of the longest par fours on the course and one of the toughest, as well as being one of the best looking holes, winding back towards the clubhouse, obscured by two huge grandstands from which you can see the 9th & 18th greens. For the Ryder Cup, the drive is 30 yards back from the normal tee, and the hole dog-legs at 200 yards from right to left with bunkers in the crook of the turn, making even the biggest hitters think twice about carrying them. Thick woodland down the right will snare anything sliced, but the real attraction is the approach into an L-shaped green. There is a very wide lake protecting both the 9th & 18th greens that cuts into the right of the green. If the pin is at the front the players don't have to carry water but the target is very thin. On the last day the pin will almost certainly be back right which leaves a very intimidating approach over water into a small, narrow section of green that slopes towards the water.

BELFRY COURSE GUIDE

HOLE 10

The great do-or-die par-four 10th is a masterfully-designed hole and probably the most memorable on the course. From the tee, there's only 210 yards of fairways, a bunker lying on either side of the short grass, with water running along the right hand side.

The green is a full 50 yards long (and 12 yards wide) on the other side of the water, some 60 yards from where the fairway runs out.

The tee shot, if you take the standard & conservative route, can be as little as a six-iron. Obviously right is a no go area. If the tee shot is straight but too short or too long, your view to the putting surface may be blocked out by large trees guarding either side of the entry. Accurate play of the approach is paramount.

If you decide to take your chances, check the pin position by walking left of the tee, and you'll need to carry 235 yards to the front of the green. In the fourballs expect one of each pairing to go for the green but in foursomes and singles, with more to lose, it will be a case of 'Who Dares Wins'.

It was the dashing Spaniard Severiano Ballesteros, who first conquered by risking all and driving the small, well guarded, tiered green on the opening morning of the 1985 contest. It's all about stretching nerves and confidence to the limit on the tee when weighing up the odds. The player with the honour knows that if he takes the cautious route then he leaves the door wide open for his opponent.

HOLE 11

The dilemma facing a player on the 11th tee is whether to arrow a drive down the heart of the fairway which bottlenecks as it approaches the green, or whether to opt for caution and thread an iron through the two bunkers which sit either side of the fairway at around 200 yards.

The small green slopes from back to front and is guarded by two bunkers but competitors have to beware the ground in front of the putting surface which tends to be bumpy, and an overhit approach shot can shoot through the green past the pin.

Considered one of the easier holes on the course, the light rough is nothing to worry about and this hole will be targeted as a definite birdie chance by the majority of players.

Beware complacency though. In 1985, on the final day, Sam Torrance was three holes down having visited the water on three different occasions already in his round but Andy North could only bogey here and a par set the Scotsman on the way to a remarkable comeback, culminating in his Cup-winning putt on the last green.

BELFRY COURSE GUIDE

The longest of the three short holes on the course has undergone dramatic surgery since the last Ryder Cup at the Belfry in 1993. The hole has actually been shortened by 20 odd yards but the flip side is that the designers have turned the old stream into a lake guarding the green which should ensure some spectacular action over the three days.

A small waterfall has been added for visual effect and players will get a fine view from the newly elevated tee position, bordered by trees on both sides. If the pin is positioned towards the back it will take a four or five-iron to get there, and there are also a couple of deep bunkers to contend with, though it is quite a large green compared to most and allows for some margin of error. This is probably the toughest of the par threes so birdies will be at a premium.

One of the shorter par fours on the course, but with out of bounds on the left hand side of the fairway, where newly crowned British Open champion Sandy Lyle hooked on the final day in 1985, most players will stick with an iron off the tee and then a short iron or wedge on a hole where accuracy is key. Twelve trees planted on the right hand side of the fairway mean there is a fairly narrow driving area from the tee should anyone be feeling bold and decide to bring out the wood.

Like most holes on the course the green has been tinkered with. In this case it has been lengthened, had slopes added, and been given extra protection with a pot bunker at the rear. But it is fairly clear why this hole is ranked as the easiest on the course. The bunkers at 200 yards shouldn't trouble many and a big drive would have to be very wayward to find more trouble than light rough – leaving just a small pitch to the green.

This links-type par three with deep rough is dominated by the huge bunker which sits on the left edge of the long, narrow two-tiered green. But there is also a smaller sand trap on the other side to catch anybody who ventures too far that way. The tee has been raised to provide a fine view of the shot, which will probably require a five or six-iron. Charismatic Spaniard Seve Ballesteros holed a typically outrageous 50-foot putt for birdie here in 1985 against Tom Kite in the singles. The pin is likely to be tucked away on the left hand side close to the bunker on the final day, where many spectators will choose to watch the action from the new mound behind the green.

In 1993, Nick Faldo's hole in one here against Paul Azinger was only the second hole-in-one during the history of the Ryder Cup.

BELFRY COURSE GUIDE

The first of two long holes in the final four, the 15th offers a good chance of making the green in two and setting up an eagle putt if the narrow fairway is played downwind. The only danger with the wind behind is that some of the bigger hitters may drive too far off the tee, which brings the stream at 370 yards into play.

If the wind is blowing into the players' faces, the hole is a totally different proposition and nearly all – perhaps Tiger Woods excepted – will have to lay up short and play a third shot with a wedge into the green.

However, problems are far from over even once the green has been reached as it is a monster three-tiered effort surrounded by three bunkers. In 1985 the unheralded Spaniard Manuel Pinero birdied here to seal a singles victory over one of the US's strongest team members Lanny Wadkins, but eight years later Chip Beck eagled the hole on his way to turning round a three-hole deficit against Barry Lane and win on the final green.

The crucial final turn home begins with the par-four 16th, which is relatively tame compared to what lies ahead at the last two holes. The wind is generally behind the players from the tee so most can leave themselves no more than a gentle short iron approach to the green.

The fairway dog-legs gently from left to right, and a steep bunker protects a small two-tiered green, with trees overhanging at the back. This is another hole where the bunker at the front left of the green has been remodelled and the pin is likely to be place in close proximity to the sand for most of the weekend.

In 1985, a remarkable 25-yard putt from the back of the green by Sandy Lyle gave the Scotsman a crucial 3&2 victory over Peter Jacobson on the final day. The approach is definitely the main feature of this hole and the pin position on this undulating green will determine how easy or hard it is to play. Birdies here and at the 17th by Howard Clark in 1989, playing with Mark James in the Saturday afternoon foursomes, led to a crucial win by one hole over Payne Stewart and Curtis Strange as Europe tied 14-14 to retain the cup.

front nine

HOLE	1	2	3	4	5	6	7	8	9	OUT
YARDS	411	379	538	442	408	395	177	428	433	3611
PAR	4	4	5	4	4	4	3	4	4	36
STROKE INDEX	9	17	13	3	11	5	15	1	7	

BELFRY COURSE GUIDE

At 564 yards, this par five is the longest hole on the course. The tee has been realigned to encourage players to drive across the bunker on the sharp right dog-leg, dangling the carrot of being able to reach the green in two if successful in doing so. There are also bunkers at the turn of the dog leg for players who hit too long.

To have any chance of making the green in two the players will have to fade a drive round the corner as the trees prevent a straight drive over it. A stream running across the fairway halfway up the hole comes into play if any of the bunkers are found from the tee, while the bunkers either side on the quite narrow approach to the green have been reshaped and deepened. Trees down the right of the fairway and a huge bunker down the left will swallow any stray approach shots.

In 1993 as Europe slipped to defeat on the final day, Constantino Rocca was one up with two to play and had two putts on the green for a par five but as his first slid down the hill from 25 feet it raced more than four feet past the hole and, almost inevitably, he missed the return. That crucial miss led to victory at the last for his opponent Davis Love III who said he had seen 'fear' in his opponent's eyes.

The par-four final is one of the most famous in the world. The tee shot is across a lake angled at 45 degrees, and for prime position the ball should be drawn slightly. The fairway runs along the far right side of the long lake. Too straight and you'll end up in the thin bunker on the far side. That, as well as a short tee shot that made the forced carry, might find reaching the 44-yards, long, three-tiered green very difficult. The same lake that intimidates the tee shot returns to haunt again in front of the green and another forced carry is required. The one thing no player will want is having the outcome of his match rest on a chip from the bank at the back of the green, steeply downhill and towards the water.

Some of the Cup's most memorable images have come from the 18th green, not least Sam Torrance standing with arms aloft in triumph after his 1985 match-winning birdie putt.

back nine

HOLE	10	11	12	13	14	15	16	17	18	IN	TOTAL
YARDS	284	419	208	384	190	545	413	564	473	3480	7091
PAR	4	4	3	4	3	5	4	5	4	36	72
STROKE INDEX	8	16	6	18	14	2	12	10	4		

TRAVEL
HOW TO GET THERE

TRAIN: Virgin Trains serve Birmingham International from all major British cities including London, Manchester, Liverpool, Leeds, Cardiff and Glasgow. Then walk onto the NEC site to catch the shuttle buses to The Belfry.

National Rail Enquiries 08457 48 49 50

CAR: The Belfry lies in Sutton Coldfield but there is no general public parking at the hotel itself.

All parking will be at Birmingham's National Exhibition Centre, better known as the NEC, from where there will be a 'park and ride' scheme in operation to transport people to The Belfry. The NEC sits next to the M6 motorway at Junction 4. A programme of road closures on sections of the A446 Litchfield Road and the A4091 Tamworth Road north of the M42, junction 9 will be in force, complimented by a series of minor road closures and through traffic routes. All traffic movements within the closed road area will be restricted to event buses, essential vehicles linked to the event and local residents. There will be no access off junction 9 of the M42 for any vehicle other than accredited coaches.

HELICOPTER: The official heliport is located at Middleton Hall Farm, adjacent to The Belfry. Landing is by prior arrangement only.

The course will be closed and all spectators asked to leave approximately 1 hour after the end of play. The park and ride will be in operation until 2 hours after the end of play, or 10:00pm, whichever is later. There will be a temporary bus terminal opposite The Belfry where coach travellers will be dropped of and picked up.

There is no direct public access to The Belfry for guests travelling by taxi or private hire vehicles.

RYDER CUP FACTS

Over the three days of the event there will be up to 40,000 visitors per day

RYDER CUP HISTORY

BY ANDY SWALES

1927

WORCESTER, MASSACHUSETTS JUNE 3-4

UNITED STATES 9½
GREAT BRITAIN 2½

CAPTAINS: WALTER HAGEN (US), TED RAY (GB)

Even before the British team set sail from Southampton to compete in the first Ryder Cup, their original choice of captain, Abe Mitchell, was forced to withdraw because of appendicitis. Fifty-year-old Ted Ray took over as skipper. This late change meant a call-up for Herbert Jolly from the Channel Islands. He was unable to meet up with the rest of the team in Southampton, so sailed alone four days later. It was hardly the best of starts for a team that would win only two of their 12 games in Worcester, Massachusetts.

Charles Whitcombe was the only Briton to remain unbeaten, thanks to a crushing 7&5 win in the foursomes and a halved singles with Gene Sarazen.

GB's only other victory came from George Duncan who beat Joe Turnesa one-up in the singles. Duncan, two down with nine to play, birdied the final hole to sneak victory.

As for replacement captain Ray, he lost both of his games and remains the oldest non-American to play in the Ryder Cup.

Ray, who with Tony Jacklin remains the only British winner of the US Open in the last 85 years, admitted that the hosts were superior on the putting green: "They holed out much better than we did. We can never hope to beat the Americans unless we learn to putt." In some games, the standard of golf was pretty poor. Sarazen and Al Watrous were well over par but still defeated Arthur Havers and Jolly 3&2.

One man who opted not to play at all, despite undergoing the six-day boat trip, was George Gadd. After failing to produce any form in practice he asked the captain to leave him out of the foursomes and singles.

The trip to North America had cost the British team around £3,000. The money was raised from donations, following an appeal in the press, with founder Samuel Ryder topping up this amount. Ryder was born in 1858, the son of a Manchester corn merchant, and had agreed to donate a trophy for the contest which cost him £250.

Ryder, an amateur golf enthusiast, employed Abe Mitchell as his personal coach, paying him £1,000 a year. And the solid gold cup is not only testimony to Ryder's love for the game, but the miniature figure on the lid of the trophy depicts Mitchell who in the 1920s was considered to be the best player never to win The Open Championship.

1929

MOORTOWN, YORKSHIRE, ENGLAND MAY 26-27

GREAT BRITAIN 7
UNITED STATES 5

CAPTAINS: GEORGE DUNCAN (GB), WALTER HAGEN (US)

The hosts recovered from a one-point deficit after the foursomes to record a resounding singles victory over the Americans in the first Ryder Cup match to be staged in Britain. Only two visitors registered wins on singles day, as Britain claimed five and a half points out of eight.

American captain Walter Hagen suffered his only ever Ryder Cup defeat in the singles, trounced 10&8 by his opposite number George Duncan. Gene Sarazen later relayed an amusing tale of how Hagen, having learnt of the singles draw, told his team-mate in the washroom that his match with Duncan would provide the United States with a definite point. Unfortunately, Hagen was unaware that Duncan was in one of the cubicles nearby and had heard every word of the conversation. Spurred on by Hagen's presumptuous comments, Duncan was five-up by lunch following a 68. It didn't get any easier for the American skipper in the afternoon as Duncan reached the turn in just 31 strokes, by which stage the match had almost run its course. It was quite a thrashing for a player who two weeks earlier had won the British Open (for a fourth time) by six shots at Muirfield.

Similarly, reigning US Open champion and Muirfield runner-up Johnny Farrell was crushed 8&6 by Charles Whitcombe, while Archie Compston trounced Sarazen 6&5. However, it wasn't all one-way traffic. Abe Mitchell, despite having played the morning round in 70, found himself five down to the red-hot Leo Diegel. He was still under par by the time Diegel registered a 9&8 win. The other US singles winner was Horton Smith, at 21 the youngest American player in Ryder Cup history, who won 4&2 against Fred Robson.

In the final match, Ernest Whitcombe was in prime position to beat Al Espinosa but halved with the American despite being two-up with two to play. Happily, the destiny of the trophy had been settled shortly before, when the youngest member of the home side, 22-year-old Henry Cotton, beat Al Watrous 4&3. Cotton had lost three of the opening four holes in the morning round but chipped-in at 18 to go into lunch all square. From there he took control before securing victory on the 33rd green.

Britain's only foursomes win came from veterans Mitchell and Robson, both in their 40s. Elsewhere, the impressive Diegel and Espinosa had raced to a seven-hole lunchtime lead over Aubrey Boomer and Duncan and eventually won 7&5.

1927 UNITED STATES 9½
GREAT BRITAIN 2½

DAY 1

FOURSOMES		GB	
TED RAY	FRED ROBSON	0	V
GEORGE DUNCAN	ARCHIE COMPSTON	0	V
ARTHUR HAVERS	HERBERT JOLLY	0	V
AUBREY BOOMER	CHARLES WHITCOMBE	1	V

DAY 2

SINGLES	GB	
ARCHIE COMPSTON	0	V
AUBREY BOOMER	0	V
HERBERT JOLLY	0	V
TED RAY	0	V
CHARLES WHITCOMBE	0.5	V
ARTHUR HAVERS	0	V
FRED ROBSON	0	V
GEORGE DUNCAN	1	V

1929 GREAT BRITAIN 7
UNITED STATES 5

DAY 1

FOURSOMES		GB	
ARCHIE COMPSTON	CHARLES WHITCOMBE	0.5	V
AUBREY BOOMER	GEORGE DUNCAN	0	V
ABE MITCHELL	FRED ROBSON	1	V
ERNEST WHITCOMBE	HENRY COTTON	0	V

DAY 2

SINGLES	GB	
CHARLES WHITCOMBE	1	V
GEORGE DUNCAN	1	V
ABE MITCHELL	0	V
ARCHIE COMPSTON	1	V
AUBREY BOOMER	1	V
FRED ROBSON	0	V
HENRY COTTON	1	V
ERNEST WHITCOMBE	0.5	V

US			WINNER	MARGIN
1	WALTER HAGEN	JOHNNY GOLDEN	USA	2&1
1	JOHNNY FARRELL	JOE TURNESA	USA	8&6
1	GENE SARAZEN	AL WATROUS	USA	3&2
0	LEO DIEGEL	BILL MEHLHORN	GB	1 HOLE

1	BILL MEHLHORN		USA	1 HOLE
1	JOHNNY FARRELL		USA	5&4
1	JOHNNY GOLDEN		USA	8&7
1	LEO DIEGEL		USA	7&5
0.5	GENE SARAZEN		HVD	–
1	WALTER HAGEN		USA	2&1
1	AL WATROUS		USA	3&2
0	JOE TURNESA		GB	1 HOLE

US			WINNER	MARGIN
0.5	JOHNNY FARRELL	JOE TURNESA	HVD	–
1	LEO DIEGEL	AL ESPINOSA	USA	7&5
0	GENE SARAZEN	ED DUDLEY	GB	2&1
1	JOHNNY GOLDEN	WALTER HAGEN	USA	2 HOLES

0	JOHNNY FARRELL		GB	8&6
0	WALTER HAGEN		GB	10&8
1	LEO DIEGEL		USA	9&8
0	GENE SARAZEN		GB	6&4
0	JOE TURNESA		GB	4&3
1	HORTON SMITH		USA	4&2
0	AL WATROUS		GB	4&3
0.5	AL ESPINOSA		HVD	–

1931

SCIOTO, COLUMBUS, OHIO JUNE 26-27

UNITED STATES 9
GREAT BRITAIN 3

CAPTAINS: WALTER HAGEN (US), CHARLES WHITCOMBE (GB)

Britain were without three of their best players when they travelled to Ohio in the summer of 1931. Not that the presence of Percy Alliss, Aubrey Boomer and Henry Cotton would have made that much difference to the final result. However, the reasons for the trio's non-appearance were contentious.

While Alliss and Boomer were ineligible, Cotton simply fell out with the authorities. Ryder Cup rules stipulated that pros had to be attached to clubs in Great Britain or Ireland to play in the match and, as Alliss was in Berlin and Boomer played in Paris, neither could face the Americans. As for Cotton, he was originally selected for the trip but fell out with the British PGA who insisted that players agree to a clause in the invitation which stated that the team must travel to and from the match en bloc. Cotton, however, wanted to remain in the United States at the conclusion of the match to further his golfing education. But the British PGA would not be swayed from its original decision. Cotton opted not to sign the contract although he said he was prepared to pay for his own ticket, to and from America. Still the PGA wouldn't accept, so Cotton didn't play. As it happened Cotton, Alliss and Boomer went to the States anyway, where they competed in a number of events. Cotton would also miss the 1933 and 1935 Ryder Cup matches because of his attachment to a club in Belgium.

HENRY COTTON'S RYDER CUP RE

FORMAT	PARTNER	F	A	OPPONENTS
FOURSOMES	ERNEST WHITCOMBE	0	1	JOHNNY GOLDEN
SINGLES		1	0	AL WATROUS
FOURSOMES	ALF PADGHAM	0	1	ED DUDLEY
SINGLES		1	0	TONY MANERO
FOURSOMES	ARTHUR LEES	0	1	ED OLIVER
SINGLES		0	1	SAM SNEAD

Cotton's Ryder Cup career actually spanned 18 years but, because of arguments, rules and the Second World War, he would appear in only three matches (1929-37-47).

Stifling heat didn't help the British cause either as the hosts led from start to finish. Denny Shute and Gene Sarazen won both of their matches without going beyond the 12th green in the afternoon rounds. In all, five of America's nine victories were won by scorelines of 7&6 or better, including a record 10&9 win in the foursomes by Hagen and Shute, George Duncan and Arthur Havers their victims. Seven of the ten Americans enjoyed 100% records from two games, leaving only Leo Diegel (a foursomes loser) and Horton Smith (who didn't play) as the only two members of the victorious team that didn't contribute even half-a-point. None of the visitors remained unbeaten.

1933

SOUTHPORT & AINSDALE, LANCASHIRE, ENGLAND JUNE 26-27

GREAT BRITAIN 6½
UNITED STATES 5½

CAPTAINS: JH TAYLOR (GB), WALTER HAGEN (US)

With the series tied at five-and-a-half points each, and only one singles left on the course, the overall result depended on the game between Britain's Syd Easterbrook and American Denny Shute. All square on the 36th tee, both players hit poor drives before reaching the final green in three shots apiece.

CORD

	WINNER	MARGIN	YEAR
WALTER HAGEN	USA	2 HOLES	1929
	GB	4&3	1929
BYRON NELSON	USA	4&2	1937
	GB	5&3	1937
LEW WORSHAM	USA	10&9	1947
	USA	5&4	1947

With each player facing a difficult par putt of around 25 to 30 feet, Easterbrook left his approach close to the hole, before Shute raced four feet past and then missed the return. Easterbrook duly tapped in for his five to win the match by one hole and give Britain the Cup.

Britain had gone into the match with only three survivors from the triumphant 1929 team – Percy Alliss, Abe Mitchell and Charles Whitcombe – even though the former didn't get a game at Moortown. Yet the hosts thoroughly deserved their victory and were a little unfortunate not to have won by a wider margin.

In the opening foursomes, Alliss and Whitcombe halved a topsy-turvy encounter with Gene Sarazen and Walter Hagen. In the morning, the British pair won four successive holes from the 13th and reached lunch three-up. But the Americans battled back from four-down with nine to play to square the match on the 34th green.

It was advantage Britain once more at the penultimate hole where the visitors hooked into trouble as Alliss and Whitcombe regained the lead. But at the 36th, Alliss bunkered his approach and later missed a short putt that allowed Hagen and Sarazen to draw level once again. Britain's only foursomes defeat came at the hands of Ed Dudley and Billy Burke. The Americans fought back from four down after 18 to edge out Alf Padgham and Alf Perry by a solitary hole.

Although it was Easterbrook who holed the Cup-clinching putt, the real hero on singles day was 46-year-old Abe Mitchell, who conquered Olin Dutra 9&8. The American had won the PGA Championship in 1932.

Dutra had started strongly, reaching the turn in 35 to go three-up. Yet Mitchell won 12 of the next 19 holes - including eight in a row - to give GB&I their first point of the second day. Another vital win came from Alliss, a 2&1 winner over Paul Runyan. After being all square with three to play, Alliss secured victory when Runyan thinned his shot from a greenside bunker at 17 where the ball flew out of bounds.

Britain were captained by 62-year-old JH Taylor who employed a fitness trainer to take his squad onto Southport beach every morning for a spot of exercise.

Less than two weeks later, Shute, whose three putts had cost his team the Ryder Cup in Lancashire, won the British Open at St Andrews, beating team-mate Craig Wood in a play-off. Five of the leading six players over the Old Course were American Ryder Cuppers, the odd man out being Easterbrook.

Easterbrook, who had gone into the final round tied for the lead, failed to join Shute and Wood in the play-off by one shot.

RYDER CUP FACTS

Christy O'Connor Sr and Neil Coles share the unenviable record for the most losses in Ryder Cup history – 21 matches each. O'Connor comes into his own when considering the most ever singles defeats, racking up a massive ten losses (from 14 matches). He's in good company though – Tony Jacklin is next on the list, with eight defeats from 11 matches

1935

RIDGEWOOD, NEW JERSEY SEPTEMBER 28-29

UNITED STATES 9
GREAT BRITAIN 3

CAPTAINS: WALTER HAGEN (US), CHARLES WHITCOMBE (GB)

Three brothers represented Britain and Ireland in 1935 – Charles, Reg and Ernest Whitcombe. But there was to be no family celebration as America swept through the foursomes 3-1 and the singles 6-2.

Of the 12 matches in New Jersey, the visitors would only win two and both of these went the full 36 holes. America's golfing superiority was beginning to take shape.

Percy Alliss was GB's only winner on singles day, beating Craig Wood 1up. Alliss had been three down at lunch against Wood, who was the Greg Norman of his era when it came to near-misses in major championships.

Wood and Norman remain the only players to lose all four majors in extra-holes. Wood suffered his fate between 1933 and 1939, and like Norman was at the wrong end of some outrageous strokes of bad luck. In 1935 at Augusta, Wood could only gasp in disbelief when told that Gene Sarazen had holed his now-famous Albatross two at the par-five 15th. Wood was being congratulated as champion in the clubhouse just as Sarazen holed his 4-wood shot from 220-yards.

After finishing runner-up in five major championships, Wood finally won the Masters and US Open in 1941 at the age of 39. In three Ryder Cup appearances (1931-33-35), Wood triumphed in only one of his four games.

Britain's only other success at Ridgewood Country Club came in the foursomes, courtesy of brothers Charles and Ernest, although they did manage to post a couple of halved games in the singles. Bill Cox battled back from five down at lunch to halve his match with Horton Smith. Cox even took the lead in the afternoon after winning six holes on the front nine. And in the battle of the British and US Open champions, Sam Parks holed from 40 feet on the final green to tie with England's Alf Perry.

There were some heavy beatings handed out by the hosts, particularly in the foursomes where none of the three American victories went beyond the 31st green.

Paul Runyan and Horton Smith trounced Cox and Edward Jarman 9&8, while captain Walter Hagen and Sarazen beat Perry and Jack Busson 7&6. It was to be Hagen's final tie in the Ryder Cup. Although he was to act as non-playing skipper two years later, he left himself out of the singles. Three months short of his 43rd birthday, Hagen's Cup career ended with seven wins, one half and one loss.

Before heading home, the British side travelled to Toronto to face the Canadians, who won convincingly, 9½-5½. Clearly, the gulf in standard between North America and Great Britain was becoming as wide as the Atlantic that separated them. For the next 40 years, visits to America would merely become exercises in damage limitation.

1937

SOUTHPORT & AINSDALE, LANCASHIRE, ENGLAND JUNE 29-30
GREAT BRITAIN 4
UNITED STATES 8

CAPTAINS: CHARLES WHITCOMBE (GB), WALTER HAGEN (US)

For the first time in Cup history, victory was achieved by the away team. It also signalled the start of American domination. Britain's next victory was 20 years away, while the Americans would lose only once in the next 48 years. Not that the hosts went down without a fight in 1937. Indeed there was much to enjoy from the contest, not least the debut of Dai Rees, who would remain unbeaten in his two matches. In the foursomes, he and skipper Charles Whitcombe halved with Gene

WALTER HAGEN'S RYDER CUP RE

FORMAT	PARTNER	F	A	OPPONENTS
FOURSOMES	JOHNNY GOLDEN	1	0	TED RAY
SINGLES		1	0	ARTHUR HAVERS
FOURSOMES	JOHNNY GOLDEN	1	0	ERNEST WHITCOMBE
SINGLES		0	1	GEORGE DUNCAN
FOURSOMES	DENNY SHUTE	1	0	GEORGE DUNCAN
SINGLES		1	0	CHARLES WHITCOMBE
FOURSOMES	GENE SARAZEN	0.5	0.5	ALLISS PERCY
SINGLES		1	0	ARTHUR LACEY
FOURSOMES	GENE SARAZEN	1	0	ALF PERRY

Sarazen and Denny Shute. The British duo won the 17th to bring the game all square and, after the Americans had enjoyed a favourable free-drop at the 18th where Sarazen's approach landed on the practice putting green, Rees was forced to hole out from six feet to tie the match. In the singles, the Welshman beat reigning Masters champion Byron Nelson 3&1, after being three down at one stage during the morning round. Britain's only other singles victory came from Henry Cotton, a 5&3 winner over Tony Manero, although Sam King did force a half against Shute. Shute, who chipped in twice during the morning round, had been four-up with 11 to play, but King grabbed half-a-point when he made a birdie at the last by holing from five feet.

One of the five singles matches that didn't go GB&I's way was Ralph Guldahl's 8&7 victory over Alf Padgham. The American was hot property during the late 1930s, and coming into the match was rated as possibly the best in the world. He won the US Open in 1937 and 1938, and added the Masters in 1939 having been a runner-up at Augusta the previous two years. In all, he won 13 times between 1936 and 1940 before retiring from pro golf at the extraordinarily early age of 31. One particularly interesting contest featured Sarazen and Percy Alliss, which the American won 1up. The key moment came at the par-three 15th where Sarazen hit an errant tee-shot. However, his ball struck a spectator and bounced onto the green from where he holed the putt for a birdie two to go one-up. Alliss, who made par, had earlier been three ahead.

From 4-4, the Americans won the last four singles to extend their winning margin to four points. As winning captain Walter Hagen explained at the prize-giving: "It was only towards the end that I was able to stop chewing the cigarettes and start smoking them."

Hagen would never be involved in another Ryder Cup. Although selected as non-playing captain for the 1939 match in Jacksonville, Florida, war broke out on September 3rd and the contest was never staged. Henry Cotton, named British skipper for the cancelled 1939 Ryder Cup, made up for the 1937 loss in Lancashire by winning the British Open at Carnoustie. Nine days after being part of a losing Ryder Cup team, Cotton carded rounds of 74-73-72-71 to win his second Open title. Every member of the triumphant American team took part, with Nelson posting the highest finish at fifth.

CORD

	WINNER	MARGIN	YEAR
FRED ROBSON	USA	2&1	1927
	USA	2&1	1927
HENRY COTTON	USA	2 HOLES	1929
	GB	10&8	1929
ARTHUR HAVERS	USA	10&9	1931
	USA	4&3	1931
CHARLES WHITCOMBE	HVD	–	1933
	USA	2&1	1933
JACK BUSSON	USA	7&6	1935

1931 UNITED STATES 9
GREAT BRITAIN 3

DAY 1	FOURSOMES		GB	
	ARCHIE COMPSTON	WILLIAM DAVIES	0	V
	GEORGE DUNCAN	ARTHUR HAVERS	0	V
	ABE MITCHELL	FRED ROBSON	1	V
	SYD EASTERBROOK	ERNEST WHITCOMBE	0	V

DAY 2	SINGLES			
	ARCHIE COMPSTON		0	V
	FRED ROBSON		0	V
	WILLIAM DAVIES		1	V
	ABE MITCHELL		0	V
	CHARLES WHITCOMBE		0	V
	BERT HODSON		0	V
	ERNEST WHITCOMBE		0	V
	HAVERS ARTHUR		1	V

1933 GREAT BRITAIN 6½
UNITED STATES 5½

DAY 1	FOURSOMES		GB	
	PERCY ALLISS	CHARLES WHITCOMBE	0.5	V
	ABE MITCHELL	ARTHUR HAVERS	1	V
	WILLIAM DAVIES	SYD EASTERBROOK	1	V
	ALF PADGHAM	ALF PERRY	0	V

DAY 2	SINGLES			
	ALF PADGHAM		0	V
	ABE MITCHELL		1	V
	ARTHUR LACEY		0	V
	WILLIAM DAVIES		0	V
	PERCY ALLISS		1	V
	ARTHUR HAVERS		1	V
	SYD EASTERBROOK		1	V
	CHARLES WHITCOMBE		0	V

US			WINNER	MARGIN
1	GENE SARAZEN	JOHNNY FARRELL	USA	8&7
1	WALTER HAGEN	DENNY SHUTE	USA	10&9
0	LEO DIEGEL	AL ESPINOSA	GB	3&1
1	BILLY BURKE	WILFRED COX	USA	3&2
1	BILLY BURKE		USA	7&6
1	GENE SARAZEN		USA	7&6
0	JOHNNY FARRELL		GB	4&3
1	WILFRED COX		USA	3&1
1	WALTER HAGEN		USA	4&3
1	DENNY SHUTE		USA	8&6
1	AL ESPINOSA		USA	2&1
0	CRAIG WOOD		GB	4&3

US			WINNER	MARGIN
0.5	GENE SARAZEN	WALTER HAGEN	HVD	–
0	OLIN DUTRA	DENNY SHUTE	GB	3&2
0	CRAIG WOOD	PAUL RUNYAN	GB	1 HOLE
1	ED DUDLEY	BILLY BURKE	USA	1 HOLE
1	GENE SARAZEN		USA	6&4
0	OLIN DUTRA		GB	9&8
1	WALTER HAGEN		USA	2&1
1	CRAIG WOOD		USA	4&3
0	PAUL RUNYAN		GB	2&1
0	LEO DIEGEL		GB	4&3
0	DENNY SHUTE		GB	1 HOLE
1	HORTON SMITH		USA	2&1

1935 UNITED STATES 9
GREAT BRITAIN 3

DAY 1

FOURSOMES		GB	
ALF PERRY	JACK BUSSON	0	V
ALF PADGHAM	PERCY ALLISS	0	V
BILL COX	EDWARD JARMAN	0	V
CHARLES WHITCOMBE	ERNEST WHITCOMBE	1	V

DAY 2

SINGLES			
JACK BUSSON		0	V
RICHARD BURTON		0	V
REG WHITCOMBE		0	V
ALF PADGHAM		0	V
PERCY ALLISS		1	V
BILL COX		0.5	V
ERNEST WHITCOMBE		0	V
ALF PERRY		0.5	V

1937 GREAT BRITAIN 4
UNITED STATES 8

DAY 1

FOURSOMES		GB	
ALF PADGHAM	HENRY COTTON	0	V
ARTHUR LACEY	BILL COX	0	V
CHARLES WHITCOMBE	DAI REES	0.5	V
PERCY ALLISS	RICHARD BURTON	1	V

DAY 2

SINGLES			
ALF PADGHAM		0	V
SAM KING		0.5	V
DAI REES		1	V
HENRY COTTON		1	V
PERCY ALLISS		0	V
RICHARD BURTON		0	V
ALF PERRY		0	V
ARTHUR LACEY		0	V

US			WINNER	MARGIN
1	GENE SARAZEN	WALTER HAGEN	USA	7&6
1	HENRY PICARD	JOHNNY REVOLTA	USA	6&5
1	PAUL RUNYAN	HORTON SMITH	USA	9&8
0	OLIN DUTRA	KY LAFOON	GB	1 HOLE
1	GENE SARAZEN		USA	3&2
1	PAUL RUNYAN		USA	5&3
1	JOHNNY REVOLTA		USA	2&1
1	OLIN DUTRA		USA	4&2
0	CRAIG WOOD		GB	1 HOLE
0.5	HORTON SMITH		HVD	–
1	HENRY PICARD		USA	3&2
0.5	SAM PARKS		HVD	–

US			WINNER	MARGIN
1	ED DUDLEY	BYRON NELSON	USA	4&2
1	RALPH GULDAHL	TONY MANERO	USA	2&1
0.5	GENE SARAZEN	DENNY SHUTE	HVD	–
0	HENRY PICARD	JOHNNY REVOLTA	GB	2&1
1	RALPH GULDAHL		USA	8&7
0.5	DENNY SHUTE		HVD	–
0	BYRON NELSON		GB	3&1
0	TONY MANERO		GB	5&3
1	GENE SARAZEN		USA	1 HOLE
1	SAM SNEAD		USA	5&4
1	ED DUDLEY		USA	2&1
1	HENRY PICARD		USA	2&1

1947

UNITED STATES 11
GREAT BRITAIN 1

CAPTAINS: BEN HOGAN (US), HENRY COTTON (GB)

Undoubtedly Britain's worst defeat during the era of 36-hole matches. But in many ways, the visitors had mitigating circumstances. Two years after the end of the Second World War, competitive golf in Britain was fairly thin on the ground. The United States' involvement in the war hadn't affected home life in quite the same way.

With the exception of 1943, the professional golf circuit in North America was fairly untouched by war, even if a number of players were called up to fight. In 1940 there were 27 pro events, with 30 (1941), 21 (1942), 3 (1943), 22 (1944) and 36 (1945) in subsequent years. So when the two nations met up for the 1947 renewal, the already professional and streetwise Americans were far more battled hardened than their allies across the Atlantic. The British team needed financial help from America to even make the trip. Robert Hudson, a fruit grower from Oregon, provided the cash and the use of his local club. He even met the team in New York as they pulled into port on the Queen Mary.

Before the match teed-off, British skipper Henry Cotton was less generous, in demanding that an official check the clubs of the American team. Having witnessed the severe amount of backspin that the home players were putting on the ball during practice, Cotton obviously believed there was something suspicious, or perhaps illegal, going on. But an inspection proved otherwise, and the superior American team proved unstoppable.

To make matters worse, Cotton was at the end of a severe beating in the opening foursomes. Together with Arthur Lees, he was thumped 10&9 by Ed Oliver and Lew Worsham – the reigning US Open champion. The scoreline equalled the widest winning margin in Ryder Cup history. Despite this, there was a glimmer of hope for Britain as they reached lunch on the first day up in two and down in two. But from there it was all downhill.

Jimmy Adams and Max Faulkner offered the best hope of a British foursomes victory, reaching the turn in 33 to go four-up on Ben Hogan and Jimmy Demaret. After 18 holes the lead was halved, and after lunch it was the turn of the Americans to go out in 33. The visitors held on until the 34th hole where despite Hogan fired a 6-iron to within 10 feet of the flag and his partner rattled home the putt for a birdie three and a decisive one-up lead.

It was left to Sam King, in the final match to save the whitewash. Thankfully, 11-0 became 11-1 as King beat Herman Keiser 4&3.

1949

GREAT BRITAIN 5
UNITED STATES 7

CAPTAINS: CHARLES WHITCOMBE (GB), BEN HOGAN (US)

On February 2nd, 1949, Ben Hogan was involved in a near-fatal road accident, when his Cadillac was struck head-on by a 10-ton greyhound bus. For over an hour, Hogan lay unconscious by the side of a dark Texas highway, while his wife Valerie waited for an ambulance. His injuries were considerable and it was touch-and-go whether he would survive. After 58 days in hospital, Hogan somehow pulled through. Yet his legs had taken a terrible hammering and it wasn't clear whether he would be able to walk again, let alone play golf. He did both, winning six Major titles in a little over three years.

In 1949, however, there was no more golf for Hogan, although he did accompany the American team to Yorkshire for the Ryder Cup as team captain. And he caused a stir when he complained about the grooves on the face of the British players' clubs, perhaps getting his own back for Henry Cotton's actions two years earlier. This time, though, an R&A rules official examined the clubs and ruled them illegal, the result being that local pro Jock Ballantine spent the night filing all the clubfaces until they met the required specifications.

It certainly annoyed the hosts who had already been insulted by the Americans' desire to bring their own food to England. Four years after the end of World War II, rationing was still in place on this side of the Atlantic and the visitors were taking no chances. They arrived with crates of steak, bacon, ribs and other meats. Upset by all of this, a determined British side raced into a 3-1 lead at the end of the foursomes. Fred Daly and Ken Bousfield were particularly impressive in beating Bob Hamilton and Skip Alexander 4&2. They scored 69 in the morning, and remained under par after lunch. America's sole victory came from Jimmy Demaret and Clayton Heafner, 4&3 winners over Charles Ward and Sam King.

But singles day belonged to the Americans, who took six out of eight ties. Only one of these victories went beyond the 33rd hole with some of the best golf played by Dutch Harrison against Max Faulkner. Harrison covered the opening six holes in 19 shots to move four ahead. After 18 holes he was seven-up, thanks to a 67. He eventually triumphed 8&7. The only Brit to win both his games was Jimmy Adams who registered a brace of 2&1 successes. In the end, a two-point loss was fairly respectable. Yet it could have been a tie had Heafner not finished 3-4-3-3 to beat former Open champion Richard Burton 3&2.

1947 UNITED STATES 11
GREAT BRITAIN 1

DAY 1

FOURSOMES		GB	
HENRY COTTON	ARTHUR LEES	0	V
FRED DALY	CHARLES WARD	0	V
JIMMY ADAMS	MAX FAULKNER	0	V
DAI REES	SAM KING	0	V

DAY 2

SINGLES		GB	
FRED DALY		0	V
JIMMY ADAMS		0	V
MAX FAULKNER		0	V
CHARLES WARD		0	V
ARTHUR LEES		0	V
HENRY COTTON		0	V
DAI REES		0	V
SAM KING		1	V

1949 GREAT BRITAIN 5
UNITED STATES 7

DAY 1

FOURSOMES		GB	
JIMMY ADAMS	MAX FAULKNER	1	V
FRED DALY	KEN BOUSFIELD	1	V
CHARLES WARD	SAM KING	0	V
RICHARD BURTON	ARTHUR LEES	1	V

DAY 2

SINGLES		GB	
MAX FAULKNER		0	V
JIMMY ADAMS		1	V
CHARLES WARD		0	V
DAI REES		1	V
RICHARD BURTON		0	V
SAM KING		0	V
ARTHUR LEES		0	V
FRED DALY		0	V

US			WINNER	MARGIN
1	ED OLIVER	LEW WORSHAM	USA	10&9
1	SAM SNEAD	LLOYD MANGRUM	USA	6&5
1	BEN HOGAN	JIMMY DEMARET	USA	2 HOLES
1	BYRON NELSON	HERMAN BARRON	USA	2&1
1	DUTCH HARRISON		USA	5&4
1	LEW WORSHAM		USA	3&2
1	LLOYD MANGRUM		USA	6&5
1	ED OLIVER		USA	4&3
1	BYRON NELSON		USA	2&1
1	SAM SNEAD		USA	5&4
1	JIMMY DEMARET		USA	3&2
0	HERMAN KEISER		GB	4&3

US			WINNER	MARGIN
0	DUTCH HARRISON	JOHNNY PALMER	GB	2&1
0	BOB HAMILTON	SKIP ALEXANDER	GB	4&2
1	JIMMY DEMARET	CLAYTON HEAFNER	USA	4&3
0	SAM SNEAD	LLOYD MANGRUM	GB	1 HOLE
1	DUTCH HARRISON		USA	8&7
0	JOHNNY PALMER		GB	2&1
1	SAM SNEAD		USA	6&5
0	BOB HAMILTON		GB	6&4
1	CLAYTON HEAFNER		USA	3&2
1	CHICK HARBERT		USA	4&3
1	JIMMY DEMARET		USA	7&6
1	LLOYD MANGRUM		USA	4&3

1951

PINEHURST, PINEHURST, NORTH CAROLINA
NOVEMBER 2-4

UNITED STATES 9½
GREAT BRITAIN 2½

CAPTAINS: SAM SNEAD (US), ARTHUR LACEY (GB)

Even with reigning British Open champion Max Faulkner in attendance, the visitors could offer little resistance to the all-conquering Americans. Faulkner, whose Open victory at Portrush in July was to be the last by a British player until Tony Jacklin's 18 years later, failed to contribute even half a point to the team's tally.

Partnering Dai Rees in the foursomes, Faulkner was unable to stop Clayton Heafner and Jack Burke winning 5&3. In the singles, the flamboyant Faulkner lost 4&3 to American captain Sam Snead, who was the reigning PGA Champion.

As it happened, Britain could only muster two victories out of 12, with both of these involving Arthur Lees.

In the foursomes Lees and Charlie Ward edged out Ed Oliver and Harry Ransom 2&1. The key moments came late in the first round when the British pair played the last five holes in only 16 shots to open-up a three-hole lead at lunch.

Oliver, nicknamed 'Porky', also fell victim to Lees in the singles as the gritty Yorkshireman won 2&1. Lees was always in control of the match, having reached the interval four up.

Britain's only other half-point came from Fred Daly in the singles. The Irishman, who had won the British Open at Hoylake in 1947, battled back from three down with three to play to tie Clayton Heafner. The American was bunkered at the last and Daly took full advantage.

In all, the hosts won nine of the dozen matches. Ben Hogan, the reigning Masters and US Open champion, was unstoppable. In the singles he beat Ward, who played under par golf for 34 holes, but still lost 3&2.

And then there was Jimmy Demaret who was playing in his third and final Ryder Cup. The extrovert American is the proud owner of a 100% Cup record, winning all of his six matches between 1947 and 1951.

In the singles he broke the heart of Welshman Dai Rees who took Demaret the distance before losing out by two holes. Rees said of Demaret: "I regard him as the greatest sand player I have ever seen. He was in 11 greenside bunkers that day and on

10 occasions got down with a splash and a putt."

The killer blow came at the 17th where the 41-year-old holed out from sand for a birdie two. At the end of the game Demaret, a three-time champion at Augusta, presented Rees with his match-winning sand wedge.

The biggest-winning margin belonged to Skip Alexander, one of the lesser-known members of the US team. Alexander, who the previous year survived serious injuries and burns from a plane crash, demolished John Panton 8&7.

The 1951 meeting was unusual in that the two-day contest lasted three days. On the rest day, both sets of players attended a college football match between North Carolina and Tennessee which, for the record, the latter won 27-0.

1953

WENTWORTH, SURREY, ENGLAND
OCTOBER 2-3

GREAT BRITAIN 5½
UNITED STATES 6½

CAPTAINS: HENRY COTTON (GB), LLOYD MANGRUM (US)

Britain snatched defeat from the jaws of victory and missed out on their first Ryder Cup triumph for 20 years. Unfortunately, Peter Alliss and Bernard Hunt went down in Ryder Cup folklore as the duo who lost their nerve while holding the destiny of the trophy in their youthful hands.

First came 22-year-old Alliss who was one-up on Jim Turnesa with three to play. At 16, the American's wild tee-shot was saved from landing in the trees when his ball bounced off a spectator. Turnesa hit his second into a greenside bunker but got up and down in two to save par and win the hole, after Alliss had played a poor pitch. The match was now all square.

Turnesa went one-up at 17 where Alliss hit his tee-shot out of bounds. But Alliss looked all set to square the match at the final hole after Turnesa sliced his drive into a wooded area down the right. The American, still well short of the green in three, could only make a bogey six, leaving Alliss needing a par to win the hole.

The young Briton had driven safely and was almost pin high in two after hitting a two-iron approach left of the green. But Alliss fluffed his first chip, leaving the ball a yard short of the putting surface. His next chip was good, running to within a yard of the pin. But his putt for par remained above ground and, after taking four shots from just off the green, Alliss had lost by one hole. The pain of this loss remained with Alliss for a long time, and despite his excellent overall record in the Ryder Cup, he is always remembered for losing this vital singles in 1953.

Next up, in the penultimate match, was Bernard Hunt who arrived at the final hole one ahead. His opponent Dave Douglas had lost the 17th after twice going out of bounds. At the concluding hole, Hunt left his second shot short, then over-hit his approach and from the back of the green three-putted for a bogey six, while Douglas took five. If Alliss and Hunt had parred the 18th, Britain would have sneaked home by a solitary point. Even one par out of two would have led to a tie.

Despite Hunt's half and Alliss's defeat, the hosts still came out on top in the singles, after losing the foursomes 3-1. Earlier on singles day, Harry Weetman recovered from four down with six to play to beat Sam Snead by one hole, while Fred Daly crushed Ted Kroll 9&7. Eric Brown beat visiting captain Lloyd Mangrum and, with just three matches left on the course, the Americans held a slender 5-4 advantage. In the final match, Ireland's Harry Bradshaw beat Fred Haas 3&2, leaving Alliss and Hunt to construct the last rites.

Skipper Mangrum admitted afterwards: "Never will I captain an American team again because of the nine thousands deaths I suffered in the last hour."

The exciting finale to the match at Wentworth eclipsed the excellent form shown by the Americans in the foursomes the previous day. Mangrum and Snead went round in 67 on the opening morning en route to beating Brown and John Panton 8&7. The result was never in doubt after Brown and Panton found themselves seven down inside nine holes. In the next match, Kroll and Jack Burke opened with a 66 to reach lunch seven up on Jimmy Adams and Hunt. They eventually triumphed 7&5.

When all the dust had settled, the only three players with 100% records from two games were Irishmen Daly and Bradshaw, along with the visiting Burke.

RYDER CUP FACTS

The fiery and committed Scot Eric Brown boasts an impressive Ryder Cup singles record. Brown won all four of his singles matches, where the US has traditionally been the stronger side, for a 100% record. He returned to the Ryder Cup as non-playing captain in the famous 1969 match when Europe earned a tie

Three sets of Uncles and Nephews have appeared in Ryder Cups: Christy O'Connor Sr and Jr; Sam and JC Snead; and Bob Goalby and Jay Haas. There have also been two father and son combinations – Percy and Peter Alliss and Antonio and Ignacio Garrido. The most frequent family bond has been brothers, though, with the Whitcombe, Hunt, Turnesa and Hebert brothers all represented over the years

1955

THUNDERBIRD, PALM SPRINGS, CALIFORNIA
NOVEMBER 5-6

UNITED STATES 8
GREAT BRITAIN 4

CAPTAINS: CHICK HARBERT (US), DAI REES (GB)

Yet another comprehensive home success for the States, who never looked in danger of losing. The highlight for Britain was the performance of rookie John Jacobs, playing in his only Ryder Cup match. Jacobs was the only visitor to win both his games. In the foursomes, he and John Fallon beat Chandler Harper and Jerry Barber one up, a scoreline that Jacobs repeated in his singles against reigning US Masters champion Cary Middlecoff.

In the foursomes victory, Fallon holed from four feet at the 36th, after Barber had chipped in. In his singles, Jacobs had to battle back from two down after 18 to hole a tricky five-footer on the final green for victory. After posting a 69 in the morning, Jacobs reached the turn after lunch in 32 strokes, before adding birdies at the 12th and 13th to go two-up. Middlecoff reduced the arrears with a monster putt for birdie at 17 but Jacobs held on after going round in 65. Strangely, Jacobs never returned to the Ryder Cup arena as a player, although he did captain the first two European teams in 1979 and 1981. He also went on to become one of the game's greatest teachers and coaches.

Arthur Lees and Eric Brown were other British winners on singles day, while Harry Bradshaw did his best to join them. Bradshaw, who lost a play-off for the Britain Open at Sandwich six years earlier, was all square at lunch against Jack Burke having made six straight threes. But the Irishman failed to maintain his momentum in the afternoon, and when Burke beat him 3&2, the Americans were home and dry. Dai Rees, the GB captain, came away empty-handed although, in his defence, he did have to face American superstar Sam Snead twice - losing 3&2 in foursomes and 3&1 at singles.

For the first time in Ryder Cup history, Britain used a points system to select its team. The leading seven in the table qualified automatically, with the final three wild cards chosen by those who had already booked their flights to California. The unfortunate Peter Alliss and Bernard Hunt, whose errors in 1953 had cost Britain victory at Wentworth, were both overlooked. Making his debut was Christy O'Connor Sr who would go on to play in 10 consecutive matches for GB through to 1973.

1957

LINDRICK, YORKSHIRE, ENGLAND
OCTOBER 4-5
GREAT BRITAIN 7½
UNITED STATES 4½
CAPTAINS: DAI REES (GB), JACK BURKE (USA)

Without the financial assistance of Sir Stuart Goodwin, Britain's momentous victory over the Americans in 1957 may not have taken place. Goodwin, a Yorkshire industrialist, offered the British PGA £10,000 to stage the event and he even allowed them to keep the gate receipts. In return, the PGA asked Goodwin to select a venue and so he chose Lindrick, close to the Nottinghamshire border.

The most remarkable aspect of GB's victory was their domination of the singles, after losing the foursomes 3-1. It would have been more in keeping with tradition had they won the foursomes handsomely, and then hung-on for dear-life in the singles. In fact, the only foursomes win came from Dai Rees and Ken Bousfield who beat Art Wall and Fred Hawkins 3&2.

Before victory could be achieved, Britain had to overcome some reported in-fighting, that in truth was exaggerated by the press. Max Faulkner and Harry Weetman, who had played together in the foursomes losing 4&3, were omitted from the singles. The following day's newspapers reported that there had been a massive argument between Weetman and his captain, regarding the former's absence from the singles.

However, Bernard Hunt, a member of the British side, believes it was comments made to the press by Weetman's wife that had been instrumental in producing these wild newspaper headlines. Hunt said that his own wife had witnessed a conversation between Rees and Weetman, who had offered to stand down in the singles.

Hunt added: "But then Harry's wife – Freda – told him he should be playing and I think that's what stirred it up. She went to the press and told someone that Dai had no right to leave her husband out. But my wife remembers the original conversation and there was never any argument between Dai and Harry."

On the course, Eric Brown won the opening match against American Tommy Bolt 4&3. Bolt, known for his explosive temper, later complained about the British crowds. He claimed: "They cheered when I missed a putt and sat on their hands if I played a good shot." It was reported that Bolt didn't even attend the prize-giving.

But the victories didn't stop there, as the British golfers grabbed the opportunity with

154

both hands. Not only did they win six of the eight singles, they triumphed with holes to spare. None of the victories (over 36 holes) reached the 16th tee in their second rounds. Christy O'Connor Sr and Rees both won 7&6, while Hunt trounced the reigning Masters champion Doug Ford 6&5.

O'Connor, all-square at lunch against Dow Finsterwald, won six of the opening eight holes in the afternoon round. As for Hunt, one-up at the interval, he put daylight between himself and Ford by reaching the turn in 32.

The Cup-clinching point arrived when Ken Bousfield beat the 1957 PGA Champion Lionel Hebert 4&3. And in the final match of the day, even the current US Open champion Dick Mayer failed to win his singles, halving with Harry Bradshaw.

The only home loss on singles day was Peter Alliss, beaten 2&1 by Fred Hawkins, who was one of only two Americans in the 1957 side that didn't win a Major championship during their career.

It was a famous final day fightback but the Americans were not to lose another Ryder Cup match for 28 years.

1959

ELDORADO, PALM DESERT, CALIFORNIA
NOVEMBER 6-7

UNITED STATES 8½
GREAT BRITAIN 3½

CAPTAINS: SAM SNEAD (US), DAI REES (GB)

Revenge for the Americans in a contest that almost never happened. While flying between Los Angeles and Palm Springs on October 29, the British and Irish team experienced a journey of sheer terror as their charter flight was tossed around in a violent storm.

Team member Bernard Hunt explained: "I had a camera on the seat next to me, and suddenly it started to float towards the ceiling. It became pinned to the roof because the plane was dropping pretty quickly. I looked around and everyone else was looking ill. Then the pilot got control again and the camera came down with a heavy bang on the seat. But suddenly the plane started dropping again and the same thing happened."

In the end the plane turned back and returned to Los Angeles, with Hunt adding: "We went to a hotel near the airport, all of us feeling bloody awful. I think everybody was physically sick after that."

Also on the flight was one member of the American team, Doug Ford, as well as Daily Express journalist Ronald Heager who wrote: "From our flying height of 13,000 feet, we dropped like a stone to 9,000 feet. It was like falling in a giant lift when the cable had snapped."

The trip to Palm Springs was finally made by greyhound bus but after this brush with death, the result hardly seemed to matter.

The foursomes was a close run affair which the Americans edged by a point. However, the visitors must have felt aggrieved at not sharing the series 2-2.

Harry Weetman and Dave Thomas were one-up on Americans Sam Snead and Cary Middlecoff as they reached the 17th green, where Thomas missed a five-footer that would have sealed a 2&1 victory. At the 18th, a difficult 470-yard par four, Thomas hit the perfect drive while Middlecoff hooked his tee-shot into the rough. Needing to make a birdie at best, or par at worst, Snead went for the green only to land in water near the putting surface. But instead of playing-safe by laying-up, Weetman opted to go for the

1951 UNITED STATES 9½
GREAT BRITAIN 2½

	FOURSOMES			GB	
DAY 1	MAX FAULKNER	DAI REES		0	V
	CHARLES WARD	ARTHUR LEES		1	V
	JIMMY ADAMS	JOHN PANTON		0	V
	FRED DALY	KEN BOUSFIELD		0	V

	SINGLES		GB	
DAY 2	JIMMY ADAMS		0	V
	DAI REES		0	V
	FRED DALY		0.5	V
	HARRY WEETMAN		0	V
	ARTHUR LEES		1	V
	CHARLES WARD		0	V
	JOHN PANTON		0	V
	MAX FAULKNER		0	V

green and ended-up joining Snead in the drink. It was an elementary error for an experienced player such as Weetman who had only needed to halve the hole to win the match.

After both teams had taken a penalty drop, the Americans chipped to 10-feet where Snead holed the putt for bogey while the Brits had to settle for a double-bogey six. It was a massive psychological blow not to end the day all square - but the British pair only had themselves to blame.

Snead, the captain, was back in the US team after missing the shock defeat in Yorkshire two years earlier. And the following day in the singles he faced Thomas again, beating him 6&5 over 36 holes. The Americans took the singles 6-2 to regain the trophy with a winning margin of five points.

The leading British player was Peter Alliss, unbeaten in two matches. The only visiting player to win on singles day was Eric Brown, who trounced Middlecoff 4&3. The fiery Scot never liked losing – particularly to Americans – and this victory maintained his 100% singles record from four Ryder Cup matches. He never played again in the Ryder Cup but 10 years later was non-playing captain when Britain pulled off a surprise 16-16 tie at Birkdale.

US			WINNER	MARGIN
1	CLAYTON HEAFNER	JACK BURKE	USA	5&3
0	ED OLIVER	HENRY RANSOM	GB	2&1
1	SAM SNEAD	LLOYD MANGRUM	USA	5&4
1	BEN HOGAN	JIMMY DEMARET	USA	5&4
1	JACK BURKE		USA	4&3
1	JIMMY DEMARET		USA	2 HOLES
0.5	CLAYTON HEAFNER		HVD	–
1	LLOYD MANGRUM		USA	6&5
0	ED OLIVER		GB	2&1
1	BEN HOGAN		USA	3&2
1	SKIP ALEXANDER		USA	8&7
1	SAM SNEAD		USA	4&3

1953 GREAT BRITAIN 5½ UNITED STATES 6½

DAY 1

FOURSOMES		GB	
HARRY WEETMAN	PETER ALLISS	0	V
ERIC BROWN	JOHN PANTON	0	V
JIMMY ADAMS	BERNARD HUNT	0	V
FRED DALY	HARRY BRADSHAW	1	V

DAY 2

SINGLES	GB	
DAI REES	0	V
FRED DALY	1	V
ERIC BROWN	1	V
WEETMAN HARRY	1	V
MAX FAULKNER	0	V
PETER ALLISS	0	V
BERNARD HUNT	0.5	V
HARRY BRADSHAW	1	V

1955 UNITED STATES 8 GREAT BRITAIN 4

DAY 1

FOURSOMES		GB	
JOHN FALLON	JOHN JACOBS	1	V
ERIC BROWN	SYD SCOTT	0	V
ARTHUR LEES	HARRY WEETMAN	0	V
HARRY BRADSHAW	DAI REES	0	V

DAY 2

SINGLES	GB	
CHRISTY O'CONNOR	0	V
SYD SCOTT	0	V
JOHN JACOBS	1	V
DAI REES	0	V
ARTHUR LEES	1	V
ERIC BROWN	1	V
HARRY BRADSHAW	0	V
HARRY WEETMAN	0	V

US			WINNER	MARGIN
1	DAVE DOUGLAS	ED OLIVER	USA	2&1
1	SAM SNEAD	LLOYD MANGRUM	USA	8&7
1	TED KROLL	JACK BURKE	USA	7&5
0	WALTER BURKEMO	CARY MIDDLECOFF	GB	1 HOLE

1	JACK BURKE		USA	2&1
0	TED KROLL		GB	9&7
0	LLOYD MANGRUM		GB	2 HOLES
0	SAM SNEAD		GB	1 HOLE
1	CARY MIDDLECOFF		USA	3&1
1	JIM TURNESA		USA	1 HOLE
0.5	DAVE DOUGLAS		HVD	–
0	FRED HAAS		GB	3&2

US			WINNER	MARGIN
0	CHANDLER	JERRY BARBER	GB	1 HOLE
1	DOUG FORD	TED KROLL	USA	5&4
1	JACK BURKE	TOMMY BOLT	USA	1 HOLE
1	SAM SNEAD	CARY MIDDLECOFF	USA	3&2

1	TOMMY BOLT		USA	4&2
1	CHICK HARBERT		USA	3&2
0	CARY MIDDLECOFF		GB	1 HOLE
1	SAM SNEAD		USA	3&1
0	MARTY FURGOL		GB	3&2
0	JERRY BARBER		GB	3&2
1	JACK BURKE		USA	3&2
1	DOUG FORD		USA	3&2

1957 GREAT BRITAIN 7½
UNITED STATES 4½

DAY 1	FOURSOMES		GB	
	PETER ALLISS	BERNARD HUNT	0	V
	KEN BOUSFIELD	DAI REES	1	V
	MAX FAULKNER	HARRY WEETMAN	0	V
	CHRISTY O'CONNOR SR	ERIC BROWN	0	V

DAY 2	SINGLES			
	ERIC BROWN		1	V
	PETER MILLS		1	V
	PETER ALLISS		0	V
	KEN BOUSFIELD		1	V
	DAI REES		1	V
	BERNARD HUNT		1	V
	CHRISTY O'CONNOR SR		1	V
	HARRY BRADSHAW		0.5	V

1959 UNITED STATES 8½
GREAT BRITAIN 3½

DAY 1	FOURSOMES		GB	
	BERNARD	ERIC BROWN	0	V
	KEN BOUSFIELD	DAI REES	0	V
	CHRISTY O'CONNOR SR	PETER ALLISS	1	V
	HARRY WEETMAN	DAVE THOMAS	0.5	V

DAY 2	SINGLES			
	NORMAN DREW		0.5	V
	KEN BOUSFIELD		0	V
	HARRY WEETMAN		0	V
	DAVE THOMAS		0	V
	CHRISTY O'CONNOR SR		0	V
	DAI REES		0	V
	PETER ALLISS		0.5	V
	ERIC BROWN		1	V

US			WINNER	MARGIN
1	DOUG FORD	DOW FINSTERWALD	USA	2&1
0	ART WALL	FRED HAWKINS	GB	3&2
1	TED KROLL	JACK BURKE	USA	4&3
1	DICK MAYER	TOMMY BOLT	USA	7&5

US			WINNER	MARGIN
0	TOMMY BOLT		GB	4&3
0	JACK BURKE		GB	5&3
1	FRED HAWKINS		USA	2&1
0	LIONEL HEBERT		GB	4&3
0	ED FURGOL		GB	7&6
0	DOUG FORD		GB	6&5
0	DOW FINSTERWALD		GB	7&6
0.5	DICK MAYER		HVD	–

US			WINNER	MARGIN
1	BOB ROSBURG	MIKE SOUCHAK	USA	5&4
1	JULIUS BOROS	DOW FINSTERWALD	USA	2 HOLES
0	ART WALL	DOUG FORD	GB	3&2
0.5	SAM SNEAD	CARY MIDDLECOFF	HVD	–

US			WINNER	MARGIN
0.5	DOUG FORD		HVD	–
1	SOUCHAK MIKE		USA	3&2
1	BOB ROSBURG		USA	6&5
1	SAM SNEAD		USA	6&5
1	ART WALL		USA	7&6
1	DOW FINSTERWALD		USA	1 HOLE
0.5	JAY HEBERT		HVD	–
0	CARY MIDDLECOFF		GB	4&3

1961

ROYAL LYTHAM & ST ANNES, LANCASHIRE, ENGLAND
OCTOBER 13-14

GREAT BRITAIN 9½
UNITED STATES 14½

CAPTAINS: DAI REES (GB), JERRY BARBER (US)

For the 14th staging of the Ryder Cup there was a new format. All matches were played over 18 holes, rather than 36. Instead of four foursomes on the first day there were now eight (four in the morning/four in the afternoon) while the number of second day singles was also doubled, from eight to 16.

All this made little difference to the outcome. The States led 6-2 after day one, and by the end of the first series of eight singles had moved 11-5 in front. This meant only one point was needed from the second round of eight singles to retain the trophy. It was duly delivered when Art Wall beat Harry Weetman by one hole.

With four matches left on the course, the US were 14-6 ahead, before the hosts made the scoreline more respectable thanks to wins from Dai Rees, Ken Bousfield and Neil Coles. Rees, the home captain, led by example, winning three of his four matches including both his singles against Jay Hebert and Doug Ford.

Peter Alliss also performed well in taking two and a half points out of four, while remaining unbeaten in the singles. His half-point came against American debutant Arnold Palmer in his opening singles. It was the only game (out of four) that Palmer didn't win. Another visitor, Billy Casper, won all three of his games.

One of Britain's rookies was Coles, who also managed to avoid defeat in two singles matches. Coles recalls his debut on the first morning: "The theory was that we must do well in the foursomes because the Americans normally dominate the singles. Our captain Dai Rees told us that we must get off to a good start. The first hole at Lytham is a par-three which on the opening day was playing into a stiff breeze. American Mike Souchak proceeded to take a one-iron off the tee and the ball never wavered from the stick, finishing about six inches away. My partner, Tom Haliburton, hit a two-wood and missed the green – just the start we wanted! And that was my baptism in the Ryder Cup." As it happened, Coles and Haliburton went the distance with Souchak and Bill Collins before losing by one hole. In fact, ten of the 24 games reached the 18th green – but GB could only come out on top in two of them.

RYDER CUP HISTORY – THE 1960s

Most of the pre-match talk concerned the absence of Sam Snead. The 49-year-old had been due to travel to England but made the mistake of playing in a low-key pro-am in Cincinnati without receiving permission. Leading pros were not allowed to compete in 'unofficial' tournaments that coincided with PGA Tour events. Yet Snead was in Cincinnati when he should have been playing in the 'official' Portland Open.

He was subsequently fined $500 and suspended from tournament play for six months. He therefore missed the Ryder Cup and his place was taken by Doug Ford. On hearing his ban, Snead said: "This is the worst slap in the face I have ever had. I went out of my way to enter enough tournaments to qualify for the Ryder Cup and I won't take it sitting down." Although the ban was reduced on appeal, Snead was never to play in the Ryder Cup again.

1963

EAST LAKE, ATLANTA, GEORGIA
OCTOBER 11-13

UNITED STATES 23
GREAT BRITAIN 9

CAPTAINS: ARNOLD PALMER (US), JOHN FALLON (GB)

The last Ryder Cup to feature a playing captain. Arnold Palmer not only skippered the American side, he also chose to play in all six sessions, winning four and losing two. For the first time, fourball matches were included, as the contest was extended from two days to three. The first 14 editions of the Ryder Cup had been two-day affairs.

While foursomes were a British invention, fourballs were said to be more American in style. But it didn't make any difference to the result, with the hosts winning both sets of eight matches 6-2, to hold a 12-4 lead going into the singles.

Although the opening morning foursomes had been shared (2-2), Britain won only one of the next 12 games. From there, the Americans claimed 11 points out of 16 on the final day, and in three of the six sessions the visitors didn't even win a single game.

The final series of eight singles was particularly disappointing as Britain picked up just half a point – courtesy of Peter Alliss, who tied with Tony Lema. Such was the American domination, that none of the other seven games even reached the 18th tee. The hosts had gone into the final session needing just half a point to retain the trophy.

163

Billy Casper led the American charge with four and a half points out of five, while team-mate Dow Finsterwald played in all six sessions and enjoyed a personal tally of four wins, one half, and one defeat.

One of Britain's few heroes was 32-year-old Alliss who, in the morning singles, had beaten US captain Palmer in front of his own adoring fans. One-down after 16, Palmer appeared to have squared the match at the penultimate hole where he made a birdie three. But Alliss followed suit with a 12-foot birdie putt of his own. At the 18th, the Briton two-putted from long range to edge out Palmer by one hole.

Yet some of the earlier play had been ragged, with a number of matches being won with over-par scores. In a first day foursomes Alliss and Christy O'Connor Senior failed to break 80 but still only lost on the final green to Billy Casper and Dave Ragan.

On the second day, however, Palmer and Dow Finsterwald produced some of the weekend's best golf. After winning their morning fourball 5&4, they needed only 30 shots to reach the turn in their afternoon encounter against Neil Coles and O'Connor Senior. These 23 holes had yielded 14 American birdies, and there was little GB could do to stem the flow. The visitors fielded brothers Bernard and Geoffrey Hunt, although they never teamed-up together in either the foursomes or fourballs. The best individual record in the British side belonged to rookie Brian Huggett, who ended with figures of two wins, one half and two losses.

The sorry display was compounded for the visiting team by the withdrawal of the British PGA's original offer to pay the airfares and expenses of the wives of players and officials. All in all, it was a trip best forgot for the British team.

1965

ROYAL BIRKDALE, LANCASHIRE, ENGLAND
OCTOBER 7-9
GREAT BRITAIN 12½
UNITED STATES 19½
CAPTAINS: HARRY WEETMAN (GB), BYRON NELSON (US)

Back in 1965, four of Royal Birkdale's final six holes were par-fives (13th, 15th, 17th and 18th). And, according to reports, this final group of holes decided the outcome of what was a fairly competitive match.

RYDER CUP HISTORY – THE 1960s

With none of these par-fives easily reachable in two, the delicate third shot proved to be the difference between the two sides. While the hosts generally preferred to use the lob, the Americans discovered that the best way to combat the coastal wind was to execute low punch shots into the green. And the US usually came out on top. According to one report, had the match been played over the front nine, Britain would have won by three points.

Much was made of two particular fourball games that were won by the Americans who snatched victory from the jaws of defeat. Dave Thomas and George Will were beaten by Don January and Tommy Jacobs despite being four up with eight to play. In the very next match, Lionel Platts and Peter Butler lost each of the last four holes to halve with Billy Casper and Gene Littler. Butler three-putted the 15th green, when he only needed two putts for a 4&3 victory, and at the next couple of holes Littler made a brace of birdies.

Even so, Britain only trailed 9-7 going into the singles. The first couple of days had been nip and tuck. Seven of the eight fourball games on day two went the distance, while the opening eight foursomes were shared 4-4.

On the first morning, Thomas and Will hammered Arnold Palmer and Dave Marr 6&5, before the Americans got their revenge after lunch. In the afternoon, Palmer and Marr made six straight threes from the second hole to reach the turn in 30. They went on to win 6&5.

The Americans made their vital victory surge early on singles day by winning the first four matches to put six-points of daylight between the two sides. They eventually triumphed by seven.

From a British perspective, it turned out to be one of Peter Alliss's finest hours. The BBC's 'voice of golf' won five of his six matches, including both his singles against Billy Casper (1up) and Ken Venturi (3&1). The latter also went on to become one of golf's most famous TV commentators.

For the States, Tony Lema was a key member, winning five out of six ties. In beating Christy O'Connor Senior 6&4 in the second series of singles, he was six-under-par for 14 holes. But Lema, the 1964 British Open champion, would never play in the Ryder Cup again. Ten months later, after competing in the PGA Championship at Firestone, Ohio, he was killed in a plane crash.

In the days before major sponsorship, Royal Birkdale member Brian Park, who was also a British PGA official, spent £11,000 of his own money to promote the match. His cash paid the way for a tented village and hospitality marquees.

But once again on the field of play, it was the Americans who were toasting success and collecting the trophy after winning 10½ points out of 16 on singles day.

RYDER CUP FACTS

Ray Floyd holds the distinction of being the oldest player to appear in a Ryder Cup. The veteran was 51 at the Belfry in 1993, where he won three of his four matches. However, over the years, Floyd has racked up the most losses of any US player – 16

1967

CHAMPIONS, HOUSTON, TEXAS
OCTOBER 20-22

UNITED STATES 23½
GREAT BRITAIN   8½

CAPTAINS: BEN HOGAN (US), DAI REES (GB)

Just another stroll in the park for the United States. In the 41 years since the introduction of 18-hole matches in 1961, this was Britain's (or Europe's) heaviest defeat.

The visitors didn't win any of the eight fourballs on day two, losing seven. And when Arnold Palmer beat Tony Jacklin 3&2 in the opening series of singles, to retain the trophy for the Americans, only 19 of the 32 ties had been completed. At this stage, the US led 16-3, with GB triumphant in only two games.

Palmer and Gardner Dickinson both recorded 100 per cent records from five matches , and the latter wasn't even taken to the 18th tee. Former PGA champion Bobby Nichols, making his only Ryder Cup appearance, was another success story claiming four wins and a half from five games.

Britain's best performer was Dave Thomas, who lost only once in five matches, of which two were won and another two halved. And in his solitary defeat, Thomas even managed to make it to the final green.

The American captain was tough-talking Texan Ben Hogan who let it be known that he was completely in charge of team affairs. Even the domineering Palmer, who back in the 1960s enjoyed the same attention as Tiger Woods does today, had to give second best to the old maestro. After hearing that Hogan had decided to use the 1.62 inch golf ball, as opposed to the more common 1.68 version that was played on the PGA Tour, Palmer questioned his captain's choice in the locker room at the Champions Golf Club. When Palmer suggested that he may not have any small balls with him, Hogan replied: "Who said you were playing, Palmer?"

At the age of 55, this was Hogan's final involvement with the Ryder Cup. For Britain it was both the start and end of eras. Dai Rees was making his fifth and last appearance as captain, having made his debut as a player 30 years earlier.

The 1967 contest also marked the beginning of Tony Jacklin's Cup career, which was to span 22 years. Jacklin teamed-up with Thomas to register Britain's only two victories on the opening couple of days. The 23-year-old from Scunthorpe lost both of his singles, although these defeats were against the in-form duo of Palmer and Dickinson. But his 42 per cent record (2-1-3) was fairly respectable given the circumstances.

The only British player to win both his singles was Neil Coles, who beat Doug Sanders 2&1 – morning and afternoon. By close of play the tourists had won just six of 32 matches, a pretty meagre showing against an American side that won 21, with five games halved. Such was the lack of interest in the game Stateside, that none of the big American television companies wanted to screen the match.

Even though TV coverage of golf was commonplace in the United States – and the box-office hit named Palmer was in attendance – the networks obviously felt that the visiting British side offered little attraction to its viewers.

1969

ROYAL BIRKDALE, LANCASHIRE, ENGLAND
SEPTEMBER 18-20

GREAT BRITAIN 16
UNITED STATES 16

CAPTAINS: ERIC BROWN (GB), SAM SNEAD (US)

One of the most exciting clashes in Cup history, with 18 of the 32 matches going down to the final hole. The match erupted on day two in a fourball game involving America's Dave Hill and Ken Still, against Britons Brian Huggett and Bernard Gallacher.

For most of the front nine, there was constant squabbling between the four players. At the first, Hill was told to stand still as Huggett putted. On the second green Gallacher was just about to putt when Still shouted to his own caddie not to hold the flag for the Scottish player. Still remarked that Gallacher's own caddie should be attending the flag. At the seventh, the British pair protested that Still had putted out of turn, and at the eighth the Americans were furious that they had been conceded a putt. Still had wanted to hole-out in order to show his partner the line. By this stage, both captains had arrived on the scene to try to calm things down. The match took a more normal route over the back nine with Hill and Still finally winning 2&1.

Huggett recalls that he and Hill even had an argument later that evening in the hotel. But the following week, when many of the British and American players were travelling together to compete in a tournament in Seattle, Hill approached Huggett on the plane and suggested they play a practice round together, which they did.

Going into the final day, the match was level at eight points apiece. In the first series of singles, Tony Jacklin beat Jack Nicklaus 4&3. And when the two captains nominated their players for the afternoon round of eight singles, Jacklin and Nicklaus were once again drawn to face each other – in the last match of the series.

By holing an enormous eagle putt to win the 17th, Jacklin had drawn level with Nicklaus. And, as they teed-up on the par-four 18th, their game was the only one left on the course. The match was tied at 15½-15½ and everything depended on this final hole. Both reached the 18th green in two. Jacklin was at the back of the green, while Nicklaus was slightly closer and to the right of the flag. Jacklin, putting first, ran his ball to within 20 inches of the cup. Nicklaus, with a putt to win the Ryder Cup, overshot by three feet before holing the return for a par four.

Nicklaus immediately picked up Jacklin's ball marker and conceded him his putt. The match ended in a tie, 16-16. As Nicklaus handed Jacklin back his marker, he said: "I don't think you would have missed but under the circumstances I'm not giving you the opportunity." It was a fine sporting gesture by the world's top golfer.

Jacklin was undoubtedly the British hero and on the crest of a wave. Less than three months earlier he had won the British Open at Royal Lytham, just a few days after his 25th birthday. The following June he would add the US Open title for good measure.

At Birkdale he played in all six sessions, winning four and halving two. In all, he covered 104 out of a maximum 108 holes. It was an incredible feat of skill, endurance and nerve. The gesture by Nicklaus on the final green, while warmly received by the hosts, angered a number of his team-mates who felt that Jacklin should have been made to putt out.

Strangely, Nicklaus was making his Ryder Cup debut at the age of 29. Despite his seven Major titles and 27 US Tour wins, a PGA rule stipulated that a player must have been a pro for five years before he could earn Ryder Cup qualifying points. The rule was changed when the match became more competitive and the Americans needed to field their strongest side. But if such a rule still applied today, Tiger Woods would not be teeing-up at The Belfry in September.

Nicklaus was one of ten US rookies in 1969, with only Billy Casper and Gene Littler having competed before.

RYDER CUP FACTS

Bernhard Langer has had more playing partners than any other player – 12. The full list reads: Manuel Pinero, Nick Faldo, Jose Maria Canizares, Sandy Lyle, Ken Brown, Ronan Rafferty, Mark James, Colin Montgomerie, Ian Woosnam, Barry Lane, Per-Ulrik Johansson and David Gilford

ARNOLD PALMER'S
RYDER CUP CAREER

FORMAT	PARTNER	F	A	OPPONENTS	WINNER	SCORE	YEAR
Foursomes	B. Casper	1	0	D. Rees & K. Bousfield	USA	2&1	1961
Foursomes	B. Casper	1	0	J. Panton & B. Hunt	USA	5&4	1961
Singles		0.5	0.5	P. Alliss	Hvd	–	1961
Singles		1	0	T. Haliburton	USA	2&1	1961
Foursomes	J. Pott	0	1	B. Huggett & G. Will	GB	3&2	1963
Foursomes	B. Casper	1	0	B. Huggett & G. Will	USA	5&4	1963
Fourballs	D. Finsterwald	1	0	B. Huggett & D. Thomas	USA	5&4	1963
Fourballs	D. Finsterwald	1	0	N. Coles & C. O'Connor Sr	USA	3&2	1963
Singles		0	1	P. Alliss	GB	1 hole	1963
Singles		1	0	G. Will	USA	3&2	1963
Foursomes	D. Marr	0	1	D. Thomas & G. Will	GB	6&5	1965
Foursomes	D. Marr	1	0	D. Thomas & G. Will	USA	6&5	1965
Fourballs	D. Marr	1	0	C. O'Connor Sr & P. Alliss	USA	6&4	1965
Fourballs	D. Marr	0	1	C. O'Connor Sr & P. Alliss	GB	2 holes	1965
Singles		1	0	J. Hitchcock	USA	3&2	1965
Singles		1	0	P. Butler	USA	2 holes	1965
Foursomes	G. Dickinson	1	0	C. O'Connor Sr & P. Alliss	USA	2&1	1967
Foursomes	G. Dickinson	1	0	M. Gregson & H. Boyle	USA	5&4	1967
Fourballs	J. Boros	1	0	G. Will & H. Boyle	USA	1 hole	1967
Singles		1	0	T. Jacklin	USA	3&2	1967
Singles		1	0	B. Huggett	USA	5&3	1967
Foursomes	G. Dickinson	1	0	P. Oosterhuis & P. Townsend	USA	2 holes	1971
Foursomes	G. Dickinson	1	0	P. Oosterhuis & P. Townsend	USA	1 hole	1971
Fourballs	G. Dickinson	1	0	P. Oosterhuis & B. Gallacher	USA	5&4	1971
Fourballs	J. Nicklaus	1	0	P. Townsend & H. Bannerman	USA	1 hole	1971
Singles		0.5	0.5	H. Bannerman	Hvd	–	1971
Singles		0	1	P. Oosterhuis	GB	3&2	1971
Foursomes	J. Nicklaus	1	0	M. Bembridge & E. Polland	USA	6&5	1973
Fourballs	J. Nicklaus	0	1	M. Bembridge & B. Huggett	GBI	3&1	1973
Foursomes	D. Hill	0	1	T. Jacklin & P. Oosterhuis	GBi	2 holes	1973
Fourballs	JC Snead	1	0	B. Barnes & P. Butler	USA	2 holes	1973
Singles		0	1	P. Oosterhuis	GBI	4&2	1973

■ **PLAYED: 32** ■ **WON: 22** ■ **HALVED: 2** ■ **LOST: 8** ■ **%: 71.88**

1961

GREAT BRITAIN 9½
UNITED STATES 14½

FOURSOMES		GB	
CHRISTY O'CONNOR SR	PETER ALLISS	1	V
JOHN PANTON	BERNARD HUNT	0	V
DAI REES	KEN BOUSFIELD	0	V
TOM HALIBURTON	NEIL COLES	0	V

FOURSOMES			
CHRISTY O'CONNOR SR	PETER ALLISS	0	V
JOHN PANTON	BERNARD HUNT	0	V
DAI REES	KEN BOUSFIELD	1	V
TOM HALIBURTON	NEIL COLES	0	V

SINGLES		
HARRY WEETMAN	0	V
RALPH MOFFITT	0	V
PETER ALLISS	0.5	V
KEN BOUSFIELD	0	V
DAI REES	1	V
NEIL COLES	0.5	V
BERNARD HUNT	1	V
CHRISTY O'CONNOR SR	0	V
HARRY WEETMAN	0	V
PETER ALLISS	1	V
BERNARD HUNT	0	V
TOM HALIBURTON	0	V
DAI REES	1	V
KEN BOUSFIELD	1	V
NEIL COLES	1	V
CHRISTY O'CONNOR SR	0.5	V

1961 RYDER CUP

US			WINNER	MARGIN
0	DOUG FORD	GENE LITTLER	GB	4&3
1	ART WALL	JAY HEBERT	USA	4&3
1	ARNOLD PALMER	BILLY CASPER	USA	2&1
1	BILL COLLINS	MIKE SOUCHAK	USA	1 HOLE
1	ART WALL	JAY HEBERT	USA	1 HOLE
1	ARNOLD PALMER	BILLY CASPER	USA	5&4
0	BILL COLLINS	MIKE SOUCHAK	GB	4&2
1	JERRY BARBER	DOW FINSTERWALD	USA	1 HOLE
1	DOUG FORD		USA	1 HOLE
1	MIKE SOUCHAK		USA	5&4
0.5	ARNOLD PALMER		HVD	–
1	BILLY CASPER		USA	5&3
0	JAY HEBERT		GB	2&1
0.5	GENE LITTLER		HVD	–
0	JERRY BARBER		GB	5&4
1	DOW FINSTERWALD		USA	2&1
1	ART WALL		USA	1 HOLE
0	BILL COLLINS		GB	3&2
1	MIKE SOUCHAK		USA	2&1
1	ARNOLD PALMER		USA	2&1
0	DOUG FORD		GB	4&3
0	JERRY BARBER		GB	1 HOLE
0	DOW FINSTERWALD		GB	1 HOLE
0.5	GENE LITTLER		HVD	–

1963 UNITED STATES 23
GREAT BRITAIN 9

DAY	FOURSOMES		GBI	
1	BRIAN HUGGETT	GEORGE WILL	1	V
	CHRISTY O'CONNOR SR	PETER ALLISS	0	V
	NEIL COLES	BERNARD HUNT	0.5	V
	DAVE THOMAS	HARRY WEETMAN	0.5	V
	DAVE THOMAS	HARRY WEETMAN	0	V
	BRIAN HUGGETT	GEORGE WILL	0	V
	NEIL COLES	GEOFFREY HUNT	0	V
	TOM HALIBURTON	BERNARD HUNT	0	V

DAY	FOURBALLS		GBI	
2	BRIAN HUGGETT	DAVE THOMAS	0	V
	PETER ALLISS	BERNARD HUNT	0.5	V
	HARRY WEETMAN	GEORGE WILL	0	V
	NEIL COLES	CHRISTY O'CONNOR SR	1	V
	NEIL COLES	CHRISTY O'CONNOR SR	0	V
	PETER ALLISS	BERNARD HUNT	0	V
	TOM HALIBURTON	GEOFFREY HUNT	0	V
	BRIAN HUGGETT	DAVE THOMAS	0.5	V

DAY	SINGLES	GBI	
3	GEOFFREY HUNT	0	V
	BRIAN HUGGETT	1	V
	PETER ALLISS	1	V
	NEIL COLES	0.5	V
	DAVE THOMAS	0	V
	CHRISTY O'CONNOR SR	0	V
	HARRY WEETMAN	1	V
	BERNARD HUNT	1	V
	GEORGE WILL	0	V
	NEIL COLES	0	V
	PETER ALLISS	0.5	V
	TOM HALIBURTON	0	V
	HARRY WEETMAN	0	V
	CHRISTY O'CONNOR SR	0	V
	DAVE THOMAS	0	V
	BERNARD HUNT	0	V

1963 RYDER CUP

US			WINNER	MARGIN
0	ARNOLD PALMER	JOHNNY POTT	GB	3&2
1	BILLY CASPER	DAVE RAGAN	USA	1 HOLE
0.5	JULIUS BOROS	TONY LEMA	HVD	–
0.5	GENE LITTLER	DOW FINSTERWALD	HVD	–
1	BILLY MAXWELL	BOB GOALBY	USA	4&3
1	ARNOLD PALMER	BILLY CASPER	USA	5&4
1	GENE LITTLER	DOW FINSTERWALD	USA	2&1
1	JULIUS BOROS	TONY LEMA	USA	1 HOLE
1	ARNOLD PALMER	DOW FINSTERWALD	USA	5&4
0.5	GENE LITTLER	JULIUS BOROS	HVD	–
1	BILLY CASPER	BILLY MAXWELL	USA	3&2
0	BOB GOALBY	DAVE RAGAN	GB	1 HOLE
1	ARNOLD PALMER	DOW FINSTERWALD	USA	3&2
1	TONY LEMA	JOHNNY POTT	USA	1 HOLE
1	BILLY CASPER	BILLY MAXWELL	USA	2&1
0.5	BOB GOALBY	DAVE RAGAN	HVD	–
1	TONY LEMA		USA	5&3
0	JOHNNY POTT		GB	3&1
0	ARNOLD PALMER		GB	1 HOLE
0.5	BILLY CASPER		HVD	–
1	BOB GOALBY		USA	3&2
1	GENE LITTLER		USA	1 HOLE
0	JULIUS BOROS		GB	1 HOLE
0	DOW FINSTERWALD		GB	2 HOLES
1	ARNOLD PALMER		USA	3&2
1	DAVE RAGAN		USA	2&1
0.5	TONY LEMA		HVD	–
1	GENE LITTLER		USA	6&5
1	JULIUS BOROS		USA	2&1
1	BILLY MAXWELL		USA	2&1
1	DOW FINSTERWALD		USA	4&3
1	BOB GOALBY		USA	2&1

1965 GREAT BRITAIN 12½
UNITED STATES 19½

DAY 1

FOURSOMES

		GB	
LIONEL PLATTS	PETER BUTLER	0	V
DAVE THOMAS	GEORGE WILL	1	V
NEIL COLES	BERNARD HUNT	0	V
CHRISTY O'CONNOR SR	PETER ALLISS	1	V
DAVE THOMAS	GEORGE WILL	0	V
CHRISTY O'CONNOR SR	PETER ALLISS	1	V
JIMMY MARTIN	JIMMY HITCHCOCK	0	V
NEIL COLES	BERNARD HUNT	1	V

DAY 2

FOURBALLS

DAVE THOMAS	GEORGE WILL	0	V
LIONEL PLATTS	PETER BUTLER	0.5	V
CHRISTY O'CONNOR SR	PETER ALLISS	0	V
NEIL COLES	BERNARD HUNT	1	V
CHRISTY O'CONNOR SR	PETER ALLISS	1	V
DAVE THOMAS	GEORGE WILL	0	V
LIONEL PLATTS	PETER BUTLER	0.5	V
NEIL COLES	BERNARD HUNT	0	V

DAY 3

SINGLES

JIMMY HITCHCOCK		0	V
LIONEL PLATTS		0	V
PETER BUTLER		0	V
NEIL COLES		0	V
BERNARD HUNT		1	V
DAVE THOMAS		0	V
PETER ALLISS		1	V
GEORGE WILL		0.5	V
CHRISTY O'CONNOR SR		0	V
JIMMY HITCHCOCK		0	V
PETER BUTLER		0	V
PETER ALLISS		1	V
NEIL COLES		1	V
GEORGE WILL		0	V
BERNARD HUNT		0	V
LIONEL PLATTS		1	V

1965 RYDER CUP

US			WINNER	MARGIN
1	JULIUS BOROS	TONY LEMA	USA	1 HOLE
0	ARNOLD PALMER	DAVE MARR	GB	6&5
1	BILLY CASPER	GENE LITTLER	USA	2&1
0	KEN VENTURI	DON JANUARY	GB	5&4
1	ARNOLD PALMER	DAVE MARR	USA	6&5
0	BILLY CASPER	GENE LITTLER	GB	2&1
1	JULIUS BOROS	TONY LEMA	USA	5&4
0	KEN VENTURI	DON JANUARY	GB	3&2
1	DON JANUARY	TOMMY JACOBS	USA	1 HOLE
0.5	BILLY CASPER	GENE LITTLER	HVD	–
1	ARNOLD PALMER	DAVE MARR	USA	6&4
0	JULIUS BOROS	TONY LEMA	GB	1 HOLE
0	ARNOLD PALMER	DAVE MARR	GB	2 HOLES
1	DON JANUARY	TOMMY JACOBS	USA	1 HOLE
0.5	BILLY CASPER	GENE LITTLER	HVD	–
1	KEN VENTURI	TONY LEMA	USA	1 HOLE
1	ARNOLD PALMER		USA	3&2
1	JULIUS BOROS		USA	4&2
1	TONY LEMA		USA	1 HOLE
1	DAVE MARR		USA	2 HOLES
0	GENE LITTLER		GB	2 HOLES
1	TOMMY JACOBS		USA	2&1
0	BILLY CASPER		GB	1 HOLE
0.5	DON JANUARY		HVD	–
1	TONY LEMA		USA	6&4
1	JULIUS BOROS		USA	2&1
1	ARNOLD PALMER		USA	2 HOLES
0	KEN VENTURI		GB	3&1
0	BILLY CASPER		GB	3&2
1	GENE LITTLER		USA	2&1
1	DAVE MARR		USA	1 HOLE
0	TOMMY JACOBS		GB	1 HOLE

UNITED STATES 23½
GREAT BRITAIN 8½

DAY 1	FOURSOMES		GB	
	BRIAN HUGGETT	GEORGE WILL	0.5	V
	CHRISTY O'CONNOR SR	PETER ALLISS	0	V
	TONY JACKLIN	DAVE THOMAS	1	V
	NEIL COLES	BERNARD HUNT	0	V
	BRIAN HUGGETT	GEORGE WILL	0	V
	MALCOLM GREGSON	HUGH BOYLE	0	V
	TONY JACKLIN	DAVE THOMAS	1	V
	CHRISTY O'CONNOR SR	PETER ALLISS	0	V

DAY 2	FOURBALLS			
	CHRISTY O'CONNOR SR	PETER ALLISS	0	V
	NEIL COLES	BERNARD HUNT	0	V
	TONY JACKLIN	DAVE THOMAS	0	V
	BRIAN HUGGETT	GEORGE WILL	0	V
	NEIL COLES	BERNARD HUNT	0	V
	PETER ALLISS	MALCOLM GREGSON	0	V
	GEORGE WILL	HUGH BOYLE	0	V
	TONY JACKLIN	DAVE THOMAS	0.5	V

DAY 3	SINGLES			
	HUGH BOYLE		0	V
	PETER ALLISS		0	V
	TONY JACKLIN		0	V
	BRIAN HUGGETT		1	V
	NEIL COLES		1	V
	MALCOLM GREGSON		0	V
	DAVE THOMAS		0.5	V
	BERNARD HUNT		0.5	V
	BRIAN HUGGETT		0	V
	PETER ALLISS		1	V
	TONY JACKLIN		0	V
	CHRISTY O'CONNOR SR		0	V
	GEORGE WILL		0	V
	MALCOLM GREGSON		0	V
	BERNARD HUNT		0.5	V
	NEIL COLES		1	V

1967 RYDER CUP

US			WINNER	MARGIN
0.5	BILLY CASPER	JULIUS BOROS	HVD	
1	ARNOLD PALMER	GARDNER DICKINSON	USA	2&1
0	DOUG SANDERS	GAY BREWER	GB	4&3
1	BOBBY NICHOLS	JOHNNY POTT	USA	6&5
1	BILLY CASPER	JULIUS BOROS	USA	1 HOLE
1	ARNOLD PALMER	GARDNER DICKINSON	USA	5&4
0	GENE LITTLER	AL GEIBERGER	GB	3&2
1	BOBBY NICHOLS	JOHNNY POTT	USA	2&1
1	BILLY CASPER	GAY BREWER	USA	3&2
1	BOBBY NICHOLS	JOHNNY POTT	USA	1 HOLE
1	GENE LITTLER	AL GEIBERGER	USA	1 HOLE
1	GARDNER DICKINSON	DOUG SANDERS	USA	3&2
1	BILLY CASPER	GAY BREWER	USA	5&3
1	GARDNER DICKINSON	DOUG SANDERS	USA	3&2
1	ARNOLD PALMER	JULIUS BOROS	USA	1 HOLE
0.5	GENE LITTLER	AL GEIBERGER	HVD	–
1	GAY BREWER		USA	4&3
1	BILLY CASPER		USA	2&1
1	ARNOLD PALMER		USA	3&2
0	JULIUS BOROS		GB	1 HOLE
0	DOUG SANDERS		GB	2&1
1	AL GEIBERGER		USA	4&2
0.5	GENE LITTLER		HVD	–
0.5	BOBBY NICHOLS		HVD	–
1	ARNOLD PALMER		USA	5&3
0	GAY BREWER		GB	2&1
1	GARDNER DICKINSON		USA	3&2
1	BOBBY NICHOLS		USA	3&2
1	JOHNNY POTT		USA	3&1
1	AL GEIBERGER		USA	2&1
0.5	JULIUS BOROS		HVD	–
0	DOUG SANDERS		GB	2&1

1969
GREAT BRITAIN 16
UNITED STATES 16

DAY 1	FOURSOMES		GB	
	NEIL COLES	BRIAN HUGGETT	1	V
	BERNARD GALLACHER	MAURICE BEMBRIDGE	1	V
	TONY JACKLIN	PETER TOWNSEND	1	V
	CHRISTY O'CONNOR SR	PETER ALLISS	0.5	V
	NEIL COLES	BRIAN HUGGETT	0	V
	BERNARD GALLACHER	MAURICE BEMBRIDGE	0	V
	TONY JACKLIN	PETER TOWNSEND	1	V
	PETER BUTLER	BERNARD HUNT	0	V

DAY 2	FOURBALLS			
	CHRISTY O'CONNOR SR	PETER TOWNSEND	1	V
	BRIAN HUGGETT	ALEX CAYGILL	0.5	V
	BRIAN BARNES	PETER ALLISS	0	V
	TONY JACKLIN	NEIL COLES	1	V
	PETER BUTLER	PETER TOWNSEND	0	V
	BRIAN HUGGETT	BERNARD GALLACHER	0	V
	MAURICE BEMBRIDGE	BERNARD HUNT	0.5	V
	TONY JACKLIN	NEIL COLES	0.5	V

DAY 3	SINGLES			
	PETER ALLISS		0	V
	PETER TOWNSEND		0	V
	NEIL COLES		1	V
	BRIAN BARNES		0	V
	CHRISTY O'CONNOR SR		1	V
	MAURICE BEMBRIDGE		1	V
	PETER BUTLER		1	V
	TONY JACKLIN		1	V
	BRIAN BARNES		0	V
	BERNARD GALLACHER		1	V
	MAURICE BEMBRIDGE		0	V
	PETER BUTLER		1	V
	NEIL COLES		0	V
	CHRISTY O'CONNOR SR		0	V
	BRIAN HUGGETT		0.5	V
	TONY JACKLIN		0.5	V

1969 RYDER CUP

US			WINNER	MARGIN
0	MILLER BARBER	RAY FLOYD	GB	3&2
0	LEE TREVINO	KEN STILL	GB	2&1
0	DAVE HILL	TOMMY AARON	GB	3&1
0.5	BILLY CASPER	FRANK BEARD	HVD	–
1	DAVE HILL	TOMMY AARON	USA	1 HOLE
1	LEE TREVINO	GENE LITTLER	USA	1 HOLE
0	BILLY CASPER	FRANK BEARD	GB	1 HOLE
1	JACK NICKLAUS	DAN SIKES	USA	1 HOLE
0	DAVE HILL	DALE DOUGLASS	GB	1 HOLE
0.5	MILLER BARBER	RAY FLOYD	HVD	–
1	LEE TREVINO	GENE LITTLER	USA	1 HOLE
0	JACK NICKLAUS	DAN SIKES	GB	1 HOLE
1	BILLY CASPER	FRANK BEARD	USA	2 HOLES
1	DAVE HILL	KEN STILL	USA	2&1
0.5	TOMMY AARON	RAY FLOYD	HVD	–
0.5	LEE TREVINO	MILLER BARBER	HVD	–
1	LEE TREVINO		USA	2&1
1	DAVE HILL		USA	5&4
0	TOMMY AARON		GB	1 HOLE
1	BILLY CASPER		USA	1 HOLE
0	FRANK BEARD		GB	5&4
0	KEN STILL		GB	1 HOLE
0	RAY FLOYD		GB	1 HOLE
0	JACK NICKLAUS		GB	4&3
1	DAVE HILL		USA	4&2
0	LEE TREVINO		GB	4&3
1	MILLER BARBER		USA	7&6
0	DALE DOUGLASS		GB	3&2
1	DAN SIKES		USA	4&3
1	GENE LITTLER		USA	2&1
0.5	BILLY CASPER		HVD	–
0.5	JACK NICKLAUS		HVD	–

1971

OLD WARSON, ST LOUIS, MISSOURI
SEPTEMBER 16-18

UNITED STATES 18½
GREAT BRITAIN 13½

CAPTAINS: JAY HEBERT (US), ERIC BROWN (GB)

After the emotional, gripping finale of 1969, normal service was resumed two years later. But, bearing in mind the strength in depth of American golf during the 1970s, the visitors did extremely well to limit the margin to just five points. In fact, Great Britain even managed to grab a one point advantage at the end of the first day (4½-3½). But on day two they could only win one of eight fourballs to fall 10-6 behind. Much of the talk on the second day concerned an unsavoury incident during a morning encounter involving Americans Arnold Palmer and Gardner Dickinson, and their opponents Bernard Gallacher and Peter Oosterhuis. The hosts were one-up when they arrived at the 207-yard, par-three seventh. Palmer played first, and as the ball came to rest beyond the hole Gallacher's caddie, an American called Jack McLeod, innocently shouted: "Great shot, what did you hit?"

Palmer replied: "A five-iron". But McLeod's instinctive inquiry had infringed the rules, which state that advice can only be transferred between partners and their caddies. Technically, McLeod had asked one of his opponents for advice, which is not permitted.

Gallacher, not as big a hitter as Palmer, took a three-iron but it mattered little. The outcome was that the British pair had to forfeit the hole. Gallacher claimed that instead of turning a blind eye to the incident, one of the Americans had complained to the referee about his caddie's remarks while walking off the green after both sides had made par. The 22-year-old Scot felt that neither Palmer nor Dickinson had played within the spirit of the law.

The Americans denied Gallacher's accusation, stressing that the match referee had heard the caddie's comments and had little option but to award the hosts the hole. As a result of this penalty, the Americans went two-up, and finally won the contest 5&4. Gallacher added that his caddie lost confidence as a result of the ruling.

Oosterhuis, a rookie, went on to win both his singles including a 3&2 victory over Palmer while Brian Barnes was another British success story on the final day with victories over Mason Rudolph and Miller Barber.

For the Americans, Dickinson triumphed in four of his five ties, while Jack

Nicklaus lost his opening game but then won the next five. Even Lee Trevino, who arrived in St Louis having just had surgery for appendicitis, won three of his five matches and halved another. In the second round of singles he trounced Brian Huggett 7&6.

Possibly the unluckiest player of the week was Englishman Peter Townsend, who lost all six of his matches. The 25-year-old reached the 18th green four times but came away pointless. And on one occasion, he and Harry Bannerman put together a better-ball score of 64 only to lose to Nicklaus and Palmer's 65. To add insult to injury Nicklaus holed a 15-foot birdie putt at 18 to win by one hole.

Among America's rookies was JC Snead, a nephew of former player and captain Sam. JC went on to to play in two more Cups and in 1971 won all four of his matches.

1973

MUIRFIELD, NR EDINBURGH, SCOTLAND
SEPTEMBER 20-22

GREAT BRITAIN & IRELAND 13
UNITED STATES 19

CAPTAINS: BERNARD HUNT (GB&I), JACK BURKE (US)

The only Ryder Cup yet to be staged in Scotland and for two days it was a competitive contest. Hopes were high when Britain led 5½- 2½ at the close of play on day one. The Americans were restricted to just two wins from eight matches as the Scottish pairing of Brian Barnes and Bernard Gallacher led from the front.

Barnes and Gallacher were the first pair out in both sessions on the opening day. In the morning they survived a tense tussle against Lee Trevino and Billy Casper. All square after 16, the Brits birdied the par-five 17th to go one-up only for Gallacher to drive into a bunker at the last. However, Gallacher made up for his earlier error with a great pitch leaving Barnes to single putt for a half, and win the match by one hole.

After lunch they demolished Tommy Aaron and Gay Brewer 5&4, thanks largely to a hat-trick of birdies from Barnes at the 8th, 9th and 10th. As the British team headed back to their hotel on day one, spirits were high within the camp. But joy turned to disappointment when Gallacher was forced to pull out of his foursomes the following morning with food poisoning. It was a critical blow for the hosts.

His replacement was Peter Butler who became the first player in Ryder Cup history to make a hole-in-one, which came at the 16th against Jack Nicklaus and Tom Weiskopf in the foursomes. Alas Butler was unable to consistently deliver the sort of golf played by Gallacher the previous day. In partnership with Barnes, Butler lost both his matches on day two, although each game did at least reach the 18th green.

The hosts still led by three points at lunchtime on the second day but then failed to win any of the afternoon's four fourballs. After two days the match was tied at 8-8 – but the British dream ended there. Once again, the Americans proved invincible in the singles, which they swept through 11-5. In the first round of eight singles Britain's only winner was Jacklin, although Peter Oosterhuis and Maurice Bembridge emerged with great credit.

Oosterhuis remained unbeaten in the singles, halving with Trevino in the morning and beating Arnold Palmer 4&2 after lunch. In all, he claimed four points out of six during the three-day match (three wins, two halves, one loss).

Bembridge, meanwhile, had two memorable singles matches against Jack Nicklaus, both of which went the distance. The morning clash was halved, while Nicklaus won the afternoon encounter by two holes. Nicklaus was on top form, winning four of his six games and losing only once while the only Americans to win both singles were Casper and JC Snead. One man who does not have happy memories of the 1973 match is John Garner who sat out all six sessions. Captain Bernard Hunt left Garner on the sidelines for the entire match while selecting Clive Clark only once.

Hunt's opposite number Jack Burke probably felt that lightening was about to strike twice when Britain led 7½- 4½ midway through day two. Burke had also been captain in 1957 when the Americans suffered a rare defeat. But he was saved on singles day as his players came to his rescue. One particular highlight for Britain came in a first day fourball when Jacklin and Oosterhuis birdied each of the opening seven holes against Weiskopf and Casper to reach the turn in 28. The Americans, who themselves had gone out in 31 to trail by three, managed to reduce the deficit to just one hole after 13, before Jacklin and Oosterhuis pulled away again to win 3&1.

RYDER CUP FACTS

Only five teams have ever won the Cup after being behind going into the final day. The Americans famously managed it in 1999, with that sensational run of singles victories. A similar fate struck the Europeans in 1949, when the Americans also won six singles matches on the bounce, to turn around a 3-1 European lead. Europe pulled off the feat memorably in 1995, turning round a 9-7 overnight deficit on a day when nine of the twelve matches went to the final hole. The earliest example comes from 1929, when the British team turned round a single point deficit to take the contest 7-5. Great Britain also reversed a losing situation in 1957, losing only one singles match on the final day

Nick Faldo boasts the most Ryder Cup appearances of any player, with 11. In fact, the Europeans hold the top four placings in this category, through Christy O'Connor Sr (10), Bernhard Langer (10 in 2002) and Dai Rees (9)

1975

LAUREL VALLEY, LIGONIER, PENNSYLVANIA SEPTEMBER 19-21

UNITED STATES 21
GREAT BRITAIN & IRELAND 11

CAPTAINS: ARNOLD PALMER (US), BERNARD HUNT (GB&I)

One of the most one-sided matches in Ryder Cup history. The Americans won all four foursomes on the opening morning, with only one game reaching as far as the 17th tee. By the end of day one they were 6½-1½ ahead, and with two days completed the Americans led 12½- 3½. The visitors won only two of the opening 16 ties, and both of these involved Tony Jacklin.

To rub salt into the wounds of the British and Irish golfers they clinched the match with more than a session to spare. By lunchtime on Sunday, the US were 17½- 6½ in front, leaving the final round of eight singles meaningless.

On Sunday morning, Brian Barnes had beaten Jack Nicklaus 4&2, so to add some spice to an otherwise low-key final session of play, it was agreed that Barnes should face Nicklaus again. According to Barnes: "It was the first time in the history of the Ryder Cup that the draw was changed after it had been made. Jack went to Arnold (Palmer, US captain) and suggested the draw be changed, so he could have the opportunity of playing me again, just to keep the crowd interested." All parties agreed and Barnes duly won again, this time by 2&1.

There were few other highlights for Britain all week. However, Peter Oosterhuis maintained his excellent singles record with victories over Johnnie Miller and JC Snead. Two down after 11 against Miller, 'Oosty' made six straight threes to win by two holes.

Tommy Horton also enjoyed singles day. In the morning he halved with Hale Irwin (the 1974 US Open winner) before beating Lou Graham (the reigning US Open champion) 2&1 in the afternoon.

GB&I won half of the eight singles on Sunday afternoon, but whether this would have happened had the match still been alive is open to conjecture.

Irwin was the week's leading player, taking four and a half points out of five, while team-mate Tom Weiskopf won all four of his games without going beyond the 16th green. Weiskopf had the honour of securing the point that regained the trophy for the Americans, covering 15 holes in six under par to beat the diminutive Guy Hunt 5&3.

Britain and Ireland's team featured six rookies, while Neil Coles – who hated flying – opted not to travel. The Americans fielded one of their strongest ever teams. Ten of the 12 had already won Major titles, the exceptions being JC Snead and Bob Murphy. It is often compared with the 1981 side which many believe to be even stronger.

1977

ROYAL LYTHAM & ST ANNES, LANCASHIRE, ENGLAND SEPTEMBER 15-17

GREAT BRITAIN & IRELAND 7½
UNITED STATES 12½

CAPTAINS: BRIAN HUGGETT (GB&I), DOW FINSTERWALD (US)

To commemorate 50 years of the Ryder Cup, the match was taken to the Lancashire coast. The contest also coincided with the Queen's Silver Jubilee (25 years on the throne). But despite Virginia Wade's singles victory at Wimbledon in July, there were no such British and Irish celebrations at Royal Lytham & St Annes.

The three-day event also used a format so unpopular that it was never considered again. For the one and only time – since matches were changed from 36 holes to 18 – there were just three sessions of play, with a grand total of just 20 games.

Day one had five foursomes, on day two there were five fourballs, with ten singles on the final afternoon. The reduced quota was obviously designed to make America's winning margin more bearable for the hosts, but such was the scheduling of matches on each of the first two days, it failed to ignite any passion.

To accommodate TV, each of the games on days one and two had 45-minute intervals. But such a gap made it difficult for spectators to move quickly between ties, and with the five games spread around the course there wasn't a great deal of atmosphere.

Yet, for a couple of hours on the first afternoon, it looked as if Britain might grab an early advantage as they led in three of the five foursomes. Debutant Peter Dawson and Neil Coles were two-up with just three holes to play against Dave Stockton and Jerry McGee. But then Stockton, one of the finest putters of his generation, holed from 24 feet at the 16th and 35 feet at 17. Coles then bunkered his drive at 18 to hand the Americans a one hole victory.

In another game, Eamonn Darcy and Tony Jacklin lost a two-hole lead with three to play, to halve with Ed Sneed and Don January. So instead of leading 3-2, they trailed 3½-1½, and never recovered. The visitors won four of the five fourballs and it was good night Great Britain and Ireland in more ways than one. Two years later a revamped

Ryder Cup would include professionals from the continent of Europe.

Britain's only stars were Peter Oosterhuis and Nick Faldo, the latter making his debut. Faldo, at 20 years, one month and 28 days, became the youngest player to compete in the Ryder Cup.

Oosterhuis and Faldo beat Ray Floyd and Lou Graham 2&1 in the foursomes, before defeating Jack Nicklaus and Floyd 3&1 in the fourballs. Both Oosterhuis and Faldo went on to win their respective singles matches on the final day. Faldo was particularly impressive in edging out the reigning US Masters and British Open champion Tom Watson by one hole, while Oosty beat Jerry McGee by two holes.

American Lanny Wadkins won all three of his games on his debut while fellow debutant Dawson, who made history by becoming the first left-hander to play in the Ryder Cup, beat 47-year-old January 5&4, while Bernard Gallacher held off a late fightback by Jack Nicklaus to win on the final green. And for those interested in rare statistics, Brian Barnes beat Hale Irwin on the 18th. It was feted to be close – the two players were born on the same day – June 3rd, 1945. The hosts managed to share the singles 5-5 but it was too little to late.

The match witnessed an unfortunate incident between Britain's non-playing captain Brian Huggett and Jacklin on day two. Huggett confronted Jacklin for not going back on to the course to support his team-mates, after his own match had ended. Huggett, who complained that Jacklin's attitude had not been right all week, then dropped him from the singles.

1979

THE GREENBRIER, WHITE SULPHUR SPRINGS, WEST VIRGINIA SEPTEMBER 14-16

UNITED STATES 17 EUROPE 11

CAPTAINS: BILLY CASPER (US), JOHN JACOBS (EUR)

The first contest to include players from the continent of Europe. By extending the Great Britain & Ireland team to incorporate professionals from continental Europe it was hoped that the match might become more competitive. In 18 meetings from 1935 through to 1977, the Americans had won 16, with one halved. Britain's solitary victory had come in 1957 in Yorkshire.

Such a change was both necessary and inevitable and as the 1970s were coming to a close, the contest was becoming even more one-sided than ever.

RYDER CUP HISTORY – THE 1970s

Jack Nicklaus, who had always believed in the value and spirit of the Ryder Cup, had suggested to the British PGA in the mid-1970s that it might be a good idea if they included players from other nations. Talk of a Commonwealth side was mooted, as was a rest of the world team.

In the end it was felt that Europe had more identity. In 1976 a 19-year-old Spaniard called Seve Ballesteros had finished second in the British Open. That year, as well as in 1977 and 1978, Ballesteros topped the European Order of Merit. To add to that, Spain, with Ballesteros and Manuel Pinero, won the 1976 World Cup in Palm Springs, California. And in 1977, Ballesteros teamed-up with Antonio Garrido to successfully defend the title in Manila.

At Augusta National, in April 1978, the British PGA met with their American counterparts to rubber stamp a new format that would include Europe. Seventeen months later, Ballesteros and Garrido were given the honour of being the first non-British, Irish or American golfers to play in the Ryder Cup.

The 1979 match also witnessed another significant event as Lee Elder became the first black golfer to tee-up in the Ryder Cup. But one name missing was Tom Watson who withdrew on the eve of the match to be with his wife Linda who was giving birth to their first child. Mark Hayes took his place.

The match was to be marred by the behaviour of two young Englishmen – Mark James and Ken Brown. The duo were involved in a number of misdemeanours during the trip. On their return, Brown was fined £1,000 and suspended from international team golf for a year, while James was fined £1,500 but was not given a suspension.

Somehow, Europe managed to overcome such internal mayhem to make a match of it – for the first couple of days at least. By Saturday night, the contest was finely balanced in favour of the Americans (8½- 7½). The golf had been of a decent standard, with the European highlight being Peter Oosterhuis and Nick Faldo's performance in a second-day foursomes in which they led Andy Bean and Tom Kite by six holes at the turn.

But on singles day it was a different story, with America taking eight and a half points out of 12. Yet Europe might have run the hosts closer, had they not lost four of the five singles that reached the 18th green.

The meeting's leading player was American debutant Larry Nelson who won all five of his matches, including four victories over Ballesteros. The Spaniard was obviously unfortunate to run into Nelson on four occasions. Seve's only victory came in an opening day foursomes when he and Garrido beat Fuzzy Zoeller and Hubert Green 3&2. As for Nelson, he never had to play the 18th hole all week.

Europe's top player was Bernard Gallacher who won four out of five, including three victories with fellow Scot Brian Barnes. Not surprisingly his only defeat involved a foursomes against Nelson, who was quite clearly the main difference between the two teams.

Faldo, one of only three European winners on singles day, won three out of four. His only defeat came on the opening morning.

WHICH WAS THE BEST TEAM EVER?

1975 US TEAM

	AGE	MAJORS (74-76)	TOUR WINS (74-76)
BILL CASPER	44	-	1
RAY FLOYD	33	1	3
AL GEIBERGER	38	-	5
LOU GRAHAM	37	1	1
HALE IRWIN	30	1	5
GENE LITTLER	45	-	3
JOHNNY MILLER	28	1	14
BOB MURPHY	32	-	1
JACK NICKLAUS	35	2	9
JC SNEAD	34	-	3
LEE TREVINO	35	1	4
TOM WEISKOPF	32	-	2
TOTAL:		**7**	**51**

1981 US TEAM

	AGE	MAJORS (80-82)	TOUR WINS (80-82)
BEN CRENSHAW	29	-	1
RAY FLOYD	39	1	7
HALE IRWIN	36	-	3
TOM KITE	31	-	2
BRUCE LIETZKE	30	-	5
JOHNNY MILLER	34	-	4
LARRY NELSON	34	1	3
JACK NICKLAUS	41	2	3
JERRY PATE	28	-	3
BILL ROGERS	30	1	3
LEE TREVINO	41	-	4
TOM WATSON	32	3	12
TOTAL:		**8**	**50**

1971

UNITED STATES 18½
GREAT BRITAIN 13½

DAY 1

FOURSOMES

		GB	
NEIL COLES	CHRISTY O'CONNOR SR	1	V
PETER OOSTERHUIS	PETER TOWNSEND	0	V
TONY JACKLIN	BRIAN HUGGETT	1	V
MAURICE BEMBRIDGE	PETER BUTLER	1	V

FOURSOMES

BERNARD GALLACHER	HARRY BANNERMAN	1	V
PETER OOSTERHUIS	PETER TOWNSEND	0	V
TONY JACKLIN	BRIAN HUGGETT	0.5	V
MAURICE BEMBRIDGE	PETER BUTLER	0	V

DAY 2

FOURBALLS

CHRISTY O'CONNOR SR	BRIAN BARNES	0	V
NEIL COLES	JOHN GARNER	0	V
PETER OOSTERHUIS	BERNARD GALLACHER	0	V
PETER TOWNSEND	HARRY BANNERMAN	0	V

FOURBALLS

PETER OOSTERHUIS	BERNARD GALLACHER	1	V
TONY JACKLIN	BRIAN HUGGETT	0	V
PETER TOWNSEND	HARRY BANNERMAN	0	V
NEIL COLES	CHRISTY O'CONNOR SR	0.5	V

DAY 3

SINGLES

TONY JACKLIN	0	V
BERNARD GALLACHER	0.5	V
BRIAN BARNES	1	V
PETER OOSTERHUIS	1	V
PETER TOWNSEND	0	V
CHRISTY O'CONNOR SR	0	V
HARRY BANNERMAN	0.5	V
NEIL COLES	0.5	V
BRIAN HUGGETT	0	V
TONY JACKLIN	0	V
BRIAN BARNES	1	V
PETER TOWNSEND	0	V
BERNARD GALLACHER	1	V
NEIL COLES	0	V
PETER OOSTERHUIS	1	V
HARRY BANNERMAN	1	V

1971 RYDER CUP

US			WINNER	MARGIN
0	BILLY CASPER	BARBER MILLER	GB	2&1
1	ARNOLD PALMER	DICKINSON GARDNER	USA	2 HOLES
0	JACK NICKLAUS	STOCKTON DAVE	GB	3&2
0	CHARLES COODY	BEARD FRANK	GB	1 HOLE
0	BILLY CASPER	MILLER BARBER	GB	2&1
1	ARNOLD PALMER	GARDNER DICKINSON	USA	1 HOLE
0.5	LEE TREVINO	MASON RUDOLPH	HVD	–
1	JACK NICKLAUS	JC SNEAD	USA	5&3
1	LEE TREVINO	MASON RUDOLPH	USA	2&1
1	FRANK BEARD	JC SNEAD	USA	2&1
1	ARNOLD PALMER	GARDNER DICKINSON	USA	5&4
1	JACK NICKLAUS	GENE LITTLER	USA	2&1
0	LEE TREVINO	BILLY CASPER	GB	1 HOLE
1	GENE LITTLER	JC SNEAD	USA	2&1
1	JACK NICKLAUS	ARNOLD PALMER	USA	1 HOLE
0.5	CHARLES COODY	FRANK BEARD	HVD	–
1	LEE TREVINO		USA	1 HOLE
0.5	DAVE STOCKTON		HVD	–
0	MASON RUDOLPH		GB	1 HOLE
0	GENE LITTLER		GB	4&3
1	JACK NICKLAUS		USA	3&2
1	GARDNER DICKINSON		USA	5&4
0.5	ARNOLD PALMER		HVD	–
0.5	FRANK BEARD		HVD	–
1	LEE TREVINO		USA	7&6
1	JC SNEAD		USA	1 HOLE
0	MILLER BARBER		GB	2&1
1	DAVE STOCKTON		USA	1 HOLE
0	CHARLES COODY		GB	2&1
1	JACK NICKLAUS		USA	5&3
0	ARNOLD PALMER		GB	3&2
0	GARDNER DICKINSON		GB	2&1

1973 GREAT BRITAIN & IRELAND 13
UNITED STATES 19

DAY 1

FOURSOMES		GBI	
BRIAN BARNES	BERNARD GALLACHER	1	v
CHRISTY O'CONNOR SR	NEIL COLES	1	v
TONY JACKLIN	PETER OOSTERHUIS	0.5	v
MAURICE BEMBRIDGE	EDDIE POLLAND	0	v

FOURSOMES			
BRIAN BARNES	BERNARD GALLACHER	1	v
MAURICE BEMBRIDGE	BRIAN HUGGETT	1	v
TONY JACKLIN	PETER OOSTERHUIS	1	v
CHRISTY O'CONNOR SR	NEIL COLES	0	v

DAY 2

FOURBALLS			
BRIAN BARNES	PETER BUTLER	0	v
TONY JACKLIN	PETER OOSTERHUIS	1	v
MAURICE BEMBRIDGE	BRIAN HUGGETT	1	v
CHRISTY O'CONNOR SR	NEIL COLES	0	v

FOURBALLS			
BRIAN BARNES	PETER BUTLER	0	v
TONY JACKLIN	PETER OOSTERHUIS	0	v
CLIVE CLARK	EDDIE POLLAND	0	v
MAURICE BEMBRIDGE	BRIAN HUGGETT	0.5	v

DAY 3

SINGLES			
BRIAN BARNES		0	v
BERNARD GALLACHER		0	v
PETER BUTLER		0	v
TONY JACKLIN		1	v
NEIL COLES		0.5	v
CHRISTY O'CONNOR SR		0	v
MAURICE BEMBRIDGE		0.5	v
PETER OOSTERHUIS		0.5	v
BRIAN HUGGETT		1	v
BRIAN BARNES		0	v
BERNARD GALLACHER		0	v
TONY JACKLIN		0	v
NEIL COLES		0	v
CHRISTY O'CONNOR SR		0.5	v
MAURICE BEMBRIDGE		0	v
PETER OOSTERHUIS		1	v

1973 RYDER CUP

US			WINNER	MARGIN
0	LEE TREVINO	BILLY CASPER	GBI	1 HOLE
0	TOM WEISKOPF	JC SNEAD	GBI	3&2
0.5	CHI CHI RODRIGUEZ	LOU GRAHAM	HVD	–
1	JACK NICKLAUS	ARNOLD PALMER	USA	6&5
0	TOMMY AARON	GAY BREWER	GBI	5&4
0	JACK NICKLAUS	ARNOLD PALMER	GBI	3&1
0	TOM WEISKOPF	BILLY CASPER	GBI	3&1
1	LEE TREVINO	HOMERO BLANCAS	USA	2&1
1	JACK NICKLAUS	TOM WEISKOPF	USA	1 HOLE
0	ARNOLD PALMER	DAVE HILL	GBI	2 HOLES
0	CHI CHI RODRIGUEZ	LOU GRAHAM	GBI	5&4
1	LEE TREVINO	BILLY CASPER	USA	2&1
1	JC SNEAD	ARNOLD PALMER	USA	2 HOLES
1	GAY BREWER	BILLY CASPER	USA	3&2
1	JACK NICKLAUS	TOM WEISKOPF	USA	3&2
0.5	LEE TREVINO	HOMERO BLANCAS	HVD	–
1	BILLY CASPER		USA	2&1
1	TOM WEISKOPF		USA	3&1
1	HOMERO BLANCAS		USA	5&4
0	TOMMY AARON		GBI	3&1
0.5	GAY BREWER		HVD	–
1	JC SNEAD		USA	1 HOLE
0.5	JACK NICKLAUS		HVD	–
0.5	LEE TREVINO		HVD	–
0	HOMERO BLANCAS		GBI	4&2
1	JC SNEAD		USA	3&1
1	GAY BREWER		USA	6&5
1	BILLY CASPER		USA	2&1
1	LEE TREVINO		USA	6&5
0.5	TOM WEISKOPF		HVD	–
1	JACK NICKLAUS		USA	2 HOLES
0	ARNOLD PALMER		GBI	4&2

1975 UNITED STATES 21
GREAT BRITAIN & IRELAND 11

DAY 1	FOURSOMES		GBI	
	BRIAN BARNES	BERNARD GALLACHER	0	V
	NORMAN WOOD	MAURICE BEMBRIDGE	0	V
	TONY JACKLIN	PETER OOSTERHUIS	0	V
	TOMMY HORTON	JOHN O'LEARY	0	V
	FOURSOMES			
	TONY JACKLIN	PETER OOSTERHUIS	1	V
	EAMONN DARCY	CHRISTY O'CONNOR JR	0	V
	BRIAN BARNES	BERNARD GALLACHER	0.5	V
	TOMMY HORTON	JOHN O'LEARY	0	V

DAY 2	FOURBALLS			
	TONY JACKLIN	PETER OOSTERHUIS	0.5	V
	TOMMY HORTON	NORMAN WOOD	0	V
	BRIAN BARNES	BERNARD GALLACHER	0	V
	EAMONN DARCY	GUY HUNT	0.5	V
	FOURBALLS			
	TONY JACKLIN	BRIAN HUGGETT	1	V
	CHRISTY O'CONNOR JR	JOHN O'LEARY	0	V
	PETER OOSTERHUIS	MAURICE BEMBRIDGE	0	V
	EAMONN DARCY	GUY HUNT	0	V

DAY 3	SINGLES			
	TONY JACKLIN		0	V
	PETER OOSTERHUIS		1	V
	BERNARD GALLACHER		0.5	V
	TOMMY HORTON		0.5	V
	BRIAN HUGGETT		0	V
	EAMONN DARCY		0	V
	GUY HUNT		0	V
	BRIAN BARNES		1	V
	TONY JACKLIN		0	V
	PETER OOSTERHUIS		1	V
	BERNARD GALLACHER		0.5	V
	TOMMY HORTON		1	V
	JOHN O'LEARY		0	V
	MAURICE BEMBRIDGE		0	V
	NORMAN WOOD		1	V
	BRIAN BARNES		1	V

1975 RYDER CUP

US			WINNER	MARGIN
1	JACK NICKLAUS	TOM WEISKOPF	USA	5&4
1	GENE LITTLER	HALE IRWIN	USA	4&3
1	AL GEIBERGER	JOHNNY MILLER	USA	3&1
1	LEE TREVINO	JC SNEAD	USA	2&1
0	BILLY CASPER	RAY FLOYD	GBI	2&1
1	TOM WEISKOPF	LOU GRAHAM	USA	3&2
0.5	JACK NICKLAUS	BOB MURPHY	HVD	–
1	LEE TREVINO	HALE IRWIN	USA	2&1
0.5	BILLY CASPER	JOHNNY MILLER	HVD	–
1	JACK NICKLAUS	JC SNEAD	USA	4&2
1	GENE LITTLER	LOU GRAHAM	USA	5&3
0.5	AL GEIBERGER	RAY FLOYD	HVD	–
0	LEE TREVINO	BOB MURPHY	GBI	3&2
1	TOM WEISKOPF	JOHNNY MILLER	USA	5&3
1	HALE IRWIN	BILLY CASPER	USA	3&2
1	AL GEIBERGER	LOU GRAHAM	USA	3&2
1	BOB MURPHY		USA	2&1
0	JOHNNY MILLER		GBI	2 HOLES
0.5	LEE TREVINO		HVD	–
0.5	HALE IRWIN		HVD	–
1	GENE LITTLER		USA	4&2
1	BILLY CASPER		USA	3&2
1	TOM WEISKOPF		USA	5&3
0	JACK NICKLAUS		GBI	4&2
1	RAY FLOYD		USA	1 HOLE
0	JC SNEAD		GBI	3&2
0.5	AL GEIBERGER		HVD	–
0	LOU GRAHAM		GBI	2&1
1	HALE IRWIN		USA	2&1
1	BOB MURPHY		USA	2&1
0	LEE TREVINO		GBI	2&1
0	JACK NICKLAUS		GBI	2&1

1977 GREAT BRITAIN & IRELAND 7½
UNITED STATES 12½

DAY 1

FOURSOMES

		GBI	
BERNARD GALLACHER	BRIAN BARNES	0	V
NEIL COLES	PETER DAWSON	0	V
NICK FALDO	PETER OOSTERHUIS	1	V
EAMONN DARCY	TONY JACKLIN	0.5	V
TOMMY HORTON	MARK JAMES	0	V

DAY 2

FOURBALLS

BRIAN BARNES	TOMMY HORTON	0	V
NEIL COLES	PETER DAWSON	0	.V
NICK FALDO	PETER OOSTERHUIS	1	V
EAMONN DARCY	TONY JACKLIN	0	V
MARK JAMES	KEN BROWN	0	V

DAY 3

SINGLES

HOWARD CLARK	0	V
NEIL COLES	0	V
PETER DAWSON	1	V
BRIAN BARNES	1	V
TOMMY HORTON	0	V
BERNARD GALLACHER	1	V
EAMONN DARCY	0	V
MARK JAMES	0	V
NICK FALDO	1	V
PETER OOSTERHUIS	1	V

1977 RYDER CUP

US			WINNER	MARGIN
1	LANNY WADKINS	HALE IRWIN	USA	3&1
1	DAVE STOCKTON	JERRY MCGEE	USA	1 HOLE
0	RAY FLOYD	LOU GRAHAM	GBI	2&1
0.5	ED SNEED	DON JANUARY	HVD	–
1	JACK NICKLAUS	TOM WATSON	USA	5&4
1	TOM WATSON	HUBERT GREEN	USA	5&4
1	ED SNEED	LANNY WADKINS	USA	5&3
0	JACK NICKLAUS	RAY FLOYD	GBI	3&1
1	DAVE HILL	DAVE STOCKTON	USA	5&3
1	HALE IRWIN	LOU GRAHAM	USA	1 HOLE
1	LANNY WADKINS		USA	4&3
1	LOU GRAHAM		USA	5&3
0	DON JANUARY		GBI	5&4
0	HALE IRWIN		GBI	1 HOLE
1	DAVE HILL		USA	5&4
0	JACK NICKLAUS		GBI	1 HOLE
1	HUBERT GREEN		USA	1 HOLE
1	RAY FLOYD		USA	2&1
0	TOM WATSON		GBI	1 HOLE
0	JERRY MCGEE		GBI	2 HOLES

1979 UNITED STATES 17 EUROPE 11

FOURSOMES

		EUR	
ANTONIO GARRIDO	SEVE BALLESTEROS	0	V
KEN BROWN	MARK JAMES	0	V
PETER OOSTERHUIS	NICK FALDO	0	V
BERNARD GALLACHER	BRIAN BARNES	1	V

FOURSOMES

KEN BROWN	DES SMYTH	0	V
ANTONIO GARRIDO	SEVE BALLESTEROS	1	V
SANDY LYLE	TONY JACKLIN	0.5	V
BERNARD GALLACHER	BRIAN BARNES	0	V

FOURBALLS

SANDY LYLE	TONY JACKLIN	1	V
PETER OOSTERHUIS	NICK FALDO	1	V
BERNARD GALLACHER	BRIAN BARNES	1	V
ANTONIO GARRIDO	SEVE BALLESTEROS	0	V

FOURBALLS

ANTONIO GARRIDO	SEVE BALLESTEROS	0	V
SANDY LYLE	TONY JACKLIN	0	V
BERNARD GALLACHER	BRIAN BARNES	1	V
PETER OOSTERHUIS	NICK FALDO	1	V

SINGLES

BERNARD GALLACHER	1	V
SEVE BALLESTEROS	0	V
TONY JACKLIN	0	V
ANTONIO GARRIDO	0	V
MICHAEL KING	0	V
BRIAN BARNES	0	V
NICK FALDO	1	V
DES SMYTH	0	V
PETER OOSTERHUIS	0	V
KEN BROWN	1	V
SANDY LYLE	0	V
MARK JAMES (INJURED)	0.5	V

1979 RYDER CUP

US			WINNER	MARGIN
1	LANNY WADKINS	LARRY NELSON	USA	2&1
1	LEE TREVINO	FUZZY ZOELLER	USA	3&2
1	ANDY BEAN	LEE ELDER	USA	2&1
0	HALE IRWIN	JOHN MAHAFFEY	EUR	2&1
1	HALE IRWIN	TOM KITE	USA	7&6
0	FUZZY ZOELLER	HUBERT GREEN	EUR	3&2
0.5	LEE TREVINO	GIL MORGAN	HVD	–
1	LANNY WADKINS	LARRY NELSON	USA	4&3
0	LEE ELDER	JOHN MAHAFFEY	EUR	5&4
0	ANDY BEAN	TOM KITE	EUR	6&5
0	FUZZY ZOELLER	MARK HAYES	EUR	2&1
1	LANNY WADKINS	LARRY NELSON	USA	3&2
1	LANNY WADKINS	LARRY NELSON	USA	5&4
1	HALE IRWIN	TOM KITE	USA	1 HOLE
0	LEE TREVINO	FUZZY ZOELLER	EUR	3&2
0	LEE ELDER	MARK HAYES	EUR	1 HOLE
0	LANNY WADKINS		EUR	3&2
1	LARRY NELSON		USA	3&2
1	TOM KITE		USA	1 HOLE
1	MARK HAYES		USA	1 HOLE
1	ANDY BEAN		USA	4&3
1	JOHN MAHAFFEY		USA	1 HOLE
0	LEE ELDER		EUR	3&2
1	HALE IRWIN		USA	5&3
1	HUBERT GREEN		USA	2 HOLES
0	FUZZY ZOELLER		EUR	1 HOLE
1	LEE TREVINO		USA	2&1
0.5	GIL MORGAN		HVD	EUR INJ

1981

WALTON HEATH, SURREY, ENGLAND
SEPTEMBER 18-20

EUROPE 9½
UNITED STATES 18½

CAPTAINS: JOHN JACOBS (EUR), DAVE MARR (US)

The 1981 match is remembered for two things. Firstly, the awesome strength of the American visitors, and secondly the farcical manner in which Europe selected its team.

Regarding the States, their group of 12 is largely believed to be the strongest side ever to compete in the Ryder Cup, although the 1975 dozen might have something to say about that. Nine of the 12 were already Major champions while two others – Ben Crenshaw and Tom Kite – would enjoy their Major success later in their careers. Only Bruce Lietzke, now on the American Senior Tour, would never win a Major.

On the other side of the coin, Europe opted not to select its strongest side by omitting their leading player, Seve Ballesteros. The Spaniard was, to all intents and purposes, the world number two behind Tom Watson but was prevented from competing because of the Tour's stance regarding appearance money.

Ballesteros, who by then was playing most of his golf on the US Tour, believed he should be offered appearance money to perform in Europe. His argument was: that if Lee Trevino or Tom Weiskopf were allowed to take sponsor's cash to compete in Europe, why couldn't he. He was, by this stage, a two-time Major champion himself.

Subsequently, he decided to contest only a handful of European events, preferring to spend most of his time across the Atlantic. So when it came to choosing the two wild cards, the three-man committee went for Mark James and Peter Oosterhuis. The latter had won the Canadian Open earlier in the summer, beating Jack Nicklaus into second place, while James had finished 11th in the qualifying table.

The committee had voted 2-1 against selecting Ballesteros, while also passing over Tony Jacklin, who had finished one place behind James in the standings. Jacklin was particularly angered at the way that James – who had been fined for his bad behaviour two years earlier – had been given the nod ahead of him. Ballesteros, on the other hand, vowed never to compete in the Ryder Cup again – just two years after the formation of a European side.

The following year Jacklin proved he was still a force to be reckoned with by winning

Europe's flagship event – the PGA Championship (now staged at Wentworth), beating Bernhard Langer in a play-off at Hillside.

As for the match itself, Europe enjoyed a surprising one point lead at the end of the first day. But they were to win only four of the remaining 20 ties. On the second day they lost seven of the eight matches while also being outplayed in the singles.

The first match out on Sunday was Trevino against Sam Torrance, with the American racing to a 5&3 victory in two hours and ten minutes. The match of highest quality featured Kite versus Sandy Lyle who was six-under-par for 16 holes, but still lost 3&2 against the American (10-under). One of the rare highlights for Europe was Howard Clark's 4&3 victory over Tom Watson, while Larry Nelson maintained his excellent Ryder Cup record with four wins out of four.

It was also the final Ryder Cup appearances – as players – for Trevino, Johnnie Miller and Jack Nicklaus. Trevino and Nicklaus ended with four wins from as many games, with the Golden Bear never having to reach the 17th tee. In more ways than one it was the end of an era. The new one, just around the corner, would finally bring glory to Europe for whom the main architects would be, ironically, Ballesteros and Jacklin, the two men who had been cast aside at Walton Heath.

1983

PGA NATIONAL, PALM BEACH, FLORIDA
OCTOBER 14-16
UNITED STATES 14½
EUROPE 13½
CAPTAINS: JACK NICKLAUS (US), TONY JACKLIN (EUR)

U nlike nowadays, when team captains are usually chosen long before the first qualifying tournament is played, the selection of Tony Jacklin as European skipper in 1983 was only decided five months before the match itself.

Jacklin made no secret of his anger when dropped for the 1981 match at Walton Heath, having played in every Ryder Cup since 1967. But now, at the age of 38, he was asked to captain the side. Having accepted the invitation, Jacklin set about persuading another 1981 absentee – Seve Ballesteros – to change his mind and return to the European fold. Political reasons had prevented the European number one from playing in 1981, and it took all of Jacklin's excellent man management skills to get Ballesteros to agree. After the debacle of two years earlier, Ballesteros vowed never to play in the Ryder Cup again. Jacklin approached him in a Southport hotel that summer and within a couple of weeks Ballesteros had said yes.

In many ways, the 1983 match signalled the start of the modern era. From now on, there would be no easy games for the Americans.

After two days of competition the sides couldn't be separated at 8-8. In the opening singles Ballesteros, who lost only one of his five matches that week, forced a half out of Fuzzy Zoeller. The tie was memorable for an incredible stroke of genius by the Spaniard at 18 where he had driven into the rough and then hit his second into a fairway bunker – some 230 yards from the green. Yet from sand he opted to take a three-wood, hitting the ball to the fringe of the putting surface. A chip and single putt later, and Seve had forced a draw.

Bernhard Langer and Nick Faldo also contributed to the European cause, each winning four of their five matches, including both singles.

With just two singles left on the course, the match score was tied at 13-all. Standing on the tee at the par-five 18th, Spain's Jose-Maria Canizares was one-up on Lanny Wadkins. But after Canizares failed to get up and down with a putt, and had to settle for a par, Wadkins knocked a 60-yard chip to within 12 inches of the pin to grab a half. The American had been three down with seven to play.

Bringing up the rear was Tom Watson and Bernard Gallacher, with the American one ahead after 16. At the par-three penultimate hole, both players missed the green with their tee-shots. Gallacher went through the back, while Watson's was pushed to the right. Gallacher then fluffed his first chip, before knocking his third shot to within four feet of the flag. Watson also messed up his second, before getting down in four. Gallacher, needing to hole out to take the game up the 18th, missed, leaving Watson the winner 2&1. Ten years later the pair would oppose each other as team captains.

However, Watson's bogey-four was enough for the States to retain the trophy. The American, who'd won his fifth and last Open title three months earlier, ended the week with four wins from five outings.

The match, despite being tense and competitive, was an extremely friendly affair. Much of the credit for this must go to American captain Jack Nicklaus who, on the eve of the match, invited both teams and their partners around to his house in nearby West Palm Beach for a meal.

RYDER CUP FACTS

Neil Coles has played in the most ever Ryder Cup singles matches – 15, just ahead of Christy O'Connor's 14. Arnold Palmer is the most experienced American singles competitor, having been involved in 11 contests. Lee Trevino, Gene Littler, Billy Casper and Jack Nicklaus have all played 10

1985

THE BELFRY, MIDLANDS, ENGLAND
SEPTEMBER 13-15

EUROPE 16½
UNITED STATES 11½

CAPTAINS: TONY JACKLIN (EUR), LEE TREVINO (US)

Victory for Europe at the fourth attempt and America's first defeat in 28 years. Yet the opening morning's play had a familiar ring to it, as the visitors raced into a 3-1 lead. But that was as good as it got for the Americans who won only four of the next 20 ties, before a late rally took their points total into double figures.

The turning point came on the second morning when Bernhard Langer and Sandy Lyle recovered from two-down with two to play, to half their fourball tie against Craig Stadler and Curtis Strange.

Lyle's lengthy eagle putt won the 17th, but at the concluding hole it appeared that the Americans would get the half they needed to win the game. Inexplicably, Stadler missed a par putt of barely two feet. In normal circumstances such a short putt would have been conceded, but as it was Europe's only hope of earning a half, the Americans were asked to play it.

European captain Tony Jacklin recalls that he was standing close to the 18th green when Stadler missed his tiddler: "That putt was no more than 22 inches. It was a very short putt. I was numb. I was standing with Seve who said: 'Don't for Christ sake feel sorry for anybody.' I think we gained momentum from that."

Another vital win on that Saturday morning came from Sam Torrance and Howard Clark, 2&1 winners over Tom Kite and reigning US Open champion Andy North. Clark holed from all of 60 feet for birdie at the 15th, and then chipped-in for another birdie at the 16th. And when Stadler suffered his calamity around an hour later, the match was level at 6-6.

From here, Europe took control. As American heads dropped, Europe won three of the afternoon's four foursomes, including a tremendous Spanish double. First, Jose Maria Canizares and Jose Rivero trounced Tom Kite and Calvin Peete 7&5, followed shortly after by Seve Ballesteros and Manuel Pinero's 5&4 victory over Hal Sutton and the luckless Stadler.

The Spaniards also played their part on singles day. First match out, Pinero beat Lanny Wadkins 3&1 to move Europe 10-7 ahead. And Ballesteros, three-down with five to play, holed putts of 40, 15 and 12 feet, at the 14th, 15th and 17th respectively, to force a half against Kite. Twelve years later at Valderrama the pair would be opposing captains.

By close of play the Spanish quartet would contribute seven of Europe's 16½ points with Pinero the unsung hero of the week, winning four of his five games.

Another continental, Langer, closed out Sutton 5&4 at the 14th where the German's tee-shot finished up five inches from the flag.

In all, Europe collected seven and a half points out of 12 on singles day, and the Cup was regained when Sam Torrance holed from around 20-feet at 18 to beat Andy North by one hole. Torrance had been three down after ten, and at the final hole North drove into the lake before reaching the green in four.

There were still five matches to complete but with a European victory assured the souvenir hunters decided to have a field day. By the time Strange and Ken Brown had completed their match, a number of tee markers had been swiped. Not that any European was going to complain.

For the first home match in almost 50 years, there was no Irishman present although Christy O'Connor Jr came mighty close to making the team. O'Connor had finished in a tie for third in that year's Open Championship at Sandwich, but at the end of qualifying had missed out on automatic selection by less than £120. Canizares had pipped him and Jacklin overlooked O'Connor for one of the wild cards too, preferring to give them to Nick Faldo, Brown and Rivero.

Jacklin later admitted that O'Connor only spoke to him once during the next four years. And when the match returned to The Belfry in 1989, it was O'Connor who played one of the greatest Ryder Cup shots of all time.

1987

MUIRFIELD VILLAGE, COLUMBUS, OHIO
SEPTEMBER 25-27

UNITED STATES 13 EUROPE 15

CAPTAINS: JACK NICKLAUS (US), TONY JACKLIN (EUR)

Seve Ballesteros contested nine Ryder Cup matches during his 18-year spell as either player or captain of the European team. And quite often he would refer to the period under Tony Jacklin's leadership during the mid-1980s as the 'Muirfield Generation'.

RYDER CUP HISTORY – THE 1980s

For him, America's first defeat on home soil coincided with Europe's best-ever performance.

As far as he was concerned Europe were at their peak in Ohio. Ballesteros, together with Nick Faldo, Bernhard Langer, Sandy Lyle and Ian Woosnam were the key members of that side and by some strange coincidence they were all born within 12 months of each other.

At the time of the match, Lyle and Woosnam were 29, the other three being 30. Faldo was the reigning British Open champion, Lyle was seven months away from wearing Augusta's green jacket, while Woosnam – a four-time winner in Europe during 1987 – was topping the Order of Merit for the first time. Ballesteros and Langer were even more established in the world of golf.

Ken Brown, Europe's next best player, was 30, while the oldest member of the team was Eamonn Darcy who had just turned 35. The youngest was 21-year-old debutant Jose Maria Olazabal.

While Europe's victory at Oak Hill in 1995 was thrilling for the very reason that the underdogs came out on top, in 1987 the visitors were expected to win. And they did.

During the opening two days of fourballs and foursomes it was Europe's cream that dominated proceedings. Ballesteros teamed-up with compatriot Olazabal to win three of their four matches. Lyle and Langer won three out of three, while Faldo and Woosnam won three out of four, and halved the other.

With the singles to be played, Europe held a commanding five-point lead (10½-5½). Yet, before the visitors could hold the trophy aloft, the Americans produced their customary fightback, taking 7½ points out of 12.

Possibly the key game for Europe was Darcy's tense victory over Ben Crenshaw, achieved in bizarre circumstances. After losing the sixth hole to go two down, the American snapped his putter in a rare display of anger. From then on he was forced to putt with a one-iron. Yet somehow he fought back to take the lead at 16, which Darcy bogied. But the Irishman struck back immediately with a tremendous six-iron approach at 17 to make birdie and level the match. At the final hole, Crenshaw drove into a water hazard but still made a bogey-five. Darcy bunkered his second, splashed out to six feet above the flag and holed the tricky downhill putt for a par to win by one.

Fittingly, it was Ballesteros who secured an historic triumph for Europe, by beating Curtis Strange 2&1. Ballesteros had won four of his five games that week.

For the States, Hal Sutton led the way by losing only one of his five games. And after a run of nine straight wins in 1979 and 1981, Larry Nelson finally lost a Ryder Cup tie. As it happened, he lost three out of four, earning a solitary half in his singles against Langer.

With the confidence of being part of a successful European team, Brown secured his first PGA Tour title just seven days later in Georgia at the Southern Open – winning by seven shots.

As for Muirfield Village, the first round of fourball games on day one probably best summed up Europe's standard of play. Not only did they win all four contests, but for the cumulative 65 holes were 29 under par. Jacklin confessed: "I never thought I would live to see the day when I would see golf played like this."

1989

THE BELFRY, MIDLANDS, ENGLAND
SEPTEMBER 22-24
EUROPE 14
UNITED STATES 14
CAPTAINS: TONY JACKLIN (EUR), RAY FLOYD (US)

Only the second tie in 28 meetings. Trailing 9-7 going into the singles, the visitors fought back to square the series 14-all, although a draw was good enough for Europe to retain the trophy. Eight of the 12 singles reached the final green, with the treacherous 18th hole causing havoc for many players.

The first to suffer was American Paul Azinger who hooked his tee-shot into the giant lake in the opening singles tie against Seve Ballesteros. Ballesteros was unable to take advantage, thinning his approach into the water in front of the green. The Spaniard was also unhappy with the 'drop under penalty' awarded to Azinger who played his third shot from the island in the centre of the lake. The American won by one hole.

Tom Kite covered the front nine in 31 strokes against Howard Clark to reach the turn six-up. He eventually won 8&7. And when Chip Beck beat an out-of-sorts Bernhard Langer 3&1, Europe's overnight lead of 9-7 had turned into a deficit of 9-10.

But just as America moved in for the kill, the 18th hole at The Belfry became a banana skin for Uncle Sam's men.

Payne Stewart's tee-shot just failed to clear the hazard, and the colourful American donned his waterproofs and attempted to hit the ball from shallow water. But Stewart took three unsuccessful swipes before conceding victory to Jose Maria Olazabal.

Next up was Mark Calcavecchia who also drove into the lake, took a drop under penalty, and promptly hit his third shot into water further up the fairway. The beneficiary this time was debutant Ronan Rafferty, who won by one hole.

Meanwhile, Mark James had had an easier time closing out Mark O'Meara 3&1 before Christy O'Connor Jr and Fred Couples got to 18. While O'Connor's safe tee shot left him with a long two-iron approach, Couples hit one of the best drives all week and was no more than a nine-iron from the putting surface.

The most dramatic moment of an emotional final afternoon belonged to the Irishman whose crisp two-iron came to rest within four feet of the flag. The shot certainly shook Couples who was unable to locate the putting surface with his lofted club, pushing it to the right of the green. His subsequent chip was poor and when he failed to make par, O'Connor didn't even have to hole out for a birdie.

And if prospects looked bad for the visitors, it got a lot worse as Ken Green three-putted the final green against Jose Maria Canizares. So when the 42-year-old Spaniard tapped-in for par from three feet, Europe had retained the trophy. In little over an hour, Europe had gone from 9-10 down to 14-10 up.

But while captain Tony Jacklin celebrated, Europe would suffer defeat in the final quartet of games. Ian Woosnam, one-up after 14, lost to Curtis Strange, who made a hat-trick of birdies from the 15th to win by two holes.

Not even Nick Faldo could secure a match-winning half. All square on the final tee against Lanny Wadkins, Faldo's hooked drive was swallowed up by the giant lake which for most of the day had been Europe's saviour. Tom Watson comfortably beat Sam Torrance and Mark McCumber edged out Gordon Brand Jr to complete the comeback.

Despite retaining the trophy, a feeling of anti-climax hung over The Belfry. While Europe's lesser-known stars had enjoyed their 15 minutes of fame, the big guns – Langer, Ballesteros, Faldo and Woosnam – were all beaten. The out-of-form Langer had suffered a pretty torrid time, losing all three of his games that week.

Jose-Maria Olazabal was Europe's key player, picking-up four and a half points out of five, while Chip Beck contributed three and a half points to the American cause.

GREAT RYDER CUP PARTNERSHIPS
SEVE BALLESTEROS & JOSE MARIA OLAZABAL

FORMAT	F	A	OPPONENTS	WINNER	MARGIN	YEAR
Foursomes	1	0	Larry Nelson & Payne Stewart	Eur	1 hole	1987
Fourballs	1	0	Curtis Strange & Tom Kite	Eur	2&1	1987
Foursomes	1	0	Ben Crenshaw & Payne Stewart	Eur	1 hole	1987
Fourballs	0	1	Hal Sutton & Larry Mize	USA	2&1	1987
Foursomes	0.5	0.5	Tom Watson & Chip Beck	Hvd	–	1989
Fourballs	1	0	Tom Watson & Mark O'Meara	Eur	6&5	1989
Foursomes	1	0	Curtis Strange & Tom Kite	Eur	1 hole	1989
Fourballs	1	0	Mark Calcavecchia & Ken Green	Eur	4&2	1989
Foursomes	1	0	Paul Azinger & Chip Beck	Eur	2&1	1991
Fourballs	1	0	Paul Azinger & Chip Beck	Eur	2&1	1991
Foursomes	1	0	Fred Couples & Ray Floyd	Eur	3&2	1991
Fourballs	0.5	0.5	Payne Stewart & Fred Couples	Hvd	–	1991
Foursomes	0	1	Tom Kite & Davis Love	USA	2&1	1993
Fourballs	1	0	Tom Kite & Davis Love	Eur	4&3	1993
Foursomes	1	0	Tom Kite & Davis Love	Eur	2&1	1993

■ PLAYED: 15 ■ WON: 11 ■ HALVED: 2 ■ LOST: 2 ■ %: 80.00

1981 EUROPE 9½ UNITED STATES 18½

FOURSOMES		EUR	
BERNHARD LANGER	MANUEL PINERO	0	V
SANDY LYLE	MARK JAMES	1	V
BERNARD GALLACHER	DES SMYTH	1	V
PETER OOSTERHUIS	NICK FALDO	0	V

FOURBALLS			
SAM TORRANCE	HOWARD CLARK	0.5	V
SANDY LYLE	MARK JAMES	1	V
DES SMYTH	J-M CANIZARES	1	V
BERNARD GALLACHER	EAMONN DARCY	0	V

FOURBALLS			
NICK FALDO	SAM TORRANCE	0	V
SANDY LYLE	MARK JAMES	0	V
BERNHARD LANGER	MANUEL PINERO	1	V
DES SMYTH	J-M CANIZARES	0	V

FOURSOMES			
PETER OOSTERHUIS	SAM TORRANCE	0	V
BERNHARD LANGER	MANUEL PINERO	0	V
SANDY LYLE	MARK JAMES	0	V
DES SMYTH	BERNARD GALLACHER	0	V

SINGLES			
SAM TORRANCE		0	V
SANDY LYLE		0	V
BERNARD GALLACHER		0.5	V
MARK JAMES		0	V
DES SMYTH		0	V
BERNHARD LANGER		0.5	V
MANUEL PINERO		1	V
J-M CANIZARES		0	V
NICK FALDO		1	V
HOWARD CLARK		1	V
PETER OOSTERHUIS		0	V
EAMONN DARCY		0	V

1981 RYDER CUP

US			WINNER	MARGIN
1	LEE TREVINO	LARRY NELSON	USA	1 HOLE
0	BILL ROGERS	BRUCE LIETZKE	EUR	2&1
0	HALE IRWIN	RAY FLOYD	EUR	3&2
1	TOM WATSON	JACK NICKLAUS	USA	4&3
0.5	TOM KITE	JOHNNY MILLER	HVD	–
0	BEN CRENSHAW	JERRY PATE	EUR	3&2
0	BILL ROGERS	BRUCE LIETZKE	EUR	6&5
1	HALE IRWIN	RAY FLOYD	USA	2&1
1	LEE TREVINO	JERRY PATE	USA	7&5
1	LARRY NELSON	TOM KITE	USA	1 HOLE
0	HALE IRWIN	RAY FLOYD	EUR	2&1
1	TOM WATSON	JACK NICKLAUS	USA	3&2
1	LEE TREVINO	JERRY PATE	USA	2&1
1	TOM WATSON	JACK NICKLAUS	USA	3&2
1	BILL ROGERS	RAY FLOYD	USA	3&2
1	LARRY NELSON	TOM KITE	USA	3&2
1	LEE TREVINO		USA	5&3
1	TOM KITE		USA	3&2
0.5	BILL ROGERS		HVD	–
1	LARRY NELSON		USA	2 HOLES
1	BEN CRENSHAW		USA	6&4
0.5	BRUCE LIETZKE		HVD	–
0	JERRY PATE		EUR	4&2
1	HALE IRWIN		USA	1 HOLE
0	JOHNNY MILLER		EUR	2&1
0	TOM WATSON		EUR	4&3
1	RAY FLOYD		USA	1 HOLE
1	JACK NICKLAUS		USA	5&3

1983 UNITED STATES 14½
EUROPE 13½

DAY 1

FOURSOMES

		EUR	
BERNARD GALLACHER	SANDY LYLE	0	V
NICK FALDO	BERNHARD LANGER	1	V
SEVE BALLESTEROS	PAUL WAY	0	V
J-M CANIZARES	SAM TORRANCE	1	V

FOURBALLS

KEN BROWN	BRIAN WAITES	1	V
NICK FALDO	BERNHARD LANGER	0	V
SEVE BALLESTEROS	PAUL WAY	1	V
SAM TORRANCE	IAN WOOSNAM	0.5	V

DAY 2

FOURBALLS

KEN BROWN	BRIAN WAITES	0	V
NICK FALDO	BERNHARD LANGER	1	V
SEVE BALLESTEROS	PAUL WAY	0.5	V
SAM TORRANCE	IAN WOOSNAM	0	V

FOURSOMES

NICK FALDO	BERNHARD LANGER	1	V
KEN BROWN	BRIAN WAITES	0	V
SAM TORRANCE	J-M CANIZARES	0	V
SEVE BALLESTEROS	PAUL WAY	1	V

DAY 3

SINGLES

SEVE BALLESTEROS	0.5	V
NICK FALDO	1	V
BERNHARD LANGER	1	V
GORDON J BRAND	0	V
SANDY LYLE	0	V
BRIAN WAITES	0	V
PAUL WAY	1	V
SAM TORRANCE	0.5	V
IAN WOOSNAM	0	V
J-M CANIZARES	0.5	V
KEN BROWN	1	V
BERNARD GALLACHER	0	V

1983 RYDER CUP

US			WINNER	MARGIN
1	TOM WATSON	BEN CRENSHAW	USA	5&4
0	LANNY WADKINS	CRAIG STADLER	EUR	4&2
1	TOM KITE	CALVIN PEETE	USA	2&1
0	RAY FLOYD	BOB GILDER	EUR	4&3
0	GIL MORGAN	FUZZY ZOELLER	EUR	2&1
1	TOM WATSON	JAY HAAS	USA	2&1
0	RAY FLOYD	CURTIS STRANGE	EUR	1 HOLE
0.5	BEN CRENSHAW	CALVIN PEETE	HVD	–
1	LANNY WADKINS	CRAIG STADLER	USA	1 HOLE
0	BEN CRENSHAW	CALVIN PEETE	EUR	4&2
0.5	GIL MORGAN	JAY HAAS	HVD	–
1	TOM WATSON	BOB GILDER	USA	5&4
0	TOM KITE	RAY FLOYD	EUR	3&2
1	JAY HAAS	CURTIS STRANGE	USA	3&2
1	GIL MORGAN	LANNY WADKINS	USA	7&5
0	TOM WATSON	BOB GILDER	EUR	2&1
0.5	FUZZY ZOELLER		HVD	–
0	JAY HAAS		EUR	2&1
0	GIL MORGAN		EUR	2 HOLES
1	BOB GILDER		USA	2 HOLES
1	BEN CRENSHAW		USA	3&1
1	CALVIN PEETE		USA	1 HOLE
0	CURTIS STRANGE		EUR	2&1
0.5	TOM KITE		HVD	–
1	CRAIG STADLER		USA	3&2
0.5	LANNY WADKINS		HVD	–
0	RAY FLOYD		EUR	4&3
1	TOM WATSON		USA	2&1

1985 EUROPE 16½ UNITED STATES 11½

DAY 1

FOURSOMES

		EUR	
SEVE BALLESTEROS	MANUEL PINERO	1	V
BERNHARD LANGER	NICK FALDO	0	V
SANDY LYLE	KEN BROWN	0	V
HOWARD CLARK	SAM TORRANCE	0	V

FOURBALLS

IAN WOOSNAM	PAUL WAY	1	V
SEVE BALLESTEROS	MANUEL PINERO	1	V
BERNHARD LANGER	J-M CANIZARES	0.5	V
HOWARD CLARK	SAM TORRANCE	0	V

DAY 2

FOURBALLS

HOWARD CLARK	SAM TORRANCE	1	V
IAN WOOSNAM	PAUL WAY	1	V
SEVE BALLESTEROS	MANUEL PINERO	0	V
BERNHARD LANGER	SANDY LYLE	0.5	V

FOURSOMES

J-M CANIZARES	JOSE RIVERO	1	V
SEVE BALLESTEROS	MANUEL PINERO	1	V
IAN WOOSNAM	PAUL WAY	0	V
BERNHARD LANGER	KEN BROWN	1	V

DAY 3

SINGLES

MANUEL PINERO	1	V
IAN WOOSNAM	0	V
PAUL WAY	1	V
SEVE BALLESTEROS	0.5	V
SANDY LYLE	1	V
BERNHARD LANGER	1	V
SAM TORRANCE	1	V
HOWARD CLARK	1	V
JOSE RIVERO	0	V
NICK FALDO	0	V
J-M CANIZARES	1	V
KEN BROWN	0	V

1985 RYDER CUP

US			WINNER	MARGIN
0	CURTIS STRANGE	MARK O'MEARA	EUR	2&1
1	CALVIN PEETE	TOM KITE	USA	3&2
1	LANNY WADKINS	RAY FLOYD	USA	4&3
1	CRAIG STADLER	HAL SUTTON	USA	3&2
0	FUZZY ZOELLER	HUBERT GREEN	EUR	1 HOLE
0	ANDY NORTH	PETER JACOBSEN	EUR	2&1
0.5	CRAIG STADLER	HAL SUTTON	HVD	–
1	LANNY WADKINS	RAY FLOYD	USA	1 HOLE
0	TOM KITE	ANDY NORTH	EUR	2&1
0	FUZZY ZOELLER	HUBERT GREEN	EUR	4&3
1	LANNY WADKINS	MARK O'MEARA	USA	3&2
0.5	CRAIG STADLER	CURTIS STRANGE	HVD	–
0	CALVIN PEETE	TOM KITE	EUR	7&5
0	CRAIG STADLER	HAL SUTTON	EUR	5&4
1	CURTIS STRANGE	PETER JACOBSEN	USA	4&2
0	LANNY WADKINS	RAY FLOYD	EUR	3&2
0	LANNY WADKINS		EUR	3&1
1	CRAIG STADLER		USA	2&1
0	RAY FLOYD		EUR	2 HOLES
0.5	TOM KITE		HVD	–
0	PETER JACOBSEN		EUR	3&2
0	HAL SUTTON		EUR	5&4
0	ANDY NORTH		EUR	1 HOLE
0	MARK O'MEARA		EUR	1 HOLE
1	CALVIN PEETE		USA	1 HOLE
1	HUBERT GREEN		USA	3 &1
0	FUZZY ZOELLER		EUR	2 HOLES
1	CURTIS STRANGE		USA	4&2

1987 UNITED STATES 13 EUROPE 15

DAY 1

FOURSOMES

		EUR	
SAM TORRANCE	HOWARD CLARK	0	V
KEN BROWN	BERNHARD LANGER	0	V
NICK FALDO	IAN WOOSNAM	1	V
SEVE BALLESTEROS	JOSE M OLAZABAL	1	V

FOURBALLS

GORDON BRAND JNR	JOSE RIVERO	1	V
SANDY LYLE	BERNHARD LANGER	1	V
NICK FALDO	IAN WOOSNAM	1	V
SEVE BALLESTEROS	JOSE M OLAZABAL	1	V

DAY 2

FOURSOMES

GORDON BRAND JNR	JOSE RIVERO	0	V
NICK FALDO	IAN WOOSNAM	0.5	V
SANDY LYLE	BERNHARD LANGER	1	V
SEVE BALLESTEROS	JOSE M OLAZABAL	1	V

FOURBALLS

NICK FALDO	IAN WOOSNAM	1	V
EAMONN DARCY	GORDON BRAND JNR	0	V
SEVE BALLESTEROS	JOSE M OLAZABAL	0	V
SANDY LYLE	BERNHARD LANGER	1	V

DAY 3

SINGLES

IAN WOOSNAM	0	V
HOWARD CLARK	1	V
SAM TORRANCE	0.5	V
NICK FALDO	0	V
JOSE M OLAZABAL	0	V
JOSE RIVERO	0	V
SANDY LYLE	0	V
EAMONN DARCY	1	V
BERNHARD LANGER	0.5	V
SEVE BALLESTEROS	1	V
KEN BROWN	0	V
GORDON BRAND JNR	0.5	V

1987 RYDER CUP

US			WINNER	MARGIN
1	CURTIS STRANGE	TOM KITE	USA	4&2
1	HAL SUTTON	DAN POHL	USA	2&1
0	LANNY WADKINS	LARRY MIZE	EUR	2 HOLES
0	LARRY NELSON	PAYNE STEWART	EUR	1 HOLE
0	BEN CRENSHAW	SCOTT SIMPSON	EUR	1 HOLE
0	ANDY BEAN	MARK CALCAVECCHIA	EUR	1 HOLE
0	HAL SUTTON	DAN POHL	EUR	2&1
0	CURTIS STRANGE	TOM KITE	EUR	2&1
1	CURTIS STRANGE	TOM KITE	USA	3&1
0.5	HAL SUTTON	LARRY MIZE	HVD	–
0	LANNY WADKINS	LARRY NELSON	EUR	2&1
0	BEN CRENSHAW	PAYNE STEWART	EUR	1 HOLE
0	CURTIS STRANGE	TOM KITE	EUR	5&4
1	ANDY BEAN	PAYNE STEWART	USA	3&2
1	HAL SUTTON	LARRY MIZE	USA	2&1
0	LANNY WADKINS	LARRY NELSON	EUR	1 HOLE
1	ANDY BEAN		USA	1 HOLE
0	DAN POHL		EUR	1 HOLE
0.5	LARRY MIZE		HVD	–
1	MARK CALCAVECCHIA		USA	1 HOLE
1	PAYNE STEWART		USA	2 HOLES
1	SCOTT SIMPSON		USA	2&1
1	TOM KITE		USA	3&2
0	BEN CRENSHAW		EUR	1 HOLE
0.5	LARRY NELSON		HVD	–
0	CURTIS STRANGE		EUR	2&1
1	LANNY WADKINS		USA	3&2
0.5	HAL SUTTON		HVD	–

1989 EUROPE 14
UNITED STATES 14

DAY 1

FOURSOMES		EUR	
NICK FALDO	IAN WOOSNAM	0.5	V
HOWARD CLARK	MARK JAMES	0	V
BERNHARD LANGER	RONAN RAFFERTY	0	V
SEVE BALLESTEROS	JOSE M OLAZABAL	0.5	V

FOURBALLS			
SEVE BALLESTEROS	JOSE M OLAZABAL	1	V
HOWARD CLARK	MARK JAMES	1	V
SAM TORRANCE	GORDON BRAND JNR	1	V
NICK FALDO	IAN WOOSNAM	1	V

DAY 2

FOURSOMES			
SAM TORRANCE	GORDON BRAND JNR	0	V
NICK FALDO	IAN WOOSNAM	1	V
RONAN RAFFERTY	CHRISTY O'CONNOR JR	0	V
SEVE BALLESTEROS	JOSE M OLAZABAL	1	V

FOURBALLS			
NICK FALDO	IAN WOOSNAM	0	V
BERNHARD LANGER	J-M CANIZARES	0	V
SEVE BALLESTEROS	JOSE M OLAZABAL	1	V
HOWARD CLARK	MARK JAMES	1	V

DAY 3

SINGLES			
HOWARD CLARK		0	V
BERNHARD LANGER		0	V
SEVE BALLESTEROS		0	V
MARK JAMES		1	V
JOSE M OLAZABAL		1	V
RONAN RAFFERTY		1	V
CHRISTY O'CONNOR JR		1	V
J-M CANIZARES		1	V
SAM TORRANCE		0	V
GORDON BRAND JNR		0	V
NICK FALDO		0	V
IAN WOOSNAM		0	V

1989 RYDER CUP

US			WINNER	MARGIN
0.5	CURTIS STRANGE	TOM KITE	HVD	–
1	PAYNE STEWART	LANNY WADKINS	USA	1 HOLE
1	MARK CALCAVECCHIA	KEN GREEN	USA	2&1
0.5	TOM WATSON	CHIP BECK	HVD	–
0	TOM WATSON	MARK O'MEARA	EUR	6&5
0	LANNY WADKINS	FRED COUPLES	EUR	3&2
0	CURTIS STRANGE	PAUL AZINGER	EUR	1 HOLE
0	MARK CALCAVECCHIA	MARK MCCUMBER	EUR	2 HOLES
1	CHIP BECK	PAUL AZINGER	USA	4&3
0	LANNY WADKINS	PAYNE STEWART	EUR	3&2
1	MARK CALCAVECCHIA	KEN GREEN	USA	3&2
0	CURTIS STRANGE	TOM KITE	EUR	1 HOLE
1	CHIP BECK	PAUL AZINGER	USA	2&1
1	TOM KITE	MARK MCCUMBER	USA	2&1
0	MARK CALCAVECCHIA	KEN GREEN	EUR	4&2
0	CURTIS STRANGE	PAYNE STEWART	EUR	1 HOLE
1	TOM KITE		USA	8&7
1	CHIP BECK		USA	3&1
1	PAUL AZINGER		USA	1 HOLE
0	MARK O'MEARA		EUR	3&2
0	PAYNE STEWART		EUR	1 HOLE
0	MARK CALCAVECCHIA		EUR	1 HOLE
0	FRED COUPLES		EUR	1 HOLE
0	KEN GREEN		EUR	1 HOLE
1	TOM WATSON		USA	3&1
1	MARK MCCUMBER		USA	1 HOLE
1	LANNY WADKINS		USA	1 HOLE
1	CURTIS STRANGE		USA	2 HOLES

1991

OCEAN COURSE, KIAWAH ISLAND, SC
SEPTEMBER 27-29

UNITED STATES 14½
EUROPE 13½

CAPTAINS: DAVE STOCKTON (US), BERNARD GALLACHER (EUR)

Kiawah Island in South Carolina is arguably the toughest venue ever to stage the Ryder Cup. The Ocean Course didn't have any bunkers, because the entire location was surrounded by sand dunes.

The event became known as the 'War on the Shore' as partisan supporters from both sides entered into the 'spirit' of the occasion and at times the match became overheated, with one or two ugly scenes.

Former player Manuel Pinero, who was part of European captain Bernard Gallacher's backroom team, admitted to fearing for the future of the competition after witnessing some of the scenes at Kiawah Island. He complained: "The fans got too close to the players. They got too involved in the matches. I was worried about the future of the Ryder Cup. We have to be sure that the Ryder Cup is played in the right spirit."

In the end the destiny of the trophy depended on the very last putt. In the final singles tie, Hale Irwin needed a half against Bernhard Langer to regain the Cup for the Americans. And with four holes left Irwin was two-up. But as the pressure built on 46-year-old Irwin, Langer drew level by winning both the 15th and 17th holes. At the final hole, Irwin's tee-shot appeared to be heading for severe trouble but such was the size of the encroaching gallery that the ball was prevented from running off the fairway. His approach was also poorly hit, flying wide of the green to the right. A nervous chip was followed by a mediocre putt to around 12 inches from the cup. Langer, who conceded Irwin his short putt, needed to make par to win his match and force a 14-14 draw which would be enough for Europe to retain the trophy. From 45 feet, Langer hit his birdie putt six-feet past the hole. But as supporters of both teams held their breath, Langer's putt for glory rolled agonisingly wide. Irwin had escaped with a half and the States had won back the Ryder Cup by a single point.

Earlier, on the last afternoon, Colin Montgomerie had fought back from four down with four to play, to halve his game with America's Mark Calcavecchia. Over those last four holes, Calcavecchia made two bogeys and two triple-bogeys while Monty covered the same stretch in a total of three over par – such was the pressure of the Ryder Cup, combined with the brutal nature of the course.

At the par-three 17th, Calcavecchia put two balls into the giant lake, while Monty also found water but still went on to win the hole.

The leading points scorer was Europe's Seve Ballesteros who contributed four and a half points out of five. Jose Maria Olazabal collected three and a half points, while the leading Americans were Fred Couples and Lanny Wadkins both of whom matched Olazabal's total.

Throughout the three days, Europe were struggling to keep pace with the hosts who led 3-1 after the first round of foursomes. By lunchtime on day two Europe were three points adrift, before drawing level in the afternoon when they allowed the Americans to claim just a single half from four fourball games.

One player who left South Carolina feeling dejected was rookie David Gilford. In a second day foursomes he teamed up with Nick Faldo against Paul Azinger and Mark O'Meara who won by a record-equalling margin of 7&6. Despite being the more experienced player, Faldo rarely communicated with Gilford who appeared a forlorn figure through the match.

To add insult to injury, Gilford was withdrawn by his captain when American Steve Pate pulled out of the singles with an injury. In cases of injury, it had been agreed that the opposing captain would select a player to step aside. Both players were awarded a half for the tie that wasn't played.

As a foot note to the match, seven days later Langer shrugged aside his Ryder Cup disappointment to win on the European Tour. The mentally tough Langer won the German Masters after a play-off – quite a feat of endurance.

1993

THE BELFRY, ENGLAND SEPTEMBER 24-26

EUROPE 13
UNITED STATES 15

CAPTAINS: BERNARD GALLACHER (EUR), TOM WATSON (US)

Will always be remembered by European followers as 'the one that got away'. At lunchtime on Saturday, the hosts held a three-point advantage, but from there, Europe could only win four of the remaining 16 ties.

RYDER CUP HISTORY – THE 1990s

Yet in the end, it was still a close run affair. Bernard Gallacher's team were left to rue the singles defeats of Barry Lane and Costantino Rocca.

Lane, who was making his Ryder Cup debut, was three-up on Chip Beck as they left the 13th green. But the Englishman proceeded to lose four of the last five holes, including the 18th. For Beck, it was his third straight singles victory, having also won in 1989 and 1991.

It also helped to erase the memories of Augusta in April of that year when he was heavily criticised for not attacking the 15th green while in pursuit of Bernhard Langer at the US Masters. The American press showed no mercy to Beck who laid up short of the water when they believed he should have attempted to hit the green in two. As it happened, his runner-up finish behind Langer (the winner by four shots) virtually guaranteed Beck his place in the US team.

Now, five months later, he was one of the heroes of the American side. Beck more than anyone probably understood the emotions suffered by Rocca who became the scapegoat for Europe's defeat.

The Italian, one-up on Davis Love after 16, was in the driving seat when he arrived at the penultimate green. With Love already finished in par, Rocca had a 20-footer for birdie and the match. His putt was smoothly struck and appeared to have a chance of dropping. But the ball missed the edge of the cup by no more than a few centimetres and rolled about three feet beyond. He then missed the return handing Love an unlikely win. Having three-putted, Rocca looked a beaten man as he teed-off on the final hole where his bogey allowed Love to snatch victory from the jaws of defeat.

Unfortunately for Rocca, the press singled him out as the man responsible for Europe's demise. But, as he vainly pointed out, the more-experienced Seve Ballesteros, Jose Maria Olazabal and Langer all lost on the final afternoon.

One of Europe's few successes on singles day was Peter Baker who ended an excellent debut by making birdie on the treacherous 18th to edge out Corey Pavin by one hole. Baker collected two and a half points from four matches and on Saturday afternoon had teamed up with Ian Woosnam to thrash Fred Couples and Paul Azinger 6&5 in a fourball.

Late in the day, Nick Faldo gave European fans something to cheer by making a hole-in-one (with a six-iron) at the par-three 14th – only the second ace in Cup history. But his half against Azinger mattered little.

For the record, Ray Floyd, 51, became the oldest competitor in Cup history. He won three of his four matches, including a singles success over Olazabal (2 holes). The best individual record for the week belonged to Ian Woosnam, who won four and a half points out of five.

Three years earlier, the decision to nominate The Belfry for a third time had caused a stir. The selection meeting was attended by three representatives from the European Tour, three members from the Professional Golfers' Association and was chaired by the late Lord Derby, who was president of the two bodies.

The Tour voted for Club de Campo in Spain, while the PGA opted for The Belfry. At 3-3, Lord Derby gave his casting vote to The Belfry and resigned from his position with the Tour. The Belfry, home of the PGA, will host its fourth Ryder Cup in 2002.

1995

OAK HILL, ROCHESTER, NY
SEPTEMBER 22-24
UNITED STATES 13½
EUROPE 14½

CAPTAINS: LANNY WADKINS (US), BERNARD GALLACHER (EUR)

I n the 75-year history of the competition there can be few contests to equal the suspense, unpredictability and ultimate surprise of the 1995 encounter in New York. Few followers from either side of the Atlantic gave Europe's 'team of old men' any chance of winning back the trophy. Eight of the 12-man team were over 37, of which three – Sam Torrance, Howard Clark and Mark James – were in their 40s. Only one, Per-Ulrik Johansson – at 28 – was under 30.

Exactly half of the victorious dozen played at Valderrama two years later but by 1999 Colin Montgomerie was the only member of Europe's triumphant Oak Hill team to feature at Brookline. Spurred on by the knowledge that it was likely to be their final chance of Ryder Cup glory, Torrance, James and Clark all won their singles on an emotional Sunday afternoon in Rochester.

Yet when Corey Pavin (playing with Loren Roberts) chipped-in from just off the green at 18 to beat Europe's Nick Faldo and Bernhard Langer by one hole in the final fourball game of the second day, the United States had held a 9-7 lead.

Never before on American soil had Europe (or GB&I) claimed most points on singles day. However, Europe performed one of the greatest Ryder Cup fightbacks of all time to sneak a one point victory.

Every game was vital, but two in particular turned out to be crucial – Brad Faxon v David Gilford; and Curtis Strange v Nick Faldo. One-up with one to play, Gilford was in trouble at the final hole where he pulled his second shot left of the green and then fluffed a chip. In the end he salvaged a bogey-five by holing a tough 12 footer.

Faxon still had a chance to halve the match, if only he could sink his par putt from around five feet. But Faxon, considered one of the best putters on the US Tour, failed in his attempt. Gilford had escaped with a narrow victory to make up for his acute disappointment four years earlier.

In the other key match, Faldo was one-down with two to play. The Englishman, however, got back to all square when he won the 17th (par four), where he got down in two from a bunker to save par. Strange had also found sand with his second shot but

219

could only make bogey. At the final hole Faldo drove into rough, from where he had to lay-up short of the green with his second. Strange, meanwhile, had hit the perfect drive only for his second shot to finish in the steep bank short of the green. Faldo then produced one of the best shots he's ever played under pressure, a high wedge to within four feet of the flag. Strange found this an impossible act to follow. He chipped poorly, then missed the return and had to settle for another bogey. Faldo held his nerve brilliantly to make par and snatch an unlikely win.

Now, with just one point needed to win, Philip Walton was in great shape to seal victory for Europe. The Irishman appeared to be coasting when he led by three with three to play. But at 16 his opponent Jay Haas holed out from a greenside bunker, while a Walton bogey at 17 reduced his lead by one.

At 18, Haas drove into trees on the left, while Walton found rough down the right from where he put his approach into the steep bank at the front of the green. It was the same location that ended the hopes of Strange. With Haas unable to make par, following his poor tee-shot, Walton knew he had to get down in three. His chip from deep rough finished 15 feet beyond the flag and his putt for par trundled up to within a foot of the pin. A bogey-five was enough to secure victory and the European celebrations began.

Corey Pavin was the leading points scorer over the three days, collecting four points out of five for the States. There were also holes-in-one for Costantino Rocca (at the 167-yard 6th) in a second day foursomes and Howard Clark (the 192-yard 11th) in his singles with Peter Jacobsen which Clark won by one hole.

1997

VALDERRAMA, SPAIN SEPTEMBER 26-28
EUROPE 14½
UNITED STATES 13½
CAPTAINS: SEVE BALLESTEROS (EUR), TOM KITE (US)

To celebrate 70 years of the Ryder Cup the match was staged in Spain, the home of European legend Seve Ballesteros. The 40-year-old Spaniard was made captain for the occasion and although he was to ultimately taste victory on home soil, the build-up to the contest was anything but smooth.

RYDER CUP HISTORY – THE 1990s

At the conclusion of qualifying, Miguel Angel Martin had edged out fellow Spaniard Jose Maria Olazabal by a handful of pounds to snatch the final automatic qualifying spot. Although desperate to have Olazabal in the team, Ballesteros chose Jesper Parnevik and Nick Faldo as his two wild cards. But there was to be a twist in the tail.

Martin, who three months earlier had looked a comfortable qualifier, injured his wrist in early summer and had not played since The Open Championship at Royal Troon in mid-July. Martin was keen to make his Ryder Cup debut while Ballesteros was anxious to bring in Olazabal as his replacement.

The Ryder Cup committee of the European Tour arranged for Martin to undergo a fitness test, which the Spaniard failed to attend. He wanted more time to prove his fitness before making a decision. The committee, no doubt influenced by Ballesteros, axed Martin from the team which opened the door for the lawyers to get involved.

Martin turned to the Tour's Tournament Committee, which included players such as Colin Montgomerie and Sam Torrance, and they agreed with the 35-year-old's argument that there was still plenty of time to make a decision on his injured wrist.

In the end Martin opted to stand down, paving the way for Olazabal to make an 11th hour appearance. A deal had been struck where Martin would receive his Ryder Cup uniform and be part of the official team photographs.

Martin would not have been fit enough to play anyway and would have been happy to have made a more dignified withdrawal – if only given the opportunity. Unfortunately, the Ryder Cup committee had handled the situation rather clumsily, as had Ballesteros.

Yet Olazabal was in, having only returned to action in March of that year after a nightmare 17 months with a career-threatening condition. He had done remarkably well to even reach 11th in the qualifying table in such a short space of time.

When the action finally began it was the first match to be played outside of Britain or the United States. It also witnessed the debut of Eldrick T Woods, the reigning Masters champion in his first full season as a pro.

On the first morning, Tiger teamed up with his great friend Mark O'Meara to beat Montgomerie and Bernhard Langer 3&2 in a fourball encounter. But that was to be Tiger's only success. He played four more times, but could only manage a solitary half.

In the singles he was beaten 4&2 by Costantino Rocca who won the opening hole and remained in front for the rest of the match.

The key session for Europe was the third, when they won three and a half points out of four in the second round of fourball matches.

With just the singles to play, Europe led 10½ to 5½ and were seemingly on course for an emphatic victory. But as is tradition, the Americans battled back superbly on the final afternoon.

Fred Couples opened with a resounding 8&7 victory over Ian Woosnam, while Tom Lehman crushed Euro debutant Ignacio Garrido 7&6. Europe survived despite losing the singles 8-4. Possibly the key to Europe's flagging fortunes was the brilliant fightback by Thomas Bjorn who lost the opening four holes to Justin Leonard. The Dane won three in a row from the eighth to level matters, only for Leonard to retake the lead on three more occasions. But Bjorn kept fighting back and finally took the lead on 17 where he made a tricky putt.

Leonard, on the verge of defeat, managed to escape with a half despite hitting his approach at 18 into a greenside bunker. While Bjorn bogied, Leonard got up and down in two. It was an epic encounter in which only two of 18 holes (6th and 7th) were halved. It was a vital half for Europe. Bernhard Langer's point against Brad Faxon (2&1) meant Europe had retained the Cup, but America could still force a tie if Scott Hoch could beat Montgomerie in the final game. Hoch had been two-up after six, but by the time they reached the final tee the game was all square.

Monty admitted later: "That's the most pressure I've ever experienced. The worst I have ever felt on a hole. I just breathed very deep and tried to focus on doing nothing more than hitting the fairway."

Hoch missed the green with his approach and chipped to 15 feet. Monty, who made a safe par to clinch the match for Europe, was then told by his captain to concede Hoch his par putt as a gesture of goodwill. Monty agreed but later admitted he was a little miffed by it all. I wonder how Seve would have reacted if one of his captains had asked him to concede his opponent a lengthy vital putt.

However, Monty still ended the match with the best individual points tally of all 24 players – three wins, one half and one defeat.

1999

THE COUNTRY CLUB, BROOKLINE, MA
SEPTEMBER 24-26

UNITED STATES 14½
EUROPE 13½

CAPTAINS: BEN CRENSHAW (US), MARK JAMES (EUR)

Much of the pre-match build-up in 1999 revolved around appearance money, and whether players should be paid for playing in the Ryder Cup. Many, including Tiger Woods, believed that the competitors should receive some sort of payment, even if most of it went to charity. One player who made it clear that he didn't want to receive any cash was Payne Stewart, who less than five weeks after playing in his fifth Ryder Cup perished in a plane crash.

Other pre-match talk concerned the absence of Nick Faldo after 11 consecutive appearances. Faldo, to his credit, made a valiant effort to qualify for the team. Although based in America, he returned to Europe to play in as many qualifying events as possible (appearing in 17 Tour events in total), but still couldn't finish inside the top 40.

Months later, a disappointed Faldo became angry when he discovered that a letter of support sent to the European team ended up in a waste bin. Captain Mark James said sorry but was probably right not to select Faldo as a wildcard. James opted for Jesper Parnevik and Andrew Coltart. The latter turned out to be a strange decision, bearing in mind that the Scot was not selected until singles day

Coltart's inclusion took Europe's rookie tally to seven. Another big name to miss out was Bernhard Langer who had finished 14th in the qualifying table. But for two days it didn't seem to matter that Europe were fielding an inexperienced team. By the end of the fourballs and foursomes, the visitors were leading 10-6. The stars of the show were Sergio Garcia and Jesper Parnevik who claimed three and a half points out of four, including a 3&2 victory over Tom Lehman and Tiger Woods on the first morning.

Woods was having a fairly difficult time, losing three of his four opening matches. His only success was a slender one-hole victory in a second day foursomes as he partnered wildcard Steve Pate against Padraig Harrington and Miguel-Angel Jimenez.

Over the opening two days, the Americans could only win four games, while halving four more. But on singles day the Americans struck back with a vengeance. Desperate not to lose the Ryder Cup for an unprecedented third straight time, the United States won the opening seven singles – and by some hefty margins too. None of these first seven games reached the 18th tee, while four didn't even make it to the 16th.

The hosts gave away only 3½ points out of 12, a combination of the Americans breaking loose from the pressure of being favourites, while taking advantage of some tired European limbs. Three of Europe's dozen (Jean Van de Velde, Jarmo Sandelin and Coltart) hadn't been used on days one and two, so it was no surprise that all three fell tamely on the Sunday. Van de Velde lost 6&5 to Davis Love, Sandelin was beaten 4&3 by matchplay expert Phil Mickelson, while Coltart fell to Woods 3&2.

Two of Europe's three victories were claimed on the final green, leaving newly crowned Open champion Paul Lawrie to register their only emphatic victory of the final afternoon. Lawrie dominated from the off in beating Andersen Consulting Matchplay winner Jeff Maggert 4&3. But by then it was too late.

The deciding moment came on the 17th green where Justin Leonard and Jose Maria Olazabal were all square. Leonard had been four down with seven to play before winning four in a row from the 12th. At the penultimate hole he sank a 45-foot putt, and was immediately mobbed by ecstatic team-mates. Leonard moved one hole ahead and although Olazabal squared matters on the final green, the damage had been done.

Although Leonard had failed to win any of his four ties, he was an all-American hero. The United States had regained the trophy and avoided suffering a second successive home defeat. Hal Sutton was their leading player with 3½ points out of 5.

Four Europeans also registered 3½ points – Garcia, Parnevik, Lawrie and Colin Montgomerie. Garcia and Parnevik both lost their singles while Lawrie and Monty suffered their only defeats when teaming up in a second day foursomes against Sutton and Maggert. The match went all the way down to the final hole where Maggert conjured up a fantastic iron shot to four feet for a match-winning birdie.

1991

UNITED STATES 14½
EUROPE 13½

FOURSOMES

		EUR	
SEVE BALLESTEROS	JOSE M OLAZABAL	1	V
DAVID GILFORD	COLIN MONTGOMERIE	0	V
BERNHARD LANGER	MARK JAMES	0	V
NICK FALDO	IAN WOOSNAM	0	V

FOURBALLS

STEVE RICHARDSON	MARK JAMES	1	V
SAM TORRANCE	DAVID FEHERTY	0.5	V
NICK FALDO	IAN WOOSNAM	0	V
SEVE BALLESTEROS	JOSE M OLAZABAL	1	V

FOURSOMES

NICK FALDO	DAVID GILFORD	0	V
SAM TORRANCE	DAVID FEHERTY	0	V
STEVE RICHARDSON	MARK JAMES	0	V
SEVE BALLESTEROS	JOSE M OLAZABAL	1	V

FOURBALLS

IAN WOOSNAM	PAUL BROADHURST	1	V
BERNHARD LANGER	COLIN MONTGOMERIE	1	V
STEVE RICHARDSON	MARK JAMES	1	V
SEVE BALLESTEROS	JOSE M OLAZABAL	0.5	V

SINGLES

DAVID GILFORD	0.5	V
DAVID FEHERTY	1	V
NICK FALDO	1	V
COLIN MONTGOMERIE	0.5	V
STEVE RICHARDSON	0	V
SEVE BALLESTEROS	1	V
JOSE M OLAZABAL	0	V
IAN WOOSNAM	0	V
PAUL BROADHURST	1	V
SAM TORRANCE	0	V
MARK JAMES	0	V
BERNHARD LANGER	0.5	V

1991 RYDER CUP

US			WINNER	MARGIN
0	PAUL AZINGER	CHIP BECK	EUR	2&1
1	LANNY WADKINS	HALE IRWIN	USA	4&2
1	FRED COUPLES	RAY FLOYD	USA	2&1
1	PAYNE STEWART	MARK CALCAVECCHIA	USA	1 HOLE
0	COREY PAVIN	MARK CALCAVECCHIA	EUR	5&4
0.5	LANNY WADKINS	MARK O'MEARA	HVD	–
1	FRED COUPLES	RAY FLOYD	USA	5&3
0	PAUL AZINGER	CHIP BECK	EUR	2&1
1	PAUL AZINGER	MARK O'MEARA	USA	7&6
1	LANNY WADKINS	HALE IRWIN	USA	4&2
1	PAYNE STEWART	MARK CALCAVECCHIA	USA	1 HOLE
0	FRED COUPLES	RAY FLOYD	EUR	3&2
0	PAUL AZINGER	HALE IRWIN	EUR	2&1
0	COREY PAVIN	STEVE PATE	EUR	2&1
0	LANNY WADKINS	WAYNE LEVI	EUR	3&1
0.5	PAYNE STEWART	FRED COUPLES	HVD	–
0.5	STEVE PATE (INJURED)		HVD	US INJURY
0	PAYNE STEWART		EUR	2&1
0	RAY FLOYD		EUR	2 HOLES
0.5	MARK CALCAVECCHIA		HVD	
1	COREY PAVIN		USA	2&1
0	WAYNE LEVI		EUR	3&2
1	PAUL AZINGER		USA	2 HOLES
1	CHIP BECK		USA	3&1
0	MARK O'MEARA		EUR	3&1
1	FRED COUPLES		USA	3&2
1	LANNY WADKINS		USA	3&2
0.5	HALE IRWIN		HVD	–

1993 EUROPE 13 / UNITED STATES 15

DAY 1

FOURSOMES		EUR	
SAM TORRANCE	MARK JAMES	0	V
IAN WOOSNAM	BERNHARD LANGER	1	V
SEVE BALLESTEROS	JOSE M OLAZABAL	0	V
NICK FALDO	COLIN MONTGOMERIE	1	V

FOURBALLS		EUR	
IAN WOOSNAM	PETER BAKER	1	V
BERNHARD LANGER	BARRY LANE	0	V
NICK FALDO	COLIN MONTGOMERIE	0.5	V
SEVE BALLESTEROS	JOSE M OLAZABAL	1	V

DAY 2

FOURSOMES		EUR	
NICK FALDO	COLIN MONTGOMERIE	1	V
IAN WOOSNAM	BERNHARD LANGER	1	V
PETER BAKER	BARRY LANE	0	V
SEVE BALLESTEROS	JOSE M OLAZABAL	1	V

FOURBALLS		EUR	
NICK FALDO	COLIN MONTGOMERIE	0	V
MARK JAMES	COSTANTINO ROCCA	0	V
IAN WOOSNAM	PETER BAKER	1	V
JOSE M OLAZABAL	JOAKIM HAEGGMAN	0	V

DAY 3

SINGLES	EUR	
SAM TORRANCE	0.5	V
BARRY LANE	0	V
COLIN MONTGOMERIE	1	V
PETER BAKER	1	V
IAN WOOSNAM	0.5	V
JOAKIM HAEGGMAN	1	V
MARK JAMES	0	V
COSTANTINO ROCCA	0	V
SEVE BALLESTEROS	0	V
JOSE M OLAZABAL	0	V
BERNHARD LANGER	0	V
NICK FALDO	0.5	V

1993 RYDER CUP

'S			WINNER	MARGIN
	LANNY WADKINS	COREY PAVIN	USA	4&3
	PAYNE STEWART	PAUL AZINGER	EUR	7&5
	TOM KITE	DAVIS LOVE	USA	2&1
	RAY FLOYD	FRED COUPLES	EUR	4&3
0	JIM GALLAGHER	LEE JANZEN	EUR	1 HOLE
1	LANNY WADKINS	COREY PAVIN	USA	4&2
.5	PAUL AZINGER	FRED COUPLES	HVD	
	TOM KITE	DAVIS LOVE	EUR	4&3
0	LANNY WADKINS	COREY PAVIN	EUR	3&2
0	PAUL AZINGER	FRED COUPLES	EUR	2&1
0	RAY FLOYD	PAYNE STEWART	USA	3&2
0	TOM KITE	DAVIS LOVE	EUR	2&1
1	JOHN COOK	CHIP BECK	USA	2 HOLES
1	COREY PAVIN	JIM GALLAGHER	USA	5&4
0	PAUL AZINGER	FRED COUPLES	EUR	6&5
1	RAY FLOYD	PAYNE STEWART	USA	2&1
0.5	LANNY WADKINS		HVD	EUR INJURY
1	CHIP BECK		USA	1 HOLE
0	LEE JANZEN		EUR	1 HOLE
0	COREY PAVIN		EUR	2 HOLES
0.5	FRED COUPLES		HVD	–
0	JOHN COOK		EUR	1 HOLE
1	PAYNE STEWART		USA	3&2
1	DAVIS LOVE		USA	1 HOLE
1	JIM GALLAGHER		USA	3&2
1	RAY FLOYD		USA	2 HOLES
1	TOM KITE		USA	5&3
0.5	PAUL AZINGER		HVD	–

1995 UNITED STATES 13½
EUROPE 14½

			EUR	
DAY 1	**FOURSOMES**			
	NICK FALDO	COLIN MONTGOMERIE	0	V
	COSTANTINO ROCCA	SAM TORRANCE	1	V
	HOWARD CLARK	MARK JAMES	0	V
	P-U JOHANSSON	BERNHARD LANGER	1	V
	FOURBALLS			
	SEVE BALLESTEROS	DAVID GILFORD	1	V
	COSTANTINO ROCCA	SAM TORRANCE	0	V
	NICK FALDO	COLIN MONTGOMERIE	0	V
	P-U JOHANSSON	BERNHARD LANGER	0	V
DAY 2	**FOURSOMES**			
	NICK FALDO	COLIN MONTGOMERIE	1	V
	COSTANTINO ROCCA	SAM TORRANCE	1	V
	IAN WOOSNAM	PHILIP WALTON	0	V
	DAVID GILFORD	BERNHARD LANGER	1	V
	FOURBALLS			
	COLIN MONTGOMERIE	SAM TORRANCE	0	V
	COSTANTINO ROCCA	IAN WOOSNAM	1	V
	SEVE BALLESTEROS	DAVID GILFORD	0	V
	NICK FALDO	BERNHARD LANGER	0	V
DAY 3	**SINGLES**			
	SEVE BALLESTEROS		0	V
	HOWARD CLARK		1	V
	MARK JAMES		1	V
	IAN WOOSNAM		0.5	V
	COSTANTINO ROCCA		0	V
	DAVID GILFORD		1	V
	COLIN MONTGOMERIE		1	V
	NICK FALDO		1	V
	SAM TORRANCE		1	V
	BERNHARD LANGER		0	V
	PHILIP WALTON		1	V
	P-U JOHANSSON		0	V

1995 RYDER CUP

US			WINNER	MARGIN
1	COREY PAVIN	TOM LEHMAN	USA	1 HOLE
0	FRED COUPLES	JAY HAAS	EUR	3&2
1	DAVIS LOVE	JEFF MAGGERT	USA	4&3
0	BEN CRENSHAW	CURTIS STRANGE	EUR	1 HOLE
0	BRAD FAXON	PETER JACOBSEN	EUR	4&3
1	JEFF MAGGERT	LOREN ROBERTS	USA	6&5
1	FRED COUPLES	DAVIS LOVE	USA	3&2
1	PHIL MICKELSON	COREY PAVIN	USA	6&4
0	JAY HAAS	CURTIS STRANGE	EUR	4&2
0	DAVIS LOVE	JEFF MAGGERT	EUR	6&5
1	PETER JACOBSEN	LOREN ROBERTS	USA	1 HOLE
0	COREY PAVIN	TOM LEHMAN	EUR	4&3
1	FRED COUPLES	BRAD FAXON	USA	4&2
0	BEN CRENSHAW	DAVIS LOVE	EUR	3&2
1	JAY HAAS	PHIL MICKELSON	USA	3&2
1	COREY PAVIN	LOREN ROBERTS	USA	1 HOLE
1	TOM LEHMAN		USA	4&3
0	PETER JACOBSEN		EUR	1 HOLE
0	JEFF MAGGERT		EUR	4&3
0.5	FRED COUPLES		HVD	–
1	DAVIS LOVE		USA	3&2
0	BRAD FAXON		EUR	1 HOLE
0	BEN CRENSHAW		EUR	3&1
0	CURTIS STRANGE		EUR	1 HOLE
0	LOREN ROBERTS		EUR	2&1
1	COREY PAVIN		USA	3&2
0	JAY HAAS		EUR	1 HOLE
1	PHIL MICKELSON		USA	2&1

1997

EUROPE 14½
UNITED STATES 13½

DAY 1	FOURBALLS		EUR	
	JOSE M OLAZABAL	COSTANTINO ROCCA	1	V
	NICK FALDO	LEE WESTWOOD	0	V
	JESPER PARNEVIK	P-U JOHANSSON	1	V
	COLIN MONTGOMERIE	BERNHARD LANGER	0	V
	FOURSOMES			
	JOSE M OLAZABAL	COSTANTINO ROCCA	0	V
	COLIN MONTGOMERIE	BERNHARD LANGER	1	V
	NICK FALDO	LEE WESTWOOD	1	V
	JESPER PARNEVIK	IGNACIO GARRIDO	0.5	V

DAY 2	FOURBALLS			
	COLIN MONTGOMERIE	DARREN CLARKE	1	V
	IAN WOOSNAM	THOMAS BJORN	1	V
	NICK FALDO	LEE WESTWOOD	1	V
	JOSE M OLAZABAL	IGNACIO GARRIDO	0.5	V
	FOURSOMES			
	COLIN MONTGOMERIE	BERNHARD LANGER	1	V
	NICK FALDO	LEE WESTWOOD	0	V
	JESPER PARNEVIK	IGNACIO GARRIDO	0.5	V
	JOSE M OLAZABAL	COSTANTINO ROCCA	1	V

DAY 3	SINGLES			
	IAN WOOSNAM		0	V
	P-U JOHANSSON		1	V
	JESPER PARNEVIK		0	V
	DARREN CLARKE		0	V
	COSTANTINO ROCCA		1	V
	THOMAS BJORN		0.5	V
	IGNACIO GARRIDO		0	V
	BERNHARD LANGER		1	V
	LEE WESTWOOD		0	V
	JOSE M OLAZABAL		0	V
	NICK FALDO		0	V
	COLIN MONTGOMERIE		0.5	V

1997 RYDER CUP

US			WINNER	MARGIN
0	DAVIS LOVE	PHIL MICKELSON	EUR	1 HOLE
1	FRED COUPLES	BRAD FAXON	USA	1 HOLE
0	TOM LEHMAN	JIM FURYK	EUR	1 HOLE
1	TIGER WOODS	MARK O'MEARA	USA	3&2
1	SCOTT HOCH	LEE JANZEN	USA	1 HOLE
0	TIGER WOODS	MARK O'MEARA	EUR	5&3
0	JUSTIN LEONARD	JEFF MAGGERT	EUR	3&2
0.5	TOM LEHMAN	PHIL MICKELSON	HVD	–
0	FRED COUPLES	DAVIS LOVE	EUR	1 HOLE
0	JUSTIN LEONARD	BRAD FAXON	EUR	2&1
0	TIGER WOODS	MARK O'MEARA	EUR	2&1
0.5	TOM LEHMAN	PHIL MICKELSON	HVD	–
0	LEE JANZEN	JIM FURYK	EUR	1 HOLE
1	SCOTT HOCH	JEFF MAGGERT	USA	1 HOLE
0.5	JUSTIN LEONARD	TIGER WOODS	HVD	–
0	FRED COUPLES	DAVIS LOVE	EUR	5&4
1	FRED COUPLES		USA	8&7
0	DAVIS LOVE		EUR	3&2
1	MARK O'MEARA		USA	5&4
1	PHIL MICKELSON		USA	2&1
0	TIGER WOODS		EUR	4&2
0.5	JUSTIN LEONARD		HVD	–
1	TOM LEHMAN		USA	7&6
0	BRAD FAXON		EUR	2&1
1	JEFF MAGGERT		USA	3&2
1	LEE JANZEN		USA	1 HOLE
1	JIM FURYK		USA	3&2
0.5	SCOTT HOCH		HVD	–

1999 UNITED STATES 14½
EUROPE 13½

DAY 1

FOURSOMES		EUR	
PAUL LAWRIE	COLIN MONTGOMERIE	1	V
SERGIO GARCIA	JESPER PARNEVIK	1	V
PADRAIG HARRINGTON	MIGUEL A JIMENEZ	0.5	V
DARREN CLARKE	LEE WESTWOOD	0	V

FOURBALLS			
SERGIO GARCIA	JESPER PARNEVIK	1	V
PAUL LAWRIE	COLIN MONTGOMERIE	0.5	V
MIGUEL A JIMENEZ	JOSE M OLAZABAL	1	V
DARREN CLARKE	LEE WESTWOOD	1	V

DAY 2

FOURSOMES			
PAUL LAWRIE	COLIN MONTGOMERIE	0	V
DARREN CLARKE	LEE WESTWOOD	1	V
PADRAIG HARRINGTON	MIGUEL A JIMENEZ	0	V
SERGIO GARCIA	JESPER PARNEVIK	1	V

FOURBALLS			
DARREN CLARKE	LEE WESTWOOD	0	V
SERGIO GARCIA	JESPER PARNEVIK	0.5	V
MIGUEL A JIMENEZ	JOSE M OLAZABAL	0.5	V
PAUL LAWRIE	COLIN MONTGOMERIE	1	V

DAY 3

SINGLES			
LEE WESTWOOD		0	V
J VAN DE VELDE		0	V
JARMO SANDELIN		0	V
DARREN CLARKE		0	V
JESPER PARNEVIK		0	V
ANDREW COLTART		0	V
MIGUEL A JIMENEZ		0	V
PADRAIG HARRINGTON		1	V
SERGIO GARCIA		0	V
PAUL LAWRIE		1	V
JOSE M OLAZABAL		0.5	V
COLIN MONTGOMERIE		1	V

1999 RYDER CUP

US			WINNER	MARGIN
0	DAVID DUVAL	PHIL MICKELSON	EUR	3&2
0	TOM LEHMAN	TIGER WOODS	EUR	2&1
0.5	DAVIS LOVE	PAYNE STEWART	HVD	–
1	JEFF MAGGERT	HAL SUTTON	USA	3&2
0	JIM FURYK	PHIL MICKELSON	EUR	1 HOLE
0.5	DAVIS LOVE	JUSTIN LEONARD	HVD	
0	JEFF MAGGERT	HAL SUTTON	EUR	2&1
0	DAVID DUVAL	TIGER WOODS	EUR	1 HOLE
1	JEFF MAGGERT	HAL SUTTON	USA	1 HOLE
0	JIM FURYK	MARK O'MEARA	EUR	3&2
1	STEVE PATE	TIGER WOODS	USA	1 HOLE
0	JUSTIN LEONARD	PAYNE STEWART	EUR	3&2
1	TOM LEHMAN	PHIL MICKELSON	USA	2&1
0.5	DAVID DUVAL	DAVIS LOVE	HVD	–
0.5	JUSTIN LEONARD	HAL SUTTON	HVD	–
0	STEVE PATE	TIGER WOODS	EUR	2&1
1	TOM LEHMAN		USA	3&2
1	DAVIS LOVE		USA	6&5
1	PHIL MICKELSON		USA	4&3
1	HAL SUTTON		USA	4&2
1	DAVID DUVAL		USA	5&4
1	TIGER WOODS		USA	3&2
1	STEVE PATE		USA	2&1
0	MARK O'MEARA		EUR	1 HOLE
1	JIM FURYK		USA	4&3
0	JEFF MAGGERT		EUR	4&3
0.5	JUSTIN LEONARD		HVD	–
0	PAYNE STEWART		EUR	1 HOLE

RYDER CUP COURSES

BY PETER LEVINGER

Verulam Golf Club

London Road, St Albans AL1 1JG, United Kingdom
Tel +44 (0)1727 853327 Fax +44 (0)1727 812201
www.verulamgolf.co.uk

front nine

HOLE	1	2	3	4	5	6	7	8	9	OUT
YARDS	365	343	312	412	384	314	433	180	545	3288
PAR	4	4	4	4	4	4	4	3	5	36
STROKE INDEX	7	11	17	3	5	15	1	9	13	

COURSE HISTORY

LOCATION St Albans, Hertfordshire, about 20 miles north of London. Easily accessible from the M1 or A1. Nearest airport London Luton.

COURSE This is not only where it all began but was also the home course of the great Abe Mitchell, mentor to the Ryder Cup founder Sam Ryder.

Ryder took up golf in 1908, while recovering from illness, and was soon elected club captain in keeping with his status as Mayor of St Albans. Never a man to do things by halves, Ryder fell in love with the game and courted the patronage of leading players including Abe Mitchell, who was to become his personal teacher. There is no doubt that the plans to create the Ryder Cup emanated at Verulam, including the unofficial matches which preceded the first tournament in 1927.

Originally formed in 1905, the club was first located in the grounds of Sopwell House. In 1912, adjacent land was purchased and architect James Braid laid out the course which has remained largely unchanged until today. The splendid clubhouse is adorned with memorabilia to Ryder and the trophy and houses the Abe Mitchell Lounge Bar (he was club captain from 1936) and the Ryder Dining Room.

The course is parkland, broken up by strategically planted stands of trees and some water. It is a delightful course to play, with frequent views of St Albans cathedral; a hidden gem.

HOLE OF THE COURSE This has to be the par-three 17th (135 yards SI 17), one of the most unusual in golf in that the tee and green are separated by a road. The tee shot is downhill so the road is not only hidden from view but is protected by a large net that does not interfere with play. This has not stopped many a wayward tee shot reaching moving traffic and there is some evidence to suggest that one such shot lodged itself in a passing lorry and ended up in Swansea-the longest tee shot at a par-three ever?

PROFESSIONAL Mick Birch

GREEN FEES Visitors and societies are welcome at specified times.

CLUB HOUSE Traditional, comfortable and steeped in history.

ACCOMMODATION Sopwell House Hotel, Cottonmill Lane, St Albans, Herts AL1 2HQ. Golf packages (incl green fees) from £293 Tel 01727 864477 Fax 01727 844741

back nine

HOLE	10	11	12	13	14	15	16	17	18	IN	TOTAL
YARDS	185	539	336	375	339	373	294	135	575	3160	6448
PAR	3	5	4	4	4	4	4	3	5	36	72
STROKE INDEX	8	14	12	10	6	2	18	16	4		

COURSE HISTORY

1927

Worcester Country Club

2 Rice Street, Worcester MA 01606 USA
Tel 001 508 853 8064 Fax 001 508 853 7056
www.worcestercountryclub.com

LOCATION Central Massachusetts about 45 minutes from Boston, on Routes 290, 9, 495 and Mass. Pike.

COURSE Another Donald Ross course, dating back to 1900. Will this genius of golf course design, whose courses will probably long outlive bricks and mortar, be remembered as will a Lutyens or other Edwardian architect? He certainly deserves to be.

At 6,422 yards, this course is not the longest, but it is well regarded for its dog leg par-fours, three par-fives and three par-threes. The course hosted one of the most famous US Opens in 1925. In the practice round, Walter Hagen recorded the first hole in one at the par-three 6th, using a one-iron after breaking the shaft of the club he was about to use!

During the tournament, Bobby Jones announced that his ball had moved while

front nine

HOLE	1	2	3	4	5	6	7	8	9	OUT
YARDS	380	558	372	232	478	179	398	177	410	3184
PAR	4	5	4	3	5	3	4	3	4	35
STROKE INDEX	13	3	9	11	7	15	5	17	1	

at address on the 11th hole. Despite being the only witness, he penalised himself one stroke. This was to cost him the Championship, as he tied scores after 72 holes before losing the play-off to Willie MacFarlane.

HOLE OF THE COURSE At 416 yards, the 12th may seem well within two comfortable shots. The approach, however, is blind to an elevated green, guarded by bunkers and sloping away front to back. The hole justly deserves its selection as SI 2.

PROFESSIONAL Allan J Belden

GREEN FEES Invitation only

CLUBHOUSE This is a private members club, the facilities steeped in traditional service and style. Famous for its summer marquee.

ACCOMMODATION Beechwood Hotel, 363 Plantation Street, Worcester, MA 01605 USA. Price range $119 - $239. Book through www.hotelroom.com

---

1927 RYDER CUP
US 9½ v GB 2½

This is where it all began – officially matchplay golf's Garden of Eden! Even in these early days, drama was not unknown, with the nominated British Captain, Abe Mitchell, struck down at the last minute with appendicitis and replaced by Ted Ray. This was the year of Charles Lindburgh's solo flight across the Atlantic; so 4-6 day boat journeys were the order of the day. By the time the boat sailed, the British were a man short so the Jersey-based Herbert Jolly was called in from the Channel Islands and followed on four days after the rest of the party.

The British team were soundly defeated, with only one match even making it to the final hole.

---

back nine

HOLE	10	11	12	13	14	15	16	17	18	IN	TOTAL
YARDS	161	388	420	196	344	534	407	462	326	3238	6422
PAR	3	4	4	3	4	5	4	4	4	35	70
STROKE INDEX	18	8	2	12	16	6	10	4	14		

1929

Moortown Golf Club

Harrogate Road, Leeds LS17 7DB, UK
Tel +44 (0)113 2683 636 Fax +44 (0)113 2680 986
www.moortown-gc.co.uk

LOCATION Six miles north of Leeds on the A61; from Leeds city centre follow Ring Road to A61, signposted Harrogate.

COURSE Moortown Golf Club was formed in 1909 with just one hole! The designer, Dr Alistair MacKenzie, completed work on the course by the 1920s and his designs were to remain virtually unchanged for the next 60 years.

The course has an international reputation and is without doubt the best known in Yorkshire. The 18 top class golf holes start, unusually, with two par-fives.

The course is mainly flat, a mixture of parkland and heathland. The 18th is a splendid closing hole, worthy of deciding the outcome of any championship.

HOLE OF THE COURSE The short par-three 10th is MacKenzie's renowned short hole – "Gibraltar" – and Moortown's

front nine

HOLE	1	2	3	4	5	6	7	8	9	OUT
YARDS	490	456	446	174	363	446	516	220	470	3581
PAR	5	5	4	3	4	4	5	3	4	37
STROKE INDEX	11	3	9	17	13	1	7	15	5	

signature hole. Four bunkers guard a green that is reached by an uphill tee shot. At SI 18, there is little forgiveness here.

PROFESSIONAL Bryon Hutchinson

GREEN FEES Week-days £55 ($85) weekends £65 ($100)

CLUBHOUSE A mixture of modern and traditional values, coupled with Yorkshire hospitality. The billiard room is a marvel in its own right.

ACCOMMODATION Haley's Hotel and Restaurant, Shire Oak Road, Headingley, Leeds LS6 2DE. Tel 0113 278 4446 Fax 0113 275 3342

Haley's is just two miles from Leeds city centre, in Shire Oak Road, Headingley – a leafy conservation area – just off the main Otley Road (A660) which is the main route from the city centre to Otley, Ilkley and Leeds/Bradford Airport. The Leeds Outer Ring Road is minutes away. Rates: Double room £125-175 inc breakfast.

1929 RYDER CUP
GB 7 v US 5

1929 at Moortown was the venue for the first series of matches on British soil. American captain Walter Hagen, in keeping with his true gentlemanly behaviour, decided to give every player on his team at least one match, whereas the British captain George Duncan selected his players on a strategic basis. In fact two, Percy Alliss (father of Peter) and Stewart Burns, did not feature at all!

In what was to be Henry Cotton's debut, the home team, in excellent weather, turned around a 1 point deficit at the end of the first day to record a winning margin of 7-5.

The highlight of the singles was the match between the two captains, with Duncan demolishing Hagen 10&8. Another interesting aspect about this series of matches was the R & A's rules on clubs. It was not until 1930 that they sanctioned the use of steel shafts, so the US team had to change to hickory. The US PGA got its own back in the 1960s with the introduction of the 'big ball' that for many years was blamed for the decline of British golf!

back nine

HOLE	10	11	12	13	14	15	16	17	18	IN	TOTAL
YARDS	176	367	564	439	437	397	417	190	436	3423	7004
PAR	3	4	5	4	4	4	4	3	4	35	72
STROKE INDEX	18	10	2	4	12	14	6	16	8		

1931

Scioto Country Club

2196 Riverside Drive, Columbus, OH 43221 USA
Tel 001 614 486 4341 Fax 001 614 486 8327

LOCATION From Interstate I-35, exit at Lane Avenue. Proceed in a westerly direction and turn onto Riverside Drive heading south; the entrance to the club is on the left.

COURSE Scioto Country Club was formed in 1916. The golf course architect was the fabled Donald Ross. It has hosted five Major championships including the US Open won by Bobby Jones in 1926.

The Golden Bear, Mr Jack Nicklaus, was taught on this course by pro Jack Grout. It is almost fitting that Nicklaus's great design, Muirfield Village, is just down the road. This is definitely in the world's top 100 courses, and is perhaps

front nine

HOLE	1	2	3	4	5	6	7	8	9	OUT
YARDS	418	459	381	188	439	527	378	509	160	3459
PAR	4	4	4	3	4	5	4	5	3	36
STROKE INDEX	9	1	11	15	7	5	13	3	17	

made more desirable by the fact that it is a private members club, thus making it exclusive to play. Even the scorecard is a thing of beauty, conjuring up a picture of an immaculately manicured course.

HOLE OF THE COURSE The par-four 459 yard 2nd (SI 1) is one of the finest in the world. Driving to an uphill plateau, bunkers on the right and trees on the left are waiting to snaffle any wayward tee shots. The green is surrounded by water, is well bunkered and elevated from the fairway, with a front to back slope.

PROFESSIONAL David Tiedmann

GREEN FEES $80 (£48) – invitation only

CLUBHOUSE A recent course reviewer describes it as "oozing tradition".

ACCOMMODATION Courtyard Columbus Dublin, 5175 Post Road, Dublin, OH 43017 USA Tel 001 614 228 3200

1931 RYDER CUP
US 9 v GB 3

In the third series of matches after one win each, 'Hagen's Heroes', in hot, humid conditions, recorded a comfortable victory.

Controversy dogged the event. The British PGA interpreted the Trust Deed as prohibiting two of their players on the grounds that they were professionals at clubs outside Britain. Percy Alliss, father of Peter, was attached to the Wansee Club of Berlin and Aubrey Boomer was attached to a Parisien club. The British sought to draft in Henry Cotton, who refused to travel with the rest of the team because of other golfing commitments, and was thus omitted.

The level of the US victory was amplified by the 10&9 margin over 36 holes between Hagen & Shute over Duncan & Mitchell.

back nine

HOLE	10	11	12	13	14	15	16	17	18	IN	TOTAL
YARDS	421	365	546	446	236	425	420	191	446	3496	6955
PAR	4	4	5	4	3	4	4	3	4	35	71
STROKE INDEX	6	8	4	14	18	10	2	16	12		

1933/37

Southport & Ainsdale

Bradshaws Lane, Ainsdale, Southport, Merseyside PR8 3LG
Tel +44 (0)1704 578092 Fax +44 (0)1704 570896
www.sandagolfclub.co.uk

LOCATION Junction 26 from M6. Closest airport is John Lennon, Liverpool.

COURSE A few miles south of Royal Lytham, equidistant between Liverpool and Blackpool, is the town of Southport. In a cluster of four magnificent links courses – Lytham, Royal Birkdale, Hillside and Formby – lies S&A, as it is affectionately known by its members. S&A shares the distinction with Royal Birkdale of hosting two Ryder Cups.

The 18 hole, 6,640 yard, par-72 links course starts and finishes at the clubhouse. Set among ranges of tall sandhills and smaller sand dunes, the course, designed by the legendary James Braid in 1906 and remodelled in the 1920s, is a true test of golf for all golfers and is famous for its heather and gorse.

Accuracy is of ultimate importance and you need to plan your drive rather than just hit it as far as possible. The par-three first (nicknamed The Trial) is a notable example and players should also watch out for the 16th – The Gumbleys.

HOLE OF THE COURSE Among many

front nine

HOLE	1	2	3	4	5	6	7	8	9	OUT
YARDS	204	520	430	350	448	386	483	153	490	3464
PAR	3	5	4	4	4	4	5	3	5	37
STROKE INDEX	13	3	11	15	1	5	6	17	7	

fine holes we have selected the 3rd, a par-four 430 yarder called 'Braids'. The hill next to the tee amplifies the beautiful surroundings from where the Welsh Hills can be seen on a fine day. The fairway is traversed at 260-280 yards (40 less from the yellows) by a diagonal ridge, making the second shot blind for the longer drives. At SI 11, the extra stroke is fairly allocated.

PROFESSIONAL Jim Payne

GREEN FEES Weekdays £50 ($75) per round, weekends £75 ($110)

CLUBHOUSE Modern, air-conditioned facilities, in traditional surroundings. Mementos from the Ryder Cup abound.

ACCOMMODATION The Scarisbrook Tel: 01704 543000
www.scarisbrookhotel.com
Ideally situated in the heart of Southport's tree-lined main boulevard, this traditional hotel offers the discerning visitor the highest standards of accommodation, cuisine and service. Close to the Promenade, Floral Hall, Arts Centre and only 12 miles from the motorway network.

1933 RYDER CUP
GB 6½ v US 5½

With 15,000 spectators following the action, the final singles match of 1933 provided one of the most exciting finishes in Cup history. Britain's Syd Easterbrook and American Denny Shute were all square on the final green facing par putts of 30 feet each. Easterbrook put his approach within tap-in range. Shute hit his first putt four feet past and missed the return. The trophy went back to Britain by 6½-5½ and tied the series, 2-2.

1937 RYDER CUP
GB 4 v US 8

1937 saw the first victory by a US team on British soil, through rookies Sam Snead, Byron Nelson and Ed Dudley. The event was played throughout in wind and rain. The singles, contested over 36 holes, saw Percy Alliss squander a three hole lead to Gene Sarazen, whose recovery was sparked when a wayward tee shot at the par-three 13th bounced back off a spectator and on to the green.

back nine

HOLE	10	11	12	13	14	15	16	17	18	IN	TOTAL
YARDS	183	442	403	155	396	343	508	443	350	3223	6963
PAR	3	4	4	3	4	4	5	4	4	35	72
STROKE INDEX	18	4	10	16	6	12	2	8	14		

1935

Ridgewood Country Club

96 West Midland Avenue, Paramus, NJ 07652 USA
Tel 001 201 599 3900 Fax 001 201 599 1457

LOCATION About 35 miles north-west of New York City off Highway 17.

COURSE The Ridgewood Country Club traces its history as far back as 1890. It is the oldest club in New Jersey.

Renowned golf course architect A.W. Tillinghast designed and oversaw construction of the 27-hole course, which opened on May 30, 1929. Although he also found fame for designs at Baltusrol, Winged Foot and Bethpage State Park,

center course

HOLE	1	2	3	4	5	6	7	8	9	OUT
YARDS	370	563	458	530	216	289	396	143	380	3345
PAR	4	5	5	5	3	4	4	3	4	37
STROKE INDEX	6	1	2	4	8	7	3	9	5	

east course

HOLE	1	2	3	4	5	6	7	8	9	OUT
YARDS	375	170	567	414	407	229	460	403	379	3404
PAR	4	3	5	5	4	3	5	4	4	37
STROKE INDEX	7	9	1	4	3	8	2	6	5	

COURSE HISTORY

Ridgewood is regarded by many as the pinnacle of Tillinghast's achievements.

The layout is divided into three courses of nine holes – Center, West and East. The Center course provides the most challenging holes. Ridgewood has staged many events using a combination of the courses and sometimes a composite course. In 1990 the US Senior Open, won by Lee Trevino, was played on Center/West while the PGA Seniors used a combination in 2001.

HOLE OF THE COURSE The challenging and picturesque par-four, 289 yard 6th on the Center Course, played to a small green. Stroke Index 7 (or 14 for 18 holes), it is nicknamed the 'five and dime' as that is what your score can vary between!

PROFESSIONAL Bill Adams

GREEN FEES Invitation only, $75 (£50)

CLUBHOUSE Restaurant and snack bar. Historic and traditional facilities for its members.

ACCOMMODATION Anywhere in Manhattan. That way, if you are not invited you will at least be in easy reach of the many other courses in the area.

1935 RYDER CUP
US 9 v GB 3

Using the combination of Center/East courses, Ridgewood played host to the 1935 series of matches. It is noteworthy that many new US courses have been used for the Ryder Cup shortly after opening – Muirfield Village, Eldorado and Kiawah Island particularly coming to mind.

American captain Walter Hagen and team member Gene Sarazen stayed in rooms above the pro shop during the matches. Not that it effected their form – the home team won the first three foursomes by comfortable margins (6&5, 7&6 and 9&8) and never looked back. In fact with two contests halved, the British prevailed in only two matches and those by the closest of margins, each being won on the last.

The Ridgewood matches are remembered as the finale of Walter Hagen's participation in an event that he had done much to inaugurate. At a time when the competition was approximately half the length of what it is today, he retired with a total of 7 wins, one half and only one defeat!

west course

HOLE	1	2	3	4	5	6	7	8	9	OUT
YARDS	371	384	202	597	413	151	420	569	427	3534
PAR	4	4	3	5	5	3	4	5	4	37
STROKE INDEX	7	5	8	2	3	9	6	1	4	

COURSE HISTORY

1939

Ponte Vedra

200 Ponte Vedra Boulevard, Ponte Vedra Beach, Florida 32082 USA
Tel 001 (904) 285 1111 Fax 001 (904) 285 2111
www.pvresorts.com

LOCATION Northern Florida near Jacksonville, located off I-A1A. Nearest airport Jacksonville.

COURSE The Ocean Course was designed in 1928 by British architect Herbert Bertram Strong.

The par-72 Ocean Course was the area's first golf resort. Strong dredged adjoining lagoons and built up a series of earth mounds that dot the fairways, creating dramatic undulations.

front nine

HOLE	1	2	3	4	5	6	7	8	9	OUT
YARDS	415	361	547	467	221	521	409	442	144	3527
PAR	4	4	5	4	3	5	4	4	3	36
STROKE INDEX	11	13	1	3	15	5	7	9	17	

COURSE HISTORY

This course has hosted the US Open on five occasions with the immortal Bobby Jones describing it as "a course to challenge professionals."

The course is noted for its elevated greens and 90 sand bunkers.

HOLE OF THE COURSE Hole number 9 is a 144 yard par-three, SI 17. It features the first ever island green.

PROFESSIONAL Jim Howard

GREEN FEES $107 (£71)

CLUBHOUSE Overlooking the 'island' 9th, the stylish clubhouse has facilities in keeping with the resort's five star approach. Excellent casual dining in the evening, superb buffet lunch.

ACCOMMODATION On site at the resort – 221 elegantly appointed guest rooms and suites set on miles of unspoiled, white Atlantic Ocean beaches. Rates from $200, with golf packages available.

1939 RYDER CUP
CANCELLED

The Ocean Course at Ponte Vedra was selected as the venue for the 1939 series of matches, but had to be cancelled because of the outbreak of hostilities. One day...!

---

back nine

HOLE	10	11	12	13	14	15	16	17	18	IN	TOTAL
YARDS	308	443	182	559	485	413	131	404	359	3284	6811
PAR	4	4	3	5	5	4	3	4	4	36	72
STROKE INDEX	18	4	12	2	8	10	16	6	14		

COURSE HISTORY

1947

Portland Golf Club

5900 SW Scholls Ferry Rd, Portland, Oregon 97225, Washington County USA
Tel 001 503 292 2778 Fax 001 503 292 9177

LOCATION Approx five miles south-west of Portland, just off Interstate 5. Portland golf club is located on Route 210 in the district of Raleigh Hills. The nearest airport is Portland International, approx 20 miles away.

COURSE A mature course dating back to 1916. Fir trees separate fairways giving each hole a character, and name, of its own.

The 7th and 11th share a lake as a hazard. The tee shot at the latter needs to carry the lake, whereas the second shot on the 7th needs to clear the water to reach the green. The best advice is to play below the hole. The greens are smooth and very fast.

front nine

HOLE	1	2	3	4	5	6	7	8	9	OUT
YARDS	413	436	339	132	524	380	351	195	361	3131
PAR	4	4	4	3	5	4	4	3	4	35
STROKE INDEX	5	1	13	17	3	9	11	15	7	

COURSE HISTORY

HOLE OF THE COURSE The par-three, 208 yard 12th plays downhill to a green guarded by four bunkers. Highly regarded by selectors of leading golf holes; anything from a three- to five-iron is required here. Beware the trees on the left, marking out of bounds.

PROFESSIONAL Chris Mitchell

GREEN FEES $135 (£90). Green times can be requested by bona fide members of other private clubs. Handicap certificate required. Reciprocal arrangements with Knole Park Golf Club in Kent.

CLUBHOUSE Timber-clad, attractive building, completely in harmony with the existing surroundings.

ACCOMMODATION Portland Marriott Downtown. 1401 SW Naito Parkway, Portland, OR 97201 USA
Tel 1 503 226 7600
Fax 1 503 221 1789

1947 RYDER CUP
US 11 v GB 1

A near whitewash in the first post-war series of matches. In fact the sole British point was scored in the final singles, when Sam King defeated Herman Keiser 4&3.

Following the war, British golf was at a low ebb both on the course and financially. An Oregon fruit farmer and grocery magnate, Robert Hudson, kindly funded the British team and arranged to stage the matches at his local club, Portland. He travelled across country to meet the Queen Mary in New York and accompanied the team on the three day trans-continental rail journey.

Arriving from the austerity of post-war Britain, the British team was shown considerable hospitality both in Portland and on a countrywide tour thereafter. Although the golf was uneven the event did much to foster true sportsmanship and encourage the British PGA to ensure that the bi-annual meetings continued as a permanent fixture.

back nine

HOLE	10	11	12	13	14	15	16	17	18	IN	TOTAL
YARDS	509	370	208	384	390	542	420	171	558	3552	6955
PAR	5	4	3	4	4	5	4	3	5	37	72
STROKE INDEX	12	6	16	2	8	4	14	18	10		

1949

Ganton Golf Club

Ganton, North Yorkshire YO12 4PA
Tel +44 (0)1944 710 329 Fax +44 (0)1944 710922
www.gantongolfclub.com

LOCATION Ganton Golf Club is located 11 miles south-west of Scarborough. From the A1, access is available to the A64.

COURSE Golf was first played at Ganton in the summer of 1891 on a course laid out by Tom Chisholm of St Andrews, who had assistance from Robert Bird, the club's first professional and head greenkeeper.

The site chosen then formed part of Sir Charles Legard's Ganton Estate and was very rough ground, covered with many varieties of grasses and wild flowers. Thousands of years previously this site had been an inlet from the North Sea, and the natural sandy subsoil was an ideal place to develop a course. Six time winner of the British Open Harry Vardon – famous for that grip – was club professional between 1896 and 1903.

front nine

HOLE	1	2	3	4	5	6	7	8	9	OUT
YARDS	373	445	334	406	157	470	435	414	504	3538
PAR	4	4	4	4	3	4	4	4	5	36
STROKE INDEX	15	7	13	5	17	9	1	11	3	

COURSE HISTORY

The course is laid out on undulating heathland with few trees, except on the boundaries. The views can be stunning, notably on the 10th hole, looking towards Ganton Village. At 6,734 yards from the white tees, this is not the longest golf course. In fact there are only two par-fives and only one over 500 yards. The wind is a major factor, blowing in from the North Sea. Accuracy is essential as wayward shots will be swallowed up by gorse which surrounds many fairways and the back of greens.

HOLE OF THE COURSE The genius of designer Harry Colt, who while not the original designer, made significant alterations in the first decade of the 20th century, marks the 406 yard, par-four 4th as one of the best holes on the outward half. The second shot is across a valley to a plateau green, where surrounding gorse punishes less than perfect shots.

PROFESSIONAL Gary Brown

GREEN FEES £60 ($90) weekdays £70 ($105) weekends and Bank Holidays

---

1949 RYDER CUP
GB 5 v US 7

Ganton was home to the Ryder Cup in 1949. The first post-war event on British soil saw the USA team, captained by the great Ben Hogan, overturn an overnight 3-1 deficit to beat the British team 7-5.

Ganton also hosted the Curtis Cup in 2000 and will be the venue for the Walker Cup in 2003.

CLUBHOUSE Ganton's website describes the clubhouse as having 'an unmistakable air of character and quality'.

ACCOMMODATION
Beiderbeckes Hotel
Tel 01723 365766
The Ganton Greyhound Hotel
Tel 01944 710116
Marriott Hotel York
Tel 01904 701000

back nine

HOLE	10	11	12	13	14	15	16	17	18	IN	TOTAL
YARDS	168	417	363	524	282	461	448	249	434	**3346**	**6884**
PAR	3	4	4	5	4	4	4	3	4	**35**	**71**
STROKE INDEX	18	6	10	2	16	4	8	14	12		

1951

Pinehurst

1 Carolina Vista Drive, P.O. Box 4000, Village of Pinehurst, NC 28374 USA
Tel 001 910 295 6811 Fax 001 910 235 8466
www.pinehurst.com

LOCATION From Raleigh, take Route 1 south to the junction with Hwy 50. Head south and the Pinehurst Resort is directed.

COURSE Golf's 'Hermitage of St Petersburg' – and with eight courses, you are unlikely to do it all in one visit.

The legendary No.2, designed by Donald Ross and home to the 1999 and 2005 US Championships, will forever take its place as a leading test of golf, if not the very best. At 6,741 yards, the course is not a monster, but is designed to test even the longest hitters while its fast greens expose all but the soundest of short games.

The course is in virtually everyone's world top ten.

front nine

HOLE	1	2	3	4	5	6	7	8	9	OUT
YARDS	391	432	327	503	442	194	397	487	165	3383
PAR	4	4	4	5	4	3	4	5	3	36
STROKE INDEX	11	3	13	5	1	15	9	7	3	

COURSE HISTORY

HOLE OF THE COURSE With no exaggeration, all of them. It's that good.

GREEN FEES $310 (£200) for guests on the no.2 course. An extra $15 (£10) for non-residents, who must book on the day of play.

CLUBHOUSE The original clubhouse serves five of the eight courses. Dine in the multi-pillared Donald Ross Grill Room for that 'Gentleman's Club' feel

ACCOMMODATION Pinehurst's award-winning accommodation will pamper you in style in a setting that combines modern convenience with incomparable service.

Over 500 sleeping rooms (including suites) in five different venues await. The complex features the Carolina hotel, the newly-restored Holly Inn, the quaint Manor Inn, four-bedroom villas, and condominiums. For rates and reservations check the website or phone 001 910 235 850.

1951 RYDER CUP
US 9½ v GB 2½

The 1951 series of matches was not so much a match as a rout. In fact, if it had not been for Arthur Lees, the British points tally would have been a mere ½! Jimmy Demaret played his last Ryder Cup, retiring with a perfect 6-0.

During his final singles match, with Dai Rees, Demaret made 10 out of 11 sand saves, including holing out from a greenside bunker on the par-three 17th. Rees was so fulsome in his praise that Demaret gave him his sand wedge as a gift.

back nine

HOLE	10	11	12	13	14	15	16	17	18	IN	TOTAL
YARDS	569	427	368	365	417	183	492	165	417	3403	6741
PAR	5	4	4	4	4	3	5	3	4	36	72
STROKE INDEX	2	8	10	14	4	12	12	18	6		

1953

Wentworth

Virginia Water, Surrey
Tel +44 (0)1344 846306 Fax +44 (0)1344 842804
www.wentworthgolfclub.co.uk

LOCATION Approx 25 miles on the A30 from south-west London.

COURSE A proliferation of televised tournaments has made the West Course at Wentworth one of the most recognised in golf. Each hole is familiar to golfers, making a visit to play the course a must.

The West Course, opened in 1926, is nicknamed the Burma Road as the layout is one continuous tree lined track, rather than the zig-zag layout of most golf courses. Once started, there is no turning back.

Everyone has their own favourite hole. Yours might be the daunting 1st; a drive in front of the clubhouse, with the concealed road beneath. There is always a starter on hand to make it feel just like a real tournament. The short tenth is a shot to an undulating, narrow green with a fearsome bunker for the wayward. The two closing holes match St Andrews for notoriety. The 570 yard 17th is Bernard Gallacher's personal favourite.

The half-way house, bizarrely at the 8th, serves a mean sausage sandwich, in

front nine

HOLE	1	2	3	4	5	6	7	8	9	OUT
YARDS	473	154	447	497	191	354	396	400	452	3364
PAR	5	3	4	5	3	4	4	4	4	36
STROKE INDEX	9	17	3	11	15	13	5	7	1	

COURSE HISTORY

contrast to the haute cuisine of the clubhouse.

HOLE OF THE COURSE We have selected the par-five 18th, a 531 yard, left-to-right dog leg. When you see how far the ball needs to be hit to have sight of the green, you then understand that the Pro's are on a different planet. The three shot strategy from tee to green has the added complication of a horizontal ditch half way up the approach. Of such insignificance to the professionals, however, it is not even seen on TV!

PROFESSIONAL Bernard Gallacher (former Europe Ryder Cup Captain 1991-1995)

GREEN FEES £210 ($375) in high Summer, £85 ($125) in mid winter

CLUBHOUSE Golfer's heaven

ACCOMMODATION On site. Four single and two double dormy rooms with en-suite bathrooms plus two-bedroomed suites, some with views over the golf courses. Dormy rooms start from £80 with the Garden Suite Rooms starting at £225.

1953 RYDER CUP
GB 5½ v US 6½

In a hotly contested series of Ryder Cup matches, the Americans opened up a 3-1 lead after the first day foursomes. The following day, captain Henry Cotton rallied the home golfers and with three singles remaining, there was just one point between the teams.

The British, with Peter Alliss losing at the last hole and Bernard Hunt halving his match, came unstuck again and although Irish rookie Harry Bradshaw won the final singles pairing 3&2 against Fred Hass, it wasn't enough to prevent the USA team scoring a 6½-5½ victory.

The new East Course was used to stage a challenge match between US and British golfers in 1926 prior to the British Open. These so-called unofficial matches were arranged by Samuel Ryder and are regarded as the pre-cursors to the first formal series of matches the following year. For the record, Britain won 10-1!

---

back nine

HOLE	10	11	12	13	14	15	16	17	18	IN	TOTAL
YARDS	184	403	509	442	179	481	383	571	531	**3683**	**7047**
PAR	3	4	5	4	3	4	4	5	5	**37**	**73**
STROKE INDEX	10	6	18	2	12	4	16	8	14		

1955

Thunderbird

Rancho Mirage, CA 92270 USA
Tel 001 760 328 2161 Fax 001 760 321 4940

LOCATION From Palm Springs, take Interstate-10, travelling east. Take the Bob Hope Drive exit and turn right onto Country Club Drive. The entrance is on the left.

COURSE Constructed in 1950, by John and Velma Dawson, this course is the first of the desert courses which now abound in the Palm Springs area. The Dawsons were also responsible for developing Eldorado.

One business backer remarked at the time that while one course was OK, he doubted whether this part of California could support two. There are now several hundred! In the early 1950s, it was THE golf course for the movie industry, with stars such as Bob Hope, Clark Gable, Bing Crosby, Judy Garland and Lucille Ball becoming members. Another prominent member was Robert Hudson, kind benefactor to the GB team, from Portland Oregon, and now vice-president on the Ryder Cup Committee of the British PGA. It is the original site of the Bob Hope Classic, while Ford named its legendary sports-car after the course.

The original course was remodelled by Ted Robinson in 1987. The course is of traditional design, with narrow fairways bordering an exclusive residential complex. Featuring rolling-to-flat terrain and Bermuda greens of

front nine

HOLE	1	2	3	4	5	6	7	8	9	OUT
YARDS	507	178	440	393	379	368	191	385	520	3361
PAR	5	3	4	4	4	4	3	4	5	36
STROKE INDEX	13	15	7	3	9	1	17	5	11	

average size, it is a pleasure to play. But beware, there are 60 sand bunkers and ten holes guarded by water!

HOLE OF THE COURSE The 201 yard, par-three 7th, the last survivor of the original 1893 six hole course, has survived the test of time and boasted the highest over par average at the 1988 US Open.

Its double plateau green is set at a 45 degree left to right angle to the tee, making a high fade the preferred shot.

When the flag is at the front, the tee shot must be played short to roll up. The apron is always kept firm to ensure that the ball will run and not simply come to a quick halt. The same applies at most holes here.

PROFESSIONAL Don Callahan

GREEN FEES $90 (£60); invitation only

CLUBHOUSE The original ranch style design has long given way to a luxurious clubhouse in keeping with this exclusive country club.

ACCOMMODATION Desert Springs Marriott Resort & Spa, Palm Desert Tel: 001 760 341 2211 www.marriotthotels.com

---

1955 RYDER CUP
US 8 v GB 4

A unique series of matches in which not one game ended in a half. The matches were much closer than the final score suggests.

The GB team actually won the first foursome. The three other pairs were closely contested, with the Lees/Weetman v Burke/Bolt contests 'yo-yoing' until the last hole. Unfortunately the GB team found itself 3-1 down after the foursomes, and lost the singles 5-3; however, all the matches were genuine contests.

At the conclusion, Lord Brabazon, president of the PGA of Great Britain, was heard to remark in best Churhillian style: "Although we have lost, we have learnt a lot and are going back to practice on the streets and on the beaches."

---

back nine

HOLE	10	11	12	13	14	15	16	17	18	IN	TOTAL
YARDS	377	438	200	510	407	391	186	430	508	3447	6808
PAR	4	4	3	5	4	4	3	4	5	36	72
STROKE INDEX	10	4	16	14	2	8	18	6	12		

1957

Lindrick Golf Club

Lindrick, Worksop, Notts, S81 8BH
Tel: +44 (0)1909 485802 Fax +44 (0)1909 488685

LOCATION Four miles west of Worksop on the A57. M1 Junction 31

COURSE Founded in 1891, this Alister Mackenzie course comprises heathland, tight, tree-lined fairways and plenty of trouble for the odd stray one. Long holes test iron play and all-round golf skills.

The greens are tricky and well protected, a good challenge to players of all levels of ability. The course is particularly noted for its bunkers.

The course crosses a road and many believe that the best holes are located in this far area. In particular the SI 1, par-four 13th, where the big hitters will be tempted to court danger with the fairway bunkers in order to shorten the approach. Hole 14 is arguably the next most testing hole on the course, a long par five with some truly excellent bunkering.

front nine

HOLE	1	2	3	4	5	6	7	8	9	OUT
YARDS	402	364	165	478	431	140	439	316	436	3171
PAR	4	4	3	5	4	3	4	4	4	35
STROKE INDEX	8	6	14	12	2	18	4	16	10	

COURSE HISTORY

HOLE OF THE COURSE Players re-cross the road to finish with the par-three short 18th. At 210 yards from the Championship tees this is a difficult par-three with a tilted green which means you really need to be below the pin to make par. At SI 15, the handicappers have given it few friends.

PROFESSIONAL P Cowen

GREEN FEES Weekdays £25 ($38), weekends £45 ($68). A handicap certificate is required

CLUBHOUSE Excellent facilities

ACCOMMODATION Portland Hall Hotel & Restaurant, Mansfield, Notts.
Grade II listed and set in 15 acres of the most beautiful parkland, once owned by the Duke of Portland. This hotel has 10 bedrooms and the guide price per person, per night for a single room is £47.00, with double rooms at £58.75. Tel 01623 452 525 Fax 01623 452 550

1957 RYDER CUP
GB 7½ v US 4½

The British team broke a seven match US winning streak, recording its first post-war success.

Golf in the British Isles was now recovering from the Second World War, and on this occasion Sir Stuart Goodwin financed the home team. This gave him the honour of selecting a venue. As a Yorkshireman, he chose his home course of Lindrick, in nearby Nottinghamshire!

Breaking with the pattern of previous (and for that matter, subsequent) matches, the Americans prevailed 3-1 in the foursomes but were blown away 6½-1½ in the singles. Notable victories came from Dai Rees over Ed Furgol (7&6), Bernard Hunt over Don Ford (6&5) and Christy O'Connor (7&6) over Dow Finsterwald.

back nine

HOLE	10	11	12	13	14	15	16	17	18	IN	TOTAL
YARDS	370	172	347	433	542	360	487	394	210	3315	6486
PAR	4	3	4	4	5	4	4	4	3	36	71
STROKE INDEX	3	17	7	1	9	13	5	11	15		

COURSE HISTORY

1959

Eldorado

46000 Fairway Drive, Indian Wells, CA 92210 USA
Tel 001 760 346 8081   Fax 001 760 340 1325

LOCATION On Highway 111, close to Palm Springs. Turn off at Eldorado Drive. The clubhouse is approx 1.5 miles.

COURSE This private and exclusive members' club became world famous when President and First Lady Eisenhower moved to Eldorado. Ike, a golf nut, had chosen wisely. Course designer Lawrence Hughes designed a narrow track, built in 1958, whose fairways are lined by houses of the exclusive residential development. The greens are small and flat. After the Ryder Cup, the Desert Classic was played here for many years, but the course is no longer used for tournaments and has been substantially remodelled since the late 1950s.

HOLE OF THE COURSE The par-four, 393 yard 4th features a dog leg left

front nine

HOLE	1	2	3	4	5	6	7	8	9	OUT
YARDS	507	178	440	393	379	368	191	385	520	**3361**
PAR	5	3	4	4	4	4	3	4	5	36
STROKE INDEX	13	15	7	3	9	1	17	5	11	

fairway and approach shot over water. At SI 3, the club golfer will need to decide whether to play safe, with the extra shot, or go for it.

PROFESSIONAL Terry Beardsley

GREEN FEES By invitation of members only. Clubhouse closed in Summer. Green fees $150. If you cannot get an invite, there are plenty of courses in the area including two Championship courses at the Desert Springs Marriott resort.

CLUBHOUSE The 1959 Ryder Cup coincided with the opening of the clubhouse at Eldorado. The building was first used to host the opening banquet arranged by Robert Hudson, our fruit grower from Portland and great friend and benefactor to the British team. The club prides itself on its facilities and cuisine.

ACCOMMODATION Desert Springs Marriott Resort & Spa, Palm Desert Tel 001 760 341 2211 www.marriotthotels.com

---

1959 RYDER CUP
US 8½ v GB 3½

The British team and travelling press corps were severally shaken when their airplane was caught in a violent storm on route from Los Angeles. The plane turned back and Captain Dai Rees decided to make the journey into the desert by coach.

From the moment the GB team lost the first two foursomes they were never in with a chance. In fact they were limited to two victories and three halves in the entire match.

The Americans recorded some emphatic wins with Sam Snead beating Dave Thomas 6&5, Bob Rosburg taking Harry Weetman by the same score and Christy O'Connor's singles match finishing even earlier, at the 12th hole.

---

back nine

HOLE	10	11	12	13	14	15	16	17	18	IN	TOTAL
YARDS	377	438	200	510	407	391	186	430	508	3447	6808
PAR	4	4	3	5	4	4	3	4	5	36	72
STROKE INDEX	10	4	16	14	2	8	18	6	12		

1961/77

Royal Lytham & St Annes Club

Links Gate, Lytham St Annes FY8 3LQ
Tel +44 (0)1253 724206 Fax +44 (0)1253 780946
www.royallythamgolf.co.uk

LOCATION Near Blackpool, Lancashire, north-west England.

COURSE An historic British links course, founded in 1886. Its close proximity to Blackpool ensures players are always likely to 'enjoy' the bracing fresh air blowing off the Irish Sea. Everything here is steeped in tradition and history, which the course and clubhouse richly deserve.

Home to many championships, the most recent being the Open in 2001, for the tenth time. Past winners include Bobby Jones, Seve Ballesteros and Gary Player. This course – complete with 200 bunkers – justly deserves the title 'world class'.

The final nine holes are described as one of the toughest back nines in the world, as was proved at the 2001 Open. Long par-fours often into the wind don't give much chance for birdie opportunities and level par is a good score for these holes. The 17th is immortalised by the Bobby Jones bunker. A plaque marks the spot from which the great amateur golfing lawyer played a remarkable 175 yard bunker shot to the heart of the green, destroying the morale of his opponent and effectively winning him the tournament.

HOLE OF THE COURSE The 414 yard par-four 18th, played back towards the

front nine

HOLE	1	2	3	4	5	6	7	8	9	OUT
YARDS	206	437	457	393	212	490	553	418	164	3330
PAR	3	4	4	4	3	5	5	4	3	35
STROKE INDEX	13	5	1	9	15	7	3	11	17	

famous clubhouse, has been party to many exciting tournament finishes.

There are no less than 15 bunkers at this hole alone. Famously, in 1974, Gary Player, well ahead in the championship, overclubbed and had to play his third left-handed with his putter butt.

Even better, Donald Beaver, playing in a club competition, thinned his ball out of a bunker, and found it lodged in the ivy on the clubroom window sill. Taking his spikes off, he played a shot from inside, through the open window and back onto the green, only to be disqualified for leaving the course!

PROFESSIONAL Eddie Birchenough

GREEN FEES Mondays to Thursdays £100 including lunch; weekends not available.

CLUBHOUSE Good enough to satisfy the world's best golfers. Noted for the staff's friendly disposition.

ACCOMMODATION Dormy House at the club can cater for 17 guests (male only) in 9 single and four twin-bedded rooms. Minimum stay is 2 nights, which includes breakfast, dinner and four rounds of golf. Prices from £354 ($530). Tel 01253 724206.

1961 RYDER CUP
GB 9½ v US 14½

A new format which effectively doubled the number of matches and points to play for, and extended the tournament to three days. Arnold Palmer's first appearance ensured another victory for the US. Sam Snead did not appear, for the first time since WW 11, due to disciplinary problems with the US PGA after playing in a non-sanctioned tournament. The US took a 3-1 lead on the first morning, and it was always a winning margin.

1977 RYDER CUP
GB&Ire 7½ v US 12½

The 1977 series of matches will be remembered for the decision by both PGAs to extend, from 1979, the tournament to players from continental Europe. Playing over a series of 20 matches, the US team, with Raymond Floyd (a future captain), Lanny Wadkins, Don January and Jack Nicklaus were too strong. Of note from the GB camp was the 3-0 success of Nick Faldo, despite his suffering from glandular fever.

back nine

HOLE	10	11	12	13	14	15	16	17	18	IN	TOTAL
YARDS	334	542	198	342	445	463	357	467	414	3562	6892
PAR	4	5	3	4	4	4	4	4	4	36	71
STROKE INDEX	10	4	14	18	6	2	16	8	12		

1963

East Lake Golf Club

2575 Alston Drive, SE Atlanta, GA 30317 USA
Tel 001 404 373 5722 Fax 001 404 373 1437
www.eastlakegolfclub.com

LOCATION From Atlanta take I-85/75 South, I-20 East, Exit 61B. Turn left at the top, and after just over a mile, turn left on 2nd Avenue. At first light turn right onto Alston Drive.

COURSE East Lake measures 7,112 yards from the championship tees and plays to par 72. The most talked about hole on the front nine is the 165-yard, par-three sixth, which plays from an elevated tee to a diagonally-angled peninsula island green. East Lake's back nine boasts one superior hole after another, but the finish is unforgettable. The 18th hole is a terrific closer, an uphill, into-the-wind 232-yard par-three.

In 1913, famed golf course architect Donald Ross redesigned the Bendelow course at East Lake and it was the course on which Bobby Jones learned to play. Ross also designed the No. 2 course in 1928, opened on May 31, 1930, to coincide with the final day of Jones' victorious British Amateur championship match. The club enjoyed a milestone that year when Bobby Jones completed the Grand Slam of US Amateur, US Open, British Amateur and British Open.

In 1963, the 15th biennial Ryder Cup matches were played over the No. 1 course. In preparation for the matches,

front nine

HOLE	1	2	3	4	5	6	7	8	9	OUT
YARDS	424	195	387	440	561	164	394	405	584	3554
PAR	4	3	4	4	5	3	4	4	5	36
STROKE INDEX	7	17	11	1	5	15	9	13	3	

COURSE HISTORY

the course went through a face lifting for three years, during which most of it was rebuilt and many of the holes changed to provide the quality of championship layout the tournament merited. The alterations were directed by George Cobb, noted golf course architect.

Not long after the club hosted the Cup, the surrounding neighbourhood fell victim to white flight and urban decay of the 1960s. The Atlanta Athletic Club became part of that flight when it sold the No. 2 course to developers and moved to its present home in Duluth. The original course and clubhouse were saved when a group of 25 members purchased them and began operation as the newly formed East Lake Country Club in 1968. In 1993, a local charitable foundation purchased East Lake with the intention to restore it as a tribute to Bobby Jones and the club's other great amateur golfers.

In 1994, Rees Jones restored Donald Ross's original golf course layout. Using the original Philip Shutze architectural drawings, the clubhouse was brought back to its 1926 design and condition. By 1995, East Lake had regained its place as one of the world's great golf clubs.

HOLE OF THE COURSE The 453-yard 17th is a marvellous hole. With the lake on the left and bunkers to the right, it

---

1963 RYDER CUP
US 23 v GB 9

Arnold Palmer as playing captain led his team to an emphatic victory in the first series of matches to include fourballs. By lunch on the final day the US team needed just half a point. The afternoon was nothing short of a massacre, with the US prevailing in seven matches and halving one to record the second largest winning margin in Ryder Cup history.

---

requires a long and accurate tee shot. The intriguing green is sloped back-to-front on the first half, then right-to-left on the back portion, making for interesting putting and causing havoc with approach shots. A par-four with stroke index 14, this is some challenge for the lower handicappers.

PROFESSIONAL Chad Parker

GREEN FEES Visitors $150 plus $55 for caddies. Tee times 8.30am – 2.30pm.

ACCOMMODATION Swissotel, 3391 Peachtree Road, Atlanta 30326. Tel 001 404 365 0065 Fax 001 404 365 8787

back nine

HOLE	10	11	12	13	14	15	16	17	18	IN	TOTAL
YARDS	516	193	391	439	442	495	481	453	232	3642	7196
PAR	5	3	4	4	4	5	4	4	3	36	72
STROKE INDEX	6	18	12	10	4	8	2	14	16		

COURSE HISTORY

1965/69

Royal Birkdale

Waterloo Road, Southport PR8 2LX
Tel +44 (0)1704 567920 Fax +44 (0)1704 562237
www.royalbirkdale.com

LOCATION The club is 1½ miles south of Southport town centre on the A565 between Southport and Ainsdale. The nearest railway station is Hillside on the Liverpool to Southport line.

COURSE This magnificent links course is set in a large area. Each hole is presenetd among large, grass-covered sand-dunes, giving the feel of playing each hole down an alley. Unlike other links courses, the fairways are relatively flat and the ball runs true. The rough is not so kind, however. The course's current layout has existed since the mid

1930s, although the club goes back to 1899. The architects Hawkins and Taylor designed the links that have been the venue for eight Open Championships between 1954-2001, two Ryder Cups and many other tournaments, both amateur and professional.

There are many great holes on this course. The 18th, with clubhouse in view, has been the scene of many a dramatic moment. Professional Brian Hodgkinson cites the 15th as the players' favourite. At 544 yards this SI 2 par five has 13 bunkers to catch drives, second shots and thirds after a lay-up.

front nine

HOLE	1	2	3	4	5	6	7	8	9	OUT
YARDS	449	421	407	203	344	480	177	457	411	3349
PAR	4	4	4	3	4	4	3	4	4	34
STROKE INDEX	11	3	7	15	13	1	17	9	5	

COURSE HISTORY

HOLE OF THE COURSE The first hole, even from the white tees at 450 yards is a serious tester of handicaps. A dog leg left with out of bounds on the right and two huge sand dunes on the left, it requires a perfectly placed tee shot to have any chance of reaching the putting surface in two. The second shot is not much easier, as two further dunes on the left partially obscure the line into the green. Just recall how many pro's have put their first ball out of bounds. Definite bogey material.

PROFESSIONAL Brian Hodgkinson

GREEN FEES
Midweek per round $180 (£120)
Midweek per day $215 (£145)
Weekend per round $200 (£135)

CLUBHOUSE Classic pre-WW11 art deco design. Could be mistaken for an airport terminal or local authority building. Such a dour exterior belies the quality of service and facilities within.

ACCOMMODATION Royal Clifton Hotel, The Promenade, Southport PR8 1RB
Tel 01704 533771
Fax 01704 500657
www.royalclifton.co.uk
Rates from £59 ($90) per person

1965 RYDER CUP
GB 12½ v US 19½

Harry Weetman's British team started brightly. Fielding Neil Coles, Bernard Hunt, Peter Alliss and Christy O'Connor the first day's foursomes ended 4-4. But Casper, Lema, Palmer and Co took over, winning the second day's fourballs 4½ – 3½. As usual the Americans dominated the singles, winning ten of the 16 matches. The US players mastered the windy conditions better than the home team, through the low punch shot.

1969 RYDER CUP
GB 16 v US 16

An epic, ending in a tie, with the US retaining the trophy as holders. The first morning could not have been better for the home team, who took a 3½-½ lead. The US soon caught up though and the second day ended all square at 8-8. On the final day the GB team opened up a 13-11 lead. The holders responded by winning four of the next six matches. The final pairings of Huggett v Casper and Jacklin v Nicklaus were both halved.

back nine

HOLE	10	11	12	13	14	15	16	17	18	IN	TOTAL
YARDS	403	408	183	498	198	544	416	547	472	3669	7018
PAR	4	4	3	4	3	5	4	5	4	36	70
STROKE INDEX	14	8	18	4	16	2	12	6	10		

COURSE HISTORY

1967

Champions Golf Club

13722 Champions Drive, Houston, Texas 77069, USA
Tel 001 281 444 6449 Fax 001 281 444 5139

LOCATION From Houston, take Hwy 249 going north, Hwy 1960 going east, drive 1 mile to the course, and look for the entrance on the left side of the road.

COURSE This club has two excellent 18 hole courses. It is not unusual to see Phil Mickelson, Hal Sutton, Peter Jacobsen, Ben Crenshaw, Tom Kite, Rocco Mediate, and country singer Clay Walker practising their swing around the course. Steve Elkington is a member and the club boasts 14 players with level or better

handicaps! In the past, the club has hosted the US Open in 1969 and the US Amateur in 1993, on the Jack Rabbit course. The Cypress Creek Course, opened in 1959, is the more challenging course with out-of-bounds stakes lining every hole. Modelled by Architect Ralph Plummer, it is a traditionally designed course with prefect greens. Golfers, of both pro and club standard, find it a joy to play.

HOLE OF THE COURSE Although the

front nine

HOLE	1	2	3	4	5	6	7	8	9	OUT
YARDS	455	450	425	221	514	424	431	186	512	3618
PAR	4	4	4	3	5	4	4	3	5	36
STROKE INDEX	7	9	3	15	11	5	1	17	13	

COURSE HISTORY

par-three 4th is famous as the hole that ended Ben Hogan's tournament career, former club assistant professional John Weir has selected the 14th – an uphill 431 yard par-four that calls for a fade off the tee into a slightly dog legged fairway, followed by a drawn mid-iron into a green protected front left by a lake and downhill into the water. Always a difficult par.

PROFESSIONAL Tad Weeks

GREEN FEES $125 (good for all day play- so try both courses); must be invited by member, reciprocal arrangements for USGA Golf Club members.

CLUBHOUSE Noted for its Southern charm and hospitality. Of particular note are the frozen Snickers at the half-way house!

ACCOMMODATION The Robin's Nest Inn offers four guest rooms, all featuring private baths. They have a lovely parlour for your enjoyment and serve breakfast daily. For reservations or more information call 001 (800) 622-8343 or 001 (713) 528-5821.

1967 RYDER CUP
US 23½ v GB 8½

This was the sixth of a thirteen match winning streak for the American team, the margin emphasising their total and sustained domination over their British and Irish rivals. This was the era of Arnold Palmer at his golfing best, winning all five matches in which he was involved. Legend has it that US non-playing Captain Ben Hogan had the visitors beaten at the pre-match dinner by simply announcing in his welcome speech "Ladies and Gentlemen, please welcome the United States Ryder Cup Team, the finest golfers in the World!"

back nine

HOLE	10	11	12	13	14	15	16	17	18	IN	TOTAL
YARDS	453	460	213	540	431	416	181	448	440	3582	7200
PAR	4	4	3	5	4	4	3	4	4	35	71
STROKE INDEX	6	2	16	14	8	10	18	4	12		

1971

Old Warson Country Club

9841 Old Warson Road, St Louis, Missouri 63124 USA
Tel 001 314 961 0005 Fax 001 314 918 8113

LOCATION From the airport take Hwy 40 going west. At McKnight Road turn left onto Old Warson Road. The course is about a mile away on the right hand side.

COURSE A Robert Trent Jones Snr course, opened in 1955, and the concept of two golfing friends, committed to build a course of championship quality, with a clubhouse of architectural note.

Tree-lined fairways border a rolling terrain. Water hazards are in play on six holes. With up to 50 sand bunkers, Old Warson justly takes it place in the US top 100.

front nine

HOLE	1	2	3	4	5	6	7	8	9	OUT
YARDS	403	379	198	389	443	532	180	450	407	3381
PAR	4	4	3	4	4	5	3	4	4	35
STROKE INDEX	13	11	15	9	3	5	17	1	7	

COURSE HISTORY

HOLE OF THE COURSE The par-five, 618 yard 16th is a spectacularly long and challenging hole. The fairway slopes right to left, offering few flat lies. The second shot is blind and the third has a water hazard on the left! If you do reach the large green in three, it slopes dramatically from back to front.

PROFESSIONAL Gareth Bayer

GREEN FEES As guest of, or accompanied by a member, $45 (£30) for 9 holes or $75 (£45) for 18

CLUBHOUSE All reviewers report a courteous and friendly welcome at this private members club. Colonial style, in keeping with the traditions of the area.

ACCOMMODATION www.sunscale.com comes recommended as a St Louis hotel reservation specialist.

1971 RYDER CUP
US 18½ v GB 13½

Paired up against the likes of Palmer, Trevino and Nicklaus, the British team put up a creditable performance and led 4½-3½ at the end of the first day. Against the tide of history, they even put up a good show in the singles, only losing the 16 matches by one point. However, the second day was to amplify the gap in quality, with the US team taking that day's tally 6½-1½. A furore erupted in the fourballs match between Bernard Gallacher/Peter Oosterhuis and Arnold Palmer/Gardner Dickinson. Gallacher's caddie was so impressed with one of Palmer's tee shots that he inadvertently asked him which club he had used. This was a clear infringement of the rule against seeking advice and the hole was awarded to the Americans who went on to win the match by one hole.

back nine

HOLE	10	11	12	13	14	15	16	17	18	IN	TOTAL
YARDS	426	436	545	184	352	444	618	211	450	3666	7047
PAR	4	4	5	3	4	4	5	3	4	36	71
STROKE INDEX	4	12	10	18	14	2	6	16	8		

1973

Muirfield

Duncur Road, Gullane, East Lothian EH31 2EG Scotland
Tel +44 (0)1620 842123   Fax +44 (0)1620 842977

LOCATION From the north and Edinburgh Airport, take the A720 city by-pass and follow signposts to Berwick-Upon-Tweed (A1). Continue on A1 and take the A198 to North Berwick. Pass through Longniddry, Aberlady and Gullane and on leaving Gullane, Muirfield is accessed from the last exit on the left. From the south, and the A1 motorway, take the A198 to North Berwick and then follow signs to Edinburgh. Muirfield is the first exit on the right when entering Gullane.

COURSE In any list of top golf courses the name Muirfield will appear. In fact it will probably appear twice, Muirfield Village in Ohio seeking to emulate this illustrious Scottish course.

As HQ of the world's oldest golf club, Muirfield is steeped in tradition. It is located in a relatively small area wherein lie no less than 20 golf clubs. At just under 7,000 yards this links course is world renowned for its deep bunkers and circular layout, which makes the wind direction different at each hole.

The fairways run true but are guarded by the fearsome pot bunkers. The rough is serious jungle and once in you will probably wish that you had not found your ball. The closing holes on the outward nine are particularly highly rated. Venue of the Open Championship on 15 occasions.

front nine

HOLE	1	2	3	4	5	6	7	8	9	OUT
YARDS	447	351	379	180	559	469	185	444	504	3518
PAR	4	4	4	3	5	4	3	4	5	36
STROKE INDEX	8	14	5	10	1	16	6	12	3	

COURSE HISTORY

HOLE OF THE COURSE The par-four, 469 yard 6th. At the extremity of the course, this hole is nearly always affected by a cross wind in either direction. One of the few tee shots where the ball is played blind over a crest. The second shot is downhill and to the left. Judging distance is made more complicated by the change of scenery from the nearby Archerfield Wood. At SI 16, it makes a very tough par for the mid-teen handicappers!

PROFESSIONAL Never had one; considered unnecessary as most members belong to more than one club in the area.

GREEN FEES By application via the club Secretary. An information pack and application form will be sent to you, which includes the regulations and format for your morning and afternoon rounds. Visitors are only permitted on Tuesdays and Thursdays. You will also be asked whether you wish to lunch in the clubhouse and the number of caddies required.

After returning the completed form, including a handicap certificate and deposit, your application will be placed on file. During November you will be informed of the tee-off time allocated to you for play during the following year.

1973 RYDER CUP
GB&Ire 13 v US 19

In 1973 Muirfield hosted the Cup for the first and so far only time in Scotland. The US team, after seven successive wins, and boasting the likes of Palmer, Nicklaus, Trevino were once again victors. The home team performed creditably in the foursomes and fourballs, going into the last day at 8-8. The singles, as in the past, proved decisive, with the US taking 11 of the 16 available points.

Current fees £95.

CLUBHOUSE Formal and traditional but friendly and courteous. Most visitors remember their lunch for its atmosphere and ambience as much as the golf. Definitely an integral part of the Muirfield experience.

ACCOMMODATION Greywalls Hotel. Designed by Sir Edwin Lutyens in 1901, owned by the Weaver family since 1924 and run as a hotel since 1948. Muirfield, Gullane, East Lothian, EH31 2EG, Scotland. Tel 01620 842144 Fax 01620 842241.

back nine

HOLE	10	11	12	13	14	15	16	17	18	IN	TOTAL
YARDS	475	385	381	152	449	417	188	550	448	3445	6963
PAR	4	4	4	3	4	4	3	5	4	35	71
STROKE INDEX	18	9	13	4	14	2	17	11	7		

1975

Laurel Valley Golf Club

PO Box 435, Ligonier, PA 15658-0435 USA.
Tel 001 724 238 9555 Fax 001 724 238 2074

LOCATION From Route 30 going east, take Route 711 going south, and the course is on the left.

COURSE The 18 holes were designed by golf architect Bill Wilson in 1960. It is described as a course you could play every day without it 'beating you up'.

Tee shots are open but if you miss the fairway you will not hit the greens in regulation. The par-fours are unique and difficult. The greens are fast and true. Fairways are cut tight. Rough is long but playable, although it can be made tougher for tournament play. Includes lots of traps that are well placed.

Golfers of every level will enjoy the

front nine

HOLE	1	2	3	4	5	6	7	8	9	OUT
YARDS	416	410	534	430	208	524	388	221	441	3572
PAR	4	4	5	4	3	5	4	3	4	36
STROKE INDEX	5	9	11	1	15	13	7	17	3	

opportunity to play here. Definitely a top 50 course.

HOLE OF THE COURSE The finishing hole is regarded as the signature hole and is the most commonly photographed. The par-four, 447 yard 12th, however, is our pick, described by one professional as picturesque, with a tight fairway, tough to par, but with spectacular views...

PROFESSIONAL Chris McKnight

GREEN FEES As member's guest, $135

CLUBHOUSE Recently rebuilt to a magnificent specification. Won architectural plaudits for its layout, with de-luxe club facilities upstairs and golf downstairs, set in a Georgian style.

ACCOMMODATION Ramada Inn at Historic Ligonier, 216 West Loyalhanna Street, Ligonier PA USA. Tel 001 724 238 9545

1975 RYDER CUP
US 21 v GB&Ire 11

At the end of the first morning's fourballs, the visitors were trailing 4-0, a deficit which emphatically demonstrated the all round superiority of a US team which included Lee Trevino and Jack Nicklaus at the height of their powers.

One of these matches included a 5&4 victory for Nicklaus and Weiskopf against Barnes and Gallacher. Against all the odds, Barnes was to extract revenge on the Golden Bear in the singles, not once but twice!

In a famous comment at the first tee of the afternoon singles Nicklaus told Barnes, "There ain't no way you are going to beat me twice in one day." Not only did he do so but he established a reputation in the US which held good today on the Seniors Tour for many years.

back nine

HOLE	10	11	12	13	14	15	16	17	18	IN	TOTAL
YARDS	432	605	447	432	205	375	437	219	537	3689	7261
PAR	4	5	4	4	3	4	4	3	5	36	72
STROKE INDEX	6	10	8	4	16	14	2	18	12		

1979

The Greenbrier

300 West Main Street, White Sulphur Springs, West Virginia 24986
Tel 001 304 536 1110 Fax 001 304 536 7854
www.greenbrier.com

LOCATION The Greenbrier is located a few minutes from Route I-64 in White Sulphur Springs, WV. The resort is around a four-hour drive from Washington D.C. The Amtrak service from New York and Chicago, with intermediate stops, brings guests to the White Sulphur Springs station, directly across from The Greenbrier's Main Entrance.

The Greenbrier has its own airfield with daily commuter services from Charlotte (US Airways) and Atlanta (Delta).

COURSE Sybaritic, colonial style, a palace of golf featuring many other leisure activities. Even includes a nuclear shelter for US Congressmen. There has been a hotel on the site since the mid-19th century.

Golf at the Greenbrier dates back to 1913 with the opening of the Old White Course. Sam Snead was the professional between 1936 and 1974. The course was first opened in 1924 and redesigned by Jack Nicklaus in 1977 for the 1979 Cup.

front nine

HOLE	1	2	3	4	5	6	7	8	9	OUT
YARDS	423	403	475	177	551	456	211	490	197	3383
PAR	4	4	5	3	5	4	3	5	3	36
STROKE INDEX	11	5	9	13	3	1	15	7	17	

COURSE HISTORY

The 6,681 yard, par 72 course is heavily wooded with tree-lined fairways, multi-levelled greens and deep bunkers. This course is regularly voted No 1 in US course listings. The 18th green is shared with the last on the Old White Course.

HOLE OF THE COURSE Professional Hill Herrick's favourite is the 403 yard, par-four 2nd. With water guarding the right side, and trees and out of bounds to the left, it is the most demanding tee shot on the course. The second shot is no bargain either – a short to middle iron over water to a well bunkered green. This hole usually plays into the prevailing wind. Birdies are rare, double bogies common.

PROFESSIONAL Hill Herrick

GREEN FEES $175

CLUBHOUSE Unsurpassable

ACCOMMODATION Golf packages start from $262. Over 640 rooms, suites and estate cottages, seven restaurants and 30 shops. Other activities include tennis, a gun club and off-road rallying.

1979 RYDER CUP
US 17 v EUR 11

The first USA v Europe series of matches took place on The Greenbrier course in 1979.

The European team was able to field the rising star Seve Ballesteros together with Antonio Garrido. Captained by John Jacobs, the Europeans surrendered three of the first four points in the morning fourballs on the opening day.

Despite Nick Faldo recording an impressive 4-1 in his matches, it was Larry Nelson's 5-0 sweep that saw the Americans win by a comfortable 17-11 margin.

back nine

HOLE	10	11	12	13	14	15	16	17	18	IN	TOTAL
YARDS	339	176	510	404	305	438	406	160	560	3298	6681
PAR	4	3	5	4	4	4	4	3	5	36	72
STROKE INDEX	12	16	8	10	14	2	4	18	6		

1981

Walton Heath

Tadworth, Surrey KT20 7TP UK
Tel +44(0)1737 812380 Fax +44(0)1737 814225
www.whgc.co.uk

LOCATION Walton Heath Golf Course is south of London, just off the M25. Exit at Junction 8 for Reigate.

COURSE Walton Heath Golf Club was founded in 1903. The two courses were designed by leading amateur golfer Herbert Fowler.

The Old Course opened in 1904 with an exhibition match between Harry Vardon, James Braid – the club's first professional – and J.H. Taylor. The great triumvirate dominated golf for some 20 years before the Great War.

In 1907 Fowler designed the New Course which opened fully in 1913. The first five holes of the New Course are intertwined with the last four holes from the Old Course, three sets of tees converging on at least two occasions. Nevertheless, the Old Course justly deserves its accolade in a listing among the World's Top 100 Golf Courses. Not bad for a near centurion.

With soft fairways, guarded throughout by gorse and thick rough, and firm greens that run true, this is an enjoyable but true test of golf. Between 1950 and 1971 the course was owned by the News of the World newspaper – not a bad company perk!

front nine

HOLE	1	2	3	4	5	6	7	8	9	OUT
YARDS	235	458	289	441	437	440	183	494	400	3377
PAR	3	4	4	4	4	4	3	5	4	35
STROKE INDEX	9	5	17	1	11	7	15	3	13	

COURSE HISTORY

HOLE OF THE COURSE Professional Ken Macpherson cites the 16th, a par-five at 510 yards, as the members' favourite.

An accurate left of centre drive is required, as the fairway slopes away to the right. The next shot is more than likely to be played from a hanging lie. In dry summer conditions a firm second shot will run, making two shots to the green possible, even for the higher handicappers.

The green runs straight and true making an eagle a real possibility. With a short hole at17 and a reachable par 4 (SI 10) at 18, there must be many happy 'bar stories' of the Old Course finish.

PROFESSIONAL Ken Macpherson

GREEN FEES Monday to Friday:
£77 ($125) before 11.30 a.m.
£67 ($135) after 11.30 a.m.
Weekend & Bank Holidays:
£87 ($145) when permitted

CLUBHOUSE The clubhouse is a traditional pavilion design overlooking the largest putting green in England. Dining facilities are excellent and in keeping with the club's illustrious image.

1981 RYDER CUP
EUR 9½ v 18½

The US comfortably recorded their 12th straight victory by a massive 9 point margin. Although the European team boasted the likes of Langer (on his home Ryder Cup debut), Faldo and Lyle, their pre-eminence was yet to come. The combined strength of a team who had won 36 majors between them including Nicklaus, Watson, Trevino and Floyd were too strong in all departments.

A 4½-3½ European lead at the end of the first day was a false dawn as the US took the second day's points 7-1. They did not quite dominate the singles in customary fashion, only winning 8 of the available 12 points but ran out winners at 18½-9½.

ACCOMMODATION
Heathside Hotel, Brighton Rd, Burgh Heath, Tadworth, Surrey KT20 6BW
Tel +44 (0)1737 353355
Surrey Hills Hotel, Horsham Road, Capel, Dorking, Surrey RH5 4PG
Tel +44 (0)870 240 7060

back nine

HOLE	10	11	12	13	14	15	16	17	18	IN	TOTAL
YARDS	417	198	396	529	569	426	510	193	404	**3642**	**7019**
PAR	4	3	4	5	5	4	5	3	4	**37**	**72**
STROKE INDEX	4	16	14	6	12	2	8	18	10		

COURSE HISTORY

1983

PGA National

400 Avenue Of The Champions, Palm Beach Gardens, FL 33418-3698 USA
Tel 001 561 627 2000 Fax 001 561 691 9133
www.pga-resorts.com

LOCATION Within the 2,340 acre PGA National Community in Palm Beach Gardens, Florida, at the northern tip of Palm Beach County. Entry on PGA Boulevard, 15 miles north of Palm Beach International Airport, two miles west of I-95, and a quarter mile west of the Florida Turnpike.

COURSE Examining the scorecard reveals the qualities of this Fazio-designed course. The card gives details of each of six pin positions changed daily, the security access code for the on-course washrooms and the location of storm shelters in case of lightning.

On the front of the card is the course plan, which is almost literally a sea of blue. That's because water hazards guard 16 of 18 holes. You will definitely need more than one ball...

Opened in 1981, the course hosted the 1983 Ryder Cup, the 1987 PGA Championship and the PGA Seniors from 1982-1997. The course was re-designed by Jack Nicklaus in 1990. It is currently undergoing further refurbishment and will re-open in December 2002.

The 15th, 16th and 17th holes were named 'The Bear Trap' by golf legend Nicklaus. The Trap was dedicated during his practice round at the 1993 Seniors Championship. He unveiled a new sign

front nine

HOLE	1	2	3	4	5	6	7	8	9	OUT
YARDS	362	418	513	355	173	478	210	398	371	3278
PAR	4	4	5	4	3	5	3	4	4	36
STROKE INDEX	14	8	16	4	18	12	10	2	6	

at the 15th hole warning golfers 'You are now entering The Bear Trap.' The four closing holes are widely regarded as the four hardest of any golf course.

HOLE OF THE COURSE The par-four 16th at 410 yards, SI 12, is a fearsome challenge. A left hand dog leg with the fairway completely divided into two. The tee shot needs to be accurately positioned as the second shot will need to carry more water than dry land to reach the green in two

PROFESSIONAL Jane Broderick

GREEN FEES $288 (£190) for guests

CLUBHOUSE Spectacular country house mansion. You will need to be invited by a member.

ACCOMMODATION 339 guestrooms in the main hotel, each with a private terrace or balcony. Each offers panoramic views overlooking the lake, pool or golf course.

One and two bedroom suites and a 2,000 sq ft Presidential Suite, complete with formal dining room, marble bath, full kitchen, wet bar and optional second bedroom.

Golf packages from $199.

1983 RYDER CUP
US 14½ v EUR 13½

What a difference two years made. The 1981 European team had been comfortably beaten by an almost embarrassing margin. Indeed the bad weather and lack of competitveness had reduced the public interest.

The newly opened PGA course had 'American Golf' stamped all over it, and nobody predicted the exciting battle that saw Europe come within a point of a first victory on US soil.

Watson, Crenshaw, Floyd and Strange could do no more than match the European challenge in the fours over the first two days, at the end of which the scores were 8-8. In the singles the next 8 points were shared, the largest margin being 3&1. Tom Watson finally gave the US the winning point in the last match on the 17th hole.

One great difference was the inclusion of Ballesteros (bizarrely voted out in 1981 for not playing enough on the European tour). His inspirational play gave him 3½ points and featured a 240 yard three-wood from fairway bunker to green.

back nine

HOLE	10	11	12	13	14	15	16	17	18	IN	TOTAL
YARDS	540	419	424	386	453	179	412	158	528	**3499**	**6777**
PAR	5	4	4	4	4	3	4	3	5	**36**	**72**
STROKE INDEX	17	1	13	7	5	11	12	15	5		

1985/89/93/02

The Belfry

Wishaw, North Warwickshire B76 9PR, UK
Tel +44 (0)1675 470301 Fax +44 (0)1675 470178

LOCATION Sutton Coldfield, West Midlands. Take M6 and M42.

COURSE Three parkland courses within the De Vere Hotel complex, all with excellent facilities. The Brabazon Course, designed by Peter Alliss and Dave Thomas, was opened in 1981 and has quickly become world famous for hosting golf tournaments including the Benson and Hedges International and three Ryder Cups, in 1985, 89 and 93.

At 7,118 yards and par 72 from the Championship tees, this course,

featuring many water hazards, is a challenging but not overly imposing test of golf. For this reason, it is enjoyed by both professionals and amateurs alike.

The par-4 18th, SI 1 (473 for the pro's but a more modest 441 yards off whites) is well known to TV viewers. An angled tee shot across a lake is required. The fairway runs along the right side of the long lake. Too straight and you'll end up in the thin bunker on the far side. The drive must be in a prime position to reach the long, three-tiered green. On in two and you will feel a million dollars at the

front nine

HOLE	1	2	3	4	5	6	7	8	9	OUT
YARDS	411	379	538	442	408	395	177	428	433	3611
PAR	4	4	5	4	4	4	3	4	4	36
STROKE INDEX	9	17	13	3	11	5	15	1	7	

COURSE HISTORY

end of the round!

HOLE OF THE COURSE The unusual par-four 10th, which at 284 yards from yellow tees – Ryder Cup configuration – is designed to tempt the big hitters to go for the green over the water. However, there's only 210 yards of fairway. Bunkers lie on either side of the short grass. Water runs along the right hand side. Watch the pro's play it this year and consider how many clubbers will stand on the tee thereafter and go for it only to overdo it and top the ball into the lake...

PROFESSIONAL Simon Wordsworth

GREEN FEES £135

ACCOMMODATION The De Vere Belfry has 324 bedrooms, all with direct dial telephone, hairdryers, tea/coffee making facilities and trouser press.
Reservations Tel 0870 606 3606
Hotel direct Tel 01675 470301
Fax 01675 470256

1985/89/93/2002 RYDER CUP
EUR 16½ v US 11½
EUR 14 v US 14
EUR 13 v US 15

By the 1970s the tournament was begining to lose its lustre, with the US teams apparently succeeding at will against GB and Ireland.

In 1979 the first European team was fielded, but even with the additional players the Americans prevailed at the next three meetings.

Finally, in 1985 an outstanding team with Faldo, Langer and Ballesteros prevailed. Who can forget Sam Torrance's tears at the 18th after holing a long putt to secure the vital winning point? 1989 saw the closest match in recent years. Europe needed just a half for an outright victory, lost the last four singles, but retained the trophy. The lucky European course was home again in 1993 but did not provide the hat-trick as the US team, led by Tom Watson, took the trophy 15-13 through a fantastic six points from the final seven singles.

back nine

HOLE	10	11	12	13	14	15	16	17	18	IN	TOTAL
YARDS	311	419	208	384	190	545	413	564	473	3507	7118
PAR	4	4	3	4	3	5	4	5	4	36	72
STROKE INDEX	8	16	6	18	14	2	12	10	4		

1987

Muirfield Village Golf Club

Muirfield Village Golf Club, 5750 Memorial Drive, Dublin, OH 43017 USA
Tel 001 614 889-6272 Fax 001 614 889 6877

LOCATION About 15 miles north-west of Columbus Ohio, near Route I-70.

COURSE The original design of this course marked the end of the Jack Nicklaus and Desmond Muirhead partnership. After the opening of Muirfield Village in 1974, their partnership dissolved, and Nicklaus began his solo golf design career.

Muirfield Village represents a bright spot in American golf course design of the 1970s. With the 'traditional' look of his favourite courses in mind, Nicklaus directed Jay Moorish (an associate at the time for Muirhead and Nicklaus) to find and design original holes across the rolling Ohio landscape. Moorish's finesse as a land planner is the real highlight and his routing makes brilliant use of the creeks

front nine

HOLE	1	2	3	4	5	6	7	8	9	OUT
YARDS	415	455	401	200	527	447	563	182	407	3633
PAR	4	4	4	3	5	4	5	3	4	36
STROKE INDEX	11	3	1	15	9	7	13	17	5	

and terrain. He is regarded by many as the Bobby Jones of the era . Muirfield Village is considered an Augusta of the second half of the 20th century. The 8th, 175 yards SI 17, amplifies the design ideals; a narrow green guarded almost entirely by bunkers. A definite case of "it's on or it's in".

Located next to the Riviera Country Club and close to Scioto – serious golf country!

HOLE OF THE COURSE 14th hole, 360 yards, SI 18: Golfers heap praise on this relatively short par-four. The fairway is left to right. The second plays to a green with severe left to right slope, making the target area a small one

PROFESSIONAL Larry Dornisch

GREEN FEES $150 (£100) with member

CLUB HOUSE Luxury facilities

ACCOMMODATION Courtyard Columbus /Dublin 5175 Post Road Dublin, OH US 43017 Tel 001 614 228 3200

1987 RYDER CUP
US 13 v EUR 15

It is ironic to record that on 'the course the Jack built' – Nicklaus's testament to the great Muirfield – the Europeans should prevail, not only retaining the Ryder Cup with an outright win but also registering their first ever on US soil! Amidst much pre-match acrimony between the European players and the European PGA Tour, there was little belief at the start that the Americans captained by Jack Nicklaus would do anything other than make short work of re-taking the trophy lost at the Belfry two years earlier. Perhaps not concentrating on the golf to come relaxed the visitors, because they got off to a terrific start winning the first day's points 6-2. They never looked back from this, taking a commanding five point lead into the singles. As usual the US dominated the last day, but seven points from 12 was not enough.

---

back nine

HOLE	10	11	12	13	14	15	16	17	18	IN	TOTAL
YARDS	441	567	163	455	363	503	215	437	444	3588	7221
PAR	4	5	3	4	4	5	3	4	4	36	72
STROKE INDEX	2	14	12	10	8	16	18	6	4		

1991

Kiawah Island

Kiawah Island Resorts, Charleston, South Carolina
Tel 001 800 576 1570
www.kiawahresort.com

LOCATION Kiawah Island Resort is located 21 miles south of Charleston, South Carolina and convenient to many other major cities.

Charleston International Airport is approximately 35 miles from Kiawah Island Resort and is served by Delta, US Airways, United, Continental, Midway and TWA. All major car rental companies as well as limousine service are available. The Charleston Executive Airport is nine miles from Kiawah and serves private aircraft.

COURSE The Ocean Course, designed by Pete Dye – one of five at The Kiawah Island Resort and 16 on the island – was the venue for the 1991 Ryder Cup. More than half the holes on the course are exposed to the Atlantic coast. Postage stamp greens, where without back spin, the ball will simply not stop, make this a daunting course for many professionals, not to mention the club golfer.

The tournament tees (Gold) make the course 7,269 yards long. The average

front nine

HOLE	1	2	3	4	5	6	7	8	9	OUT
YARDS	395	528	390	432	207	455	527	197	464	3595
PAR	4	5	4	4	3	4	5	3	4	36
STROKE INDEX	13	3	7	1	9	11	17	15	5	

golfer might be better suited to the 6,031 yards off the white tees.

HOLE OF THE COURSE The par-three 17th at 192 yards has water on the right, two sand traps at the front left and sand dunes behind. If you do hit the green the ball has to stop (which many players, Ian Woosnam included, found to their cost during the Ryder Cup). That's the easy bit, because the green is undulating, fast and downhill from the left. A gross bogey four is definitely a respectable score.

PROFESSIONAL Brian Gerard

GREEN FEES $199 (£120) on the Ocean Course for guests, $245 (£160) for others, packages available.

CLUBHOUSE Colonial Style building at Osprey Point, with porches and terrace overlooking the lagoon. Superb dining.

ACCOMMODATION Kiawah Island Inn, from $139 daily. Phone the resort for a copy of 'Travel Planner' which contains a comprehensive list of rates and special golf packages.

1991 RYDER CUP
US 14½ v EUR 13½

An epic battle dubbed by the popular Press (rather unfortunately in hindsight) 'The War on the Shore', the contest was highly charged throughout.

The lead changed hands several times over the first two days with the teams ending the fours locked at 8-8. In the singles the Europeans opened up a two point lead only to be pegged back and find themselves one down with two matches remaining.

Who can ever forget the dramas at the 17th or Bernhard Langer's six foot downhill putt at the last, which missed and cost him the half point that would have ensured that Europe retained the trophy?

back nine

HOLE	10	11	12	13	14	15	16	17	18	IN	TOTAL
YARDS	439	562	466	404	194	421	579	197	439	3701	7296
PAR	4	5	4	4	3	4	5	3	4	36	72
STROKE INDEX	8	12	2	4	14	18	16	10	6		

1995

Oak Hill Country Club

346 Kilbourn Road, Rochester, New York 14618 USA
Tel 001 716 3811900 Fax 001 716 586 7102
www.oakhillcc.com

LOCATION Rochester is in up state New York, a 200 plus mile drive from NYC. It is located on the southern shore of lake Ontario, mid-way between Buffalo and Syracuse.

COURSE A Donald Ross course, one of two designed in 1923. The East course is used for tournaments, though there is nothing second rate about the West.

At par 71 and 7,000 yards, this course is long but fair to the average player. During the 1980 PGA Championship and the 1989 US Open, the conditions were warm but also very wet. Jack Nicklaus was the only player under par in 1980, finishing with a 6-under 274. Curtis Strange finished 2-under at 278 when he captured the 1989 US Open. Oak Hill's main challenge is always off the tee. It is a difficult driving course, with fairway widths averaging only around 23 yards and many trees just off the landing areas.

front nine

HOLE	1	2	3	4	5	6	7	8	9	OUT
YARDS	460	401	211	570	436	177	460	430	454	3599
PAR	4	4	3	5	4	3	4	4	4	35
STROKE INDEX	1	13	15	9	11	17	3	7	5	

If the course plays 'fast' with dry conditions the best driver of the ball will win the tournament. Oak Hill will be hosting the PGA Championship in August 2003.

HOLE OF THE COURSE No 17 – a 460 yard par-four. This dog leg right hole is one of the toughest on the course. The tee shot must be hit left to right, close to the right side or it will go through the fairway on the left side and into the rough. From here you will probably be chipping out to the fairway.

The undulating green makes it difficult to stop your second shot close to the hole. This hole traditionally gives up the fewest birdies and allows for the most bogeys. Most players will be hitting a longer iron onto this green, which is well bunkered on both sides.

PROFESSIONAL Craig Harmon

GREEN FEES $100

CLUBHOUSE Spectacular country house mansion. You will need to be invited by a member.

1995 RYDER CUP
US 13½ v EUR 14½

A see-saw match, played in cold, wet conditions in which, unusually for them, the US took a respectable lead of 9-7 into the final day's singles.

After pulling back to 10-10, the heroes for the Europeans were Ireland's Philip Walton and Englishman David Gilford, both of whom prevailed at the last hole of their respective matches. The match was also notable for the debut of left hander Phil Mickleson, who recorded an impressive 3-0, the only player to do so.

ACCOMMODATION There are many hotels in Rochester that can be found on www.rochester.com

We have chosen a location known as the Finger Lakes, about 30 miles away. Canadaigua Inn on the Lake, 770 S Main Street, Canadaigua, New York. Tel 001 716 394 7800

back nine

HOLE	10	11	12	13	14	15	16	17	18	IN	TOTAL
YARDS	432	222	372	594	323	177	439	460	480	3499	7098
PAR	4	3	4	5	4	3	4	4	4	35	70
STROKE INDEX	8	16	12	2	10	18	6	14	4		

1997

Valderrama Golf Club

Avenida de los Cortijos, 1, 1130 Sotogrande, Cadiz, Spain
Tel 0034 956 79 12 00   Fax 0034 956 79 1200
www.valderrama.com

LOCATION In Andalucia, southern Spain, 100 km from Malaga, 120 km from Jerez. Taking the N-340 Cadiz-Malaga road, turn left at Sotogrande and then head straight for 2.5 km. Nearest airports are Gibraltar or Malaga.

COURSE Robert Trent Jones designed this superb course in 1974 and re-modelled it in 1985. It has consistently and deservedly received accolades and is regarded as the leading continental European course. Noted for the variety of trees, pine, cork and eucalyptus. Set in

beautiful surroundings, it is maintained to the highest standard, and compared by leading professionals to Augusta. Nevertheless, the course is open to approximately 30 visitors per day, teeing off between 12 noon and 2.00pm.

Valderrama achieved international recognition in 1989 when it became the venue for the Volvo Masters. Hosted the Ryder Cup in 1997 and holds the World Championship of Golf in November each year. The 4th hole is the signature hole and carries all the characteristics of a great Trent Jones hole, with a well

front nine

HOLE	1	2	3	4	5	6	7	8	9	OUT
YARDS	391	401	173	538	383	164	463	346	443	3302
PAR	4	4	3	5	4	3	4	4	4	35
STROKE INDEX	13	7	17	3	11	15	1	9	5	

COURSE HISTORY

protected, raised green which makes for a tough second shot if you go for it.

HOLE OF THE COURSE The par-five 17th is the most famous, and is the hole at which even the Pro's struggle. Indeed, Valderrama's own website has a special section on this hole.
From the tee, there is out of bounds on the right and the fairway disappears down a slope to the left. The second shot has out of bounds on both sides and a huge carry over water to reach the green. The handicappers have kindly given this SI 12

PROFESSIONAL Miguel Sedeno

GREEN FEES
Jan-Sept 2002, 220 Euros (£145)
Oct 2002-Sept 2003, 240 Euros (£160)

CLUBHOUSE For much of 2002 the clubhouse has been undergoing refurbishment, and the restaurant and Masters Bar were temporarily housed in a marquee on the front lawn. With the clubhouse re-opening in July, fully refurbished, it now once again provides a gracious and inviting setting for members and visitors alike.

1997 RYDER CUP
EUR 14½ v US 13½

After a long campaign by captain Seve Ballesteros, the Ryder Cup was played on continental Europe for the first time. Europe's win epitomised its team spirit, with the home team prevailing in the pairs 10½ -5½.

Seve captained from the heart more than the head, and urged his team on as the US mounted its expected fightback in the singles. Even though the visitors won 8 points, with Costantino Rocca beating Woods 4&2, the European team held out for a one point win.

ACCOMMODATION
Kempinski Resort, Ctra. de Cádiz 29680 Estepona, Málaga
Tel 952 80 95 00 Fax 952 80 95 50
Guests qualify for special rates at: Estepona Golf, Paraíso, Atalaya, La Quinta, Los Naranjos, San Roque, Valderrama, Alcaidesa, Montemayor, Los Arqueros, Sotogrande, La Duquesa, Santa Maria, etc.
Room with green fee: 3 nights from 74.300 ptas – 2 pax + 2 green fees p.p.

back nine

HOLE	10	11	12	13	14	15	16	17	18	IN	TOTAL
YARDS	391	550	213	404	376	226	424	513	456	3553	6855
PAR	4	5	3	4	4	3	4	5	4	36	71
STROKE INDEX	18	10	2	14	6	16	4	12	8		

1999

The Country Club at Brookline

191 Clyde St, Brookline, Massachusetts 02467 Norfolk County, USA
Tel 001 617 566 0240 Fax 001 617 739 3531

LOCATION Approx seven miles south-west of Boston.

COURSE Willie Park, the Scots Golf architect, designed the 'Main' course, as it is known, in 1894, following the opening of Brookline as America's first Country Club some 12 years earlier. It became a full 18 hole course in 1899, and was soon honoured by hosting the 1913 US Open Championship. In 1927 a further 9 holes were added, now known as the Primrose course. For Major championships, three holes from the Primrose, some overlapping fairways,

and 15 from the Main are used to create a special Championship course. So you will have to play all 27 if you play the Ryder Cup course.

Make no mistake, this course is magnificent to play and is set in beautiful, classic New England surroundings. A definite top 20 in anyone's list, the course has hosted US Amateur Championships, Walker Cup, US Women's Amateur Championships and two other US Opens, in 1963 and 1988, the last an epic play off duel between Nick Faldo and Curtis Strange, won by the latter.

front nine

HOLE	1	2	3	4	5	6	7	8	9	OUT
YARDS	452	185	448	338	439	312	201	385	510	3270
PAR	4	3	4	4	4	4	3	4	5	35
STROKE INDEX	5	15	1	13	7	17	11	9	3	

COURSE HISTORY

HOLE OF THE COURSE The 7th, at 201 yards, SI 11. This hole is the last survivor of the original 1893 six hole course and proved its toughness as the highest over par average at the 1988 US Open.

Its double plateau green is set at a 45 degree left to right angle to the tee, making a high fade the preferred shot. When the flag is at the front the tee shot must be played short to roll up. The apron is kept firm to ensure that the ball will run and not simply come to a quick halt. The same applies at most holes.

PROFESSIONAL Brendan Walsh

GREEN FEES Weekdays $75 (£50), weekend $100 (£62); must be introduced by member. Course closed December to mid-April.

CLUBHOUSE Distinctive yellow paint adorns a cross between classic New England and Colonial design. Superb facilities. The club is particularly noted for its tennis facilities.

ACCOMMODATION Holiday Inn, 1200 Beacon Street, Brookline MA. Tel 001 617 277 1200

1999 RYDER CUP
US 14½ v EUR 13½

Amid scenes of incredible excitement bordering on hysteria (some of it by the teams themselves) the US regained the famous gold trophy for the first time since 1993.

Incredibly, the last three meetings have been decided by just one point, which has undoubtedly led to tension. This exploded at Brookline with scenes at times bordering on displays of partisanship which some argued were not in the spirit of the game.

Among the recriminations, who will forget Justin Leonard's fightback against Olazabal, culminating in an astonishing 45 foot birdie putt on the 17th? Despite the antics of the other US players on the green, José-Maria composed himself and nearly holed his 25ft putt for birdie, before holing out on the 18th for a half. Alas, it wasn't enough, and as has been a common pattern over the years, the Europeans' lead after the fours (10-6) was rendered insufficient by the US winning 8 of the 12 singles.

back nine

HOLE	10	11	12	13	14	15	16	17	18	IN	TOTAL
YARDS	439	453	131	433	527	434	185	381	438	3740	7010
PAR	4	5	3	4	5	4	3	4	4	36	71
STROKE INDEX	18	8	16	2	10	4	14	12	6		

FUTURE
RYDER
CUP
VENUES

2004 Oakland Hills Golf Club

3951 West Maple Rd, Bloomfield Hills, Michigan 48301, Oakland County,
United States Tel 001 248 6442500

A Donald Ross course that has already hosted six US Open Championships. The Ryder
Cup matches will be played on a special par 70 configuration measuring 6,974 yards.

COURSE HISTORY

Built in 1917 there are two courses – North and South. The latter is normally used for Championships. The North course is designed in classic Scottish links style with rolling terrain and water on four holes. The South course was redesigned by Robert Trent Jones in 1952 and hosted the US Open in the same year. The last five holes are nicknamed 'the fearsome fivesome'. The clubhouse is styled after George Washington's Mount Vernon home!

"We believe that golf fans should be able to see the world's greatest golfers playing the world's greatest courses," said PGA of America President Ken Lindsay, when he announced the decision to award the 2004 contest to Oakland Hills.

"Oakland Hills Country Club is synonymous with championship golf and plays a critical role in the history and tradition of our game. We are pleased to be able to incorporate this world-caliber site into our long-range plans."

The most recent Major held there was the 1996 US Open. Known as the original 'Monster' course, it was so dubbed by Ben Hogan after he won the 1951 US Open there thanks to a brilliant final-round 67. "I'm glad that I brought this monster to its knees," Hogan said after he finished with a total of 287, seven over par. "This kind of completes the cycle for us," says Pat Proswell, Oakland Hills' head professional since 1987. "We'll have held every Major championship golf tournament possible." This is what architect Donald Ross had in mind when he first saw the rolling woodland in 1917. "The Lord intended this for a golf course," he said. Ross and the Lord may have laid the original blueprints for this course in 1917, but it was Robert Trent Jones who modernised it after World War II. How much of the 'monster' side of its nature Oakland Hills will reveal for the 2004 Ryder Cup will be left to the American captain who has the responsibility of setting up the course. He might make the course play easier, but it will never play easy. Not as long as it has what Jack Nicklaus describes as "the toughest set of greens in the United States".

Jones was also astute enough to leave room for certain holes to stretch to combat continual technological advances in equipment. "It's still a monster," Proswell says. "Even if it rains and makes the course play soft, they can always put the pins on ledges and ridges on the greens."

2006 K Club

Straffan, Co. Kildare, IRELAND
Tel +353 (0)1 627 3111, Fax +353 (0)1 6273990
www.kclub.ie

There is already great excitement in Ireland over the award of the Ryder Cup to the Kildare Country Club. And bearing in mind the contribution that the likes of Eamonn Darcy, Christy O'Connor Jnr and Darren Clarke have made to the European triumphs in recent years it was only right that the contest should go to the 'Emerald Isle'. This luxurious resort, just outside Dublin, has already hosted numerous tournaments and is well worth a visit long before 2006. The Arnold Palmer designed Championship course at 7178 yards is immaculately maintained, beautifully verdant and one of the best in Europe. Ryder Cup packages are already being offered on the clubs website www.kclub.ie The US players should feel at home here – the course is more reminiscent of an American-style parkland course than many older Irish venues. Barely ten years old, the par-72 course features mature woodland, wide flat bunkers and lots of water – including the signature 7th hole where the green is on an island in the middle of the River Liffey.

2008 Valhalla Golf Club

15503 Shelbyville Road, Louisville, Kentucky, United States
Tel 001 502 245 1238 Fax 001 502 245 1157

Recently known for Tiger Woods' dramatic play-off win over Bob May in the 2000 PGA. Host for several Majors. Contrasting course of links style on the front nine and tree-lined fairways on the back nine. The Jack Nicklaus designed course, opened in 1986 and rated as one of the top 50 in the US, has two contrasting styles. The links feel of the outward nine holes is replaced by a change of layout on the inward nine. When the USPGA first went to Valhalla in 1996, the course was just ten years old, brand new in golfing terms, untried and untested. Sceptics viewed it with disdain, and the result – Mark Brooks ousting fellow journeyman pro Kenny Perry in a play-off – hardly elevated its status. But the PGA of America likes to take championship golf around the country and was rewarded both times with a passionate response from the public.

2010 Celtic Manor

Coldra Woods , Newport, Gwent , Wales . NP18 1HQ
Tel +44 (0)1633 413 000 Fax +44 (0)1633 412 910
e-mail postbox@celtic-manor.com www.celtic-manor.com

Eight holes from the original Wentwood Hills course (opened in 1999) will form the backbone of the Ryder Cup layout, with special holes created for the 2010 matches. With three excellent golf courses and superb facilities, a must to visit.

Celtic Manor won the battle to host the match after a conflict as fierce as anything to be seen on the golf course took place within the United Kingdom over a prize with a value conservatively estimated at £100 million – the right to host the 2010 Ryder Cup. The European Tour and the Professional Golfers' Association, who jointly manage the match on this side of the Atlantic, had to decide between three countries. It was Wales, and the Celtic Manor resort near Newport which eventually came out on top, ahead of England, in the shape of Slaley Hall in the north-east, and Scotland. However, some European Tour pros dislike the hillier part of the Wentwood Hills course and the seven new holes which millionaire owner Terence Matthews has pledged to add to the existing 11 in the Usk Valley in order to placate those gripes are not yet completed. Matthews has said he will shell out whatever it takes to provide the Ryder Cup committee with the quality of course it requires. His bulldozers will rebuild the entire terrain if necessary, which is, after all, what happened when Sotogrande New turned from an ugly duckling into a swan called Valderrama at the behest of Bolivian billionaire Jimmy Patino.

2012 Medinah Country Club

6N001 Medinah Road, Medinah, Illinois 60157, United States
Tel 001 630 773 1700
www.medinahcc.com

Already the venue of 12 championship events, the no. three course is currently undergoing re-modelling to host the 2006 PGA and 2012 Ryder Cup. Its clubhouse, built by the Shriners – members of the Ancient Arabic Order of Nobles of the Mystic Shrine, an association not unlike Freemasonry – is a mock-Moorish structure at once imposing and lavish. But its No 3 course, originally designed in the 1890s by expatriate Scot Tom Bendelow, is still considered by many golfers to be among America's finest. Medinah's championship course tracks through a landscape of oaks, elms and hickories whose leaves form a palette of greens, golds and ambers in the autumn. Much of the course is in sight of Lake Kadijah (named after Mohammed's wife) and two holes, the 2nd and the 17th, are played across it. Medinah hosted the USPGA in 1999 which witnessed the epic battle between Woods, who clung on for victory (just), and young Spanish star Sergio Garcia, who famously produced a miracle six-iron shot from the roots of an oak tree onto the 16th green during the last round. Hardly surprising, therefore, that visitors, on leaving the club, pass the only sign on an American golf club that urges them: 'Allah be with you.'
On the No 3 course the ladies tees are used almost exclusively by men!

CLASSIC
RYDER
CUPS
MATCHES

BY GUY WOODWARD

1969

ROYAL BIRKDALE, ENGLAND
GB 16 USA 16

O ver the passage of time, details are erased from the memories of great events, and only the strongest images remain ingrained on the mind. Frequently, these recollections are the result of positive discrimination, with the mind – and the media – shutting out negative thoughts in favour of a rose-tinted perspective.

Such is the case with the 1969 Ryder Cup, which will forever be remembered for a single act of chivalry on the part of Jack Nicklaus on the 18th green. Looking back, however, the contest was layered with notable incidents, many of them spiced with a much more bitter taste than that left by Nicklaus' moment of unique sportsmanship.

Even Nicklaus' gracious conceding of Tony Jacklin's final putt – which, had he missed it, would have cost Britain (the team had not yet expanded to include the rest of Europe) a tie of the match – was frowned upon by some present, notably among his team-mates. The US captain Sam Snead for one, was said to be furious at Nicklaus' decision, which floated uneasily on an undercurrent of bad blood that had surfaced regularly during the contest.

In truth though, while much was made, quite rightly, of Nicklaus' sportsmanship, the act arguably had little bearing on the ultimate result. Jacklin was the Open champion, and faced a routine two foot tap-in to tie the contest. Nicklaus had already made his four footer, thus ensuring the US would retain the trophy whether or not Jacklin holed out. All that was at stake was pride, and having been neck and neck throughout their final round, Nicklaus admirably ensured that both men's honour remained in tact.

Jacklin had put in a stellar performance, playing in all six rounds and never losing. "I didn't think you'd miss it," Nicklaus said at the time. "But I wasn't going to give you the chance." Years later, he explained his reasons: "Tony was the new figurehead of British golf. It wouldn't have been right for him to have missed a short putt to lose the Ryder Cup. That is the spirit of the Cup, which I think was the real reason why Sam Ryder started it all."

Snead had already been irked by a report on the second day that he felt went against such a spirit, which had the British captain Eric Brown ordering his team not to help the Americans search for balls lost in the rough. Not surprisingly, the visitors were put out at such an attitude, and the atmosphere between the two camps never recovered, remaining far from cordial for the event's duration.

In all likelihood, Snead was probably smarting at his own error of judgement on the first day, when he had chosen to blood two newcomers, Ray Floyd and Miller Barber, in the opening pairing, where they promptly lost. Their compatriots fared little better, with the British team winning 3½ of the first 4 points. To compound matters, the American Ken Still lit the blue touchpaper with some unseemly behaviour on the 13th hole of his match. Having been asked by Maurice Bembridge to move from his line of vision at the tee, Still found it necessary to make an overly dramatic demand that caddies, officials and spectators also move. Then, when playing out of a bunker on the same hole, Still appeared to make contact with his ball as he shot it out, though he made no such acknowledgement to Bembridge or Bernard Gallacher. It was left to Lee Trevino to ask his teammate whether he had made contact. On failing to give a reply, Still suffered the humiliation of Trevino picking his ball up and conceding the hole.

Things continued in much the same vein throughout the three days, with the hostile atmosphere often overshadowing some fine golf, and an even finer contest. Given that Britain had lost 10 of the last 11 events, often by wide margins, the closeness of the match defied all expectations. After the most recent thrashing, in 1967, the Cup's future was thrown into doubt, with US television companies declining the chance to cover such a one-sided show, and financial backers equally indifferent. Previous British captain Dai Rees suggested, unsuccessfully, limiting the teams to eight players in an effort to make the contest more competitive, while the British authorities moved to introduce the slightly larger US ball into PGA competitions in an attempt to level the playing field.

In the end, both associations agreed to expand, rather than reduce the size of the teams, heralding the debut of a number of young players, including the 20-year-old Scotsman Bernard Gallacher. The new approach paid off, with the teams rarely separated by more than a point throughout, and more than half the matches going to the final hole.

For the home team, fiery Welshman Brian Huggett played a pivotal role. He had kicked off proceedings with the opening win for Britain over the American debutants, had played in every intervening round, and was also there at the end, in the penultimate singles match. Playing against Billy Casper, Huggett was level pegging on the final green when an almighty cheer rose from the 17th, where Jacklin and Nicklaus were locked in their epic tussle. Assuming a Jacklin victory, Huggett mistakenly concluded that his five foot putt would win the cup. Upon holing it, he collapsed to the turf in tears before embracing Brown, only to be told that Jacklin had merely levelled his match with a long eagle putt, and the true climax was still to come.

Huggett had also been to the fore off-course, following an altercation with Dave Hill during the previous afternoon's foursomes. Playing with Still, Hill accidentally played out of turn, an error which Huggett immediately informed the referee of, and was thus awarded the hole. The Americans were so incensed that they were heard to tell Huggett he could have the hole, "and the Goddamn Cup", as they stormed off the green. The quartet then proceeded to argue openly for much of the match, with the bad blood boiling over again that night when Huggett and Hill continued their dispute in even more animated fashion in the hotel corridors.

Amid the turmoil, it should be pointed out that the American team deserved great credit for their doggedness in the face of such fervour for a home victory. Britain and Ireland were ahead for much of the contest, and needed to win just one of the final four singles contests to pinch the trophy. While Neil Coles and Christy O'Connor's games fell apart under the pressure, Casper and Nicklaus both had to hole five foot putts at the last to see off the home challenge. All of which makes Nicklaus' actions in the circumstances all the more commendable. Amazingly, it was his first Ryder Cup. Despite having already won all four majors, he had previously been prevented from playing by the US PGA's requirement that all professionals serve a five-year probation before being considered.

1983

PALM BEACH, USA
USA 14½ EUROPE 13½

Approaching the 1983 event, there was little to suggest that the Americans' hold on the trophy was under threat. After yet another routine victory in 1977, Jack Nicklaus had even spoken about how hard it was to get charged up for the matches. "British professional golf simply hasn't developed a sufficient depth of good players to make a true contest out of the event," he said.

The result of such criticism was an expanded format which would see the US take on a European, rather than solely British and Irish team. The addition of a mainly Spanish contingent had made little difference in either of the intervening match-ups, however, with the US scoring convincing wins in each. Worse still, internal tensions had plagued the European selection process in 1981, with two of Europe's leading lights – Tony Jacklin and Seve Ballesteros – being omitted, a decision which met with harsh criticism from commentators and players alike. Both vowed never to play in the Ryder Cup ever again, and Europe suffered a crushing defeat on home soil. While various theories about technique, style and type of course were bandied about to explain the American dominance, the fact remained that America's top players were simply better than their European counterparts, and by some distance. The omens were not good for the coming years.

As it turned out, never again would one side enjoy such dominance. 1983 was a watershed, Europe's coming of age, where foundations were laid for future victories. Amazingly, the architect was the previously spurned Jacklin, installed as captain by executive tour director Ken Schofield.

Even more surprising was the return to the fold of Ballesteros, whom Jacklin courted personally. It's possible that the two shared a common bond, having both felt hard done by two years' previously. The more likely reason for the Spaniard's about-turn, however, was Jacklin's effort in ensuring the players' wishes came ahead of those of the officials. Consequently, it was a happy European team that flew to Florida first class on Concorde, together with their own caddies, wives and girlfriends.

The scene was in contrast to the last trip, in 1979, when internal bickering soured the European challenge. Mark James and Ken Brown were both criticised for their behaviour, from not wearing the team uniform on the flight, appearing disinterested at the opening ceremony and then missing a team meeting to go shopping. Brown later compounded matters with a petulant display towards his partner, Des Smyth, in a heavy foursomes loss as the whole team returned with its tail between its legs. Ironically, it was James who was selected over Jacklin and Ballesteros in 1981.

Given this context, Jacklin's achievement in compiling a credible challenge on American soil was worthy of high praise. In the event, the European challenge was its strongest yet, with the result in doubt right up until the final singles' pairing. It was in the fourballs and foursomes that Jacklin showed his tactical savvy, though. He thought long and hard about his pairings, in an effort to maximise his resources. In opting to combine the steely resolves of Nick Faldo and Bernhard Langer, a formidable partnership was formed which went on to win three of its four games. Similarly, the decision to pair Paul Way, a 20-year-old making his Ryder debut, with the guiding hand of Ballesteros reaped dividends via 2½ points.

It didn't all go according to plan, however. In the opening foursomes, Bernard Gallacher and Sandy Lyle were plainly ill at ease, and were dismissed 5&4 by Ben Crenshaw and Tom Watson. Despite having been pencilled in to resume their pairing in the afternoon fourballs, both requested to be excused, on account of their poor form and their discomfort in the sweltering 95 degree heat. Their last minute replacements, Brian Waites and Ken Brown, came straight off the practice grounds to register an impressive victory over Gil Morgan and Fuzzy

Zoeller and lead Europe to a one point lead at the end of day one.

Unfortunately, Jacklin's golden touch couldn't last. Overnight, he faced a tough decision. He desperately wanted to play his strongest players throughout, but could he expect them to produce their finest golf over the course of five rounds in three days in these conditions?

Having opted to preserve the improvised Waites/Brown partnership in the next morning's fourballs, Jacklin watched in disbelief as a three hole lead came and went. To add insult to injury, Craig Stadler produced a stunning chip-in to take the match at the last hole. Ballesteros and Way also let a lead slip, and were one-down at the last before the Spanish master produced a sublime birdie on the 578 yard par-five 18th for a half.

With the Americans having drawn level, Jacklin opted to shuffle his pack slightly in the final fourballs, replacing Ian Woosnam as Sam Torrance's partner with the Spaniard, José-Maria Canizares. The move backfired, the pair going down to a 7 & 5 loss to Morgan and Lanny Wadkins. But with Ballesteros and Way, and Langer and Faldo holding firm for victories, the teams were level going into the singles.

The final day was nip and tuck throughout, with the Americans pegging back Europe every time the visitors got their nose in front. A strong opening trio of Ballesteros, Langer and Faldo returned 2½ points, but the next three games all went the Americans' way. Sam Torrance looked to have won a big point for Europe as he stood one-up on the 18th green, only for Tom Kite to pitch his ball out of the rough, stone dead next to the hole for a half.

The key match looked likely to be José-Maria Canizares' tussle with Lanny Wadkins, and again, Europe were ahead at the 18th, only for the US to produce another astonishing escape at the last. This time it was Wadkins, who served up one of the greatest shots in Ryder Cup history, a full pitching wedge to within inches of the hole for a half, prompting Nicklaus to kiss the spot from where the shot had been played.

Wadkins' moment of magic was made all the more notable when compared to the collapse under pressure of the final pairing, Bernard Gallacher and Tom Watson. Having bogeyed the 16th to drop a shot, Watson again looked vulnerable at the par 3 17th, missing the green in two and leaving the door open for Gallacher to tie up the match going to the last. Europe had to win it to win the Cup, but the Scot seemed as affected as Watson by the tension, and having also taken three to get onto the green, his missed putt sealed Europe's fate.

Having come so close to an historic first win Stateside, Jacklin was distraught. "We did everything right, but it was snatched away from us at the end," he reflected. One thing had been achieved, though. Never again would a player struggle to "get charged up for the matches".

1985

THE BELFRY, ENGLAND
EUROPE 16½ USA 11½

While the 1983 contest may have been the one to finally stimulate the appetite of the players, it was the contest two years later that fired the public imagination, particularly in Europe. For this reason alone, The Belfry will always hold a special place in the affections of home fans, and it is no coincidence that the course was selected to host the event on the next two occasions it was held in Europe, as well as again this year.

It was not always this way, however. The course was the original choice of the British PGA for the 1981 event, but the association faced such widespread criticism from all quarters in the aftermath of its decision that it eventually bowed to its sponsor's wishes and turned instead to Surrey's Walton Heath course.

The chief criticism of the course in 1981 was its youth. Many commentators felt at the time that the four-year-old venue lacked the required definition to host an event of this stature, and such concerns had not been entirely allayed four years on. Even Tony Jacklin, reprising his role as captain, had reservations over the American feel of The Belfry. But thanks to the extensive planting and fertilising to have taken place in the intervening years, the course did at least look the part and this time, the show would go on.

As it turned out, no-one worked the Belfry grounds as enthusiastically as Jacklin, who must have considered this stretch of Warwickshire as a second home by the end of the weekend, such was his familiarity with its contours. As the drama unfolded across the various greens and fairways, Jacklin was everywhere. Displaying an uncanny knack of always being in the right place at the right time, the captain zoomed across the course in his buggy, dispensing advice when it was needed and a simple, but supportive presence when it wasn't.

The result was an inspired European team, and a suitably inspired performance. Having taken the Americans so close two years previously, the European contingent, with two recent major winners – Sandy Lyle and Bernhard Langer – in its ranks, felt capable of turning the tables on home soil. Responding in kind, the British public turned out in force with opening day projections of 20,000 fans rising to 27,000 and finally 30,000 turning out on the last day to cheer Europe to victory.

Yet the match started inauspiciously for the home team. The opening foursomes saw the US take three out of four points, with only the Spanish pairing of Manuel Pinero and Seve Ballesteros enjoying any success. As it turned out, the pair would have an overwhelming influence on the destiny of the match, providing a stable influence around which the Europeans could base their challenge.

The Spaniards won again in the afternoon and, gradually, the Europeans clawed back the deficit. Halfway through the morning of the second day, they looked to have turned the corner, as Sam Torrance and Howard Clark, and Paul Way and Ian Woosnam secured successive victories in the fourballs. However, Pinero and Ballesteros couldn't reproduce their heroics of the previous day, going down 3&2 to Mark O'Meara and Lanny Wadkins. With Langer and Lyle two down with two to play against Craig Stadler and Curtis Strange, it looked as though the American lead would be preserved. Worse still, Europe would have nothing to show from their two strongest pairings.

Then came the turning point. Lyle rolled in a 25 foot eagle putt on the 17th to take the hole and suddenly, there was a glimmer of hope. Maybe, just maybe, the Americans would feel a little pressure. Certainly Strange appeared to buckle, finding a bunker with his approach to the last and putting himself out of contention. But Stadler was holding firm, matching Lyle and Langer shot for shot, and leaving himself an 18 inch tap-in to claim the match. Amazingly, he missed it, allowing Europe to sneak a half, and thus square the match.

More tellingly, the European team came out for the afternoon foursomes in buoyant mood, while the Americans were suddenly in a state of shock. It showed, as Europe scored three convincing wins to establish a two point lead going into the singles.

Pinero, who was by now in unstoppable form, opened up on the final day against Wadkins, a match-up he relished. "It was very important for the team to get a good start," he said. Pinero did just that, and describes his 3&1 victory as his greatest Ryder Cup memory, adding, "It was a great feeling having so many people there supporting you."

Whether Stadler was feeling so great after his capitulation the previous day is doubtful, but he rallied admirably to see off Ian Woosnam 2&1 and give the US fresh hope. However, Jacklin had chosen to play his trump cards early on, and reaped the benefits, as Way, Lyle and Langer reeled off victories, while Ballesteros produced a stunning comeback against Tom Kite, from three-down. A curling 50 foot putt, followed by an 18 footer gave Seve the adrenaline to reach the par-five 17th in two and secure an inspirational half, just when the Americans were threatening to mount a revival.

As the omnipresent Jacklin spread the good news, so he urged his men to greater efforts, with particular effect on Sam Torrance, who himself had been three down to US Open champion Andy North. Having clawed back the deficit, the now on fire Torrance hit a majestic drive at the last, while his jittery opponent splashed into the water. Having hit his second to 20 feet, Torrance marched triumphantly to the green, knowing he had two putts to win the trophy. At around the same time, Howard Clark actually had a single, shorter putt at the 17th, to close out his match with O'Meara, and clinch overall victory, but missed.

Torrance the showman was not to be so denied, holing for a birdie and cueing mass celebrations on the picturesque 18th. Afterwards he joked that the script had been pre-ordained to feature such a climax. Yet ultimately, Europe secured two further victories to end up comfortable winners. Whether Torrance would have been quite so relaxed had his match been the final one on course with the scores level, we will never know. One can only hope that he's celebrating in similar fashion this year.

1991

KIAWAH ISLAND, USA
USA 14½ EUROPE 13½

The 'War on the Shore' is generally remembered, on this side of the Atlantic at least, as the time when a great competition descended into gamesmanship, anarchy and ugliness. Certainly the combative approach of the American team, spurred on by a fiercely nationalistic crowd, itself fuelled by a jingoistic media, irked many of the European contingent. Several commentators attributed the overly aggressive approach to the coincidence of the contest with the US' successful military operation in Iraq. But golf and international warfare have never been likely bedfellows before or since. And while feelings of patriotic fervour may have been increased at such a time, the US team was desperate to win the Cup back on home soil for simpler, sporting reasons: Europe had held it for the last six years, something the US wasn't used to. Furthermore, they had retained it twice in a fashion the US found hard to bear – on American soil in 1987, under the captaincy of Jack Nicklaus on the course that he designed; and at The Belfry in 1989 through a tie that, as Paul Azinger commented, "Europe celebrated like a victory".

After the loss in '87, Jack Nicklaus had suggested, innocently, that American fans should learn from their European counterparts and start to really cheer on their fans. The profile of the crowd can even be traced back to Europe's historic win in 1985, when the Americans were taken aback by the home crowd's vociferous support. "All that cheering when we missed shots," said Peter

Jacobsen. "I've never seen anything like it before, especially from British crowds. You expect so much more from them."

In truth, the Cup had been fiercely contested ever since the first time Europe put up a credible challenge to American supremacy, in 1983, the last time the US won it. It was no surprise that they were so desperate to win it back eight years on. What was surprising was how the hostile atmosphere got to the players. While intimidating tactics on the part of the crowd were to be expected (even if a local radio presenter's successful campaign to persuade listeners to ring the European team's hotel and 'Wake the Enemy' was taking things a little far) the same could not be said for the players.

Yet it soon became clear that the intensity of the whole event had got to the Americans, who adopted a battle zone mentality from the start. Corey Pavin fanned the flames by turning up in combat gear, while his captain, Dave Stockton, treated the Europeans to a video of US victories and celebrations at the pre-competition gala dinner that was so one-sided, it had Nick Faldo threatening to walk out.

By the time the match commenced, there was a tangible air of confrontation surrounding the event, which was to linger throughout. Initially, it was the pumped up Americans who profited, winning three of the first four foursomes from a shell-shocked European team. It was nearly four, with Seve Ballesteros and José-Maria Olazábal three-down after the front nine of their match with Azinger and Chip Beck. That they managed to turn the deficit round and register a 2&1 victory was testament to the Spanish pair's strength when paired in Ryder Cups. They went on to win 3½ of 4 points in 1991, part of an overall record of 11 wins, 2 halves and 2 losses in 15 matches together.

On this occasion, however, their victory was tainted by accusations of gamesmanship from Azinger. Ballesteros had cast the first stone, claiming that the Americans had been playing the wrong ball. Although the referee ruled otherwise, Ballesteros continued his protest, which seemed to unsettle the American pair. When the Spaniard sunk a long putt on the 17th to take the match, his and Azinger's handshake was conducted dismissively, without so much as a glance.

They hadn't seen the last of each other however, since, in a further twist, the quartet was reformed in the afternoon's fourballs. Once again it was the Spanish who emerged on top, setting the tone for an afternoon when the Europeans enjoyed a happier time. Ryder Cup debutant Steven Richardson teamed up with Mark James to record a notable 5&4 win over Pavin and Mark Calcavecchia and Europe finished the day just one point down.

The good work was in danger of being in vain, however, when the Americans once more burst out of the traps on the second day to take command. Nick Faldo lost his third straight match (this time with rookie David Gilford) by a humbling 7&6, in a partnership where hardened veteran and nervous debutant never gelled. Gilford had a miserable first Ryder Cup, his only other involvement, in the singles, being denied him when the American Steve Pate withdrew with an injury.

Europe were on the verge of giving up the ghost as they lost the first three matches of the second morning, before Ballesteros and Olazábal again saved the day, with their third straight win, this time over Fred Couples and Ray Floyd. The pair had earned three of Europe's 4½ points thus far.

The foothold seemed to give Europe the belief that they could make up the lost ground, and sure enough, the afternoon saw the visitors haul themselves back into contention. Captain Bernard Gallacher made wholesale changes to his pairings and the players finally came good. In particular, Ian Woosnam and Paul Broadhurst combined superbly, with the Englishman's short game instrumental in a 2&1 victory over Azinger and Hale Irwin. Bernhard Langer and Colin Montgomerie followed up by defeating Pavin and the injured Pate and then James and Richardson won their second point of the week, over Lanny Wadkins and Wayne Levi. When the redoubtable Olazábal holed a six-footer at the last to secure a half against Couples and Payne Stewart, Europe had drawn level and the singles would be decisive.

The final day was a see-saw affair, with the balance of power constantly changing. Europe started well, and with Faldo finally finding form to beat Floyd, and David Feherty defeating Payne Stewart, the pressure was suddenly on the home team, who were behind for the first time in the match. Suddenly, defeat loomed large. And when Calcavecchia squandered a four shot lead over the last four holes to halve with Montgomerie, it looked like the pressure was getting to the Americans. Couples, Wadkins, Pavin and Azinger hit back, but victories for Ballesteros and Broadhurst meant the contest would be decided by the final match, between Hale Irwin and Bernhard Langer. Europe had to win it.

With four holes to play, the American was two up. But Langer is a master under pressure and after he took the 15th, Irwin played the last three holes in a visibly shaken state. The German nervelessly sank a six footer to halve the 16th, before Irwin three-putted on 17 to square the match. If Langer could win the last hole, his, and Europe's comeback would be complete. With Calcavecchia's collapse in mind, Team USA feared the worst.

Sure enough, Langer was ice-cool off the tee, drilling his drive into the heart of the fairway. Irwin, by now racked with nerves, yanked his drive left into the crowd, from where it miraculously reappeared on the fairway. No definitive explanation has ever surfaced for such an irregular trajectory, the obvious conclusion being that the partisan US crowd played its part. At the time, Langer was totally concentrated on his own game, and had eyes only for the green, to where he arrowed his second shot.

Much has been said, and written, however, about events on the green. Despite his good fortune, Irwin was unable to get himself together, and scrambled two unconvincing approach shots followed by two putts, for bogey. Langer, 30 feet away, had two putts for the match. In his first, he attacked the hole, but sped six feet past. Given the situation, it was generally agreed among players, fans and the media alike, that no-one would have holed the second. The steely Langer, who had been haunted by problems with his putter throughout his career, was no exception, and the Americans had their victory.

When the dust settled on this most intensely fought of contests, much had been said about the atmosphere in which it had been played. Manuel Pinero, who had acted as Gallacher's right hand man throughout, spoke of his concern for the Cup's future, pointing out that golf is a game where the public can get directly involved, because they share the course with the players. "We have to make sure the Ryder Cup is played in the right spirit," he said. Many would argue that the right spirit is to play to win. But not at any cost.

1997

VALDERRAMA, SPAIN
EUROPE 14½ USA 13½

With a European-hosted Ryder Cup being staged outside of the British Isles for the first time – in Spain – it was only fitting that a Spaniard take centre stage. And there was no more fitting candidate that Severiano Ballesteros. In truth, from the moment he was installed as European captain, there was never any doubt that Seve would be to the fore. At one stage, he had hoped to qualify through the ranking system as playing captain, an indication of the self-belief naturally ingrained in his psyche.

As it turned out, Ballesteros had enough on his plate without having to worry about his own game. He would need all of his famed resolution – some would say stubbornness – to withstand the rigours that come with the responsibility of captaincy. But Seve had turned the event in to a personal crusade for victory in his home country, and he would not be denied.

From the very onset of his stewardship, it was evident that the charismatic Spaniard would be doing everything his way. And doing everything was Seve's style, down to reshaping the Valderrama course so as to negate the Americans' firepower and famously insisting on which colours his team would wear.

In the lead-up to the event, however, Seve had somewhat more pressing, and challenging issues to attend to. Such as picking a team. Under the rules of the

CLASSIC RYDER CUPS

European selection process, the top ten money earners of the preceding European season were guaranteed a place. The captain would then select the final two players. Predictably, Ballesteros decided he wanted a greater say in affairs, pressing for an 8-4 balance.

"It ties my hands in so many ways," he said at the time. "I have no flexibility with only two picks. There is every chance that one, two or even three players I would like in my side are going to miss out." Advocates of the system argued that while this may have been the case, it was no bad thing, since it ensured players qualified on merit, and not through personal preference. Yet when Ballesteros tried to alter the system mid-way through the season, he won support from several leading players. Despite this, the authorities deemed his protest too late to change things.

The problem the skipper faced was that there were three players he desperately wanted in his team – Nick Faldo, Jesper Parnevik and José-Maria Olazábal – who were unlikely to qualify, the first two because they played most of their golf in America and the latter due to his poor form after injury problems. Not wanting to be accused of favouritism to his compatriot and long time Ryder Cup partner, captain Seve picked the two form players. But he wasn't finished there, and desperately looked for a way to include Olazábal.

His chance came when the unheralded, but in form Spaniard Miguel Angel Martin, having already qualified, suffered a serious wrist injury mid-summer, keeping him out of action right up until the start of the Cup. Ballesteros was unhappy with such a preparation and deemed Martin unfit to play, selecting Olazábal in his place.

Even with his preferred team, Seve's problems didn't disappear. There were a number of strong characters in the European team, at least two of whom, in Bernhard Langer and Nick Faldo, had not always seen eye to eye with the Spanish maestro. Langer it was who had denied Ballesteros a place in the 1981 Cup when given the casting vote on the selection panel. Yet the captain also had to consider the fragile nature of the likes of Darren Clarke, Ignacio Garrido, Lee Westwood and Thomas Bjorn, all making their debuts.

There was only ever going to be one way in which Ballesteros would handle the equation. The only way he knew – by totally immersing himself in the action, with a thoroughly hands-on approach. If Tony Jacklin had been impressive in his coverage of the Belfry by buggy in 1985, Ballesteros was manic at Valderrama. And while the ever forthcoming advice to players wasn't always appreciated – one player described it as like having a headmaster always looking over your shoulder – the overriding emotion given off by Seve was that of overwhelming desire, total intensity and a massive will to win. Such emotions radiated through the team and undoubtedly outwards to an American team that, at least initially, was relying solely on individual brilliance, rather than teamwork and solidarity, to succeed.

In the end, it was teamwork that won the day, with the famed American excellence in the singles unable to overcome an inspired European team performance in the foursomes and fourballs. For this, Ballesteros must take his share of the credit.

The golf was keenly fought, with almost half the four player matches going

CLASSIC RYDER CUPS

to the final hole. Yet Europe emerged from the first two days with a five point lead.

Tom Kite later attributed his team's ultimate defeat to local knowledge, particularly on the greens. But although the American press berated its team's putting, it had a simpler reason for their loss: Europe had shown a greater passion and commitment to the cause. Having been told that, man for man, the Americans were better than them, the European players had shown an overwhelming hunger to better their much vaunted opponents on every shot and every hole. "My players played with their hearts and that is why they won," said Ballesteros.

It wasn't only the captain's motivational ability that provided the difference however. He showed great tactical awareness in his reading and knowledge of the course, even going so far as to have fairways narrowed at the exact distance he envisaged the longer American hitters driving to. While such tactics were frowned upon by the visitors, they couldn't argue with his inspired choices in pairing his players, extracting fine performances from Langer and Montgomerie, Faldo and Westwood, Parnevik and Garrido and Olazábal and Rocca.

Tom Kite, by comparison, turned to former US president George Bush for his inspiration, with the statesman giving an impromptu pep-talk on the Saturday evening to a dispirited team. It obviously had the desired effect, with the American big-guns of Fred Couples, Phil Mickelson, Mark O'Meara, Jeff Maggert, Jim Furyk and Tom Lehman all posting victories early on to suggest an unlikely recovery. Ironically, perhaps their biggest guns of all, recent major winners Davis Love, Tiger Woods and Justin Leonard, failed to live up to their billing, with Woods having a particularly disappointing match. He went down in the singles to Costantino Rocca, for whom the match provided sweet recompense for the last European-hosted Ryder Cup, in 1993, when the Italian had been blamed for slipping to defeat from one-up with two to play against Love.

But if there was any man who deserved the chance to banish bad memories and secure victory, it was Langer, who suffered such a cruel fate in 1991. Sure enough, his 2&1 victory over Brad Faxon, secured in front of a huge gallery on the 17th, ensured the Cup would be retained, though it took a half from Colin Montgomerie over Scott Hoch to secure outright victory. Hoch had levelled the match at the 17th with a pitch to within a foot, meaning Monty suddenly needed a half at the last.

Europe had been criticised in some quarters for overly celebrating the retention of the Cup in 1989 when the match had finished in a tie, and there was no doubt that they were desperate to win it outright this time. The burly Scot ensured this was achieved, playing the hole in text book fashion for par, and then graciously conceding his opponent's testing par putt, knowing a half was sufficient. Such generosity would be conspicuously lacking in two years time...

1999

BROOKLINE, USA
USA 14½ EUROPE 13½

In all the furore surrounding the highly controversial 'Battle of Brookline', the achievements of certain players on both sides, in producing stunning golf in high pressure situations, are often overlooked. Judged purely on golfing prowess, however, the 1999 contest featured some exquisite moments.

The Americans went into the event in much the same frame of mind as they had in 1991, having lost two contests in a row. Convinced they had the better players (a claim borne out by the world rankings, which had the likes of Woods, Duval, Mickelson and O'Meara to the fore), the US team was under pressure from its own public to deliver.

By comparison, the European team featured a number of lesser lights, fresh to the Ryder Cup scene, and unheralded in the States. Jarmo Sandelin, Jean van de Velde and Andrew Coltart were virtual unknowns on the other side of the Atlantic, leaving European captain Mark James open to criticism for not selecting at least one more experienced campaigner, such as Langer or Faldo, in his wildcard picks.

James was protective of his young protegees, and held three of them back right up until the singles, a policy for which he was later criticised when the trio failed to withstand the intensity of the final day. In his defence, few did, and James could point to the astonishing performance of his other nine players in outplaying their hosts over the opening two days.

Given the expectancy of the American players and public, the European display in the foursomes and fourballs was nothing short of exceptional. The US opened up with their big guns, pairing David Duval with Phil Mickelson, and the solid Tom Lehman with the awesome Tiger Woods. Both pairs lost. What's more, they lost to what were considered risky pairings – Colin Montgomerie contending with a hostile crowd to superbly shepherd rookie Paul Lawrie, with the mavericks Sergio Garcia and Jesper Parnevik playing off each other's spontaneity to produce some mesmeric golf. The two pairs remained together throughout the first two days, to massive effect, with the latter picking up 3½ points out of 4.

Although the strong pairing of Jeff Maggert and Hal Sutton redressed the balance somewhat, the afternoon fourballs were a disaster for the home team, with Europe taking 3½ of 4 points, and the US' star pairing – Duval and Woods, the no's 1 and 2 in the world – humbled by Darren Clarke and Lee Westwood. Overnight, Europe had a four point lead.

Although the Americans regained some respectability on the second day, they couldn't claw back any of the deficit, with Lawrie and Montgomerie ensuring the four point lead would be retained going into the singles by clinching a superb 2&1 victory over Woods and Steve Pate in the face of increasingly vocal home support.

In the aftermath, Montgomerie cast the first stone in a debate which would rage for some time, accusing Maggert and Sutton of encouraging the crowd towards unsavoury heckling. Three times Montgomerie was forced to back off putts in his approach as the crowd disturbed him, and he and Lawrie lost their only match of the quartets, by one hole.

It is difficult to quantify exactly what effect the American players had in geeing up the crowd to what was a highly intimidating level of support on the final day. Certainly the players were fired up, inspired by a level of pride engendered through a number of factors. Just as George Bush had attempted to rally the troops prior to the final day in 1997, so this time his son, the then Texan Governor George W, instilled some fight into the US team, by reading excerpts from the memoirs of a soldier at the Siege of the Alamo. Captain Ben Crenshaw then reminded his players of their belief that, man for man, they were better than their European counterparts and if each of them lived up to their billing, they would win. If they needed any further motivation, he handed them vivid shirts decorated with photos of past American triumphs to wear. Crenshaw loaded the opening matches with his best players. James, perhaps sensing that he could afford to lose a couple of points early on, exposed his debutants to what was a cauldron of American fervour. It proved to be a mistake, as the US came out with all guns blazing. The tone was set early on when Jesper Parnevik expected a two foot putt to be conceded by David Duval on the second hole. It wasn't, the Swede missed, and Duval gestured to the crowd to increase the volume.

While there is no doubt that certain sections of the crowd overstepped the mark in their response, the fact remains that the Americans, individually, produced a stunning display. Their first six players won convincingly and suddenly America was in the lead. Having only needed four points, Europe were now scratching around to find them. Padraig Harrington produced one, beating Mark O'Meara, while Paul Lawrie was well on his way to chalking up another, in a 4 & 3 defeat of Jeff Maggert. It would be down to Europe's two most experienced campaigners – Colin Montgomerie and José-Maria Olazábal – to attain the others. Both were up coming down the back nine, and it looked, briefly, as if Europe would scramble home. But then an inspired Justin Leonard began a momentous comeback against the Spaniard, culminating in that astonishing, twisting, 45 foot putt on the 17th for birdie, to take him one up with one to play, and guaranteeing the half that the US needed to regain the Cup by one point. Olazábal's recovery to take the 18th and Montgomerie's brave win over Payne Stewart was rendered immaterial.

It was unfortunate that the brilliance of the American team's golf that day was overshadowed by the unsavoury behaviour of some of their contingent. Running across the green after Leonard's putt, but before Olazábal's, was instinctive, rather than malicious. The same cannot be said about the whooping up of the crowd into such a frenzy that players were suffering personal insults and Colin Montgomerie's father felt compelled to leave the course rather than witness any further abuse to his son.

Some said at the time that the spirit of the Ryder Cup had been lost forever. At the Belfry this year, players and spectators alike will have the chance to prove them wrong.

RYDER CUP RECORDS

OVERALL MATCH TABLE

	PLD	WON	HLVD	LOST		
UNITED STATES	33	24	2	7		
EUROPE/GB&I	33	7	2	24		

SINCE 1983.	PLD	WON	HLVD	LOST	F	A
UNITED STATES	9	4	1	4	124	128
EUROPE	9	4	1	4	128	124

MOST MATCH APPEARANCES

UNITED STATES	8	Lanny Wadkins (1977-79-83-85-87-89-91-93)
		Ray Floyd (1969-75-77-81-83-85-91-93)
		Billy Casper (1961-63-65-67-69-71-73-75)
EUROPE/GB&I	11	Nick Faldo (1977-79-81-83-85-87-89-91-93-95-97)
	10	Christy O'Connor Sr (1955-57-59-61-63-65-67-69-71-73)
	9	Bernhard Langer (1981-83-85-87-89-91-93-95-97)
	8	Dai Rees (1937-47-49-51-53-55-57-59-61)

YOUNGEST COMPETITORS

UNITED STATES   Horton Smith (21 yrs, 4 days in 1929)
Tiger Woods (21 yrs, 8 mths, 27 days in 1997)

EUROPE/GB&I   Sergio Garcia (19 yrs, 8 mths, 15 days in 1999)
Nick Faldo (20 yrs, 1 mth, 28 days in 1977)

OLDEST COMPETITORS

UNITED STATES   Ray Floyd (51 yrs, 20 days in 1993)
Don January (47 yrs, 9 mths, 26 days in 1977)

EUROPE/GB&I   Ted Ray (50 yrs, 2 mths, 6 days in 1927)
Christy O'Connor Sr (48 yrs, 8 mths, 30 days in 1973)

MOST GAMES PLAYED

UNITED STATES		
	37	Billy Casper (1961-75)
	34*	Lanny Wadkins (1977-93)
	32	Arnold Palmer (1961-73)
	31	Ray Floyd (1969-93)

* Includes a singles that was credited with a half, although not played in 1993, when Sam Torrance was injured.

EUROPE/GB&I		
	46	Nick Faldo (1977-97)
	40	Neil Coles (1961-77)
	38	Bernhard Langer (1981-97)
	37	Seve Ballesteros (1979-95)

MOST POINTS WON

UNITED STATES		
	23½	Billy Casper (Out of 37)
	23	Arnold Palmer (32)
	21½*	Lanny Wadkins (34)

* Includes a singles that was credited with a half, although not played in 1993, when Sam Torrance was injured.

EUROPE/GB&I		
	25	Nick Faldo (Out of 46)
	22½	Seve Ballesteros (37)
	20½	Bernhard Langer (38)

ALL-TIME RYDER CUP PLAYER RECORDS

PLAYER RECORDS
1927-1999

PLAYER	TEAM	FIRST	LAST	TIES	PTS	%
Aaron Tommy	USA	1969	1973	6	1.5	25.00
Adams Jimmy	GBI	1947	1953	7	2	28.57
Alexander Skip	USA	1949	1951	2	1	50.00
Alliss Percy	GB&I	1933	1937	6	3.5	58.33
Alliss Peter	GB&I	1953	1969	30	12.5	41.67
Azinger Paul	USA	1989	1993	14	6	42.86
Baker Peter	EUR	1993	1993	4	3	75.00
Ballesteros Seve	EUR	1979	1995	37	22.5	60.81
Bannerman Harry	GBI	1971	1971	5	2.5	50.00
Barber Jerry	USA	1955	1961	5	1	20.00
Barber Miller	USA	1969	1971	7	2	28.57
Barnes Brian	GB/E	1969	1979	25	10.5	42.00
Barron Herman	USA	1947	1947	1	1	100.00
Bean Andy	USA	1979	1987	6	4	66.67
Beard Frank	USA	1969	1971	8	3.5	43.75
Beck Chip	USA	1989	1993	9	6.5	72.22
Bembridge Maurice	GBI	1969	1975	16	6.5	40.63
Bjorn Thomas	EUR	1997	1997	2	1.5	75.00
Blancas Homero	USA	1973	1973	4	2.5	62.50
Bolt Tommy	USA	1955	1957	4	3	75.00
Boomer Aubrey	GBI	1927	1929	4	2	50.00
Boros Julius	USA	1959	1967	16	11	68.75
Bousfield Ken	GBI	1949	1961	10	5	50.00
Boyle Hugh	GBI	1967	1967	3	0	0.00
Bradshaw Harry	GBI	1953	1957	5	2.5	50.00

ALL-TIME RYDER CUP PLAYER RECORDS

PLAYER	TEAM	FIRST	LAST	TIES	PTS	%
Brand Gordon J	EUR	1983	1983	1	0	0.00
Brand jnr Gordon	EUR	1987	1989	7	2.5	35.71
Brewer Gay	USA	1967	1973	9	5.5	61.11
Broadhurst Paul	EUR	1991	1991	2	2	100.00
Brown Eric	GBI	1953	1959	8	4	50.00
Brown Ken	GB/E	1977	1987	13	4	30.77
Burke Billy	USA	1931	1933	3	3	100.00
Burke Jack	USA	1951	1957	8	7	87.50
Burkemo Walter	USA	1953	1953	1	0	0.00
Burton Richard	GBI	1935	1949	5	2	40.00
Busson Jack	GBI	1935	1935	2	0	0.00
Butler Peter	GBI	1965	1973	14	4	28.57
Calcavecchia Mark	USA	1987	1991	11	5.5	50.00
Canizares J-M	EUR	1981	1989	11	6	54.55
Casper Billy	USA	1961	1975	37	23.5	63.51
Caygill Alex	GBI	1969	1969	1	0.5	50.00
Clark Clive	GBI	1973	1973	1	0	0.00
Clark Howard	GB/E	1977	1995	15	7.5	50.00
Clarke Darren	EUR	1997	1999	7	3	42.86
Coles Neil	GBI	1961	1977	40	15.5	38.75
Collins Bill	USA	1961	1961	3	1	33.33
Coltart Andrew	EUR	1999	1999	1	0	0.00
Compston Archie	GBI	1927	1931	6	1.5	25.00
Coody Charles	USA	1971	1971	3	0.5	16.67
Cook John	USA	1993	1993	2	1	50.00
Cotton Henry	GBI	1929	1947	6	2	33.33
Couples Fred	USA	1989	1997	20	9	45.00
Cox Bill	GBI	1935	1937	3	0.5	16.67
Cox Wilfred	USA	1931	1931	2	2	100.00
Crenshaw Ben	USA	1981	1995	12	3.5	29.17
Daly Fred	GBI	1947	1953	8	3.5	43.75
Darcy Eamonn	GB/E	1975	1987	11	2	18.18
Davies William	GBI	1931	1933	4	2	50.00
Dawson Peter	GBI	1977	1977	3	1	33.33
Demaret Jimmy	USA	1947	1951	6	6	100.00
Dickinson Gardner	USA	1967	1971	10	9	90.00
Diegel Leo	USA	1927	1933	6	3	50.00
Douglas Dave	USA	1953	1953	2	1.5	75.00
Douglass Dale	USA	1969	1969	2	0	0.00
Drew Norman	GBI	1959	1959	1	0.5	50.00
Dudley Ed	USA	1929	1937	4	3	75.00

ALL-TIME RYDER CUP PLAYER RECORDS

PLAYER	TEAM	FIRST	LAST	TIES	PTS	%
Duncan George	GBI	1927	1931	5	2	40.00
Dutra Olin	USA	1933	1935	4	1	25.00
Duval David	USA	1999	1999	4	1.5	37.50
Easterbrook Syd	GBI	1931	1933	3	2	66.67
Elder Lee	USA	1979	1979	4	1	25.00
Espinosa Al	USA	1929	1931	4	2.5	62.50
Faldo Nick	GB/E	1977	1997	46	25	54.35
Fallon John	GBI	1955	1955	1	1	100.00
Farrell Johnny	USA	1927	1931	6	3.5	58.33
Faulkner Max	GBI	1947	1957	8	1	12.50
Faxon Brad	USA	1995	1997	6	2	33.33
Feherty David	EUR	1991	1991	3	1.5	50.00
Finsterwald Dow	USA	1957	1963	13	9.5	73.08
Floyd Ray	USA	1969	1993	31	13.5	43.55
Ford Doug	USA	1955	1961	9	4.5	50.00
Furgol Ed	USA	1957	1957	1	0	0.00
Furgol Marty	USA	1955	1955	1	0	0.00
Furyk Jim	USA	1997	1999	6	2	33.33
Gallacher Bernard	GB/E	1969	1983	31	15.5	50.00
Gallagher Jim	USA	1993	1993	3	2	66.67
Garcia Sergio	EUR	1999	1999	5	3.5	70.00
Garner John	GBI	1971	1971	1	0	0.00
Garrido Antonio	EUR	1979	1979	5	1	20.00
Garrido Ignacio	EUR	1997	1997	4	1.5	37.50
Geiberger Al	USA	1967	1975	9	6.5	72.22
Gilder Bob	USA	1983	1983	4	2	50.00
Gilford David	EUR	1991	1995	7	3.5	50.00
Goalby Bob	USA	1963	1963	5	3.5	70.00
Golden Johnny	USA	1927	1929	3	3	100.00
Graham Lou	USA	1973	1977	9	5.5	61.11
Green Hubert	USA	1977	1985	7	4	57.14
Green Ken	USA	1989	1989	4	2	50.00
Gregson Malcolm	GBI	1967	1967	4	0	0.00
Guldahl Ralph	USA	1937	1937	2	2	100.00
Haas Fred	USA	1953	1953	1	0	0.00
Haas Jay	USA	1983	1995	8	3.5	43.75
Haeggman Joakim	EUR	1993	1993	2	1	50.00
Hagen Walter	USA	1927	1935	9	7.5	83.33
Haliburton Tom	GBI	1961	1963	6	0	0.00
Hamilton Bob	USA	1949	1949	2	0	0.00
Harbert Chick	USA	1949	1955	2	2	100.00

ALL-TIME RYDER CUP PLAYER RECORDS

PLAYER	TEAM	FIRST	LAST	TIES	PTS	%
Harper Chandler	USA	1955	1955	1	0	0.00
Harrington Padraig	EUR	1999	1999	3	1.5	50.00
Harrison Dutch	USA	1947	1949	3	2	66.67
Havers Arthur	GBI	1927	1933	6	3	50.00
Hawkins Fred	USA	1957	1957	2	1	50.00
Hayes Mark	USA	1979	1979	3	1	33.33
Heafner Clayton	USA	1949	1951	4	3.5	87.50
Hebert Jay	USA	1959	1961	4	2.5	62.50
Hebert Lionel	USA	1957	1957	1	0	0.00
Hill Dave	USA	1969	1977	9	6	66.67
Hitchcock Jimmy	GBI	1965	1965	3	0	0.00
Hoch Scott	USA	1997	1997	3	2.5	83.33
Hodson Bert	GBI	1931	1931	1	0	0.00
Hogan Ben	USA	1947	1951	3	3	100.00
Horton Tommy	GBI	1975	1977	8	1.5	18.75
Huggett Brian	GBI	1963	1975	25	12	48.00
Hunt Bernard	GBI	1953	1969	28	9	32.14
Hunt Geoffrey	GBI	1963	1963	3	0	0.00
Hunt Guy	GBI	1975	1975	3	0.5	16.67
Irwin Hale	USA	1975	1991	20	14	70.00
Jacklin Tony	GB/E	1967	1979	35	17	48.57
Jacobs John	GBI	1955	1955	2	2	100.00
Jacobs Tommy	USA	1965	1965	4	3	75.00
Jacobsen Peter	USA	1985	1995	6	2	33.33
James Mark	GB/E	1977	1995	24	8.5	35.42
January Don	USA	1965	1977	7	3	42.86
Janzen Lee	USA	1993	1997	5	2	40.00
Jarman Edward	GBI	1935	1935	1	0	0.00
Jimenez Miguel A	EUR	1999	1999	5	2	40.00
Johansson P-U	EUR	1995	1997	5	3	60.00
Jolly Herbert	GBI	1927	1927	2	0	0.00
Keiser Herman	USA	1947	1947	1	0	0.00
King Michael	EUR	1979	1979	1	0	0.00
King Sam	GBI	1937	1949	5	1.5	30.00
Kite Tom	USA	1979	1993	28	17	60.71
Kroll Ted	USA	1953	1957	4	3	75.00
Lacey Arthur	GBI	1933	1937	3	0	0.00
Laffoon Ky	USA	1935	1935	1	0	0.00
Lane Barry	EUR	1993	1993	3	0	0.00
Langer Bernhard	EUR	1981	1997	38	20.5	53.95
Lawrie Paul	EUR	1999	1999	5	3.5	70.00

ALL-TIME RYDER CUP PLAYER RECORDS

PLAYER	TEAM	FIRST	LAST	TIES	PTS	%
Lees Arthur	GBI	1947	1955	8	4	50.00
Lehman Tom	USA	1995	1999	10	6	60.00
Lema Tony	USA	1963	1965	11	9	81.82
Leonard Justin	USA	1997	1999	8	2.5	31.25
Levi Wayne	USA	1991	1991	2	0	0.00
Lietzke Bruce	USA	1981	1981	3	0.5	16.67
Littler Gene	USA	1961	1975	27	18	66.67
Love Davis	USA	1993	1999	17	7.5	44.12
Lyle Sandy	EUR	1979	1987	18	8	44.44
Maggert Jeff	USA	1995	1999	11	6	54.55
Mahaffey John	USA	1979	1979	3	1	33.33
Manero Tony	USA	1937	1937	2	1	50.00
Mangrum Lloyd	USA	1947	1953	8	6	75.00
Marr Dave	USA	1965	1965	6	4	66.67
Martin Jimmy	GBI	1965	1965	1	0	0.00
Maxwell Billy	USA	1963	1963	4	4	100.00
Mayer Dick	USA	1957	1957	2	1.5	75.00
McCumber Mark	USA	1989	1989	3	2	66.67
McGee Jerry	USA	1977	1977	2	1	50.00
Mehlhorn Bill	USA	1927	1927	2	1	50.00
Mickelson Phil	USA	1995	1999	11	7	63.64
Middlecoff Cary	USA	1953	1959	6	2.5	41.67
Miller Johnny	USA	1975	1981	6	3	50.00
Mills Peter	GBI	1957	1957	1	1	100.00
Mitchell Abe	GBI	1929	1933	6	4	66.67
Mize Larry	USA	1987	1987	4	2	50.00
Moffitt Ralph	GBI	1961	1961	1	0	0.00
Montgomerie Colin	EUR	1991	1999	23	14	60.87
Morgan Gil	USA	1979	1983	6	2.5	41.67
Murphy Bob	USA	1975	1975	4	2.5	62.50
Nelson Byron	USA	1937	1947	4	3	75.00
Nelson Larry	USA	1979	1987	13	9.5	73.08
Nichols Bobby	USA	1967	1967	5	4.5	90.00
Nicklaus Jack	USA	1969	1981	28	18.5	66.07
North Andy	USA	1985	1985	3	0	0.00
O'Connor jr Christy	GB/E	1975	1989	4	1	25.00
O'Connor Sr Christy	GBI	1955	1973	36	13	36.11
O'Leary John	GBI	1975	1975	4	0	0.00
O'Meara Mark	USA	1985	1999	14	4.5	32.14
Olazabal Jose M	EUR	1987	1999	28	17.5	62.50
Oliver Ed	USA	1947	1953	5	3	60.00

ALL-TIME RYDER CUP PLAYER RECORDS

PLAYER	TEAM	FIRST	LAST	TIES	PTS	%
Oosterhuis Peter	GB/E	1971	1981	28	15.5	55.36
Padgham Alf	GBI	1933	1937	6	0	0.00
Palmer Arnold	USA	1961	1973	32	23	71.88
Palmer Johnny	USA	1949	1949	2	0	0.00
Panton John	GBI	1951	1961	5	0	0.00
Parks Sam	USA	1935	1935	1	0.5	50.00
Parnevik Jesper	EUR	1997	1999	9	5.5	61.11
Pate Jerry	USA	1981	1981	4	2	50.00
Pate Steve	USA	1991	1999	5	2.5	50.00
Pavin Corey	USA	1991	1995	13	8	61.54
Peete Calvin	USA	1983	1985	7	4.5	64.29
Perry Alf	GBI	1933	1937	4	0.5	12.50
Picard Henry	USA	1935	1937	4	3	75.00
Pinero Manuel	EUR	1981	1985	9	6	66.67
Platts Lionel	GBI	1965	1965	5	2	40.00
Pohl Dan	USA	1987	1987	3	1	33.33
Polland Eddie	GBI	1973	1973	2	0	0.00
Pott Johnny	USA	1963	1967	7	5	71.43
Rafferty Ronan	EUR	1989	1989	3	1	33.33
Ragan Dave	USA	1963	1963	4	2.5	62.50
Ransom Henry	USA	1951	1951	1	0	0.00
Ray Ted	GBI	1927	1927	2	0	0.00
Rees Dai	GBI	1937	1961	18	7.5	41.67
Revolta Johnny	USA	1935	1937	3	2	66.67
Richardson Steve	EUR	1991	1991	4	2	50.00
Rivero Jose	EUR	1985	1987	5	2	40.00
Roberts Loren	USA	1995	1995	4	3	75.00
Robson Fred	GBI	1927	1931	6	2	33.33
Rocca Costantino	EUR	1993	1997	11	6	54.55
Rodriguez Chi Chi	USA	1973	1973	2	0.5	25.00
Rogers Bill	USA	1981	1981	4	1.5	37.50
Rosburg Bob	USA	1959	1959	2	2	100.00
Rudolph Mason	USA	1971	1971	3	1.5	50.00
Runyan Paul	USA	1933	1935	4	2	50.00
Sandelin Jarmo	EUR	1999	1999	1	0	0.00
Sanders Doug	USA	1967	1967	5	2	40.00
Sarazen Gene	USA	1927	1937	12	8.5	70.83
Scott Syd	GBI	1955	1955	2	0	0.00
Shute Denny	USA	1931	1937	6	3	50.00
Sikes Dan	USA	1969	1969	3	2	66.67
Simpson Scott	USA	1987	1987	2	1	50.00

ALL-TIME RYDER CUP PLAYER RECORDS

PLAYER	TEAM	FIRST	LAST	TIES	PTS	%
Smith Horton	USA	1929	1935	4	3.5	87.50
Smyth Des	EUR	1979	1981	7	2	28.57
Snead JC	USA	1971	1975	11	9	81.82
Snead Sam	USA	1937	1959	13	10.5	80.77
Sneed Ed	USA	1977	1977	2	1.5	75.00
Souchak Mike	USA	1959	1961	6	5	83.33
Stadler Craig	USA	1983	1985	8	5	62.50
Stewart Payne	USA	1987	1999	19	9	47.37
Still Ken	USA	1969	1969	3	1	33.33
Stockton Dave	USA	1971	1977	5	3.5	70.00
Strange Curtis	USA	1983	1995	20	7	35.00
Sutton Hal	USA	1985	1999	14	8	57.14
Thomas Dave	GBI	1959	1967	18	5.5	30.56
Torrance Sam	EUR	1981	1995	28	10	35.71
Townsend Peter	GBI	1969	1971	11	3	27.27
Trevino Lee	USA	1969	1981	30	20	66.67
Turnesa Jim	USA	1953	1953	1	1	100.00
Turnesa Joe	USA	1927	1929	4	1.5	37.50
Van De Velde J	EUR	1999	1999	1	0	0.00
Venturi Ken	USA	1965	1965	4	1	25.00
Wadkins Lanny	USA	1977	1993	34	21.5	63.24
Waites Brian	EUR	1983	1983	4	1	25.00
Wall Art	USA	1957	1961	6	4	66.67
Walton Philip	EUR	1995	1995	2	1	50.00
Ward Charles	GBI	1947	1951	6	1	16.67
Watrous Al	USA	1927	1929	3	2	66.67
Watson Tom	USA	1977	1989	15	10.5	70.00
Way Paul	EUR	1983	1985	9	6.5	72.22
Weetman Harry	GBI	1951	1963	15	3	20.00
Weiskopf Tom	USA	1973	1975	10	7.5	75.00
Westwood Lee	EUR	1997	1999	10	4	40.00
Whitcombe Charles	GBI	1927	1937	9	5	55.56
Whitcombe Ernest	GBI	1929	1935	6	1.5	25.00
Whitcombe Reg	GBI	1935	1935	1	0	0.00
Will George	GBI	1963	1967	15	3	20.00
Wood Craig	USA	1931	1935	4	1	25.00
Wood Norman	GBI	1975	1975	3	1	33.33
Woods Tiger	USA	1997	1999	10	3.5	35.00
Woosnam Ian	EUR	1983	1997	31	16.5	53.23
Worsham Lew	USA	1947	1947	2	2	100.00
Zoeller Fuzzy	USA	1979	1985	10	1.5	15.00